IRELAND'S EVOLVING CONSTITUTION, 1937–97

Ireland's Evolving Constitution, 1937–97: Collected Essays

Edited by

TIM MURPHY and PATRICK TWOMEY

·HART·
PUBLISHING

OXFORD
1998

Hart Publishing
Oxford
UK

Distributed in the United States by
Northwestern University Press
625 Colfax
Evanston
Illinois 60208–4210 USA

Distributed in Australia and New Zealand
by Federation Press Pty
PO Box 45 Annandale, NSW
2038, Australia

Distributed in Netherlands, Belgium and Luxembourg by
Intersentia, Churchillaan 108
B2900 Schoten, Antwerpen
Belgium

Hart Publishing is a specialist legal publisher based in Oxford, England. To order further
copies of this book or to request a list of other publications please write to:
Hart Publishing, 19 Whitehouse Road, Oxford, OX1 4PA
Telephone: +44 (0)1865 434459, Fax: +44 (0)1865 794482 or 434459
e-mail: hartpub@janep.demon.co.uk

British Library Cataloguing in Publication Data
Data Available

ISBN 1-901362-16-7 (cloth)
1-901362-17-5 (paper)

Typeset in 10/12 pt Sabon
by Hope Services (Abingdon) Ltd.
Printed in Great Britain on acid-free paper
by Biddles Ltd., Guildford and Kings Lynn

Foreword

When I first studied law at Trinity College, Dublin in the mid-fifties there were no textbooks on Irish public law for us to study; there were relatively few decisions by the Irish courts on constitutional matters for us to consider; and constitutional issues were not the centre of vital controversy by philosophers or politicians. All that has now changed. This is partly because of several generations of able and innovative Irish judges, who have moulded and developed Irish public law into the most active and exciting branch of Irish law. A key role too was played by the late Professor John Kelly, who first began the serious study of Irish public law in his books *Fundamental Rights in the Irish Law and Constitution* (1961) and *The Irish Constitution* (1980). One can obtain some idea of the importance of Irish constitutional law today by observing that the third edition of Professor Kelly's book now runs to over 1300 pages.

Following Professor Kelly, there came a second generation of Irish public lawyers, in particular, Professor James Casey, Dr Gerard Hogan, Professor David Gwynn Morgan and Gerry White (one is glad to see that the last two are contributors to this book). The publication of this book, edited by two young Irish academic lawyers, gives further evidence of the maturity of Irish public law and of the ability of the current generation of Irish academics.

The contents of this book range from the highly philosophical to the very pragmatic examination of issues. While it is invidious to comment on particular issues or, contributions in this book, there are some matters on which I should like to briefly dwell. First of all, there is the relationship between the Catholic Church and State. The Constitution has been profoundly influenced by Catholic doctrine, evidenced, for example, by the former constitutional ban on divorce, now replaced after a referendum by provisions which lay down, in the Constitution itself, the grounds upon which alone a divorce may now be obtained in the Irish Republic (raising incidentally a recurring theme in some contributions of the appropriateness of including certain matters at all in a constitution). The contribution on public education in Ireland by Professor Clarke shows how Irish law has entrenched Church control of public education, in contrast with the US division of Church and State in this area. The late Dr Browne has contributed an important historical account of the Church-State relationship in Ireland. There is now less overt (and covert) interference by the Church in governmental issues than Dr Browne suggests. This is for a variety of reasons, including the Presidency of Mary Robinson. On the other hand, it needs to be recorded that in December 1997 the Catholic Archbishop of Dublin condemned the action of the current

President, Mary McAleese, a Catholic herself, in making the appropriate gesture (in the light of the on-going peace process in Northern Ireland) of taking Holy Communion in one of Dublin's two Protestant Cathedrals.

The problem of the extent to which social and economic rights ought to be or are protected by the Constitution is discussed by Tim Murphy. Issues of the extent to which the Constitution embodies old-fashioned views of gender relations are discussed by Dolores Dooley and Leo Flynn. Valuable contributions are made by Anthony Whelan and Síofra O'Leary on the relationship between the Constitution and the law of the European Union. Contrasting judicial approaches to the interpretation of a constitution are discussed by Professor Morgan. The problems that arise under constitutional provisions giving some recognition to the linguistic rights of people who use a language spoken only by a tiny minority of the community are discussed by Niamh Nic Suibhne and Michael Cronin. These have relevance for Constitutions that provide for two or more official languages.

Inevitably any critique of the Irish Constitution raises, if only by implication, the extent to which the provisions of the Constitution ought to be changed. The problems that arise by amending a constitution are discussed, in particular, by Adrian Hunt.

Irish constitutional law has not yet aroused as much interest abroad as it should. Irish courts have had to consider many issues, for example, whether citizens may waive their rights under a constitution, what range of defendants may be sued for violations of Bills of Right's provisions, and the proper kind of judicial approach to be adopted when interpreting basic rights, which are of general relevance to written constitutions. All these are also issues which may arise before UK courts when the European Convention on Human Rights is incorporated into UK law.

This book discusses a wide range of issues arising under the Irish constitution. Many of them have a relevance not only for lawyers but also for philosophers and political scientists, not only in Ireland but elsewhere. It shows the danger of attaching too much importance to written constitutions on their own as a means of ensuring liberty and social justice, but at the same time shows the enormous advantage of having a written constitution with the Bill of Rights, which is subject to judicial supervision, as compared to systems without a Bill of Rights, or with a Bill of Rights not subject to judicial supervision.

Paul O'Higgins,
Member of the Royal Irish Academy;
Honorary Fellow, Trinity College, Dublin.

January 1998

Christ's College,
Cambridge.

Contents

Introduction

TIM MURPHY and PATRICK TWOMEY

Throughout the world, the present time is one of particular importance for constitutions and constitutionalism. The dissolution of the Soviet Union and the subsequent adoption of new constitutions in several states has meant that questions of constitutional import, both theoretical and practical, are receiving much attention.[1] Despite this high level of interest, it is not always clear what precisely is meant when the term "constitution" is used, or indeed whether it has more than one meaning. In fact, most constitutional commentators distinguish between two basic senses of the word "constitution". First, "constitution" normally represents a document (the United Kingdom, with its unwritten constitution, is a notable exception here) that comprises a number of articles governing the State, laying down rules which State institutions are obliged to follow in their activities and also in relations with the citizens of the State. To give an example of this understanding of the term:

> "Constitutions are codes of norms which aspire to regulate the allocation of powers, functions, and duties among the various agencies and officers of government, and to define the relationship between these and the public."[2]

However, in cases where such a constitutional text exists, there is an acknowledged dissonance between many constitutional provisions and actual constitutional practice. The constitutional law of most States also includes other features, notably constitutional conventions, constitutional decisions by which the courts interpret the constitution, and ordinary statute laws with constitutional implications. Further, the documents themselves typically say little of *extra-constitutional* organisations and activities. In most cases, political parties, churches, business corporations, ethnic and other minorities, the

---

[1] See, generally, R. R. Ludwikowski, *Constitution-Making in the Region of Former Soviet Dominance* (Durham and London, Duke University Press, 1996) and U. K. Preua, "Constitution-making and Nation-building: Reflections on Political Transformations in Eastern and Western Europe" (1993) 1 *European Journal of Philosophy* 81. It has further been suggested that "constitutional problems have also become highly relevant in the so-called First and Third Worlds. In many Third World countries there is institutional reform on a major scale in order to improve the performance of the State in a search for a stable democratic regime. In the OECD countries there is a debate about the pros and cons of various basic institutions, as the welfare state is assessed in a climate where market values are given more and more attention." J. Lane, *Constitutions and Political Theory* (Manchester, Manchester University Press, 1996), 4.

[2] S. E. Finer, V. Bogdanor and B. Rudden, *Comparing Constitutions* (Oxford, Clarendon Press, 1995), 1.

media and pressure groups are among these external influences on constitutional practice. A second sense of the term "constitution" thus emerges: "the actual principles or maxims in terms of which a country is ruled ... 'Constitution' here refers not to a written document, but to the actual manner in which a country is ruled, the regime or the set of fundamental state institutions."[3]

This second sense, of course, has not always been adequately acknowledged. In 1951, for example, Karl Loewenstein, referring to the "epidemic of constitution-making in the wake of World War II", noted that the interpretation and application of constitutions is "usually monopolized by relatively small groups of technicians—politicians, lawyers, judges, [and] civil servants".[4] Since that time, however, there has been a general movement away from this situation, guided primarily by an increasing appreciation of the second sense of "constitution" referred to above. It was with this in mind that this project—a collection of essays marking the sixtieth anniversary of the 1937 Constitution of Ireland, *Bunreacht na hEireann*—was conceived and undertaken. It is designed to provide insights into both senses of "constitution" and indeed this is implied by the notion of the "Evolving Constitution" in the title. The collection is therefore by no means confined to legalistic or textual analyses. Like many other collections on similarly broad themes, it seeks to highlight the fact that constitutions, as fields of study, are essentially interdisciplinary: in addition to legal analyses, they also require to be viewed from philosophical, historical, political, economic, sociological and other perspectives.

Loewenstein suggested that the "monopoly" he referred to had come to overshadow:

> "what may be called the ontology of constitutions, that is, the investigation of what a written constitution really means within a specific national environment; in particular, how real it is for the common people, who after all are everywhere, in this alleged age of the common man, the addressees of political power."[5]

Fortunately, these ontological questions now receive a greater deal of attention than was previously the case and this has been very apparent in the Republic of Ireland during recent years. Public debates about social issues have frequently been "constitutionalised"—one need only consider how questions relating to European integration, abortion, divorce, personal liberty and freedom of information have been placed before the voting public to realise

---

[3] J. Lane, *supra* n.1, 9.

[4] K. Loewenstein, "Reflections on the Value of Constitutions in Our Revolutionary Age" in A. J. Zurcher (ed.), *Constitutions and Constitutional Trends since World War II: An Examination of Significant Aspects of Postwar Public Law with Particular Reference to the New Constitutions of Western Europe* (New York, New York University Press, 1951), 191-3. Loewenstein makes reference here to "some fifty-odd nations" that had equipped themselves with new constitutions between 1945 and 1951.

[5] *Ibid.*, 193.

how often "political debate" has been converted into "constitutional debate". Jan-Erik Lane has described this general phenomenon as follows:

"A constitutional document may play a major role in political life due to the fact that it may take on a charismatic aura or because its interpretation may be essentially contested. In some countries politics is to an extraordinary degree constitutional politics. Political conflict involves to a considerable extent constitutional conflict."[6]

In the Republic of Ireland, this has meant that there has occurred, to some degree at least, a "demystification" of the Constitution and Irish constitutionalism, and one of the main objectives of this collection is to further encourage this process. While the collection makes no claim to being in any way exhaustive, it does bring together commentaries on a wide range of important constitutional issues which we sincerely hope will provide a contribution of some value to ongoing debates related to *Bunreacht na hEireannn* and indeed to public law debates elsewhere.

The main body of the book opens with a philosophical essay by Garrett Barden on the "discovery" of constitutions, which addresses some crucial questions relating to the legitimacy or otherwise of *Bunreacht na hEireann*. This is followed by two historical perspectives: John A. Murphy, academic historian and former Senator, casts an experienced eye over the political dynamics surrounding the framing of the Constitution in 1936–7, while Garret Fitzgerald draws on a long career both in public office and in academic life to provide an overview of the history of Irish constitutionalism generally and also of various provisions of the present Constitution.

The major concern of the next three essays is the relationship between the Catholic Church and faith and the Constitution. Noel Browne's death, before the publication of this collection, robbed Ireland of one of its most important and consistent "awkward voices": a voice which applied the Constitution's paper guarantees to the ongoing litmus-test of their significance to the everyday life of the "common people". Dr. Browne's essay, *Church and State in Modern Ireland*, is a salutary reminder of the extent of the power of the

---

[6] J. Lane, *supra* n.1, 13. Lane also remarks that in these contexts, "[c]hanges in the formal constitution may be difficult to achieve". *Bunreacht na hEireann* also falls into this category: it is a "rigid" as opposed to a "flexible" constitution in this sense. Art. 46 of the Irish Constitution declares that the only method of amending it is by referendum. For an analysis of Irish constitutional referendums in a comparative essay on direct democracy, see V. Bogdanor, "Western Europe", in D. Butler and A. Ranney (eds.), *Referendums around the World: The Growing Use of Direct Democracy* (Washington, American Enterprise Institute Press, 1994), 78–87. Bogdanor's general conclusion is worth quoting in full: "It is of course far too early to tell whether the increasing incidence of the referendum since the 1970s signals a genuine turning point in democratic politics or whether the referendum will remain a subordinate instrument in Western European political systems. But as we reach the end of the twentieth century, signs indicate that the mass party as we have known it since the beginning of the century, far from being inherent to any democratic system of government, may represent merely a phase of democratic development that is passing away. If that is so, we may confidently expect a more widespread use of the referendum in the twenty-first century than we have seen in the twentieth." (97).

Catholic Church during Ireland's history. From a different generation and perspective, Gerry Whyte adopts a less hostile stance in his analysis of the role of religious morality in the constitutional order. Finally, in his treatment of two "high-profile" constitutional matters, religion and education, Desmond Clarke elaborates on one of Dr. Browne's central concerns: religious control of education in Ireland. In some respects, Frank Martin's essay on the Constitution's provision on the Family mirrors earlier observations on education, particularly in terms of his account of the input of the Catholic Church. This essay also highlights the divergence between modern social conditions and the aspirations associated with the Family's special constitutional status.

In a particularly timely piece, Anthony Carty draws on the principles of international law to offer a revised, partitionist solution to the situation in Northern Ireland. In stressing the existence of two "peoples" on the island, he eschews the constitutional imperative of Articles 2 and 3 in favour of a pragmatic resort to a new boundary commission. David Gwynn Morgan's essay, taking as case-studies the themes of international affairs, the demise of the Prerogative and specific examples of constitutional interpretation, warns of some dangers associated with overly-zealous judicial activism.

There then follow two pieces on the theme of gender and the Constitution: Dolores Dooley presents a feminist critique of the provisions of the Constitution and Leo Flynn examines the constructions of masculinity in two major interpretations of constitutional provisions. Siobhán Mullally's discussion of equality and the public/private divide in Irish constitutional law addresses fundamental questions regarding the alleged "neutrality" of the Irish liberal State. Tim Murphy's essay then examines the non-recognition of economic rights in Irish constitutional law and places this examination in the context of the extremely high levels of poverty in the State.

Paul O'Mahony postulates that the Constitution has been a "mixed blessing" on matters of criminal justice. While approving the judicial development of a "meta-Constitution" relating to otherwise vague constitutional provisions, he is highly critical of the extent to which political expediency often trumps constitutional guarantees in what he terms the "rhetoric-reality gap". Patrick Twomey, in his essay on the right to freedom of expression, similarly highlights how a weakness of constitutional formulation, compounded by a range of external factors, created another such "gap" in the context of the situation in Northern Ireland. Analysing a related right, that of freedom of association, Irene Lynch considers the tension between the focus on individual rights in the Constitution and the collective interest of trade unions in the wider context of the historical relationship between Irish law and the trade union movement.

Drawing on a career as a social activist and politician, Brendan Ryan is critical of the failure of the Constitution to play a central role in the quest for social justice in Irish society. At the same time, he identifies extra-constitutional causes of this conservativism and sectarianism in Irish society and advises against any presumption that a new Constitution would necessarily be more progressive. In a comparative essay which draws on the Polish experience of constitutionalism, Bozena Cierlik highlights a darker road that might have been followed by the Irish State in the 1930s.

The next two essays explore different aspects of the public debate on the Irish language from a constitutional perspective. Niamh Nic Shuibhne considers both the terms of the constitutional guarantee in Article 8 and the resulting case-law in maintaining that the reality of the Irish language as a "minority" language provides a truer reflection of the current position and more possibilities in terms of the protection of linguistic rights than the current constitutional pedestal. Michael Cronin's essay also highlights the reality of current Irish language usage in analysing what he terms the "status without substance" afforded by Article 8 and the failure of government policy to match this constitutional rhetoric. The following two pieces share as a theme the European dimension of the Constitution. Anthony Whelan addresses the question of the inherent tension between the Constitution's assertion of national sovereignty and membership of the European Union, while Siofra O'Leary looks at the reciprocal relationship between Irish constitutional law and European Union law in the context of individual rights.

The two concluding essays provide reflections on the extra-constitutional realm. Stephen Livingstone examines political participation in Ireland beyond the sphere of party politics and suggests that Ireland's modern civil society requires fresh thinking about the involvement of non-governmental groups to compensate for the declining influence of the Constitution's vocationalism. In a similar vein, Adrian Hunt delves behind formal appearance to ask fundamental questions about the limits of constitutionalism and constitutional law in the Irish context.

In conclusion, we would like to thank Richard Hart for his enthusiasm right from the time when this project was first mooted and for being a pleasure to work with throughout, Paul O'Higgins for his scholarly foreword, and all the contributors, for their essays and their patience and understanding! We would also like to extend our gratitude to Leysa Day and Clare Jennings at Nottingham Law Department for their invaluable secretarial assistance and for the magic that occasionally had to be worked on troublesome computer discs, to Karen Kenny for her editorial assistance with several contributions, to our students for their stimulation and suggestions, and finally, to our families, friends and colleagues for their continued support and encouragement.

Tim Murphy   *Patrick Twomey*
Department of Law   *Department of Law*
National University of Ireland,   *University of Nottingham*
Cork

December 1997

1

Discovering a Constitution

GARRETT BARDEN

INTRODUCTION

It is entirely coincidental that 1997 is the sixtieth anniversary of the 1937 Constitution and the two hundredth anniversary of the death of Edmund Burke, but the coincidence prompts reflection on a written, invented Constitution.

Behind a written, invented, modern constitution, such as the Irish Constitution, more or less clearly, is the idea that it "founds" the polity. However, it is brought into effect following a plebiscite or referendum or some other method of election. Such a constitution can, and often does, define who or what kind of person will comprise the electorate once the constitution has been put in place. Such a constitution can, and often does, define how it may itself be altered.

Questions arise as to how the electorate that elects the constitution is to be determined. Who are to be the electors and who is to choose them? This cannot be done by the proposed constitution itself, since it is not yet in force. The electors who vote the constitution into being are not constituted as an electorate by it. The manner in which they vote the constitution into being is not determined by it. By their adoption of a constitution the electors will establish themselves as living under it, but they do not yet live under it. Accordingly, the electors are already, and must already be, an electorate before they choose their invented constitution. In other words, the adoption of an invented constitution does not, and cannot, establish its electorate for the first time—for the electorate is already established.

This is by no means a newly discovered dilemma. Rousseau quotes Grotius to the effect that a people can give itself a king and comments:

"According to Grotius a people is a people before giving itself a king. This giving of a king to itself is already a civil act and supposes public deliberation. Accordingly, before examining the act by which a people elects a king, it behoves us to examine the act by which a people is a people. For this act necessarily precedes the other and is the true foundation of society."[1]

[1] J. Rousseau, *Du Contrat Social*, I, v.

If "king" is replaced by "constitution" one has the dilemma outlined above.

Hobbes, in *Leviathan*, faced a similar problem, to solve which he relied on the myth or assumption of a natural condition in which humans lived individually but with the desire for peace to overcome the incessant war of all against all, and with the possibility of discovering civil society which is brought into being by the *unanimous* consent of those who enter it. Hobbes adopts here a method which, in this present century, became known as methodological individualism. For Hobbes, civil society is not alone founded on, but also maintained by, the agreement of each member to the establishing "contract"—a position fully accepted and more clearly articulated in such different works in modern political philosophy as Collingwood's *The New Leviathan*[2] and Buchanan and Tullock's *The Calculus of Consent*.[3]

Buchanan and Tullock clearly and explicitly take civil society as given and their analysis concerns how the members of this already constituted civil society would rationally make certain decisions. They also expressly accept that anyone may withdraw from, or not enter into, the contract.

The question in this essay, however, concerns the original electorate that votes a written constitution such as the Constitution of Ireland into being. That electorate necessarily precedes the establishment of the written constitution. How does this electorate come about? In Hobbes' brilliant logical solution to an aporia within his model, the question of the establishment of civil society is assumed to be addressed to all, and each person becomes a member of the electorate by his agreement to its establishment. Even so, the assumption remains: the question is assumed to be addressed to all.

Hobbes' answer demands consideration. The person becomes a member of the electorate by agreeing to the establishment of civil society; those who do not agree remain outside the newly founded civil society and do not form part of its electorate. Written constitutions are often so imagined. They are imagined to establish, to found, the polity and, so to speak, to render obsolete whatever political associations went before them. Thus, whoever does not accept them remains outside the newly founded polity. In other words, the bringing into being of a constitution renders obsolete the electorate that brought it into being, in favour of a new electorate that is established by it.

Edmund Burke is sometimes thought of as an irrationalist with an organic conception of society.[4] He is better understood as one trying to clarify and to argue in favour of the constantly changing lived constitution that precedes the written. For Burke, a constitution is not an invented ideal of what society should be, but is the tentative, uncertain and critical discovery of the polity that is brought about by intelligently and sensitively living in society as it is.

---

   [2] R. G. Collingwood, *The New Leviathan* (Oxford, Clarendon Press, 1942).

   [3] J. M. Buchanan and G. Tullock, *The Calculus of Consent: Logical Foundations of Constitutional Democracy* (Ann Arbor, Mich., University of Michigan Press, 1965), 262.

   [4] See J. M. Buchanan and G. Tullock, *supra* n. 3, at 317. This essay is not intended to be, nor is it, a study of Burke—as will shortly become patent.

Everyone, including Hobbes, accepts the mythical character of the natural condition of solitary humans wandering about the woods and brought together by the rhetorical persuasion of some great orator statesman. The fable does not begin with Hobbes but is found in Plato and comes to Hobbes through Cicero's version in the *De Inventione* [I, 2] and the *De Oratore* [I, 33]. Foundational written constitutions tend covertly to rely upon that fable. They tend also to bring about the mythical situation; the foundational written constitution constitutes the future society but also, precisely because it surpasses and renders obsolete the electorate that brought it into being, in imagination converts the past into a pre-constitutional repudiated natural condition.

The written constitution brings about in imagination a specious unanimity that negates and forgets the differences that existed before its establishment. Sometimes the new unanimity is brought about by the elimination, whether by execution or exile, of dissenters. The great examples of this elimination are the Constitutions following the revolutions in France and America. But the Constitution of Ireland is not an exception.

Against the images of an age that saw the constitution as a formal and explicit founding contract, Burke sets the image of a constitution as that imperfectly known order—an order that none directly intends—that is set up between people as they live together. Certainly, Burke's imagery is sometimes organic; he may sometimes seem to reject "all attempts to explain collective activity on the basis of rational individual choice".[5] His supposed irrationalism is not the repudiation of intelligence and reason; it is the refusal to consider as reasonable and rational the attempt to direct human affairs by proceeding abstractly from axioms and to impose on circumstances the dictates of a reason unencumbered by experience. A polity is found and established over centuries, not, by abstract reason, founded.[6]

There are contrasting images of unanimity. The first, and more common, is of the formal contract, in which the unanimity is clear, known and, in the constitution, founded. The polity is imagined as the product of a single idea. The second image is of a polity developing through the daily interaction of many people. No single act constitutes the political order, as no single act constitutes the economic order. The constitution is the daily accommodation that

---

[5] J. M. Buchanan, "Marginal Notes" in J. M. Buchanan and G. Tullock, *supra* n. 3, at 317. In fact, Burke does not reject individual choice as an explanation of collective action. He thinks that the actual political order comes about through the interaction of many individual decisions. What he rejects is the idea that the political order is the product of a single decision or set of decisions designed to bring it about. For Burke, as for Adam Smith, the political economy is an order that none intended, but that does not make it irrational. The political economy is not a *nomos* but a *taxon*, an order, not an organisation.

[6] Hobbes was not the first to start the fiction of a state of nature, as Hume remarks in *An Enquiry into the Principles of Morals*, 1777, 151, n. 1 (Oxford, 1988, 189). The fiction is nonetheless used as a model, and as such can be useful. What I have called the Burkean perspective is the effort to work with another model.

arises between those who live together, the lived agreement to live here and with these people.[7]

There is a contingency in human affairs with which a certain and common type of rationality is ill at ease. The Burkean constitution is the lived, disputed, developing order that cannot be perfectly known but, as intelligently lived, is, in two ways, the context within which a written constitution emerges. First, a written constitution, being a linguistic instrument, cannot but presuppose an entire language and operative background of political aspirations, ideas and agreements that cannot be made totally clear. A written constitution will express part of this background in its provisions. Necessarily, this expression will be partial, will suggest a clear unanimity that does not and cannot exist and will divide those whom it purports to constitute. Necessarily, the written constitution will conceal and sometimes destroy the ambiguous and fragile accommodation upon which it arises. Secondly, and precisely because it arises within a context that cannot be fully expressed, a written constitution cannot express fully the interpretative context that is needed for it to be intelligible. No language, no linguistic instrument, can be expressed totally; every language, every linguistic instrument, requires for its interpretation the inexhaustible and developing context of its listeners. Thus, in two intertwined ways, a written constitution rests upon the anterior, inexhaustible, lived constitution that it, by its rhetorical form, often pretends to supplant.

The need for this background or context may be recognised in a written constitution and, to the extent that this recognition occurs, the written constitution acknowledges openly its own partial character. The Dutch civil code, the *Burgerlijk Wetbok*, refers to the "common opinions held about law by the Dutch people" of which the written constitution and code are a partial expression.[8] The provisions may be conceived less as deductions from abstract principles than as attempts to discern and express the developing sense of justice.

It is not that there are no principles or that these cannot be expressed. The suggestion is that the sense of what is just is incompletely specified. The opposing rationalist temptation to which we are prone is to suppose that this sense of justice can be expressed precisely and fully. The rationalist fear—a fear that is by no means unfounded—is that imprecision and incompleteness will allow judges to import their own prejudices under the guise of being the common opinions held about law by the people. This is the ancient and proper concern that the rule of law be not supplanted by the rule of man. Hence, in *Pure Theory of Law*, Kelsen's suggestion is that lacunae can be elim-

---

[7] The idea of an order "that none intendeth", that comes about through many interactions, is due to Adam Smith. It has been in recent times the constant theme of Friedrich von Hayek. Burke, particularly in his writings and speeches on taxation in America, espoused the same notion.

[8] *Burgerlijk Wetbok*, Preliminary Title, s. 7. See J. L. M. Elders, "Equity in Dutch Law" in R. A. Newman (ed.), *Equity in the World's Legal Systems* (Brussels, Bruylant, 1973), 355–65.

inated, in principle, by a rule permitting whatever is not explicitly forbidden or forbidding what is not explicitly permitted.[9]

There are two ways in which a written constitution and, indeed, any set of legal provisions will be incomplete. First, ordinary living will throw up situations that have not been envisaged, and these will demand reform and extension of the explicit law. Secondly, any set of legal or constitutional provisions will be incomplete because it will require the originating and not fully expressible context for its interpretation. It is this common opinion about law, this sense of justice, that gives rise at once to the developing corpus of law and to the possibility of its interpretation.

What is this shadowy sense of justice? Since, by hypothesis, it cannot be articulated fully in advance, the answer to that question cannot be a list of established and known provisions. Is there, then, any alternative to the nagging suspicion that it is no more than the prejudices of judges?

The sense of justice operates and, for the moment, becomes specified in particular cases. Since it is judges who judge, it must be their sense of justice that appears and prevails. It must be obvious that neither in theory nor in practice are judges infallible expressions of the sense of justice. Still, their judgments enter the community and are there subject to acclaim, acceptance, criticism and even to outrage. The sense of justice will appear in the developing juridical conversation of a people. "To carry out the judge's task in each temporal situation [in each particular case] there is a method—supple, prudent, approximative—inherited from the ancients: the method of *discussion*."[10]

In the *Digest*, it is said that lawyers are called by some the priests of justice whose task is to discover the just and the unjust,[11] to discover, in the old common law phrase, the law. They are not infallible but they are learned where learning is not simply a sophistic command of the legal texts but an appreciative understanding of the sense of justice that lies behind them. Beyond Roman law, the idea goes back to Aristotle, by whom, through Cicero, the Roman lawyers were influenced—who makes it clear, particularly in his account of *epieikeia* and *suggnome* and in the whole examination of prudence, that to learn the legal provisions is a means towards the objective, not the objective itself.[12]

"The sense of justice" is prior to the explicit provisions of a written constitution which partially expresses it. That sense of justice is the original constitution and that sense of justice is ever-changing as people live together and

---

[9] It must be remembered that, in *Pure Theory of Law* (Berkeley, Cal., California University Press, 1970) (English translation 1967 of second and enlarged edn. of *Reine Rechtslehre*, 1960), Kelsen is inventing a positivist model, not describing an actual legal system. See also J. Miedzianogora "Juges, Lacunes et Ideologie" in C. Perelman (ed.), *Le Problème des Lacunes en Droit* (Bruxelles, Bruyant, 1968), 513–20.

[10] M. Villey, *Critique de la pensée juridique moderne* (Paris, Dalloz, 1976), 136.

[11] *Digestorum*, Lib. I, Tit. I, 2.

[12] See G. Barden, "Aristotle's Notion of *Epieikeia*" in M. Lamb (ed.), *Creativity and Method* (Milwaukee, Marquette Press, 1981), 355–66; P. Aubenque, *La Prudence chez Aristote* (Paris, PUF, 1963); J. P. Rentto, *Prudentia Juris* (Turku, Turun Yliopistu, 1988).

deal with the continual jural demands that ordinary living imposes upon them.

The Irish Constitution does not speak of the sense of justice of the Irish people. But neither does it assume that all relevant entitlements are precisely and clearly expressed. What are those entitlements that are not yet expressed? There are those who seem to think that behind the Irish Constitution is another, unwritten but articulated, constitution or set of provisions which, although not expressed in the *Constitution of Ireland* are, none the less, guaranteed by it. This unwritten yet articulated constitution is sometimes thought to be the "natural law". The argument of this essay is not that there is a "natural law" so understood with explicit and already articulated provisions to which appeal may be made. Were such a thing to exist it would simply be a super-ordinate law the provisions of which would either supplement or overcome the provisions of the subordinate law and, as such, it would itself be subject to the analysis put forward here in which any articulated set of provisions, written or unwritten, requires a background that cannot be fully and precisely expressed in advance: the background or context that is referred to as "the sense of justice" and is the Burkean constitution of a people.[13]

Law is to be discovered. Like all discoveries, jural discoveries are tentative and fragile. They are submitted to the test of use, sometimes corroborated, sometimes refuted. Constitutions are to be discovered, that is, the constitution that people have given themselves in their interaction with one another is to be discovered. Still, commonly constitutional provisions are thought to differ from other laws. Commonly, in modern times, but not inevitably, the difference is marked in as much as constitutions are established and amended in referenda, whereas other laws are legislated in parliament. Commonly, too, the provisions of a written constitution are held to be superordinate to legislation or tradition. Perhaps there is no single way of understanding what a constitution is or should be. Depending on the practices of the particular State, citizens will use constitutions to attain very different ends. Thus, in recent times in Ireland, attempts have been made to amend the Constitution precisely in order to prevent anticipated legislation, and this practice suggests that the Constitution is thought of both as a curb on parliamentary legisla-

[13] See G. Barden, "Two Versions of Natural Justice" in G. Quinn, A. Ingram and S. Livingstone (eds.), *Justice and Legal Theory in Ireland* (Dublin, Oak Tree Press, 1995). As far as I can see much opposition to "natural law", here and elsewhere, as well as much support for it, rests on the idea the natural law is a collection of injunctions that happen, perhaps conveniently, to be unwritten but which could, in principle, be written. See the articles by D. M. Clarke, "Natural Law and Constitutional Consistency" and A. Whelan, "Constitutional Amendment in Ireland: The Competing Claims" in *Justice and Legal Theory in Ireland*. Natural law, so conceived, does not exist. Neither, conceived in that way, do natural or human rights. What exists is the nature of the jural situation and the task is to understand it and to come to a judgment. That judgment will not be infallible. It will be the best available opinion. For those who reject the natural law so conceived, the more common solution seems to be to conceive the legal system as closed and to stay within the written law: I suggest that a closed legal system is a chimera and confinement to written law an impossibility.

tion and powerful sectional interests and as a means of imposing one's own sectional desires. The effort to enshrine human rights in a constitution (not always the same or even compatible rights) is of the same character and, of course, the modern constitutional movement stemming from the revolutions in France and America follows this course.

It is possible to think otherwise of a written constitution. One may think of it as the effort to express in as inclusive a way as is possible some fundamental characteristics of the already constituted polity. One may think of it not as the attempt to found and establish the polity but as the attempt to discover and express the characteristics of the polity that already exists. Thought of in this way, the constitution will be inclusive. It will not attempt to decide between elements that are antagonistic, yet not so antagonistic as to wrench the polity asunder. The constitution will attempt to discover the sufficient unanimity that already exists and without which no polity survives except in appearance and through force.[14]

Many modern constitutions have neither done nor attempted to do this. The Declaration of 1789 tore French society apart to such an extent that it has not yet been completely healed. The founding declaration of the United States deliberately excluded the Empire Loyalists. Neither was an effort to discover and implement the unanimity of a people. Each intended to establish a new polity that would supplant the old. This was, perhaps, inevitable. It was, perhaps, already the case that the old unanimity had collapsed. Indeed, the fear of this collapse is behind Burke's speech on *Taxation in America*. Similarly, the secession of Ireland from the United Kingdom of Great Britain and Ireland inevitably divided a polity, the sufficient unanimity of which had been under strain. Precisely because the sufficient unanimity is lost, because the antagonisms, the contrasting images and desires, the conflicting symbols have become so extreme, in many cases the intention of inclusiveness is forgotten and the written constitution becomes, more than it need be, the expression of factional interests.

Ironically, even the, perhaps inevitably, exclusive character of the American Constitution vindicates Burke's and Rousseau's contention.[15] The written constitution does not found or constitute a people. Rather, the people that expresses itself in a constitution already exists. The Empire Loyalists who departed for what was then called Upper Canada, now Ontario, were already not part of the people for whom the new constitution would be written.

---

[14] It is worth noting that the sufficient unanimity may be democratically established without having been the matter of formal referenda. It is also worth noting that referenda decided by simple or even qualified majority voting are democratic only in a specialised sense, and that the agreement to decide issues by simple or qualified majority is not itself an agreement that can be reached by simple or qualified majority. The voting rule must be unanimously accepted. See J. M. Buchanan and G. Tullock, *supra* n. 3.

[15] There is no suggestion here that Burke and Rousseau were otherwise close. Nor is it suggested that their idea of the founding act was the same. They agree about what is not the case rather than about what is.

Yet, the effort to be inclusive has some practical purchase. Articulation makes clear what may have been suspected or feared. The refusal to enshrine a particular factional interest may bring about an inclusion that might otherwise have been lost. To yield to the temptation to include factional interest may exclude where exclusion might have been avoided. Thus, to take three examples from the Irish Constitution, the provisions (1) regarding the extent of the national territory, (2) regarding the special position of the Roman Catholic Church (now deleted), (3) regarding the Irish language, exclude where exclusion could have been avoided. It is very understandable that these provisions should have been put in the constitution and it is true that the Constitution was chosen by the majority of those who voted in the establishing referendum, but neither of these is the present issue. It is also true that the exclusions brought about by these provisions were insufficient to wrench the polity apart in any very obvious way. There are other cases of the same kind within the constitution and attempts, sometimes successful, have been made to introduce still more.

About the three exemplary cases it is important to note a crucial distinction. It is a distinction perhaps difficult to see and certainly difficult to live by. To agree or disagree with any one of them, apart from their place in the Constitution, is quite distinct from deploring the place of any one of them within the Constitution. Thus, it would be perfectly reasonable for someone passionately to desire the union of Northern Ireland with Ireland while at the same time utterly repudiating the constitutional provision. The same is true of the other exemplary cases. For someone who considers that the purpose of a written constitution is to discover and express as best as may be the already existing unanimity, the introduction of divisive features is a failure—even if sometimes an unavoidable failure. Faced with any suggested provision or amendment to a written constitution, this person will ask three questions: (1) does this provision discover and express the existing unanimity? (2) if it does not, is it avoidable? (3) if it neither expresses the existing unanimity nor is unavoidable, do I want the exclusion which it will bring about?

The now-deleted provision establishing the special position of the Roman Catholic Church Article 44.1.2 is instructive. It is implausible to suppose that anyone ever considered that it expressed the existing unanimity—although it did, of course, express the unanimity of those who identified "being Irish" with "being Roman Catholic" (by no means all Roman Catholics did this). It is plausible therefore to suppose that those who accepted it wished to bring about the exclusion. It is important to notice that by no means all who voted in favour of the Constitution of 1937 were in favour of this provision, since the Constitution was not established provision by provision and one may presume that there were many who favoured the whole yet did not approve every part. It is plausible to suppose that those who favoured the deletion of the provision (most of whom were themselves Roman Catholics) did so because, more or less explicitly, they realised that its presence brought about an exclusion that they did not want and behind that reasoning is the implicit presupposition that a prime function of a written constitution is to express unanimity.

What, finally, is this "sufficient unanimity"? Here again there is a contrast between the "rationalist" and the Burkean perspective. From the rationalist perspective, the unanimity is to be clear, precise and fully expressed. The imagery of contract theory is clear agreement about propositions both clear and agreeable. Political contract is a metaphor from commercial contract which does, indeed, strive for clear, precise, unambiguous provisions. From the Burkean perspective, the unanimity is the accommodation that people living together have made and continue to make. The discovery of what is just within the common law tradition is the gradual, developing discernment in disputed cases of the jural meanings of that lived accommodation. A similar attitude appears in the *Institutes* [Lib. I, Tit. II, 9; see also 8]: *ex non scripto jus venit, quod usus comprobavit. Nam diuturni mores consensu utentium comprobati legem imitantur*[16] (*from the unwritten comes what usage has established as just. For daily customs established by the consensus of their users imitate law*). Again, and here from the modern civil law tradition, Belgian constitutional lawyers write of custom as "a direct source of law, if not exactly as the constitutional text itself, still, like it, an immediate source" ("*une source directe de droit, sinon au même titre que le texte constitutionelle lui-même, du moins, comme lui, d'une manière immédiate.*").[17] The sufficient unanimity, then, is a continuous accommodation. The task of the Court, in so far as it is not confined to statute or explicit constitutional provision, will be to discern and, in its *sententiae*, to express that accommodation. The task of legislators will be not simply to invent and impose but also to discover in that constitutional accommodation that is daily living the lineaments of what is just. The task of the framers of constitutions will be to discover and express the fundamental jural presuppositions of the lived accommodation.

[16] *The Institutes of Justinian* (trans. T. C. Sanders, London, Longmans, 1922) Sanders' translation runs: "*[t]he unwritten law is that which usage has established; for ancient customs, being sanctioned by the consent of those who adopt them, are like laws.*" This translation is clear enough but, for present purposes, it has some flaws, by commission and omission. Sanders translates *jus* in the first sentence and *legem* as "law", but there is an important distinction; the function of *lex* (law, statute, formulation) is to express the jurisprudents' fallible discovery, initially expressed in *sententiae* and *opiniones*, of *jus* (the just, what is just). He translates the one word, *comprobare*, (*comprobavit, comprobati*), first as "established", then as "sanctioned"; "established" is the better. Finally, I have taken *diuturnus* to mean "daily" rather than "ancient". I propose a less elegant but closer translation: "*[f]rom the unwritten comes what usage has established as just. For daily customs established by the consensus of their users imitate law.*" On the distinction between the written and unwritten see Lib. I, Tit. I, 3, where again the distinction between *ius* (the just) and *lex* (law) occurs. In modern English it is difficult to translate *Scriptum ius est lex . . .* precisely because we no longer easily use the distinction between "right" or "the just" and "law" in this context. An acceptable paraphrase might be: "*[w]hat is just, when written, is law . . .* "

[17] A. Vanwelkenhuyzen, "Du Droit Constitutionelle Belge" in C. Perelman (ed.), *supra* n. 9, at 341.

2

The 1937 Constitution—
Some Historical Reflections

JOHN A. MURPHY

INTRODUCTION

The long-term historical context of *Bunreacht na hÉireann* 1937 is the whole Irish parliamentary tradition stretching back to the middle ages. That tradition is part of Ireland's British heritage, absorbed into, and given distinctive shape by, the Irish experience, particularly in the nineteenth century. Well before that period, however, the constitutional debate was centrally concerned with the question, in one form or another, of what should be the Irish polity's relationship with the British crown. In the modern revolutionary period and after, say from 1919 to 1949, that question was bitterly contested before being finally resolved, the "crown" being meanwhile extended to include "empire" and "commonwealth". Though (or perhaps because) the 1937 Constitution made no reference to these controversial terms (nor to the emotionally-charged "republic" word), it provided the largely acceptable answer to the long-standing question.

SOVEREIGNTY: AN ANCIENT CONCEPT

Another historical context in which to view the Constitution is that of the concept of sovereignty. Since the constitution-makers of the 1916–37 period were anxious to establish (admittedly somewhat tenuous) links with the Gaelic past—the more venerable, the better—they would have liked to dwell on the immemorial concept of sovereignty in early Irish political culture. The accession of a *rí* or king to power in his *tuath* or territory was characterised by his ritual marriage to the sovereignty queen or goddess who was the perennial personification of the territory and who was rejuvenated by each succeeding accession. Peace and prosperity would ensue only if the rightful king ruled: any usurpation or violation of sovereignty would have disastrous consequences.[1]

---

[1] For the sovereignty theme in early Ireland, see M. Herbert, "Goddess and King: The Sacred Marriage in Early Ireland" in L. O. Fradenburg (ed.), *Women and Sovereignty* (Edinburgh,

As the prospective first *Taoiseach*, or powerful head of government, under the new constitutional dispensation, Eamon de Valera might imaginatively have regarded the outcome of the plebiscite on the draft Constitution as the latter-day equivalent of the symbolic marriage of the *rí* to his *tuath*. He might have been puritanically uneasy with the fertility undertones of the pagan ritual but nonetheless pleased to have an ancient Gaelic lineage invoked for his modern Constitution. Indeed, he was to hail Douglas Hyde ceremonially as the Gaelic chieftain of old, newly incarnated as the first President of Ireland—"the successor of our rightful princes"[2] (De Valera could afford to make this ostensibly generous, but essentially meaningless, gesture in the confident awareness it was the office of *Taoiseach* and not that of President which was the real seat of power.)

SOVEREIGNTY *VIS-À-VIS* BRITAIN

In the more immediate context, the new Constitution was all about sovereignty. In the first place, as de Valera would argue, the whole purpose of the independence movement, the central issue of the civil war and the unilateral, piecemeal undoing of the Treaty's shackles in the 1920s and 1930s—all related to the fundamental question: was Ireland (or for the moment that part of it under Irish control) to be autonomous, sovereign, mistress of her own destinies, independent of foreign, that is to say British, interference? *Bunreacht na hÉireann*, de Valera would maintain, unequivocally affirmed that sovereignty, a sovereignty which would soon successfully pass its greatest test—neutrality in a world war. After all, foreign affairs *is* sovereignty, in Pandit Nehru's phrase.[3]

SOVEREIGNTY OF THE PEOPLE

But there was yet another, and perhaps the most important, dimension of sovereignty in the Constitution. It meant the supreme authority of the people (Article 6.1), not the dominance of the State over its citizens.[4] The point has been made that in a unicameral parliament (the "obstructive" Senate had been abolished) a powerful de Valera could have enacted his Constitution legisla-

Edinburgh University Press, 1992), 264–75 and references therein; A. D. Rees and B. Rees, *Celtic Heritage: Ancient Tradition in Ireland and Wales* (London, Thames and Hudson, 1961), 73–6.

[2] Cited in M. Moynihan (ed.), *Speeches and Statements by Eamon de Valera 1917–73*, (Dublin, Gill and Macmillan, 1980), 353–4. The inauguration took place on 25 June 1938 in Dublin Castle, the actual and symbolic seat of British rule in Ireland.

[3] Quoted in R. Fanning, *Independent Ireland* (Dublin, Helicon, 1983), 120.

[4] Cf. J. M. Kelly, *The Irish Constitution* (2nd edn., Dublin, Butterworths, 1984), 28 ff. Kelly quoted (28) Henchy J to the effect that the dominant role of the people is "a central feature of the ideological rationale and political philosophy underlying the Constitution".

tively, without recourse to popular endorsement.[5] Given the fascistic and dictatorial climate of so much of contemporary Europe, he could have carved out an authoritarian power base for himself, had he been so inclined. And those opponents who had long distrusted and demonised him were vociferously suspicious of his sinister intentions, alleging that the Constitution (particularly, the new and strange office of the Presidency) would be in the last analysis, simply a front for personal aggrandisement.[6] Yet the truth is that this new basic document, however much it might reflect the values of contemporary Catholic sociology, bore witness to Eamon de Valera's commitment to liberal democratic principles and to the British parliamentary heritage. These principles are exemplified both in the Articles (15–28) dealing with the organs of government and parliament, and in that (Article 40) proclaiming "personal rights".

De Valera ringingly affirmed that the Constitution clearly upheld the sovereignty of the people. "If there is one thing more than another that is clear and shining through this whole Constitution, it is the fact that the people are the masters."[7] In expounding such a principle at this stage of his political and constitutional development, de Valera was also exorcising the ghost of one ignoble phase of his past. Ten or fifteen years earlier, in what was for him a period of demoralisation and debacle (say, 1921 to 1926), de Valera seemed to be rejecting contemptuously the majority verdict of the electorate who had "no right to do wrong".[8] He appealed rather to a mythical and mystical Irish people whose wishes could be determined through auto-cardiac inspection,[9] not by vulgar head-counts at the ballot box. By the mid-1930s, as an accomplished and successful parliamentarian, he was only too willing to proclaim the sovereignty in the Constitution of flesh-and-blood people rather than the idealised projection of his own egoism and pride. This political pilgrimage is not only an interesting personal odyssey but an individual experience of a central historical dynamic.

REPUBLICANISM AND "O'CONNELLISM"

Since the 1790s, and certainly since the mid-nineteenth century, there have been two different, and often conflicting, philosophies in mainstream Irish

---

[5] B. Farrell, "From First Dáil Through Irish Free State" in B. Farrell (ed.) *De Valera's Constitution and Ours* (Dublin, Gill and Macmillan, 1988) at 30.

[6] See below, n. 48.

[7] *Dáil Éireann* debates Vol. 67, col. 40, 11 May 1937.

[8] See T. P. Coogan, *De Valera, Long Fellow, Long Shadow* (London, Hutchinson, 1993), 313. Outlining the aims of his new *Fianna Fáil* party in 1926, de Valera said: "in forcing acceptance of the Treaty, majority rule ran counter to the fundamental rights of the nation": Moynihan, *supra* n. 2, at 137.

[9] The celebrated utterance was, "whenever I wanted to know what the Irish people wanted, I had only to examine my own heart and it told me straight off what the Irish people wanted": *Dáil Éireann*, Treaty Debates, 6 Jan. 1922, 274.

nationalism. One is republicanism, which proclaims the abstract rights of the nation and the inalienable and non-debatable right of "the Irish people" to separation and complete independence, irrespective of the ballot box, counting of heads and majorities or minorities: self-determination is a pre-ordained right which admits of no compromise, since compromise is betrayal. Those who promote the republican cause constitute an elite, a "prophetic shock minority" whose dedication and sacrifices give them the authority to act on behalf of "the Irish people", a rather abstract and idealized entity, an ideological construct, as it were.

The other nationalist tradition, pragmatic if not mundane, can best be described as democratic and parliamentarian: the term "O'Connellism" has been suggested.[10] Here the players are the flesh-and-blood "people of Ireland" rather than the mystical "Irish people".[11] The national goal is advanced gradually through the mobilisation of voters (on a widening franchise) who support a leader and party working for the amelioration of grievances and, ultimately, for Irish self-government through legislation (Home Rule) by the imperial Parliament. The early Sinn Féin movement also belongs to this tradition since it, too, envisages a democratic and parliamentary solution, albeit of a more radical kind, viz. the withdrawal of elected representatives from Westminster to form an independent Irish parliament, linked to Britain only through a common monarch. The parliamentary version of nationalism further presupposes that, post-independence, the will of the majority, as electorally expressed, will prevail.

Republicanism has traditionally disdained parliamentarianism as self-serving, compromising and corrupt. Yet, there are also links between the two traditions. The Irish Republican Brotherhood espoused the idea of "the Irish Republic now virtually established", having its own absolute existence, irrespective of parliamentary movements, parties and leaders. The president of the IRB (Michael Collins, in his time) was also president of the *de iure* Irish Republic, according to republican theology. The IRB ethos had an intermittent existence from the late 1850s down to the dissolution of the Brotherhood in 1924. Yet, the IRB could and did form tactical alliances with parliamentarians (as in the New Departure) and it could make pragmatic, *realpolitik* decisions about accepting measures of Home Rule, and the Anglo-Irish Treaty of 1921. Conversely, it should be borne in mind that parliamentarians could also be IRB men.

On the face of it, the 1916 Proclamation—indeed the 1916 Rising itself—seems to be a classic instance of the self-mandated republican elite arrogantly

---

[10] T. Garvin, *1922: The Birth of Irish Democracy* (Dublin, Gill and Macmillan, 1996), 2, where he defines O'Connellism as "a blend of Catholicism, democracy, nationalism and liberalism that characterises independent modern Ireland".

[11] The distinction here drawn between the actual "people of Ireland" and the mystical "Irish people" corresponds to Rousseau's contrast between the "will of all" (counting of heads) and the "general will" (interpreted and determined by the republican elite): see Garvin, *ibid.*, at 18. In his chap. 2, Garvin develops the theme in the context of the Treaty split and Civil War.

disregarding constitutional or parliamentary norms. And yet, the Proclamation was published by a "Provisional Government" which would exist only until "the establishment of a permanent National Government, representative of the whole people of Ireland, and elected by the suffrages of all her men and women".

Here we see republicanism's unwitting tribute to constitutionalism and parliamentarianism, again suggesting that the dualism was by no means absolute. Conversely, when the first *Dáil Éireann* issued its Declaration of Independence on 21 January 1919,[12] it did so primarily as a ratification of "the establishment of the Irish Republic" in 1916, and only secondarily by virtue of the general election triumph of December 1918. This interplay in Irish nationalism, as well as the dominance of the democratic tradition, is once again evident in the attitude of republican diehards from 1922 to 1926 (and, in some cases, long thereafter). True, they evinced an elitist contempt for "the will of all", or the will of the majority expressing itself through the ballot box in 1922–3 in support of the Treaty compromise. But the republicans' insistence that their loyalty was to the Second *Dáil*, now unlawfully usurped in their view, was in itself a backhanded tribute to the strength of the parliamentary or constitutional tradition.

SQUARING THE CIRCLE

Nonetheless, Irish nationalism was profoundly split after 1921 on the issue of "the will of all" versus "the general will" as determined by republican absolutes. Though the great majority of republicans, led by Eamon de Valera, entered and "worked" the Irish Free State system in 1927, real consensus on the legitimacy of the State was not achieved until ten years later, with the adoption of the 1937 Constitution. (An embittered republican[13] remnant took much longer to come in from the cold, but this was an insignificant factor post-1937 as far as consensus was concerned.) The Constitution, primarily designed for domestic consumption (within the twenty-six counties) and aimed at the republican core, succeeded in gaining the allegiance of all but the most fanatical. It reconciled the erstwhile diehards and convinced them that de Valera had made an honest woman of the Free State (another marital symbol!). For de Valera himself, as has been said above, the Constitution exorcised the demon of his own ambivalence to "the will of all" in 1921–3, when he appeared to be flouting the electorate's wishes. But, as well as reconciling republicans and setting to rights his own democratic credentials, Eamon de Valera in securing popular consent for the Constitution could be said to have given national sovereignty a democratic mandate. Put another way, the

---

[12] *Dáil Éireann Proceedings 1919–21* (Dublin, n.d.), 14–17.
[13] In the 1930s, "republican" meant separatist, anti-crown and anti-Commonwealth. Today, it is virtually identical with "irredentist".

Constitution largely succeeded in squaring the circle between the parliamentary "will of all" and the republican "general will", thus healing (as far as the twenty-six-county State was concerned) a nationalist schism of long standing. In the historical perspective, perhaps this is the most significant achievement of the enacted Constitution.

THE DE VALERA PAPERS

The drafting process and the thinking behind the Constitution were considerably illuminated for historians by the opening (in time for the fiftieth anniversary of *Bunreacht na hÉireann* in 1987) of the relevant sections of the de Valera Papers at the Franciscan house of studies, Killiney, Co. Dublin. Professor Dermot Keogh has made a study in depth of these papers and has incorporated them in his extensive writings on the historical background to the Constitution.[14] My own observations here are confined to what struck me personally, in the course of reading the Papers at Killiney.

First of all, they bring out the almost pedantic preoccupation of the architects of the Constitution[15] with the concept of sovereignty. There are drafts all over the place, sometimes in extravagant phraseology, on the absolute and indefeasible nature of the people's right to determine the forms of state and government, both in regard to internal and external policy. De Valera had deliberately exaggerated the shortcomings of, and British influence over, the 1922 constitution,[16] in order to exalt the supremacy of the people in the 1937 document, and to demonstrate beyond doubt that the exercise of political authority derived from no outside source whatsoever. (Even the hostile *Irish Times*[17] conceded the clarity of the document in this respect.) Republicans felt that sovereignty had been abandoned or compromised in 1922 because of a British-dictated constitution imposed on a divided national movement, and it was now essential to omit the symbols of king and empire from the new Constitution, the ground having been cleared by the External Relations Act of 1936.

We may note that, in hallowed nationalist doctrine, sovereignty connoted not only political independence but, as consequences thereof, social justice and harmony, economic prosperity and cultural autonomy. Thus, the

[14] See his lengthy essay, "The Irish Constitutional Revolution: An Analysis of the Making of the Constitution" in F. Litton (ed.) *The Constitution of Ireland* (Dublin, Institute of Public Affairs, 1988), 4–84: the emphasis throughout is on the religious/ecclesiastical dimension. See also D. Keogh, "Church, State and Society" in B. Farrell *supra* n. 5, at 103–22.

[15] De Valera's assistants and advisers included Maurice Moynihan, secretary to the Government; John J. Hearne, legal adviser in the Department of External Affairs; Philip O'Donoghue, Attorney-General's office; and Arthur Matheson, parliamentary draftsman.

[16] which, however, despite the monarchical trappings, expressed the essential autonomy of the Irish Free State, and which, as events were to prove, was vigorously evolutionary: cf. Garvin, *supra* n. 10, at 16 ff.

[17] Editorial, 1 May 1937.

Constitution articulated anew the Irish-Ireland vision splendid, resoundingly proclaimed in 1916 and 1919, but thereafter dimmed and blighted by civil war, partition, British intrusion and economic depression. Interestingly, one of the Irish-language drafts of what eventually became Article 5, read as follows: *Ard-Fhlaitheas is ea Stát na hÉireann gurab iad muintir na dúithche atá ina cheannas*.[18] "*Flaitheas*" is also the Irish word for "Paradise" which would undoubtedly be the state (State?) arrived at, were the multi-faceted visions of sovereignty to be realised!

The emphasis in the drafts on sovereignty, *nominatim* and otherwise, is to be found in various articles of the final Constitution text. The concept was also invoked during the plebiscite campaign, and people were asked to support the document on the "self-determination" basis of Article 1 ("The Irish nation hereby affirms its . . . sovereign right to choose its own form of Government . . ."). A newspaper advertisement on the very day of the plebiscite asserted that Ireland, like other named countries, should command its own destiny.[19] Interestingly, Articles 2 and 3 were not the subject of any advertisements during the campaign.

The de Valera Papers indicate that there was discussion on whether the *Dáil* should enact a new Constitution (which would have been perfectly in order) and also on whether a constituent assembly should be convened. In the end, the overriding factor was the need to give the Constitution strong popular credentials, by having it endorsed in a plebiscite. However, popular sovereignty was not to be allowed to run wild at the expense of representative democracy: there was to be no restoration of the power of popular referendum and initiative provided for in the *Saorstát* Constitution (1922) but abolished by the Cosgrave Government in 1928. Similarly, de Valera's Constitution was at pains to proclaim democratic rights in an age of fascism (in the fancy nationalist rhetoric, "to enshrine those ideas of liberty and justice embraced by the Gael") and to distance itself from the notorious Public Safety Act of 1931: still, de Valera's conservatism and concern for public order were given expression in Article 28.3.3 of the new document which provided that there could be no constitutional challenge to "any law . . . for the purpose of securing the public safety and the preservation of the State in time of war or armed rebellion".

---

[18] "The State of Ireland is a supreme sovereignty (*Ard-Fhlaitheas*) under the leadership of the people of the country" (author's translation): de Valera Papers 1060/1. Those involved in drawing up the Irish language version of the Constitution were Micheál Ó Gríobhtha (1869–1946) and the scholar, Risteard Ó Foghludha ("*Fiachra Éilgeach*") 1872–1957.

[19] Advertisement, *Irish Times*, 1 July 1937. Also, see a speech by Eamon de Valera in Seanad Éireann (vol. 22, cols. 988–90, 7 Feb. 1939) asserting that 26-county sovereignty could not be sacrificed for 32-county unity.

THE ABSENT "REPUBLIC"

One final point may be made in reference to sovereignty in the sense of autonomy *vis-à-vis* the British power. Though sovereignty was of supreme importance it was not identified by de Valera with the notion of "republic". Unlike many of his comrades of the revolutionary generation, de Valera was not a doctrinaire republican, and that by his own admission. Indeed, he was not even a doctrinaire separatist, being prepared to consider at different times such accommodations as external association, a defence pact with Britain and local autonomy for Northern Ireland.

Yet, nobody was more aware of the dynamic, not to say sacrosanct, connotations of the term "Republic" for Irish revolutionaries who believed the Irish Republic was baptised in the blood of the 1916 martyrs and made imperishable thorough the sacrifices of 1919–21 before being betrayed in 1922. And had not de Valera himself had his glorious hour as President of the Republic? It is hardly surprising then (especially given the need to reconcile extra-parliamentary republicans) that, in drafting the Constitution, he should have considered using explicit "republican" terminology. He himself had no doubt that the successive unilateral constitutional changes of the 1930s, particularly the legislation of December 1936, had made the twenty-six-county State a *de facto* republic. Thus, the self-satisfied annotation appears in his Papers in his own hand: "We are a Republic."[20] Eight or nine years later, under pressure in the *Dáil* concerning the anomalous status of the State, de Valera was to insist stubbornly that by any definition (of which he gave numerous examples) the State *was* a republic, thus provoking taunts about a "dictionary" republic.[21]

The description *"Poblacht na hÉireann"* appearing in constitutional drafts[22] in the de Valera Papers was not eventually used, and the Republic was not formally proclaimed nor even mentioned in the Constitution. De Valera would claim, of course, that the Constitution was republican in spirit, but why this reluctance by the leader of Fianna Fáil, "the Republican party", to use the term "Republic", *nominatim*?

In the first place, de Valera correctly interpreted (without necessarily sharing) republican feeling that the revered Republic could be acclaimed only in a unified thirty-two-county context: using the sacred term to describe a partitioned State would be a betrayal of the republican dead and of their ideals. De Valera himself had a rather different slant, being an "implicit" republican: the *locus classicus* of the expression of this philosophy is the Arbour Hill

---

[20] De Valera Papers, 1972/1. "On December 11th 1936 we passed an amendment of the constitution deleting all the King clauses remaining at that date and transferring to the Executive Council."

[21] *Dáil Éireann*, vol. 97, cols. 2570–2, 17 July 1945.

[22] De Valera Papers 1029/2. "Éire" and "Saorstát Éireann" are used in other drafts (1029/3/1 and 1029/6 respectively).

speech of 23 April 1933 where he referred to the need to get rid of objection-able forms and symbols:

> "Let us remove these forms one by one, so that this State that we control may be a Republic in fact and that when the time comes, the proclaiming of the Republic may involve no more than a ceremony, the formal confirmation of a status already attained".[23]

Another reason for the omission of "Republic" from the Constitution was the need to have some regard for Ulster unionist sensitivity, as de Valera understood it. Incredible as it may seem to a later generation, he claimed he was keeping the unionists sympathetically in mind in drafting the Constitution and that "You cannot go farther than we have gone in this Constitution to meet the view of those in the North, without sacrificing, to an extent they are not prepared to sacrifice, the legitimate views and opinions of the vast major-ity of our people here".[24] Indeed, de Valera admitted that only for the Northern dimension there would have been a flat, downright declaration of a Republic in the Constitution.[25]

Finally, he avoided using the term "Republic" on pragmatic and prudent grounds—the wish not to provoke the British Government unduly, a reaction which might have had undesirable consequences, *inter alia*, for the Irish com-munity in Britain. De Valera was never an anglophobe[26] and did not deliber-ately seek to aggravate Anglo-Irish relations, or altogether to eliminate the Commonwealth. The constitutional changes he had effected from 1932 to 1936, though dramatic in their cumulative impact, were also gradualist and circumspect, and if part of the object of the exercise was to tweak the lion's tail, then this was to be done judiciously and with nice calculation. Conversely, this mentality was understood by the British side, as the absence of any retaliation showed.

AN INWARD-LOOKING DOCUMENT

By and large, the Constitution was conceived and born as a unilateral, internal process, with only secondary regard for Northern, British or Commonwealth reaction. It contained only oblique references to external rela-tions (Article 29.4), such matters continuing to be relegated to the legislative provisions of the External Relations Act (1936). There was no direct mention

[23] Moynihan, *supra* n. 2, at 237.

[24] *Dáil Éireann* Debates vol. 68, col. 429, 14 June 1937. In support of his argument, de Valera would doubtless point to such "conciliatory" gestures as the 26-county *de facto* jurisdiction of his government; the pacific principle of Art. 29; the retention of the (very nebulous) links with crown and commonwealth; and the omission of the term "republic" from the Constitution.

[25] *Dáil Éireann* Debates vol. 68, col. 430, 14 June 1937.

[26] *Seanad Éireann* Debates, vol. 22, col. 990, 7 Feb. 1939. See also Moynihan, *supra* n. 2, Index, *sub* Anglo-Irish relations at 65 to the effect that, even in Aug. 1921, de Valera expressed his wish for good neighbourly relations with Britain.

of king or crown any more than there was of republic. The Constitution was drafted, complained one leader writer, "as if Great Britain were a million miles away".[27] That was not altogether fair or correct: at least, Edward VIII was informed that the Constitution would provide peace and harmony in Ireland and a more secure basis for friendship and co-operation with Britain. However, it was King George VI who observed drily to C. W. Dixon, in regard to Article 29.4.2 , that he did not mind being called an "organ" or even an "instrument" but drew the line at being described as a "method of procedure"![28]

It may have been a coincidence, or cock-a-snook timing, that the *Dáil* debates on the Constitution (Second Stage concluded, 11 May 1937) took place against the background of George VI's coronation (13 May) and the Commonwealth prime ministers' conference at which the Irish Government was unrepresented. The *Dáil* finally approved the draft Constitution, by sixty-two votes to forty-eight, on 14 June, the day the premiers met in London. Alvin Owsley, the US minister in Dublin, believed the timing was deliberate "to precipitate the fullest surprise from all quarters and create the widest discussion".[29]

Regrettably, de Valera had always been indifferent to the potential of the Commonwealth dimension, seeing it only in the context of his "external association" concept. His indifference turned to antagonism because of what he took to be the hostile attitude of the Dominions at the Ottawa conference of 1932.[30] His view was that the State was in the Commonwealth but not of it. Still, he was aware that total secession from the Commonwealth would deprive him of any room for manœuvre. For their part the Dominions, for their own good reason, indulgently regarded de Valera's constitutional ambitions. Article 28.3.1 ("the State shall not participate in any war save with the assent of *Dáil Éireann*") was certainly to their liking. The right of each Dominion to decide on peace or war was the principle being discussed at the London conference in 1937 by such statesmen as Hertzog of South Africa and Mackenzie King of Canada, and it would be implemented on the outbreak of World War II in 1939, thus putting the sovereignty of the Commonwealth nations beyond doubt.

WEAK POPULAR ENDORSEMENT

Given de Valera's preoccupation with the people as masters of the Constitution, it is interesting to note the unimpressive nature of the popular

---

[27] Editorial, *Irish Times*, 1 May 1937.
[28] "Dixon Memoirs" quoted in D. McMahon, *Republicans and Imperialists: Anglo-Irish Relations in the 1930's* (New Haven, Conn., Yale University Press, 1984), 220.
[29] *Ibid.*, at 214.
[30] For details of the Ottawa conference, see McMahon, *supra* n. 28, at 74–9.

endorsement. After the long public debate in May and June, inside and out-side the *Dáil*, the people were at last asked the question on 1 July 1937: "Do you approve of this draft constitution which is the subject of this plebiscite?" There was a 75 per cent turnout with the plebiscite being carried by 685,105 to 526,945, (57 per cent of voters saying "yes" and 43 per cent "no") while the spoiled votes amounted to an extraordinary 104,805.[31] The supporters of the Constitution could console themselves that the "yes" vote was somewhat more than a partisan Fianna Fáil one (only 45 per cent of voters supported the party in the concomitant general election), but the result was nevertheless disappointing, especially since the largest possible "yes" vote in the twenty-six counties was needed to counteract, so to speak, the objection that a parti-tioned electorate could not speak for all the people of Ireland.[32] In the event, the resounding phrase "Enacted by the People", which appears in the text of the Constitution, just before the Preamble, sounds rather hollow in the light of the actual results.

De Valera made no secret of his disappointment, but he paternalistically (and rather unconvincingly) explained the result by claiming that the people as a whole had not understood the importance of this fundamental measure. It was his own fault, he added, as the voters had not been given "sufficient opportunity, in the rural districts especially, for its meanings to penetrate into the minds of the average person in Ireland".[33] This reflected the kind of naïveté or arrogance that prompted such descriptions of de Valera as a cranky professor with a metaphysical mind. Still, it was now the *people*'s State, and subversion and treason had henceforth a new meaning.

A TWENTY-SIX-COUNTY CONSTITUTION

For all his genuine depth of feeling about the partition issue—and it was his frustration over its apparent copperfastening in 1925 that finally drove him into the constitutional politics of the Irish Free State—de Valera was too much, and too good, a practitioner of *realpolitik* not to accept the twenty-six-county area as his pragmatic field of political endeavour. Where the priorities of culture, the economy, party organisation and security were concerned, de Valera throughout his active political career put the interests of the twenty-six-county State under his control above the aspirational thirty-two-county nation. So it is that *Bunreacht na hÉireann* is essentially a document for the area under de Valera's jurisdiction: once the irredentist aspirations of THE NATION (Articles 1–3) are flourished, the body of THE STATE (Articles 4 ff.) is

---

[31] R. Sinnott, *Irish Voters Decide: Voting Behaviour in Elections and Referendum since 1918,* (Manchester, Manchester University Press, 1995), 220–1.

[32] De Valera had claimed that the 26-county electorate would be acting "on behalf of the whole nation": *Dáil Éireann*, vol. 67, col. 1913, 4 June 1937.

[33] Quoted in McMahon, *supra* n. 28, at 221.

then delineated in detail.[34] Some sections reflect the values of what was in 1937 a homogeneously Catholic twenty-six-county society, and much of the document is strongly influenced by the then fashionable principles of Catholic sociology: for example vocationalism is manifest in the articles providing for the born-again Senate (*Seanad Éireann*, Articles 18–19) and there is an elaborate window-display of social policy in Article 45—non-binding, however, and "not cognisable by any Court". The other main influence on the Constitution was the liberal tradition of parliamentary democracy, the political culture inherited by post-independence parties from Parnell and Redmond and formed in a general British context.

TERRITORIALISM AND THE NORTH

If republicans were to be reconciled through a new constitution, an expression of territorial nationalism in some form or other was inevitable in the document. The acceptance of partition after the Boundary Commission debacle had to be challenged and de Valera had promised "there would be no words in the new Constitution that could possibly place bounds to the march of a nation".[35]

In the de Valera Papers, what was to be the territorial claim in the finalised Constitution (Articles 2 and 3) does not appear in earlier drafts. But de Valera was trying out other formulations, one of which intriguingly reads: "the territory of Éire shall be such as from time to time may come within the jurisdiction of Éire". Was the notion of a gradually expanding jurisdiction linked to some vague idea of re-partition through county-based plebiscites?[36]

It was self-deception on a heroic scale for de Valera to think that his Constitution was "the only basis for unity", that the document could go no further to attract or placate Northern unionists and that it would not need a comma of alteration for a united Ireland! And this with reference to a constitution which the unionists could reasonably complain was threatening territorial aggrandisement by a Catholic State over the Protestant north-east.

The Independent TD, Frank MacDermot, took almost a lone, anglophile pro-Commonwealth stance in the Dáil during the debate on the Constitution.[37] De Valera never really faced up to the prophetic questions raised by MacDermot (though he did agree, to everybody's surprise, to the

---

[34] Interestingly, the Arts. dealing with the flag (Art. 7) and the Irish language (Art. 8) come under "State" rather than "Nation".

[35] Quoted in J. Bowman, *De Valera and the Ulster Question, 1917–93* (Oxford, Clarendon, 1982), 149.

[36] De Valera Papers, 1029/1 (in his own hand). In this connection, it may be noted that de Valera in 1923 had proposed a six-county plebiscite to determine what areas might be represented in the *Dáil*; by 1937 he obviously no longer favoured this idea. See J. Bowman, *supra* n. 35, at 150.

[37] For MacDermot, see J. Bowman, *supra* n. 35, at 128–9.

deputy's suggested addition—"or, in the English language, Ireland"—to Article 4's "the name of the State is Éire"[38]). MacDermot believed that the king and Commonwealth should be constitutionally retained in the interests of North–South, British–Irish and Commonwealth–Ireland relations.[39] In particular, MacDermot felt that the king should be used as an instrument of Irish unity, but he got no support in the *Dáil* for this approach. And he certainly did not move de Valera. Replying to him on the last day of the debate, de Valera was adamant that the majority should not be asked to make sacrifices all the time, and "we cannot go one inch farther than what is provided for in the Constitution" in respect of making sacrifices for unity.[40]

REACTION: NORTHERN IRELAND, BRITAIN, COMMONWEALTH

Predictably, the leaders of Ulster unionism were contemptuously dismissive of the new Constitution. Their leader, Craigavon, called the Irish claims presumptuous and described the Constitution as objectionable but, secure in the knowledge of British support, he was confident it "made not a pin of difference".[41]

In regard to the British themselves, de Valera's approach was relatively prudent and statesmanlike. His masterly strategy was to put the popularly-endorsed Constitution in place and then negotiate on other areas of British–Irish conflict (having sent out signals from late 1937) without having to run risks on the constitutional issue. This situation was in sharp contrast to the Treaty negotiations in 1921 when the Irish had failed to secure any constitutional recognition beforehand. Moreover, in 1938 the British side was mindful of the critical European situation, and the Irish benefited from the prevailing mood of appeasement. Thus, the British reaction to the Constitution was a mixture of phlegm and relief. Seeing *"Éire"* as the old Irish Free State writ new, Chamberlain and his colleagues made an identification between the two terms that was to be subsequently copied by the British and unionist media, to the not inconsiderable (but unjustifiable) irritation of the Irish in subsequent decades. Reciprocating fudge and ambivalence in British–Irish relations, the Chamberlain Government saw no reason to regard *"Éire"* as a foreign State or to expel it from the British Commonwealth of Nations. For various reasons, this ambivalent position also suited the Dominions. Malcolm McDonald, the Dominions Secretary, assured the South Africans that the new Constitution would not be a source of encouragement to republicanism in their country; Canada, South Africa and Australia all had problems with minorities and counselled caution on the Irish question; and,

---

[38] *Dáil Éireann*, vol. 68, col. 115, 9 June 1937.
[39] *Dáil Éireann*, vol. 67, cols. 953 ff., 25 May 1937.
[40] *Dáil Éireann*, vol. 68, col. 429, 14 June 1937.
[41] *Irish Times*, 6 May 1937. Also see J. Bowman, *supra* n. 35, at 157.

in any case, Mackenzie King believed the new Irish document to be "of no great importance".[42] For their part, the Irish rightly hailed the Anglo-Irish Agreement of 1938 as a triumph, despite the lack of progress on the partition question.

REACTION: DOMESTIC

At home, reaction to the Constitution took numerous forms. Many of the adverse attitudes were influenced by hostility to, or suspicion of, Eamon de Valera, so powerfully did the Fianna Fáil leader polarise feelings in the bitterly divided political scene. On the "national" aspects of the Constitution, the small remnant of republican diehards like Mary MacSwiney were not seduced by the new document: as guardians of the holy flame of the "usurped" Second *Dáil*, they continued to maintain that the State had no legitimacy. *Sinn Féin* flew black flags to mark the passing of the "bogus" Constitution.[43] Northern nationalists like Eamon Donnelly who wanted representation in the *Dáil* regretted that the Constitution had been enacted before an anti-partition drive could be mounted.[44]

On the conservative side of the political spectrum, Articles 2 and 3 provoked scepticism rather than furious rejection. Fine Gael spokesmen like James Dillon, Paddy McGilligan and Desmond Fitzgerald maintained that the Constitution would not promote national unity[45] while their leader, W. T. Cosgrave, referred to the "make-believe" nature of the territorial clauses[46] about which J. J. McElligott, the secretary of the Department of Finance, was robustly critical.[47]

By and large, however, such was the strong and instinctive nationalist consensus on Ireland's right to unity that Articles 2 and 3 generated far less debate than a latter-day observer might expect. The loudest objections to the Constitution, whether voiced inside or outside the *Dáil*, were about very different matters. Fears were expressed about perceived limitations on the freedom of the press and of popular assembly (Article 40.6.1). Other causes for (real or simulated) concern included the role of women in society (Article 41.2), the provision for special courts (Article 38.3), the electoral system (Article 16.2.5) and the qualification of the right to private property (Article 43.2).

What most provoked de Valera's opponents, however, was the new office of the Presidency (Articles 12–14). This led to an extensive debate. Fine Gael

---

[42] For the Commonwealth reaction, see McMahon, *supra* n. 28, at 47–50 and ch. X.

[43] See statement by "Second Dáil", *Irish Freedom*, June 1937; Sinn Féin statement, *Irish Press*, 16 June 1937.

[44] For Donnelly's views, see J. Bowman, *supra* n. 35, in Index, but particularly 149–50.

[45] *Dáil Éireann*, vol. 67, cols. 249, 373, 413, 12–13 May 1937.

[46] *Irish Times*, 3 May 1937.

[47] See R. Fanning, "Mr De Valera drafts a Constitution" in B. Farrell, *supra* n. 5 at 37–9.

approached the issue on a party and personal basis: de Valera was simply not to be trusted. Lending some semblance of substance to the opposition's expressed fears was the inordinate length of the section on the Presidency and (in the context of the fascist Europe of the 1930s) the apparently considerable powers of the office (for example, Article 13.4: "The supreme command of the Defence Forces is hereby vested in the President"). According to Dr T. F. O'Higgins, "the whole document was designed to build an edifice for one man to rest on, and the powers that were to be given to that individual were to be filched from the parliament of the people". O'Higgins's Fine Gael colleague, Desmond Fitzgerald, painted a lurid scenario: de Valera planned to win the election, become Taoiseach for a year, give extra powers to the presidency, and then take over the office: "most people know perfectly well that de Valera proposed to take the office himself".[48]

De Valera very sensibly pooh-poohed all this paranoia: he asserted that the President would be the ultimate guardian of the people's rights[49] and, besides, much of presidential activity was designed to be in the realm of the ceremonial—shaking hands with golfers and other visitors.

THE CONSTITUTION: CHANGE AND NO CHANGE

The foremost expert commentator on the Constitution, the late Professor John Kelly, used to scorn the idea that the document needed replacement because it had reached a certain age. The durability of the US Constitution would seem to refute effectively the notion that a constitution, like an aircraft frame, is susceptible to fatigue after a given period in service. On the other hand, it could be argued that the US Constitution needed various amendments in order to be able to survive, and in any case it enshrines fundamental principles of liberty and democracy guaranteed to stand the test of time. When Irish people say "hasn't our Constitution served us well?", they are really referring to the provisions about representative government and individual rights which would have to appear in *any* Irish constitution as long as the State remains part of Western democracy—and indeed of the European Union. And even the provisions on personal rights have needed the process of judicial review for their effectiveness.

In other respects, especially where the 1937 Constitution reflected the particular political preoccupations of the day and the values of a then dominant ethos, it could be argued that the document has not served us all that well in the vastly changing circumstances of the last thirty years. The 1996 Whitaker Report on the Constitution has suggested that some of the factors now influencing possible constitutional change would include "the evolution of socio-political thinking, the desire for greater inclusiveness, the implications of

[48] *Dáil Éireann*, vol. 67, cols. 268–9, 381–2, 12–13 May 1937.
[49] *Dáil Éireann*, 11 May 1937.

membership of the European Union".[50] (Indeed the State's membership of the European Community, dating from 1973, necessitated a most significant constitutional change: cf. Article 29.4.3). The Constitution has been, or needs to be, altered to reflect popular thinking on Church–State relations;[51] the changing position of marriage and the family; denominational ethos and public morality; the ongoing abortion debate; and women's rights. In the latter connection, the Constitution Review Group recommended that the gender-inclusiveness principle should be observed in the wording of the Constitution—a recommendation in itself reflecting a profound change in attitudes to women since 1937.

The greatest transformation of all in the State's political circumstances has been in the linked areas of nationalism, sovereignty, and North–South and British–Irish attitudes and relationships. Here is constitutional change waiting to happen, so to speak. The concept of national sovereignty, with its economic and cultural concomitants, was central to the 1937 Constitution, as we have seen, but it has since been eroded by numerous developments, particularly increasing European integration. Culturally, the linguistic form of sovereignty in Article 8.1 (" . . . Irish . . . is the first official language") was pious aspiration to begin with, and is even more so now: the Whitaker Report recommends a "more realistic" approach here.

Public debate, often painful, over the period of the Northern Ireland conflict, has created a general awareness of how inadequate, to say the least, the opening clauses of the Constitution now are. It is becoming increasingly difficult to defend the proposition that there is one Irish nation coterminous with the whole island pursuing a single destiny (Article 1). Even before the outbreak of the Northern "Troubles", an all-party 1967 *Oireachtas* committee, in the buoyant atmosphere of the mid-1960s, made a reconciliatory recommendation on the aggressively irredentist Articles 2 and 3, suggesting they should be replaced by a fraternal affirmation: "The Irish nation hereby proclaims its firm will that its territory be re-united in brotherly affection between all Irishmen."[52] This was, for the period, a remarkably liberal sentiment, particularly in the immediate aftermath of the triumphalist fiftieth anniversary celebrations of the 1916 Rising.

However, no government has acted on this recommendation, and it is significant that, in setting up the Whitaker Review Group in April 1995, the present Government took care to exclude consideration of Articles 2 and 3 from the Group's purview, thus emasculating it to some extent. However, in a related connection the Group favours the retention of the constitutional title

[50] *Report of the Constitution Review Group* (Dublin, Stationery Office, 1996).

[51] The deletion in 1972 of the clause recognising "the special position" of the Catholic Church (Art. 44.1.2) reflected the more liberal position of the post-Vatican II Church, and the Government's wish, in the North–South context, to modify the perceived Catholic image of the State.

[52] *Report of the Committee on the Constitution*, Dec. 1967 (Dublin Stationery Office, 1967), 5–6.

of the State as "Ireland", and recommends keeping the territorial title of the President "of Ireland", although such titles are obviously anomalous, as being incompatible with the legal designation of the State as the "Republic of Ireland" and with its actual territorial jurisdiction.[53] Thus the Group appears to have done nothing to challenge the "make-believe", all-Ireland pretensions of the Constitution.[54]

As a historian, my principal concern in this essay has been to supply a historical context for the 1937 Constitution or at least to provide an informative commentary on its background. As a former member of the Oireachtas, and as someone still intermittently involved in public debate, my views on the need for constitutional change, particularly on the "national clauses", are on the public record.[55]

Constitutional amendments will continue to occur piecemeal, but at some stage a new basic document may well replace the 1937 version. If that happens, there will be continuity as well as change. The best constitutional values and the insights and enlightenments of the last several decades must be further preserved, just as all that was worthwhile in the Irish Free State Constitution of 1922 received renewed expression in *Bunreacht na hÉireann*, 1937.

---

[53] *Supra* n. 50, at 10, 11, and 28.

[54] The Group's deliberations were intended to "assist" (Foreword, p. *x*) the all-Party Committee on the Constitution now charged with considering the Constitution.

[55] See, in particular, *Seanad Éireann* Debates, vol. 96, Oct. 1981 (Constitutional and Legislative Review), 143–68; vol. 97, Mar. 1982 (Constitutional Review), 460 ff.; vol. 116(a), June 1987, 634 ff.; vol. 118, Feb. 1988 (50th Anniversary Debate), 1120 ff.

3

The Irish Constitution in its Historical context

GARRET FITZGERALD

INTRODUCTION

The Irish Constitution is—necessarily—a product of its time: the immediate post-revolutionary period of Irish history. To a greater extent than is perhaps generally appreciated, the 1937 Constitution re-enacted that of 1922—with a re-ordering of the contents which served partially to disguise its provenance. Thus, although the more obvious anomalies it contains are those deriving from the circumstances in which the 1937 Constitution was drafted and put to the people, others find their origins in the conditions in which our State was founded.

Our Constitution must be seen in this historical perspective, and the task of changing it, either by way of amendment or, less probably, by way of an enactment of a third Constitution, to provide a basic law more appropriate to modern Ireland, must be seen as a necessary price to be paid by this generation for the very specific and essentially transient conditions in which our present Constitution and its predecessors were enacted.

THE 1919 AND THE IRISH FREE STATE CONSTITUTIONS

As Alan J. Ward has pointed out,[1] Ireland's first exercise in constitution-making—the document adopted by *Dáil Éireann* at its first session on 21 January 1919—retained most of the characteristics of what he describes as "British responsible government". It provided for untrammelled parliamentary sovereignty, including parliamentary control over the Constitution itself, and cabinet government subject to parliamentary support and ultimate control. In the revolutionary situation, created by a declaration of independence by Irish members elected to the Westminster Parliament, this concentration of power was inevitable. There was clearly no room for any form of judicial constraint

---

[1] A. J. Ward, *The Irish Constitutional Tradition: Responsible Government and Modern Ireland, 1782–1992* (Dublin, Ireland Academic Press, 1994), 158.

on the power of the elected representatives, of the kind that became a key feature of subsequent Irish Constitutions.

The Irish Free State Constitution derived from one of three drafts prepared by a committee theoretically under the Chairmanship of Michael Collins but in practice chaired by Darrell Figgis. The draft preferred by the Provisional Government was an essentially republican document, with only two Articles relating to the Treaty and the Crown. Article 74 provided that the new State should do whatever was necessary to implement the Treaty—although the preceding Article 73 could be read as giving power to the *Oireachtas* to determine unilaterally how far the Treaty was binding. Reference to the Crown was confined to a provision in Article 75 that there should be a "Commissioner of the British Commonwealth", to be appointed with the prior assent of the *Dáil*. He would be required to give the assent of the Crown to all legislation passed by the *Oireachtas*.[2] This draft was unacceptable to the British Cabinet—as might, indeed, have been foreseen given the importance accorded by the British during the Treaty negotiation to the monarchical principle, which they saw as the "cement" binding their Empire together.

In the subsequent negotiations with the British, many changes were made in the draft, giving to the Free State Constitution a monarchical veneer. Nevertheless, the *substance* of the Constitution remained republican to an extent not generally appreciated.

Thus, whereas other Dominion constitutions derived the authority for government from the Crown—for example, the Canadian Constitution stated that "the Executive Government and authority over Canada is hereby declared to continue and to be vested in the Queen"—Article 2 of the Irish Free State Constitution as enacted stated unambiguously that "[a]ll powers of government and all authority legislative, executive and judicial in Ireland, are derived from the people of Ireland". Strong opposition from the British Government to this wording was overcome during these negotiations.

THE ROLE OF THE HEAD OF STATE

While provision was made that the Representative of the Crown should, in the name of the King, summon and dissolve the *Oireachtas*, the dates for the conclusion of sessions of the Houses and for re-assembly were to be fixed by the *Dáil* itself. Moreover, the President of the Executive Council (Prime Minister) was to be appointed on the nomination of *Dáil Éireann*—thus reversing the monarchical practice under which the Crown nominated a Prime Minister subject to approval by the Commons. The other Ministers were to be appointed on the nomination of the President of the Executive Council, subject to the assent of *Dáil Éireann*.

[2] J. M. Curran, *The Birth of the Irish Free State 1921–1923* (Birmingham, Ala., University of Alabama Press, 1986), 206–7.

This arrangement, which excluded the Head of State from any role in the choice of Head of Government, was maintained by the 1937 Constitution. It is not clear to what extent this may have been simply a matter of continuing the previous practice, or may have been due to a concern to limit the role of the new President or, perhaps, to the consideration that the external standing of the *Taoiseach* might be affected by his appointment by a President who was not internationally recognised. For, until the declaration of the Republic in 1949, the King remained Head of the Irish State so far as the rest of the world was concerned.

The Constitution Review Group has described this arrangement as "quite unusual in parliamentary government systems", but added that "it is not clear that the intervention of the President would secure more quickly the emergence of a Government after an election that failed to yield an overall majority".[3] They proposed the removal of the President's power to refuse a dissolution to a *Taoiseach*,[4] and its replacement by a provision that votes of no confidence in a Government should take the form only of a "constructive" vote, which would have to include the name of an alternative *Taoiseach*.

Thus, the pattern established in 1922, when the role in internal affairs of the Head of State, then the King, was strictly limited by our first Constitution, seems likely to be continued for other reasons into the next century. It was probably this provision that led Dr Leo Kohn, in his book on the Irish Free State Constitution,[5] to describe that document as an "essentially republican Constitution along continental lines"—one which "reduced to precise terms the conventional rules of the British Constitution". While the "archaic symbols" of that unwritten Constitution had to be incorporated, "their meaninglessness for Ireland was writ large on every page. The monarchical principle paled into insignificance in the light of the formal enunciation of the people as the fundamental and the exclusive source of political authority".[6]

CONTINUITY BETWEEN THE 1922 AND 1937 CONSTITUTIONS

Among the many changes required by the British Government in May–June 1922 was the dropping of the clause which the Provisional Government had proposed to insert as a new Article 1 before the revised property clause, *viz.* "Ireland is a free and sovereign nation." Instead our State was to be described as "a co-equal member of the Community of Nations forming the British Commonwealth of Nations." But this attempted assertion of freedom and sovereignty surfaced fifteen years later in a slightly modified form, for Article 5

---

[3] *Report of the Constitutional Review Group 1996* (Dublin, Stationery Office, 1996), 37.
[4] Art. 13.2.2.
[5] L. Kohn, *The Constitution of the Irish Free State* (London, G. Allen and Unwin Ltd, 1932), 81.
[6] *Ibid.*

of the 1937 Constitution reads, "Ireland is a sovereign, independent, democratic State."

This is yet another example of the extent to which a very large part of our present Constitution is in fact the Constitution of 1922, with the language in many cases unchanged—some of it as drafted by the Constitutional Committee of 1922 and some of it exactly as re-drafted by the Provisional Government. The extent to which this is true has, however, been partially obscured by the manner in which the content of the Constitution has been re-ordered as between the 1922 and 1937 versions.

Nevertheless, this does not diminish in any way the political significance of the 1937 Constitution, nor the ingenuity with which it was drafted, nor the extent to which most of it, including much of the new material in it, has stood the test of time.

Not all of it, of course. Subsequent generations have found some Articles of the 1937 Constitution unacceptable, or at best dated and irrelevant to contemporary concerns. However, if the contribution of the 1937 Constitution to the stabilisation of the new Irish State is to be appreciated, those now-deleted provisions of the 1937 Constitution need to be seen in their historical context.

It must be recalled that, while in recent General Elections less than 2 per cent of the electorate in the State have voted for candidates put forward by a non-constitutional party, Sinn Féin, in 1923 30 per cent of the electorate had voted for such candidates. And even after *Fianna Fáil*'s formation in 1926 and its entry into the *Dáil* in 1927 a large minority of the population continued to withhold its full consent from the constitutional structure that had been established following the Anglo-Irish Treaty of 1921.

Now, many of those who found the 1922 Constitution unacceptable, but nevertheless voted for *Fianna Fáil* after that party's decision to enter the *Dail* and to play its part in constitutional politics, did so with considerable reservations. This was exemplified by Seán Lemass' reference in the late 1920s to *Fianna Fáil* as a "slightly constitutional party". Many others did not vote at all but, to an extent impossible to quantify for obvious reasons, maintained an abstentionist stance, refusing to participate in the political process during the decade that followed *Fianna Fáil*'s decision to take its seats in *Dáil Éireann*.

When Mr de Valera came to power in 1932, he saw as his primary role the creation of circumstances in which all people of the State, with only the most minuscule exceptions, could give their acceptance and loyalty to a Constitution upon which a stable and peaceful democracy could be built. To achieve this purpose he believed that he had to "repatriate" the 1922 Constitution, by having it re-enacted by the people themselves. This had not taken place, nor could it have, in 1922. In this process he made certain adjustments designed to remove from the Constitution the monarchical forms which, under the terms of the Treaty, were required to be incorporated in the 1922 Constitution.

It is clear, at least in retrospect, that de Valera believed that if he could accomplish this task successfully he would bring back into the constitutional fold the vast majority of those who had felt unable to accept the Treaty and the 1922 Constitution.

Of course he was not 100 per cent successful in this attempt, but during the Second World War the existence of the new Constitution probably helped to minimise the danger of destabilisation arising from IRA activity in co-operation with Germany—and, as the most recent General Election has shown, over the longer term his repatriation of the Constitution was 98 per cent successful in weaning voters away from unconstitutional parties.

THE CONSTITUTIONAL AMBIGUITY: REPUBLIC OR DOMINION?

However, a price had to be paid for achieving this objective. At one level, this price involved a period of constitutional ambiguity of a quite profound kind, involving a dichotomy between the domestic and the international status of the Irish State. For, while the 1937 Constitution was republican in form, and included provision for the election of a President—it also had to include an Article providing for the exercise of the executive function of the State in, or in connection with, its external relations by "any organ, instrument or method of procedure used or adopted for the like purpose by the members of any group or league of nations with which the State is or becomes associated for the purpose of international co-operation in matters of common concern".[7]

This contorted language was necessitated by the need to continue to accommodate the King in the Irish constitutional structure—albeit in a heavily disguised form. For no domestic Act of the Irish Parliament or people could, without the consent of the other countries in the Commonwealth of Nations, alter the international status of Ireland as a member of that Commonwealth. Nor could any such domestic Act prevent the King of the United Kingdom of Great Britain and Northern Ireland being recognised by all foreign countries as the Head—the *only* Head—of the Irish State, to whom, and by whom, Ambassadors had to be accredited.

Mr de Valera's solution—introducing a Constitution that was republican in form, for a State whose Head remained the King and whose international status remained that of a Dominion of the Commonwealth—was ingenious, to say the least. But it was also seen by many people as a demeaning solution, and in the years that followed the enactment of the Constitution, the role of the President as a domestic Head of State who could have no official relationship with the Head of any other State in the world was open to a degree of ridicule that was scarcely consistent with the dignity of a sovereign independent State. Ireland had, of course, become such a State in the eyes of the

---

[7] Art. 29.4.2.

world by the enactment, after the 1930 Imperial Conference, of the Statute of Westminster in 1931. In these circumstances an eventual declaration of a Republic, which took place in 1949, was probably inevitable.

ARTICLES 2 AND 3

Mr de Valera's commitment to the concept of Irish unity required that the Constitution contain the celebrated Article 2 which, under the heading of "[t]he Nation" (as distinct from "[t]he State" to which Articles 4 to 11 relate), asserted that the national territory consists of the whole island of Ireland, its islands and territorial seas. Article 3 went on, however, to provide simultaneously that "without prejudice to the right of the Parliament and Government established by this Constitution to exercise jurisdiction over the whole of that territory, the laws enacted by that Parliament shall have the like area and extent of application as the laws of *Saorstat Éireann* and the like extra-territorial effect".

These provisions could, perhaps, be defended, even if tenuously, in terms of international law, by reference back to the terms of the Anglo-Irish Treaty of 1921. That document created an Irish Free State comprising the whole island of Ireland, its islands and territorial seas, whilst making provision that six counties in the north-east of the island—but not the territorial seas of that part of the island!—could, by the vote of the Home Rule Parliament that had been established in that part of the island in 1920, opt out of the Irish Free State and back into the United Kingdom. This left open, so it could be asserted, the question whether the "national territory" established by the Treaty excluded these six counties permanently, or merely for an indefinite period, pending a later decision of the Northern Ireland Parliament, also envisaged by the Treaty, to join together with the rest of the island in establishing in due course a single polity.

Such an argument could certainly be made, and Articles 2 and 3 certainly reflect in a particular way the aspiration of the majority of Irish people to national unity. But the actual wording of these Articles came to be seen by Northern unionists as a "territorial claim". They can thus be argued to have both a negative effect on unionists' attitude to a future relationship with the rest of the island, and also—by not excluding specifically the use of violence to achieve national unity—to have encouraged in some measure the use of unconstitutional methods against the organs of government in Northern Ireland.

THE PROPERTY ISSUE

The original draft of the 1922 Constitution took a very radical view of the property issue. This may have reflected the input of C. P. France, an American socialist lawyer who was appointed legal advisor to, and later a member of, the drafting committee. But clearly the rest of the committee and its chairman, no doubt influenced by memories of the seventeenth-century settlements and the nineteenth-century Land War, must have shared his commitment to an approach that emphasised the need to give priority to the rights and interests of the community as against individual property rights.

The authors of this Draft emphasised their predominant concern with this issue by devoting the first of two Articles to a series of declarations about sovereignty of the nation over all its material possessions, its soil, its resources and all the wealth and wealth-producing processes within the nation—and to stating the reciprocal duties of the citizens and the State to each other in the service of the commonwealth (small "c") and of the people.

What happened to these radical—one is tempted to say socialist—declarations of the Collins Draft Constitution? The Provisional Government, under Arthur Griffith's presidency, sought external advice on the draft. This led to changes in no less than two-fifths of its Articles, many of them on the proposal of 30-year-old George O'Brien, a barrister and latterly an economic historian.[8]

Perhaps on George O'Brien's advice, the Provisional Government condensed these radical declarations into a single phase, "[t]he sovereignty of the nation extends to all the possessions and resources of the country"—which was still fairly strong stuff. But it also demoted this clause from its position of primacy in the Constitution and introduced a new political (rather than economic) Article 1, to the effect that: "Ireland is a free and sovereign nation."

Although the version of the Draft Constitution in the British Cabinet papers contains the earlier extended version of the property clause, it seems likely that when the two Governments met on 25 May 1922 to discuss the compatibility of the Draft with the Treaty, the more condensed version was before them. However that may be, the version of the Constitution that emerged from this confrontation dropped even this condensed Article relating to the sovereignty of the nation over all the possessions and resources of the country. In the 1922 Constitution, as finally enacted, it appeared only in a substantially modified form as Article 11. That Article stated "all the natural resources of the . . . [T]erritory [including the air and all forms of energy], and also all royalties and franchises within that territory shall . . . belong to the Irish Free State (*Saorstát Éireann*), *subject to any trusts, grants, leases or concessions then existing in respect thereof or any valid private interest therein* . . . ".[9]

This qualifying clause, which effectively entrenched private property rights, seems to have reflected British concern lest an independent Irish Government

---

[8] Four years later he was appointed Professor of Political Economy at University College Dublin, a post he held for 36 years, and one in which he secured the affectionate regard of generations of students.

[9] Author's italics.

to be tempted at some point to overturn the seventeenth-century land confiscations.

This entrenchment of private property rights in the 1922 Constitution, probably imposed by a British Government in defence of a three-century-old colonisation, was pushed very much further by de Valera. He was presumably unconscious of the irony of his actions in so doing. His overriding, and understandable, concern at that time, which was even more evident in the wording of the (long since amended) Article 44 on Religion, was to ensure that his new Constitution would not be put at risk as a result of being denounced by the Holy See. At that time the latter was deeply preoccupied not alone with the idea of a Catholic State but also with what it saw as a global threat of socialism and communism.

Article 40.3.2 of de Valera's Constitution accordingly states that "[t]he State shall, in particular, by its laws protect against unjust attack . . . the property rights of every citizen". As if that were not enough, Article 43 "acknowledges that man . . . has the natural right, antecedent to positive law, to the private ownership of external goods" adding that "[t]he State accordingly guarantees to pass no law attempting to abolish the right of private ownership or the general right to transfer, bequeath, and inherit property".

This double coverage of property rights in two separate Articles has been a potential source of confusion. Moreover, although qualified by a provision that the exercise of private property should be regulated by the principles of social justice and that for that purpose these rights may be delimited by law, these Articles have been open to very restrictive interpretations.

The 1996 Constitution Review Group recommended[10] an amendment under which property rights would be safeguarded by a single Article providing that "[e]very natural person shall have the right to the peaceable possession of his or her own possessions or property"—going on to provide, as in the present Constitution, that no law may be passed attempting to abolish the right of private ownership.

However, the Review Group also recommended the addition of a clause to the effect that, provided "they are duly required in the public interest and accord with the principles of social justice . . . legal restrictions, conditions and formalities may be imposed which may, in particular, but not exclusively, relate to the raising of taxation and revenue, proper land use and planning controls, protection of the environment, consumer protection, and the conservation of objects of archaeological or historical importance".

Such an addition, if accepted by the *Oireachtas* and the people, would be immensely valuable, for I can testify from personal experience in government that concern about possible restrictive interpretations of the Articles on private property has been a major impediment to legislation required in the

---

[10] *Supra* n. 3, at 31.

public interest in the areas listed above—for example in relation to the treatment of windfall profits from development land.

It could now be time to exorcise from our Constitution these ghosts of past British concerns about the preservation of the seventeenth-century land settlements and of past Catholic Church fears of socialism and communism.

THE ROMAN CATHOLIC ELEMENT IN THE CONSTITUTION

The other way in which this Constitution is very clearly the product of its time is the manner in which its terminology, and some of its provisions, were deeply influenced by a particular form of Catholic social teaching prevalent in the 1930s.[11] These include Article 44.1.2 which recognised the special position of the Holy Catholic Apostolic and Roman Church as the guardian of the faith professed by the great majority of the citizens, while also recognising a number of other named churches existing in Ireland at the date of the coming into operation of the Constitution. In addition, Article 41.3.2 stated that no law shall be enacted providing for the grant of a dissolution of marriage.[12]

But, over and above this, the influence of Roman Catholic teaching of the 1930s is visible in the tenor and tone both of the Preamble and of the formulations of fundamental rights in relation to the Family, Private Property and Education, as well as in the "Directive Principles of Social Policy" contained in Article 45. These Directive Principles are, however, primarily decorative rather than operational, because they are not justiciable.

The inclusion of these various provisions was necessitated by the uncertainty in Mr de Valera's mind as to whether a new Constitution could be successfully enacted if it were opposed *both* by the political Opposition of the day *and* by the Roman Catholic Church. In the light of more recent referenda in the 1980s he cannot reasonably be accused of having been over-cautious in taking precautions against such a double challenge when he drafted the Constitution in 1936!

THE CONSTITUTION AS A PRODUCT OF HISTORY

There is therefore not much point in complaining that the Constitution takes the form it does in these various respects, because, if it had not, it would have failed to secure the objective towards which Mr de Valera was bending all his efforts—the creation of circumstances in which all but the smallest handful of

---

[11] See generally, G. Whyte, "Some Reflections on the Role of Religion in the Constitutional Order"; N. Browne, "Church and State in Modern Ireland"; and D. M. Clarke, "Education, the State and Sectarian Schools" in this volume.

[12] These provisions were removed by referenda in 1972 and 1995, respectively.

extremists would be able to give their full allegiance to a new Constitution successfully enacted by a majority of the Irish People.

Our Constitution is as it is to-day because the State came into existence in particular circumstances which involved deep divisions amongst the Irish people, the healing of which was certainly a legitimate objective of public policy, and one that might not readily have been achieved if a price had not been paid in a number of respects.

Moreover, at least one of the anomalous features of the new Constitution was removed as early as 1949, when an inter-party Government strongly opposed to Mr de Valera's Constitution decided to declare a republic and negotiated international recognition of this new constitutional status, together with Ireland's departure from the Commonwealth of Nations. This was effected just one year before India also declared itself a republic, but India was not similarly required by the British Government to leave the Commonwealth as the price of its having the temerity to become a republic.

Thus, while Ireland's membership of the Commonwealth from 1922 until 1949 may have been seen by Irish people as anomalous, its departure from the Commonwealth can also be said to have been anomalous. This is because it is doubtful whether the issue of Ireland leaving the Commonwealth would have been raised at all if its declaration of the Republic had come *after*, rather than *before*, that of India.

THE PROTECTION OF RIGHTS

In conclusion, it should be remarked that the Irish Constitution offers very powerful protection for human rights *vis-à-vis* the Executive and the Legislature—probably stronger protection than in any other parliamentary democracy. For decades, the courts have been vigilant in upholding individual rights against inadvertent and unintended legislative breaches. This series of decisions mainly involved constitutional challenges by individuals or corporations, although there have also been a small number of Presidential references of Bills to the Supreme Court.

The roots of this system of protection of rights lie in the 1922 Constitution, where Articles 6 to 10 set out fundamental rights to liberty of the person, inviolability of citizens' dwellings, freedom of conscience and of the profession and practice of religion, and the right to free elementary education—as well as a guarantee against religious discrimination.

These constitutional provisions for the protection of personal rights represented a revolutionary change from the situation that had existed under British rule when, in common with the rest of the people of the United Kingdom, Irish people had been *subjects* of the Crown rather than *citizens* with rights. As subjects they had lacked any protection for their rights *vis-à-vis* a Parliament that had acquired the absolute power formerly exercised by the monarch. After independence, as citizens, they could appeal to the courts against decisions of the Executive and Legislature that infringed their rights entrenched in the Constitution.

However, during the lifetime of the 1922 Constitution there were relatively few attempts to overturn legislation. In the early decades of the 1937 Constitution there were, however, several very important decisions, for example one which required the re-formulation of the Offences Against the State Act of 1939;[13] another dealing with the right of free association, which restricted severely the Government's power to seek a rationalisation of the trade union movement;[14] and another on education, which limited the power of the Executive and Legislature to restrict the right of the choice of parents in regard to primary schooling.[15] The actual number of such decisions was however, fairly limited in the early years of the 1937 Constitution.

As the decades passed, the number of constitutional decisions which overturned, in whole or in part, various Acts of the *Oireachtas* increased in number quite substantially. This development was accepted with relative equanimity, both by politicians and by public opinion, because in most cases people saw the decisions in question as safeguarding various personal rights which had, without malicious intent, been weakened or undermined by certain legislation.

I think it is fair to say that up to relatively recent times there were only two decisions of significance which gave rise to significant concern or public disquiet. One was the decision in *O'Callaghan*[16] that bail could not be refused to an accused person merely on the ground that he or she was likely to commit another offence, but only in cases where the court was given reason to believe that the person concerned would "jump bail" and leave the jurisdiction, or would seek to intimidate witnesses. The other was a decision in relation to adoption of children that was seen as casting doubt on the validity of many thousands of adoptions, undertaken in good faith.[17]

In the bail case, the delay in offering the electorate an opportunity to reverse the court's decision reflected a feeling that public opinion was fairly deeply divided on the question whether priority should be given to the safety of people and property from onslaughts by people awaiting trial for serious offences, or to the preservation of the principle that an accused person is innocent until proven guilty. Eventually, after thirty years, a change in the bail provision was proposed by the *Oireachtas* and adopted by the people in a referendum.[18]

---

[13] *The State (Burke) v. Lennon* [1940] IR 136.

[14] *NUR v. Sullivan*,[1947] IR 77; see I. Lynch, "Lawyers and Unions—The Right to Freedom of Association in the Irish Constitution" in this volume.

[15] *In Re Article 26 and the School Attendance Bill 1942* [1943] IR 334.

[16] *The People (Attorney General) v. O'Callaghan* [1966] IR 501.

[17] *M v. An Bórd Uchtála* [1977] IR 287.

[18] See further on the issue of bail and the Constitution, P. O'Mahony, "The Constitution and Criminal Justice" in this volume.

In the second case, relating to adoption, immense public disquiet was immediately aroused, reflecting a quite fundamental change in public attitudes regarding the relative rights of "The Family" and children in the period since the Constitution had been adopted. A constitutional amendment was accordingly put to the people in 1979 and was approved by an overwhelming majority, albeit in a very low poll.[19]

These instances (albeit with a long delay in the case of bail) demonstrated the capacity of the political system, through the referendum process, to react adequately to a significant shift in public attitudes concerning the balance of personal rights between different groups.

What is particularly interesting about this process, as it has operated in Ireland, is that it seems to provide a better system of checks and balances than exists elsewhere. The Houses of the *Oireachtas* have the function of monitoring and controlling the Executive's legislative proposals—a role that is, however, constrained by the Executive's command of a majority in the *Dáil* and normally also in the *Seanad*. The courts in turn monitor and control the legislation enacted by the *Oireachtas*. And if the Executive and Legislature are unhappy with decision of the courts they can appeal to the people by way of referendum—and the electorate has the last word. In theory something similar exists in the United States, but the need to secure a majority in thirty-six of the fifty-one States for a constitutional amendment that would overturn a Supreme Court decision effectively rules out an appeal to the electorate in such cases.[20]

Thus, the way in which the checks and balances in the Irish Constitution work in practice can be argued to be uniquely effective in securing the rights of individuals within a representative democratic system. English common and Irish constitutional law have combined in a remarkable way to produce this fortunate outcome.

[19] The 6th Amendment of the Constitution inserted Art. 37.2 which expressly protected the constitutionality of adoption decisions by the Adoption Board despite its non-judicial nature.

[20] See generally L. Tribe, *American Constitutional Law* (2nd edn., New York, Foundation Press, 1988), 65.

4

Church and State in Modern Ireland

NOEL BROWNE[1]

INTRODUCTION

It is impossible for a nation to endure over a period of centuries the violent and repressive destruction of its own unique ethos and sense of nationhood, and to emerge with its political self-assurance and national identity undamaged by the experience. The loss—culturally, intellectually, artistically and politically—was devastating for the Irish people. In 1922, finally liberated from colonial oppression, we were totally inexperienced in the exercise of power in a popular democracy. Moreover, because of our long dependent colonial status, unique in Western Europe, we in Ireland did not share in the rich intellectual, academic, political or artistic advances enjoyed by the rest of the nations of Europe, associated with the Renaissance, the Reformation, the Enlightenment and the French Revolution. Thus on independence, in the majority, an embittered, illiterate peasantry, unprepared for the complexities of our new freedom and taking the easy option, we shed the oppressive restrictions of British imperial power only to slide willingly into the secure, welcoming, anti-democratic and totalitarian cocoon of Rome rule. One possibility for a more enlightened beginning for the state was frustrated when, prior to independence, Rome thwarted an attempt by the British Government to introduce a non-denominational, secular, pluralist and democratic system of education in Ireland in the form of the "Macpherson proposals".[2] With its immediate consolidation as our exclusive educator, in the new "Free" State, the process, according to Professor John Whyte, of "making Irish society [Roman] Catholic was to culminate in the late 1940s" and left an indelible mark on Irish society and political life.[3]

---

[1] This paper was first presented at University College, Cork in 1990 and later published as part of the Queen's University Belfast, Department of Politics' *Occasional Paper Series*. Dr Browne was rewriting the paper for inclusion in this collection at the time of his death on 22 May 1997. The editors have amended and referenced the text while seeking to retain its original style and content.

[2] See further *infra*.

[3] See J H Whyte, *Church and State in Modern Ireland 1923–1979* (2nd ed.) (Dublin, Gill and Macmillan, 1980).

THE DEVELOPMENT OF ROMAN DOMINATION

Since the Middle Ages, Norman, British, and latterly, Roman Catholic impe-
rialism, precluded the evolution of either a truly Republican or uniquely
Gaelic ethos in Ireland. It is an historical fact that, from the time of the
Norman invasion to the Reformation, Rome supported the claims of the
English monarchy over Ireland. It was only after the Reformation that an
influential counter-revolutionary movement in Europe sought to develop in
Ireland a powerful, conservative force, sympathetic to the Church of Rome.
The aims of this movement were the restoration to the English throne of a
Catholic monarchy under papal influence. For Rome, England was the lost
jewel to be won back and it was in pursuit of this that it set out to win control of Ireland and the Irish. Prior to that, Rome had regarded Ireland as a
backward, Atlantic island of little importance.

To win the Irish race over to Rome, the Catholic Church concentrated on
a powerful, proselytising, revivalist movement. Over a period of roughly one
hundred years this evangelical movement was remarkable for its fundamentalist vigour and, as Professor Whyte observes, its level of success in captur-
ing the minds of the Irish population.[4] The period from the end of the
Eighteenth Century throughout the Nineteenth, saw extraordinary Roman-
inspired activity, with the establishment of Churches, clerically-controlled
schools and seminaries. These schools and colleges played a central role in
moulding the minds of their Irish subjects according to the teachings of Rome.
At the same time, the existing lax social behaviour of the priests was replaced
by a new discipline. A carefully-trained elite was formed, as priests, teaching
and nursing orders of nuns and brothers were turned out in enormous numbers. During a period when the population generally was ravaged by emigration, between 1861 and 1901, the numbers of priests, nuns and brothers rose
from 5,955 to 14,145. In 1861 there were a mere 1,160 Sisters of Charity: in
1976 there were numbers had risen to 13,978. In 1920, the Holy Ghost Fathers
totalled one hundred and forty-three rising to six hundred and twenty in 1939.
The Irish presence in African missions rose from forty in 1920 to four hundred in 1939. In what de Valera described as "the Irish spiritual mission
abroad", Rome used the Irish to populate the United States, Latin America,
Africa and China with priests, nuns and brothers. Enthusiastic, dedicated
young Irish men and women became recruits in that great imperial army of
Rome. Training began at the earliest possible age with children between the
ages of twelve and fourteen being taken into special "juniorate" schools as
part of training for the priesthood.

> "... there were missions, novenas, masses, benedictions, Holy Hours, sermons, con-
> fraternities and sodalities. But most important of all, under the control exclusively
> of religious teachers (all loyal to Rome), there were the schools. New well-stocked

[4] *Supra* n.3 at p.54.

libraries, with carefully-chosen books, became available. A printing press run by the Catholic Trust Society was established."[5]

A leading authority motivated their lives, and determined their behaviour. For the cynical wealthy few in power, it has, to this day, been a useful vehicle for discipline over the many. In Professor Titley's words:

"In the hierarchical power structure of the church, the laity constitute a kind of disenfranchised mass. Theological suppositions are not the product of consensus opinion, but of revelation which comes down through the clerical hierarchy. In a world of unquestionable eternal verities there is little room for individual inquiry or democratic debate".[6]

But, to be systematic and effective, the takeover of the Irish nation also had to encompass the native middle-class. As early as 1873, Diocesan colleges were established in Wexford, Waterford, Navan, Tuam and Carlow. The late Bishop of Limerick, Jeremiah Newman, outlined the importance of these colleges as having the:

" . . . merit of being the breeding ground of a close understanding between the diocesan clergy and the rural middle classes. The advantages of this type of '*co-education*' are later reaped in co-operation in parish life. Parish clergy, farmers, rural businessmen, white-collar workers, speak the same language, as it were, or, to put it differently, are on the same wave-length. The pastoral advantages of this situation are immeasurable".[7]

While in the first instance, these residential colleges educated men for the priesthood, an equally important role was the political indoctrination of the governing middle class. This was the small, privileged, carefully indoctrinated, native leader-class, who had benefited most from the Catholic Emancipation in 1829, brought about by Roman agitation and Daniel O'Connell's orchestration of the masses. It was an "emancipation" that did not substantially change the overall class nature of Irish society. Its ultimate social effect was the replacement of the British by an equally insensitive and uncaring Irish ruling class. In time, these were the de Valeras, Mulcahys, Ryans, McGraths, and in contemporary Ireland the governing millionaire class—the Haugheys, Brutons, and Reynolds', Smurfits, and O'Reillys.

After the repeal of the Penal Laws and the establishment of elite secondary schools in the early 1800's, such as Clongowes, Belvedere and Blackrock, the Diocesan Colleges ensured a continuous flow of recruits to the priesthood, the professions, commerce, and later, most significantly, to political life. Meanwhile, the threat of starvation and more immediate economic needs

---

[5] N Browne, *Against The Tide* (Dublin, Gill and Macmillan, 1986) pp.223–224.

[6] E B Titley, *Church, State, and the Control of Schooling in Ireland 1900-1944*, (Kingston and Montreal, McGill-Queen's University Press, 1983) at p.142.

[7] J Newman, "The Priests of Ireland: A Socio-Religious Survey—Patterns of Vocations" (1962) 5/98 *Irish Ecclesiastical Record* 73, quoted in E B Titley *supra* n.6 at p.154.

denied educational opportunity to the masses. The Dale-Stephens' enquiry[8] had disclosed that Irish standards of education were far inferior to those in Britain. Figures from 1905 showed that, in the province of Connaught, with a population of 646,932, only 7,238 pupils attended intermediate schools. But, pressure by the British in the early 1900's, in the form of the "Macpherson proposals",[9] to establish a non-denominational educational system in Ireland produced a fusion of interests between the Irish middle class and Rome. To Rome, this British attempt to secularise education was seen as a challenge to her authority by a competing imperial culture. Thus, in a masterpiece of rhetorical hyperbole, Rome accused Macpherson of "forcing Irish children into the Irish school system at the point of a bayonet".[10] Ultimately, opposition from the Church led by Cardinal Logue and from the newly-founded *Sinn Féin* halted the Bill and forced the resignation of Macpherson. Shortly afterwards the new State came into being.

ROME RULE AFTER INDEPENDENCE

The Free State's first Education Minister, Eoin MacNéill, and his successor, John Marcus O'Sullivan, both adopted a policy of non-state involvement in education, leaving it to the control of Rome. The hegemony was all but confirmed when the closure of Ireland's only non-denominational teacher-training college, in Marlborough Street, Dublin, was announced in the Dáil in 1922. This was the beginning of a Government policy that endowed Rome with effective political power over the state through its control of our schools. Both the Government and the Opposition agreed that changes to the status quo in education were both undesirable and politically inexpedient. In espousing such views, the Ministers for Education in the new state reflected those of the state's founding revolutionaries.[11] Despite his trenchant criticism of the educational system in Ireland, which he labelled "The Murder Machine",[12] the 1916 leader, Padraic Pearse, like de Valera, believed in a sectarian education system, where school managers would be members of religious orders. State control of education led, according to Pearse, to "anarchy and irreligion".[13] As Professor Titley has noted:

---

[8] See generally, E B Titley *supra* n.6 at pp.18–25.

[9] *Ibid* at pp.59–70.

[10] Quoted in N Browne, *supra* n.5 at p.224.

[11] The tempering of the "republicanism" of the leaders of the 1916 Rising with the influence of the Catholic Church is evident in the fact that, with the exception of Tom Clarke, all of the executed leaders, even the Marxist James Connolly, died as loyal members of the Roman Catholic Church. See R Dudley Edwards, *Patrick Pearse: The Triumph of Failure* (London, Victor Gollancz Ltd, 1977) pp.285–286.

[12] In a pamphlet published in 1915 entitled *The Murder Machine*.

[13] P H Pearse, *The Murder Machine* quoted in E B Titley *supra* n.6 at p.74

"[Pearse's] emphasis on the central role of religion in education, his abhorrence of state control, his guarantee of the survival of the managerial system, and his unfettered admiration for the Middle Ages all underlined the harmony of his thought with that of the Church".[14]

Tentative steps at reform saw a struggle of remarkable tenacity in which Rome opposed attempts to secularise teaching personnel, even where it was proposed to use Catholic lay people. Such steps, as indeed the most innocuous of reforms generally, were resented by the Church as an attempt to deny its existing exclusive control over the school system. During the brief period in the 1950s when I served as Minister for Health, the Minister of Education, General Mulcahy, summed up his perspective on his ministerial role as being akin to the "the plumber, who's only called in when something goes wrong".[15] When finally compelled to accept lay teachers, the Church insisted, that teacher-training colleges be under its control, a phenomenon that remains the case to this day.[16] Inevitably, then, our teachers, historians, politicians, and journalists, our Cabinets, the electorate and, as a consequence, all our laws, have reflected the fundamentalist, anti-Republican, anti-democratic, anti-pluralist, and reactionary social attitudes fed to us by Rome.

Central to the maintenance of this level of control was the nature of religious affiliation in the Republic with its overwhelming Catholic majority. Not surprisingly, perhaps, Rome appears to have favoured a partitioned Ireland, in which unchallenged, it would lord it over a predominantly illiterate peasant population in the 26-county State. It had no wish for the inclusion of a million Northern Protestants, many of whom were members of an industrial proletariat, often radical and politically conscious. In the newly-established confessional state the first *Taoiseach*, W T Cosgrave saw fit to offer a constitutional amendment by which the state would guarantee not to introduce any law which was "contrary to Catholic social teaching".[17] He even went so far as to offer to establish a higher theological body of Bishops, as a constituent part of Parliament with powers to veto laws which it might adjudge to be contrary to Catholic social teaching.[18]

Nothing changed with the hand-over of power between the Civil War protagonists. With the approval of de Valera, who on taking power in 1932 declared Ireland to be a Catholic nation, the growth and influence of an arrogant, triumphalist, ultramontane Roman Catholicism was maintained. Under de Valera's influence, Irish Republicanism was literally turned inside-out. It became anti-democratic, xenophobic, philistine, anti-intellectual, opposed to secularism, pluralism and any ideas that had so much as a hint of socialism.

---

[14] E B Titley, *supra* n.6 at p.75.

[15] See N Browne, *supra* n.5 at p.225.

[16] See generally, E B Titley *supra* n.3 at pp.110–119.

[17] Cosgrave's religious conviction has been described as "the bedrock of his life". See S Collins, *The Cosgrave Legacy* (Dublin, Blackwater Press, 1996) at p.44.

[18] *Ibid* at pp.42–55.

Welcoming the Papal Legate, Cardinal Lauri, to Dublin for the Eucharistic Congress in June 1932, de Valera claimed, "we remain ever firm in our allegiance to our ancestral faith, answering unto death to the See of Peter"[19] and he was to maintain this line of priority in his principle legacy, the 1937 Constitution, which echoed Cosgrave's earlier promise that the law of the land would comply with Catholic teachings. While all the major Churches in Ireland were consulted before the publication of the 1937 Constitution and Cardinal MacRory was to hail it as "a great Christian document",[20] it was the Catholic Church that played the central role in its drafting. A Jesuit priest, Father Edward Cahill SJ, was asked by de Valera to frame a preamble "that would ensure all laws passed by the Oireachtas would be in accordance with Catholic social teaching" and the text of the Constitution was forwarded to Rome for the Pope's opinion in advance of publication.[21] The Preamble provides in part:

> "In the name of the Most Holy Trinity, from Whom is all authority and to Whom, as our final end, all actions both of men and States must be referred,
> We, the people of Éire,
> Humbly acknowledging all our obligations to our Divine Lord, Jesus Christ, Who sustained our fathers through centuries of trial . . ."

The nature of the resulting constitutional order was confirmed, when the Preamble, together with the constitutional provision proclaiming "the special position of the Holy Catholic Apostolic and Roman Church",[22] proved critical in the custody decision in the *Tilson* case.[23] In that case the Supreme Court upheld Judge Gavan Duffy's ruling in the High Court that, because of the special position of the Church of Rome in the Constitution, the child in a failed inter-Church marriage ought to be awarded to the mother, contrary to practice at the time, because she was a Catholic, as against the claims of the child's Protestant father.[24]

The Church of Rome was also complicit in the continued subjugation of women in the Irish State. Its opposition to women's dignity and rights derived from a perception of woman as having but one role, mere breeding stock, was endorsed by a Constitution that replaced an existing constitutional commit-

---

[19] M Moynihan, *Speeches and Statements by Eamon de Valera, 1917-1973* (Dublin, Gill and Macmillan, 1990) at p.218.

[20] Quoted in The Earl of Longford & T P O'Neill, *Eamon de Valera* (Dublin, Gill and Macmillan, 1970). Nevertheless, Cardinal MacRory had fought the inclusion of reference to the other principle, including Christian, religions in the state.

[21] On the influence of the Catholic Church on the drafting of the 1937 Constitution, see T P Coogan, *De Valera: Long Fellow, Long Shadow* (London, Hutchinson, 1993) pp.489–490.

[22] Art. 44.1.2. This provision remained in place until 1972 when, with the support of the Catholic Church, it was removed by the Fifth Amendment to the Constitution passed by 721,003 to 133,430 votes in a referendum.

[23] *In Re Tilson, Infants* [1951] IR 1, see also J H Whyte, *supra* n.3 at pp.169–171..

[24] See Gavan Duffy J at 13–15 (HC).

ment to equality "without distinction of sex"[25] with an effective endorsement of domestic servitude.[26] In the words of feminist writer Ursula Barry;

" . . . women are forced unto the margins of a debt-entangled economy. [This] position is reinforced by a range of socially repressive laws, covering family law, reproductive rights, and welfare entitlements. This combination of severely depressed economic conditions and anti-women legislation serves to intensify the burden for women in poverty. Large families, inadequate health services, dependence on welfare, violence in the home and on the streets, care of the ill and the elderly, constant wrangling with state agencies, the tragedy of seeing reared children taking the emigrant boat, train or plane, stretching hopeless pay packets in too many directions and all the time responsible for keeping the show on the road. The Irish Republic is a textbook case of the feminisation of poverty."[27]

GOVERNMENT FROM ROME AND MAYNOOTH

As a nation proud of its history and its independence, there is a tragic irony in that neither in the North nor in the South do the Irish people govern themselves. By choice, in the North, government is from London. In the South, by virtue of the mind-moulding influence of the Church we are governed by a politico-religious institution based in Rome with its local power-base in Maynooth serving as the real base of political power in our society. An undemocratic secretariat and governing bodies lie in a small state in faraway Italy. Our regional governors, the Bishops are appointed by the Pope in Rome without reference to their flock. Meanwhile in the secular sphere, in spite of its declared democratic institutions, the Republic is, effectively, a conservative, one-party, Roman Catholic State with identical political "think-alikes" for public representatives. Only in their ideologically meaningless names do the two major parties, *Fianna Fáil* and *Fine Gael*, differ from one another—at heart their policies are identical.

For a short three year period in the 1950's, I was, as Minister for Health, privileged to observe the perverse system of delegated government operating in the Republic. One incident in particular stands out as illustrative of a general deference in government circles to the Church. A member of the Cabinet, General MacEoin, the renowned "freedom fighter", entered a Cabinet meeting, threw his brief down, in some disgust, on the table, and muttered "he won't allow it". There was no discussion. It was some time before I gathered that what "he" would not allow was a Government Bill permitting the introduction of adoption, then forbidden by Rome, in the Republic. The "he" of MacEoin's remark was Rome's Archbishop of Dublin, Dr McQuaid. I was

[25] Art. 3 of the Free State Constitution.
[26] Art. 41.2.1 of the Constitution provides that ". . . the State recognises that by her life within the home, woman gives the State a support without which the common good cannot be achieved".
[27] "Plight of Women in Ireland", Women's International Studies Lecture, Dublin, 1987.

surprised by the failure of any of my then Cabinet colleagues to demur at this insolent summary rejection of a government proposal by a non-elected member of an outside pressure group, the Roman Catholic Hierarchy.

Possibly the most authoritative documentation of the Irish Republic's capitulation of sovereignty to Rome, is contained in a note made by a civil servant in April 1953 only recently revealed in the release of Cabinet Papers. This occurred shortly after the submission of the first Coalition Government to Rome on the issue of the free no-means-test of the mother and child health service.[28] At a meeting of the new Government in April 1953, de Valera on behalf of himself and his cabinet was to maintain this line of acquiescence despite the measures being authorised by an Act of the *Oireachtas*, introduced and passed by an earlier *Fianna Fáil* Government in 1947. The civil servant's note states in clear terms de Valera's acceptance of his, and his Government's, subordinate role to Rome. His position, he said, had been confirmed in a speech made by the then Archbishop of Cashel, Dr Kinane in which he pronounced that:

> "God is the author of organised civil society; hence political and social activities are subject to God's moral law, of which Rome is the divinely constituted interpreter and guardian. It is the province, then, of Rome, to decide authoritatively whether political, social and economic theories are in harmony with God's laws".[29]

In societies where Rome rules, it is its practice to establish its writ by the enforcement of one general principle: the notion of the "common good". Under this simplistic, yet powerful, principle, Rome ordains that whatever doctrine it teaches, whatever laws it makes, whatever conduct it considers necessary, are ordained by God's will, and are "in the common good". Inevitably, on the important issues that affect our lives, all the social, ethical, political, religious conventions or attitudes held by other religious or non-religious leaders are deemed "contrary to the common good". How can a politician, leader of a minority church or individual citizen publicly advocate a pattern of human behaviour which they are authoritatively informed by the government, the highest courts and by its dominating religious institution that what they advocate is "contrary to the common good"? Thus, did Republicanism became transformed into the narrow, conservative, sectarian, Catholic nationalist movement it is today.

THE PROTESTANT MINORITY IN THE NEW STATE

Explicit in his Constitution and his pronouncements throughout his career, de Valera's conception of Irish society and the Irish State was an exclusively

---

[28] On the mother and child scheme generally see J H Whyte *supra* n.3 at pp.196–272 and N Browne *supra* n.5 ch.9.

[29] Reported in the *Irish Independent* 2 June 1951, quoted in N Browne *supra* n.5 at p.218.

Catholic one. Hostage to this conviction was a significant, if dwindling, number of Protestants residing in the new state. In addition, the constitutional claims of Articles 2 and 3 encompassed over one million members of Protestant religions to whom Rome rule was, and would continue to be, anathema. Their fears as to the nature of the Southern State would be confirmed when, instead of constructing a genuinely fair and pluralist society, in which members of minority religions could live in dignity, and in the words of the 1916 Proclamation, "enjoy freedom of religious expression, freedom of conscience, freedom of information, equal rights, and equal opportunities", de Valera gave Rome a free hand over a crude, system of "separate development" and religious "apartheid". Over a period of years, the slow, inexorable and inevitable consequence of this policy was the progressive de-population of the new Irish state of its Protestant population.

By virtue of the Maynooth Decree of 1929, under pain of mortal sin, no Catholic could attend a non-Catholic primary or secondary school, or the internationally respected Trinity College, Dublin, which at the time, had a majority of Protestant undergraduates. This Decree, which survived into the 1970's, had serious consequences: whoever broke this commandment was in contempt of Rome, and therefore not eligible for employment in many positions of both state and local authority. The clear inference was that at all stages in their education, members of the minority religions were being dangerously misinformed. This was of particular importance in the case of secondary school and university education, where future teachers, lawyers, academics, doctors, midwives and nurses, as well as librarians were involved. In effect, in de Valera's new Republic, they could not find employment, carrying, as they did, the indelible stigma of a "non-Catholic" Protestant education. I recall but one medical graduate of my time at Trinity who managed to survive in private practice. One particular high profile controversy concerning religious affiliation in employment occurred in 1930 when the sacking of an appropriately-qualified librarian[30] was "justified" on the grounds that she was a Protestant. In effect, "Protestants need not apply" signs went up all over the Republic.

A similar message was sent to members of the minority religion in their family and private lives. For those Protestants who persisted in remaining in the Republic, there was the uncompromising *"Ne Temere"* decree of 1907. Under this decree, in cases where permission for an inter-Church marriage was finally given by Rome, an undertaking,[31] was demanded from the partner of the non-catholic faith, to bring up their children as members of the Church of Rome. Outside of the capital, isolated communities of Protestants dwindled and entire congregations disappeared as the message regarding the

[30] The Mayo Library Committee at the centre of the appointment controversy consisted of a Catholic Bishop, five Catholic priests, a Christian Brother, a Protestant rector, and four laymen. The voting was ten to two in favour of revoking the librarian's appointment.

[31] Which, at least according to the principle Catholic newspaper *The Catholic Standard*, 21 June 1957, was a legally binding undertaking.

Catholic nature of the state was reinforced at every turn; through its laws, its social policy, and its education policy, all of which reflected a general malaise and lack of imagination by the state's rulers.

In the tragic fiasco of seventy-five years of "freedom" in the South, we have created a manifestly unjust and ineptly-run society, in which an immorally high rate of unemployment is tolerated and one in three of our people live at, or below, the poverty line. The social and economic reality of so many citizens belies the pious commitments of the Constitution's Directive Principles of Social Policy to "promote the welfare of the whole people" and to ensure that the material resources of the state are distributed "as best to subserve the common good"[32] O'Connell Street, Dublin might well be described as the largest psychiatric out-patient clinic in the country. The unwanted elderly are tumbled onto the streets where, with young children, in their hundreds, they beg to survive for the day, and sleep rough at night in all weather. Without work, in their thousands, our unwanted young men and women emigrate, disappearing from our national unemployment register and conscience.[33] If they succeed in their enforced exile we are quick to claim them as our own: but if they fail, and disappear amongst the population of London's "cardboard city", we disown them just as quickly.

Meanwhile, the Church of Rome, once hunted and penniless in Ireland, became the single most powerful and feared institution in the state, as the largest single owner of property and one of the wealthiest institutions in the Republic. Inevitably, because of these enormous material interests it is implicitly precluded from giving real and effective leadership in the campaign for the abolition of poverty and the removal of the existing grossly unequal distribution of wealth in the state. Rather, its perpetuation of authority is inextricably linked to the denial of human rights that persist in our society. The poorer the people become, the more dependent they are on the Church, and its charitable institutions. The more inept and inadequate the state services, the more the Church thrives. Thus, was the welfare state anathematised by the Church as creeping Communism.

If there ever was a possibility of a union of minds and people in a united Ireland, then surely that possibility has been wantonly and knowingly squandered by our political leaders in the Irish State over the last 75 years. Until our politicians of all parties, finally accept the responsibilities of self-government, choose to establish a true democracy with a Constitution and laws that reflect the radical, secular, pluralist reality of a genuine independent Republic, declare that their first and only loyalty is to that Republic and abandon their suffocating dependence on Rome to rule them, we should not expect—and will not see—a United Ireland.

[32] Art. 45. See generally, T Murphy "Economic Inequality and the Constitution" in this volume.

[33] See generally, J MacLaughlin, *Ireland: The Emigrant Nursery and the World Economy* (Cork, Cork University Press, 1994).

5

Some Reflections on the Role of Religion in the Constitutional Order

GERARD F WHYTE

INTRODUCTION

"The premier and special position accorded to the Catholic Church as 'guardian of the Faith of the great majority of the citizens' will mean in practice that the Catholic Church will be the Church associated with the State on all public occasions.

Under our democratic Constitution the vast majority of the Ministers of State are certain to be Catholic, who will profess their religion openly and will attend religious functions in a Catholic Church on all occasions in which a manifestation of religious belief is called for.

In the past Ministers in a body have annually attended Mass on St. Patrick's Day at the Catholic Pro Cathedral; the Government and Members of Parliament have attended a special Mass on each occasion in which a new parliament meets after the dissolution. At the Eucharistic Congress the State was officially represented by all the Ministers."

Thus read is an extract from a document prepared on behalf of Eamon de Valera for the benefit of the secretary of the then Department of External Affairs, Joseph Walshe, who had been sent to Rome in April 1937, charged with the task of securing papal support from the proposed new Irish Constitution.[1]

---

[1] Extracts from this document, including the section set out above, are reproduced in D. Keogh, *Ireland and the Vatican: The Politics and Diplomacy of Church-State Relations, 1922–1960* (Cork, Cork University Press, 1995), 133–4. It is a measure of the temper of the times that, despite this assurance of a special place for the Catholic Church in the proposed Constitution, the Vatican refused to move beyond a position of strict neutrality in respect of the new constitutional arrangements because the draft Constitution recognised other Christian Churches and because it failed to state that the Catholic Church had been founded by Jesus. While the Catholic influence on certain provisions of the Constitution cannot be denied, it would be a mistake to characterise that document as ultramontane. Thus, Keogh comments that "[the 1937 Constitution], framed in difficult times, did not bear the hallmark of extremist confessional influence", in "The Role of the Catholic Church in the Republic of Ireland in 1922–1995", *Building Trust in Ireland: Studies Commissioned by the Forum for Peace and Reconciliation* (Blackstaff Press, 1996), 127. In a similar vein, the Constitution Review Group remarked that "The Review Group is, of course, aware that it has been frequently suggested that the State has

Sixty years later, this close association between Catholic Church and Irish State looks decidedly out of place in a society many of whose citizens have very different attitudes to religion compared to those prevalent in 1937.[2] An MRBI poll has indicated that, among Catholics, there has been a significant falling off in weekly Mass attendance since 1990, the numbers declining from 85 per cent in 1990 to 66 per cent in 1996.[3] Moreover, almost 70 per cent of those polled believed that Ireland would be Catholic only in name in twenty years time. There is therefore a growing number of people for whom religion has very little meaning and for whom the benefit of the influence of religious values on the constitutional order is, to put it mildly, far from self-evident. Even for many of those for whom religion continues to be important, the present constitutional provisions cannot be regarded as completely satisfactory insofar as they are, in some respects, offensive and divisive.

Thus, a re-examination of the relationship between law and religion in the Irish constitutional order would appear to be timely, all the more so, given the on-going process of constitutional review initiated by the Report of the Constitution Review Group.[4] Here, in a tentative attempt at such a re-examination, two issues are addressed. First, are there any compelling reasons, in terms of political morality, for excluding religious values from the Constitution simply on the ground that the values are religious in origin? Secondly, and more briefly, I attempt to evaluate the implications for Irish society of the removal of the existing endorsement of religious values from the Constitution. As will soon become apparent, this article draws heavily on the work of a US constitutional scholar, Professor Michael Perry. Though he writes primarily for a US audience, I believe that Perry's work has a particular resonance for those of us in Ireland who wish to retain the benefits of our religious heritage while at the same time promoting pluralist values. As a Christian with a strong commitment to pluralism and liberal democracy, he sees himself as "one who stands between all religious non-believers on the one

a confessional ethos which tends to favour the majority religion at the expense of religious minorities. If this is so, the fault lies elsewhere than with [the constitutional provisions on religion]": *Report of the Constitutional Review Group* (Dublin, Stationery Office, 1996), 369. For a detailed account of the process of drafting the Constitution, in particular the Article on religion, see Keogh, "The Constitutional Revolution: An Analysis of the Making of the Constitution" in F. Litton (ed.), *The Constitution of Ireland 1937–1987* (Dublin, Institute of Public Administration, 1988), 4–84.

[2] For sociological analysis of this development, see Hornsby-Smith and Whelan, "Religious and Moral Values" in C. Whelan (ed.), *Values and Social Change in Ireland* (Dublin, Gill and Macmillan, 1994) and Nic Ghiolla Phadraig, "The Power of the Catholic Church in the Republic of Ireland" in P. Clancy, S. Drudy, K. Lynch and L. O'Dowd (eds.), *Irish Society: Sociological Perspectives* (Dublin, Institute of Public Administration, 1995).

[3] *Irish Times*, 16 Dec. 1996.

[4] *Supra*, n. 1. I argue in "Discerning the Philosophical Premises of the Report of the Constitution Review Group: An Analysis of the Recommendations on Fundamental Rights" in *Irish Human Rights Yearbook 1996*, that the Review Group did not adequately address this issue, even though the effect of a number of its recommendations would appear to be to purge the Constitution of any religious influence.

side and many religious believers—especially theologically conservative believers—on the other".[5]

SHOULD THE CONSTITUTION BE PURGED OF RELIGIOUS LANGUAGE?

The question considered in this section is very specific. It is whether religious values or statements should be excluded from the Constitution simply because they are religious in origin and regardless (for the moment) of their content or effect. A good starting point for this discussion is Perry's latest book, *Religion in Politics: Constitutional and Moral Perspectives*,[6] in which he identifies—and rebuts—two reasons offered for excluding religious argument from public debate. The first reason is that religious debates about controversial political issues can be quite divisive, to which he responds that secular debates about controversial issues can be just as divisive and that consequently one cannot exclude religious argumentation on this ground alone. The second argument advanced for denying individuals the right to adduce religious argument in public debate is the suggestion that religious believers cannot engage in truly deliberative dialogue because they cannot gain a critical distance from their religious beliefs. While accepting that some religious believers may not be open to real debate with persons of differing views, Perry rejects the suggestion that this is true of all religious believers:

> "Although no one who has lived through recent American history can believe that religious contributions to the public discussion of difficult moral issues are invariably deliberative rather than dogmatic, there is no reason to believe that religious contributions are never deliberative. Religious discourse about the difficult moral issues that engage and divide us citizens of liberal democratic societies is not necessarily more problematic . . . than resolutely secular discourse about those issues. Because of the religious illiteracy—and, alas, even prejudice—rampant among many non-religious intellectuals, we probably need reminding that, at its best, religious discourse in public culture is not less dialogic . . . than is, at its best, secular discourse in public culture."[7]

Moreover, he points out that fanaticism in the holding of views is not the prerogative of religious believers:

> "As so much of the twentieth century attests, . . . one need not be a religious believer to adhere to one's fundamental beliefs with close-minded or even fanatical tenacity."[8]

On a more positive note, Perry has defended, at some length, the use of disputed beliefs about human good, including religious beliefs, in public debate.

---

[5] *Religion in Politics: Constitutional and Moral Perspectives* (New York and Oxford, Oxford University Press, 1997), 7.
[6] *Ibid.*, at 44–9.
[7] *Ibid.*, 46.
[8] *Ibid.*, 46.

In an earlier book, *Love and Power: The Role of Religion and Morality in American Politics*[9] he argues that politics from which such beliefs are excluded are:

> "bereft of the normative resources required for addressing, much less resolving, the most fundamental political-moral issues that engage and divide us. . . . [In particular] politics from which disputed beliefs about human good are excluded cannot address a political-moral question that, at the close of the twentieth century, is indisputably and appropriately at the very heart of domestic and international politics: Are there human rights and, if so, what are they?"[10]

Moreover, he also contends that politics from which religious beliefs are excluded discriminate against those who subscribe to such beliefs and as such are not truly neutral as between religious believers and non-believers.[11] Later, in *Religion in Politics*, he adds the further argument that public culture in the USA is so infused with religiously based moral discourse that it is impossible to maintain a wall of separation between such discourse and public political debate, a point which would appear to have equal validity in Ireland.[12]

Now, of course, the issue which we are considering in this section is whether the inclusion of religious language and values in the Constitution is morally permissible. This question transcends the issue of whether individuals should be permitted to rely on religious argumentation in public debate in this sense, that the latter issue is concerned only with the rights of individuals in public debate, whereas the former question raises the possibility that religious argumentation might provide justification for (or part of the justification for) action on the part of the State. Are there any reasons why the State, acting through its legislators and judges, should forego reliance on religious argument as a basis for political decision-making?

MAY THE STATE USE RELIGIOUS NORMS TO JUSTIFY POLITICAL CHOICE?

In considering this issue, I will follow Perry's lead in distinguishing between two different situations. One is where the legislator or judge relies solely on religious belief or argument as a basis for political choice; the other is where he or she relies on both secular and religious argument as a basis for such choice.

There are both secular and (perhaps, for some, paradoxically) religious reasons for rejecting the proposition that agents of the State should be permitted to rely solely on religious belief as a basis for their decisions. The secular argument is that to do otherwise would be, at best, to discriminate against

---

[9] (New York and Oxford, Oxford University Press, 1991).
[10] *Ibid.*, 29.
[11] *Ibid.*, ch. 1.
[12] *Supra* n. 5, 47–9.

non-believers, of adherents or other religious beliefs, at worst, to coerce them into acting contrary to their conscientious beliefs. Either eventuality undermines freedom of religion, either directly, through coercive legislation, or more subtly, by creating an environment in which social pressures may inhibit the expression of beliefs which do not receive the positive support of the State.[13]

The reason from within certain religious traditions[14] for denying legislators and judges the right to rely solely on religious beliefs as a basis for decision-making is that such traditions believe that their normative claims can be adequately defended on grounds of reason, in other words, on grounds which can address a secular audience. Professor Pat Hannon puts it thus, in respect of the Catholic tradition:

"The Catholic theological tradition has always argued its normative or substantive ethical claims on grounds of 'reason'. That is, even when a norm is said to be part of revelation, it is also based on arguments which do not appeal to a purely religious authority. . . .

. . . [O]ne must further ask whether, above all in a Catholic theological approach, the question [whether one should be precluded from adducing religious consideration in advocating a political choice] needs even to arise. For if, as in the natural law/human rights tradition in Catholic theology, a moral position may be accounted for without referring to divine revelation, why should one even think of having to do so in making one's case in the public square?"[15]

Perry makes the same point perhaps even more forcefully:

"[E]ven for religious believers . . . any religious argument about the requirements of human well-being should be a highly suspect basis of political choice if no persuasive secular argument reaches the same conclusion about the requirements of human well-being as the religious argument. Given the demonstrated, ubiquitous human propensity to be mistaken and even to deceive oneself about what God has revealed, the absence of a persuasive secular argument in support of a claim about the requirements of human well-being fairly supports a presumption that the claim is probably false, that it is probably the defective yield of that demonstrated human

---

[13] Robert Audi puts it as follows: "[Governmental] preference of the religious as such can also reduce the level of free *exercise* of liberty, as opposed to its mere legal *scope*. What is legally permitted, or even solicitously protected by law, may still seem to many people too troublesome to be worthwhile in day-to-day life. If, for example, exercising a freedom goes against governmental policy or even social tradition, it may be costly. Consider someone who declines to participate in state-sponsored patriotic activities; here, and surely even in absenting oneself from state- or community-sponsored voluntary prayer sessions, one might conspicuously separate oneself from most others." See "The Separation of Church and State and the Obligations of Citizenship" (1989) 17 *Philosophy and Public* and *Affairs* 259 at 267, reproduced in W. Sadurski (ed.), *Law and Religion* (Aldershot, Dartmouth, 1992), 29 at 37.

[14] This argument would not be endorsed by those religious traditions that eschew the use of reason to test the validity of what appears to be divine revelation.

[15] "On Using Religious Arguments in Public Policy Debates" in B. Treacy and G. Whyte (eds.), *Religion, Morality and Public Policy* (Dublin, Dominican Publications, 1995), at 69–70.

propensity. At least, it fairly supports a presumption that the claim is an inappropriate ground of political choice, especially coercive political choice."[16]

So much for the proposition that the State should be permitted to rely exclusively on religious grounds as a basis for political choice. However, if a secular justification for a policy exists, should the State be precluded from invoking, in addition, a religious reason which supports the same policy? To take a concrete example, is there any reason in principle why legislators or judges should avoid any reference to the religious values in the Preamble to the Constitution to bolster decisions for which there is already secular justification?[17]

The principle of State neutrality towards religion—that the State should regard religion as essentially a private matter—is offered by some commentators as one such reason. Audi argues that there is both a libertarian and an egalitarian rationale for this principle.[18]

> "[R]eligious liberty, broadly conceived, includes the freedom to reject religious views. If the state shows preference for religious institutions as such (or for religion in general) there may well be pressure to adopt a religion, and quite possibly discrimination against those who do not."

It is, however, submitted that Audi overstates the danger to liberty presented by state endorsement of religious values. Much surely depends on the nature of that endorsement, but if the State contents itself with a statement that all powers of government derive, under God, from the people—such as is to be found in Article 6 of the Constitution—how does that impinge upon the liberty of an individual to deny the existence of God and to order his life accordingly?[19]

Nor is it clear that state neutrality is capable of ensuring equality as between religious believers and non-believers insofar as there may be no

---

[16] *Supra* n. 5, *Religion in Politics*, 75. In one important instance, however, Perry argues that a State should be permitted to rely on a religious belief in the absence of a secular equivalent. In a closely reasoned article, he argues that the belief that every human being has an inherent dignity can only be inferred from a cosmological perspective which sees existence as ultimately meaningful, see "Is the Idea of Human Rights Ineliminably Religious?" in A. Sarat and T. Kearns (eds.), *Legal Rights: Historical and Philosophical Perspectives* (Ann Arbor, Mich., University of Michigan Press, 1996).

[17] There may, of course, be tactical reasons for a decision-maker to eschew reliance on religious values. Hannon comments, "[F]or I may arrive at the conclusion that human dignity requires a particular political choice at least partly in virtue of a conviction that we are each equally made in the image of God. But when I come to advocate that choice in the public forum, my interlocutor who is not a religious believer will either accept the ideas of human dignity and equality on other grounds or not. If not, unless I hope for a religious conversion, I can usefully address her or him only in secular terms and upon any common secular ground that there may be between us": *supra* n. 15, 70.

[18] *Supra* n. 13, 265–8. For a sophisticated analysis of the different theories underpinning State neutrality towards religion, and ultimately a defence of such neutrality on libertarian grounds, see Mark, "Liberalism, Neutralism and Rights" in J. R. Pennock and J. W. Chapman (eds.), *Nomos XXX: Religion, Morality and the Law* (1988), reproduced in W. Sadurski, *supra* n. 13, 3.

[19] Recall that the suggestion that the State could rely exclusively on religious beliefs for the formulation of policy has already been rejected above.

neutral territory for the State to occupy between belief and non-belief. Hitchcock argues that such neutrality is impossible to attain inasmuch as all public policy is based on value-judgements and the rejection of religion by the state is itself a value-judgement:

> "To maintain that such neutrality is possible seems to require postulating that public policy is somehow arrived at in a 'value-free' manner. Yet it would be difficult to show any policies which are in fact completely neutral. . . . The minimal government envisioned by classical conservative theory might conceivably claim the kind of neutrality which pluralism postulates. The modern, activist, liberal, welfare state cannot be neutral and does not aim to be."[20]

A related problem here is that the idea of State neutrality presupposes that it is possible to distinguish between religious and secular belief. This in turn raises the very difficult question of how to define religion.[21] Buddhism is generally recognised as a religion and yet, insofar as it is predominantly non-theistic, this would suggest that the term "religion" cannot be restricted to systems of belief in God. In that case, is transcendental meditation a religion? Is scientology a religion? And, more germane to the present discussion, is secular humanism a religion?[22] For if it is, then that surely makes a nonsense of any attempt by the State to be neutral as between religious and secular belief.

Perry also rejects the idea of State neutrality in this context as impossible to attain.[23] So, while he cautions against a public official making political choice *exclusively* on religious grounds,[24] he would not preclude such a person from replying on his or her religious beliefs where the political choice could also be supported by persuasive secular argument:

> "[I]t seems unrealistic to insist that legislators and others support a political choice about the morality of human well-being only on the basis of a secular argument they find persuasive if they also find persuasive a religious argument that supports the choice. How could such a legislator be sure that she was replying *only* on the secular argument, putting no weight whatsoever on the religious argument? She could ask whether she would support the choice even if the religious argument were

[20] Hitchcock, "Church, State and Moral Values: The Limits of American Pluralism" [1981] *Law and Contemporary Problems* 3, at 14–18, reproduced in W. Sadurski, *supra*, n. 13, 115, at 166–70. Commenting on two conflicting judicial opinions as to whether the provision of campus facilities to student religious groups was an impermissible establishment of religion, Johnson commented, "[b]oth decisions are equally rational in terms of conventional constitutional law. Providing facilities such as meeting rooms certainly aids the religious activity, much as if the state were to make a direct cash grant to pay the rent on a church building. Yet one can hardly describe as 'neutral' a state policy that provides meeting rooms to Republicans, communists, musicians and stamp collectors, but denies similar facilities to religious groups. Such discrimination seems to imply that religion is a peculiarly disfavoured activity": P. Johnson, "Concepts and Compromise in First Amendment Religious Doctrine" (1984) 72 *California Law* Review 817 at 820, reproduced in W. Sadurski, *supra* n. 13, 175 at 178 (footnotes in the original quotation have been omitted).

[21] And one which I am content to raise without exploring in detail.

[22] For an attempt to argue that it is, see Hitchcock, *supra* n. 20, at 18–19.

[23] *Morality, Politics and Law: A Bicentennial Essay* (New York and Oxford, Oxford University Press, 1988), ch. 3.

[24] Subject to the caveat described *supra* in n. 16.

absent, solely on the basis of the secular argument. However, trying to ferret out the truth by means of such counterfactual speculation is perilous at best and would probably be, as often as not, self-deceiving and self-serving.

More fundamentally, the relevant question for a legislator . . . is not whether she would find persuasive a secular argument about the requirements of human well-being if she did not already find persuasive a religious argument that reaches the same conclusion as the secular argument. To ask herself that question would be for the legislator to ask herself whether she would find the secular argument persuasive if she were someone other than the person she is, someone without the particular religious beliefs she has. Such a counterfactual inquiry is not only often hopelessly difficult, but, more importantly, beside the point: the proper question is not whether someone else would find the secular argument persuasive, but whether, on reflection, *she* finds it persuasive. The question she should ask herself is whether, in addition to the religious argument she accepts, she finds persuasive a secular argument that reaches the same conclusion about the requirements of human well-being."[25]

However, if the principle of State neutrality fails to offer a satisfactory reason for precluding a public official from invoking, in addition to secular argument, his or her religious beliefs as a basis for political choice, it seems to me that two other considerations, one pragmatic, one principled, may succeed where the principle of State neutrality fails. The pragmatic consideration here is that if there is a secular argument available to justify the political choice, why should the public official needlessly antagonise his or her protagonists by citing, in addition, religious arguments which are not shared by all participants in the debate? So, for example, in the recent public debate on the merits or otherwise of the constitutional ban on divorce, supporters of the ban, for the most part, eschewed any reliance on religious arguments in support of their position. The principled consideration is that religious values should not be used to support a policy which results in coercion of conscientious beliefs. This is not to say coercion of such beliefs is always impermissible—the law must be permitted to restrain human sacrifice, for example, even if belief in the necessity of such sacrifice is conscientiously held by the adherents of a particular religion[26]—rather it is to insist on very strong secular justification for such coercion. Nor does my position imply that religious beliefs have no public significance. Rather, what I argue for here is that the proper role for religious beliefs in social and political discourse is prophetic, rather than coercive. Such a restriction on the use of religious values is necessary in order to promote freedom of thought, in particular, to promote freedom of religious thought.[27] Indeed, certain religious traditions would regard the use

---

[25] *Supra* n. 5, at 77.

[26] A more prosaic example of this point is *DPP v. Draper*, where the Court of Criminal Appeal upheld a conviction of causing malicious damage to religious statues, even though the accused was genuinely motivated by religious beliefs in what he did: *Irish Times*, 24 Mar. 1988.

[27] In *Religion in Politics*, *supra* n. 5, Perry considers a similar argument that government, in making a coercive political choice, should not rely on a moral argument which some persons subject to the choice reasonably reject because to do so would be to deny such persons the respect that is their due as human persons. This he rejects it as "deeply problematic", at 64–5. However, my

of religious values in a coercive manner as an abuse of religion.[28] In this regard one would have to call into question the propriety of the constitutional requirement that the President and members of the judiciary must make a religious declaration on taking office.[29] Such a requirement inhibits, for no good reason, non-believers from taking up these public offices and as such effects religious discrimination.[30]

Summarising the argument so far, there would not appear to be any principled reason for precluding the use of religious language in the Constitution, provided that such language is not used, either on its own or in conjunction with secular argument, as the justification for a policy which is coercive of conscientiously held beliefs. Is there any inconsistency between the two limbs of this argument? I think not. The exclusion of religious argument from political debate can very quickly create the impression that religious beliefs are in some way tainted, eccentric, irrational. The inclusion of religious argument in public debate counters that impression and, in addition, as Perry argues, allows that debate to tap into the rich resource of moral norms contained in the religious experience. At the same time, the pursuit of religious truth must, by its very nature, be assumed voluntarily by the individual and is likely to be impeded by the coercive imposition of religious norms to which one does not subjectively subscribe.

Applying this argument to the role of religion in the Constitution, one could carve out a role for religious language as a means of deepening the sense of loyalty of the citizenry to the State. Of course, to do so effectively would

argument is based on a perceived threat to freedom of thought, which Perry does not appear to address. Consider, for example, the following comments, from a unionist perspective, about the Constitution—"The source of Catholic social teaching *is* sufficient grounds for unionists to reject the Constitution; and the content of the Constitution does *not* matter . . . because the common good it seeks may be admirable in itself but it is estranged from unionists": Arthur Aughey, "Obstacles to Reconciliation in the South" in *Building Trust in Ireland, supra* n. 1.

[28] Thus, from within my own religious tradition, one can point to the *Declaration on Religious Freedom* of the Second Vatican Council, 1965, in which it is stated, in para. 2, that "[religious freedom] means that all should be immune from coercion on the part of individuals, social group and every human power so that, within due limits, nobody is forced to act against his convictions nor is anyone to be restrained from acting in accordance with his convictions in religious matters in private or in public, alone or in association with others": see A. Flannery O. P. (ed.), *Vatican Council II: The Conciliar and Post-conciliar Documents* (Dublin, Dominican Publications, 1975), i, 801. For a discussion of this principle, see P. Hannon, *Church, State, Morality and Law* (Dublin, Gill and Macmillan, 1992), 91–5.

[29] See Arts. 12.8 and 34.5.1, respectively. Indeed the Human Rights Committee of the United Nations has indicated that this requirement violates Art. 18 of the International Covenant on Civil and Political Rights on freedom of thought, conscience and religion: see *Irish Times*, 15 July 1993.

[30] Thus one would endorse the recommendation of the Constitution Review Group that Art. 12.8 should be amended to provide for a choice of alternative declarations for the office of Presidency: *supra* n. 1, 33. However, a majority of the Review Group recommend that, as far as the judiciary is concerned, a non-religious declaration only should be required on the ground that "[t]he daily exercise of the judicial function requires that a judge's impartiality should not be put in doubt by a public declaration of personal values": *ibid.*, 179. The inference in this recommendation that religious believers could not act impartially as judges is very questionable, to say the least.

require the use of religious language which is as inclusive as possible. In this regard, the current Preamble to the Constitution gives rise to serious concern. Not only is it explicitly Christian, it is also sectarian in the context of the Christian tradition, in that it implicitly identifies the Irish people with the Roman Catholic tradition. Should the People decide to retain religious references in the Preamble, one would expect that such references would be formulated so as to have the support of all theistic religions. This, of course, immediately leads to the question of the offence caused to people who do not subscribe to theistic beliefs by inclusion of such religious language in the Constitution. Such offence, while regrettable, may be unavoidable. Insofar as there may not be any neutral territory for the State to occupy between those who advocate the use of religious language in the Constitution and those who oppose such use, and insofar as one accepts that it is therefore legitimate, in terms of political morality, for the People to decide this issue one way or another, then it would appear that the fact that non-believers will be offended by the outcome should not be sufficient reason to prevent the People from deciding to include religious language in the Constitution if that is their wish.[31]

THE IMPLICATIONS FOR IRISH SOCIETY OF REMOVING THE RELIGIOUS INFLUENCE FROM THE CONSTITUTION

This final section moves from considering what ought to be, to considering what is. Briefly, some of the implications for Irish society which follow from the use of religious language in the Constitution are highlighted. This does not necessarily amount to an argument in favour of retention of such language in the Constitution; rather it is an attempt to highlight those secular values which are currently buttressed by the existing use of religious values in the constitutional order and which would require new constitutional foundations in the event of there being acceptance of the view, argued above, that the proper role for religious views in political debate is inspirational or prophetic rather than coercive.

Perhaps the most profound implication of any change in the *status quo* is that it could remove the existing constitutional foundations for a communitarian understanding of society. The present Constitution derives its philosophical inspiration from two very different sources—liberal democracy and Christian democracy. Quinn usefully summarises the tenets of liberalism as follows:

"(1) That the world can be imagined as divided between two mutually exclusive spheres designated the 'public' (State) and the 'private' (civil society) respectively;

---

[31] Equally, it follows that religious believers cannot insist on the inclusion of such language in order to protect their sensitivities.

(2) that the first important point of departure in all meaningful political and legal debate is the sense of the primacy of the individual in the 'private' sphere over all sources of 'public' (but only 'public') power and (3) that the public sphere is legitimate only to the point that it represents a consensual delegation of a limited and well-defined amount of private sovereignty."[32]

According to Grasso, the "inner logic" of liberalism results in:

"the rejection of any substantive conception of the good life. Substantive conceptions of the good life are nothing more than 'value judgments'—mere expressions of the subjective desires, the personal preferences, of the individual—with no objective foundation in reality. If, as a result, liberalism at first glance appears to exhibit an agnosticism on the question of the good, closer examination reveals that absent a substantive conception of the human good, liberalism—either implicitly or explicitly—elevates individual choice to the status of the human good, of the highest good for man."[33]

Catholic social teaching, in contrast, argues that it is possible to discern, through reason and revelation, the existence of an objective moral order and that a key element in such order is the recognition of the mutual interdependence of individual and social progress:

"The social nature of human beings makes it evident that the progress of the human person and the advance of society itself hinge on each other. From the beginning, the subject and the goal of all social institutions is and must be the human person, which for its part and by its very nature stands completely in need of social life. This social life is not something added on to human beings. Hence, through dealings with others, through reciprocal duties, and through fraternal dialogue they develop all their gifts and rise to their destiny."[34]

This rejection of individualism has very important implications for one's understanding of human rights.[35] Thus Hollenbach argues:

"Basic to [the Catholic] interpretation [of human rights] is the primacy granted to the idea of rights as positive empowerments over rights as negative immunities. In classical liberalism rights are identified with certain freedoms that are protected against coercion or interference by others. . . . The argument for a communitarian understanding of rights questions whether this view of the political rights stressed by classical liberalism does justice to their true importance and meaning."[36]

---

[32] "The Nature and Significance of Critical Legal Studies" (1989) 7 *ILT* 282, at 283.

[33] K. Grasso, "Beyond Liberalism: Human Dignity, the Free Society, and the Second Vatican Council" in K. Grasso, G. Bradley and R. Hunt (eds.), *Catholicism Liberalism and Communitarianism: the Catholic Intellectual Tradition and The Moral Foundations of Democracy* (Lanham, Rowman and Littlefield Publishers, 1995), 45–6.

[34] *Gaudium et Spes*, no. 25.

[35] For an examination of this issue in the context of the Irish Constitution, see Quinn, "Legal Change, Natural Law and the Authority of the Courts" in B. Treacy and G. Whyte (eds.), *supra* n. 15, 97, especially 102–13.

[36] "A Communitarian Reconstruction of Human Rights: Contributions from Catholic Tradition" in R. B. Douglas and D. Hollenbach (eds.), *Catholicism and Liberalism: Contributions to American Public Philosophy* (Cambridge, Cambridge University Press, 1994), 141.

In particular, and here we move on to a second implication of any move to purge the Constitution of religious language, the Catholic understanding of human rights promotes the value of social inclusion and has direct implications for the status of socio-economic rights in our constitutional order in that "[i]t shows why economic rights are indispensable conditions for any sort of life in common with other human beings".[37] Turning to Hollenbach again:

> "These economic rights also have a positive dimension that expresses the fact that all rights are rights to participation in community. First, respect for these rights means that individuals and society as a whole have obligations to take the positive steps necessary to assure that all persons obtain the nutrition, housing and employment necessary if they are to live minimally decent and active lives. Some of these steps will take the form of direct acts of assistance by one person to another. Others will be indirect, such as the creation of the social and economic institutions needed to secure these rights in a stable way for all over time.
>
> Second, these economic rights call for enabling persons to express their agency through positive participation in the life of society . . . [R]espect for human agency demands . . . that people not only be maintained alive, but alive as active agents of their own well-being through participation in social life, for example, through being able to get a job with adequate pay and decent working conditions."[38]

Purging the Constitution of religious language would, therefore, remove the existing philosophical basis for a communitarian reading of the Constitution, a reading which produces very different results in relation to the protection of socio-economic rights than an understanding of the Constitution inspired by liberal democratic principles.[39] Consequently, should it be felt desirable to retain such communitarian perspective on the Constitution, then in the event of a decision being made to delete all religious language from the Constitution, a secular statement of communitarian values would be required, such as is suggested by Lynch in the context of reformulating the directive principles of social policy in Article 45.[40]

Perry's work helps us to identify one further implication of change. As we have already noted,[41] Perry defends the thesis that the conviction that every human being is sacred is inescapably religious in that it is intelligible only in the context of a cosmology which views the world as ultimately meaningful. Of course, this is not to say that non-religious legal orders cannot decide to affirm a similar conviction; Perry simply argues that there is no non-religious cosmology from which one can infer the concept of universal human rights. What this means, in the context of the Irish Constitution, is that the use of

---

[37] *Catholicism and Liberalism: Contributions to American Public Philosophy* (Cambridge, Cambridge University Press, 1994), 145.

[38] *Ibid.*, 146.

[39] This point is developed in greater detail in my analysis of the *Report of the Constitution Review Group, supra* n. 4.

[40] See K. Lynch, "The Value of Retaining an Updated Article 45", appended to the *Report of the Constitution Review Group* (Dublin, Stationery Office, 1996), 637.

[41] *Supra* n. 16.

religious language in the Constitution implicitly commits Irish society to the belief that all individuals everywhere possess inherent rights. If such language is to be removed, an alternative affirmation will be required if this commitment is to be retained.

The role of religion in Irish history has been a chequered one. There is much of which to be ashamed, but equally much to cherish. However, the dominance of the Roman Catholic Church in the Republic until recent times and the hostile reaction to that dominance have arguably impoverished debate about the role of the religion in our society. Debate on the appropriate role, if any, of religion in our constitutional order is certainly underdeveloped. This essay attempts to make a fairly modest contribution to such a debate by sketching the arguments for and against the retention of religious language and values in the Constitution. In so doing, I share the hope expressed by Fintan O'Toole when he wrote:

> "If Catholics can bring [the] tradition of Christian morality to bear on their society, rather than be content with a bleak reiteration of the incomprehensible into the void, then they have a real moral agenda to offer to a secularised society. And if secular liberals can see that the minimalism of their own morality, which is a morality for tolerable coexistence rather than for changing things for the better, has useful things to learn from the larger ambitions of the older tradition, then there are at least grounds for a dialogue. This might well be too much to hope for, but when the alternative is a series of sterile replays of the 1980s referendums, it is a hope worth entertaining."[42]

[42] *Black Hole, Green Card: The Disappearance of Ireland* (Dublin, New Island Books, 1994), 148–9.

6

Education, the State and Sectarian Schools

DESMOND M. CLARKE

INTRODUCTION

Article 42 of the Constitution is entitled "Education". This is almost a mis-
nomer, for reasons which emerge below. Article 42 does not establish explicitly a right to education. Nor does it impose on the State a constitutional duty
to provide education for citizens; the State merely has a duty "to provide for"
free primary education, to "*endeavour* to supplement . . . private and corporate educational initiative" and "in exceptional cases to *endeavour* to supply
the place of the parents" (author's italics). In fact, anyone reading this Article
for the first time would be struck most forcefully by the number of qualifications and disclaimers and by the frequency of its deference to the rights of the
family, of parents and of children. For example, "the State acknowledges that
the primary and natural educator of the child is the Family" (not parents);
"The State shall not oblige parents . . . to send their children to schools established by the State"; "parents shall be free to provide this education in their
homes"; the "State shall provide for free primary education . . . with due
regard, however, for the rights of parents, especially in the matter of religious
and moral formation"; "in exceptional cases . . . the State . . . shall endeavour to supply the place of parents, but always with due regard for the (unspec-
ified) natural and imprescriptible rights of the child". In contrast, the
Universal Declaration of Human Rights (1948) states: "Everyone has the right
to education."[1] Likewise, the European Convention on Human Rights is
explicit: "No person shall be denied the right to education."[2] According to the

---

[1] Art. 26. See also the International Covenant on Economic, Social and Cultural Rights, 1966,
Art. 13, which begins: "The States Parties to the present Covenant recognise the right of everyone [not just children—author's insertion] to education" and the International Covenant on Civil
and Political Rights 1966, Art. 18(4) by which states undertake to " . . . have respect for the liberty of parents and, when applicable, legal guardians to ensure the religious and moral education
of their children with their own convictions".

[2] Protocol No 1 (1952), Art. 2.

Irish Constitution, however, a citizen does not have a constitutional right to education.[3]

One would have to be historically insensitive in the extreme not to recognise that the Constitution was drafted and enacted at a time when almost all education at primary level in Ireland, and most education at secondary level (with the exception of Vocational Education schools), was provided in schools which were owned and managed by religious denominations and that the vast majority of such schools were Roman Catholic.[4] Educational initiatives taken by Churches in the nineteenth century in Ireland had been extremely beneficial to many young students who, otherwise, would not have had access to any kind of formal schooling. However this evangelically motivated beneficence was compromised when the same churches resorted to political action to maintain their control of schools and refused to co-operate with the State when, eventually, it came to recognise its duties in this area. Meanwhile the British government had established some "godless" third-level colleges (i.e. the Queen's Colleges) in Belfast, Cork and Galway, and these were reluctantly tolerated by Roman Catholics as being at least less objectionable than Trinity College, Dublin (because of the latter's historical connections with the Church of Ireland).[5] The obstructive and unco-operative political action by the Churches prior to partition was intensified in the period after 1922.[6] By the time Church and State considered the proposed constitutional provisions for education in 1937, the denominational control of schools was so entrenched that the only outstanding issues for educational policy seemed to be: how to secure the *status quo* for the churches and, at the same time, provide constitutional protection for a system of public funding for private schools. Hence

---

[3] The Constitution of the Irish Free State (1922) did guarantee a right to elementary education. Art. 10 stated: "All citizens of the Irish Free State (Saorstát Éireann) have the right to free elementary education." This was explicitly amended in 1937 to a constitutional requirement on the State "to provide for" free primary education. See *Crowley* v. *Ireland* [1980] IR 102, at 122: "it cannot be doubted that citizens have the right to receive what it is the State's duty to provide for under Art. 42, s. 4." In other words, the State has a duty to put in place the arrangements by which it provides for free primary education, and citizens have a right to those arrangements. The unreported judgment of O'Hanlon J in *O'Donoghue* v. *Minister for Health* (27 May 1993) was appealed to the Supreme Court but the appeal was withdrawn on 6 Feb. 1997; according to this judgment, the definition of "education" in *Ryan* v. *Attorney General* [1965] IR 294 includes a right to the provision by the State of appropriate educational facilities even for severely or profoundly retarded children: "there is a constitutional obligation imposed on the State by the provisions of Art. 42.4 of the Constitution to provide for free basic elementary education of all children and [that] this involves giving each child such advice, instruction and teaching as will enable him or her to make the best possible use of his or her inherent and potential capacities, physical, mental and moral, however limited these capacities may be" (at 94).

[4] The figures for 1992–3 indicate that the current situation has not significantly changed: 2,988 (93.1%) of 3,209 primary schools were Roman Catholic, and 74% of second-level students attended denominational schools.

[5] See J. Lydon, "The Silent Sister: Trinity College and Catholic Ireland" in C. H. Holland (ed.), *Trinity College Dublin and the Idea of a University* (Dublin, Trinity College Dublin Press, 1991), 29–53.

[6] See e.g. M. Harris, *The Catholic Church and the Foundation of the Northern Irish State 1912–30* (Cork, Cork University Press, 1993).

the narrow perspective of Article 42: citizens had no right to education, the State had no duty to provide educational facilities directly to citizens, and the privileged role of the churches in schools would remain unchallenged by competition from publicly funded schools.

While this brief sketch is essentially correct, it omits the wider European context in which the 1937 discussions took place. It was clear from the aftermath of the Russian revolution, and from the subsequent emergence of fascism in Europe, that many states tried to substitute ideological indoctrination for genuine education at school and that the spectre of a state which penetrated into the very minds of citizens through a widespread and effective control of education was a much greater threat than it might seem sixty years later.[7] This historical reality was acknowledged as the greatest source of concern in the Council of Europe, when drafting the provisions of the European Convention on education, and was the primary motivation for putting the rights of parents above those of the State.[8] The danger of a State exceeding its legitimate authority in education had already been recognised in a landmark US Supreme Court decision as early as 1925, and in a series of subsequent US decisions which continued to limit the educational jurisdiction of States.[9] This was not an imminent danger in Ireland in 1937. However, the historical experience raises a fundamental question about what precisely we expect a State to do, in respect of education, at the end of the twentieth century. And whatever that is, there is a further question about what should be specified in a constitution, rather than is legislation which varies from one generation to another.

The State is financially and administratively involved in education in Ireland, as in most Western democracies, at three levels; primary, secondary and third. It is also involved in a significant level of professional training which is designed to prepare people (in most cases adults) for employment. Not only does education continue into adulthood, but the ordinary meaning of the term suggests that education is not identical with schooling. Education is a life-long process, and much of it takes place independently of any formal schooling, well beyond the scope of any State's jurisdiction. Unfortunately, despite the obviously wide scope of the term "education" and despite the fact that people of all ages are being educated in an untold variety of contexts, the

---

[7] Perhaps there is a slight whiff of the spirit of fascism in the word chosen by the Constitution as the official title of the prime minister. Art. 13.1.1 provides that "the head of the government or the Prime Minister" shall be called the *Taoiseach*, which may have unwelcome connotations of *Il Duce*. Given that the President is head of state, it might seem more appropriate to call the prime minister exactly what he, or she, is, *viz.* the "Prime Minister" or first among those who serve the people.

[8] See D. M. Clarke, "Freedom of Thought and Educational Rights in the European Convention" (1987) 22 *Ir. Jur.* 28 at 34.

[9] *Pierce* v. *Society of Sisters*, 268 US 510 (1925). The nub of the issue here was whether children in the State of Oregon could be compelled to attend state schools rather than schools owned and managed by a religious order.

Constitution focuses almost exclusively on children,[10] and on the State's limited role in schools at primary and second level.

Some might argue that the State has no role at all in education and that it should mind its own business (whatever that is). But that is hardly plausible. The operation of a modern State presupposes that its citizens are educated at least to a level at which they can participate meaningfully in the democratic institutions which underpin it. We have accepted the theory that individuals have rights, that a society collectively is responsible for guaranteeing those rights for its members, and that the State is the complex of legal and administrative structures by which a society arranges for and protects the civil life of citizens. In this sense, a society makes provision for its members—minimally, to enjoy basic human rights and, ideally, to prosper and develop as members of society. It is for that reason that there are significant transfers of resources between members within any modern State. Thus the imperative for the State to provide educational opportunities for citizens derives from a general obligation on a society to care for its members. Once the generality and vagueness of this rationale is recognised, it is obvious that people may adopt rather different political theories about the role of the State, the limits of its jurisdiction, and the powers that it needs in order to implement agreed objectives. Thus, within the wide scope of what is meant by a democracy, political convictions may vary from, on the one hand, a theory of the minimal State to, on the other hand, a form of intrusive socialism which is involved in almost every aspect of people's lives, including the specification and satisfaction of their educational and cultural interests.

This highlights one of the essential features of a constitution: the extent to which it should differ from specific legislation and from the variety of political philosophies which are compatible with a broad understanding of democracy. As John Rawls has argued, a modern State should be capable of including people with incompatible comprehensive theories and, in the interests of stability, it needs structures which can accommodate policy changes over time which are reflected in changing legislation.[11] For this reason, a constitution should express very general principles which are not manifestly the voice of one particular comprehensive doctrine among others.

By these criteria, the Irish Constitution fails because it reflects too narrow an understanding of the nature of education, and it relies too exclusively on the educational theory of one particular comprehensive theory, namely, that of the Roman Catholic Church. This might seem initially like a harsh judgment and readers might even wonder whether there is such a thing as a Roman Catholic philosophy of education.

---

[10] Art. 42 provides that: "The . . . primary and natural educator of the *child*; the religious and moral . . . education of their *children*; the state shall not oblige parents . . . to send their *children* . . . ; the state shall . . . require . . . that the *children* receive a certain minimum education; in exceptional cases, . . . the State shall . . . with due regard for . . . the rights of the *child*" (author's italics).

[11] J. Rawls, *Political Liberalism* (New York, Columbia University Press, 1993).

According to Roman Catholic theology, the dominant objective in any human enterprise is the "salvation of souls". There is one true Church, and the salvation of souls is conditional on membership of this Church. This is so sectarian and blatantly pre-ecumenical that one might balk at such a stark statement of principle and look for a softer focus for the same basic assumption. But if salvation could be realised just as easily through membership of other Churches or of none, how could one explain the evangelical zeal with which the Catholic Church sends missionaries far afield into other countries and cultures to convert them to the "true faith" while it refuses to co-operate locally with other churches, even other Christian Churches, in the development of interdenominational schools? Without the theological assumption about the uniqueness of the path to salvation, one would have to fall back on other explanations, such as the financial benefits for a church from increased membership or a totalitarian mission to dominate the minds and hearts of people at the expense of other values.

This evangelical motive is translated into a policy on schools by imposing a moral duty on members of the Catholic Church to send their children to exclusively Catholic schools, if they are available. What is meant by a Roman Catholic school is discussed further below. The moral pressure on members to proselytise the next generation is transformed into a claim that Roman Catholics have a *right* to send their children to such schools. However, the alleged right is based on nothing more than the theology of that particular church. Assuming a theologically-based right, Roman Catholics then look to the state to secure their rights. They are encouraged by Canon Law to press their theological rights until the State provides them, at public expense, with the kind of schools which their Church requires them to attend. The Code of Canon Law tells parents to "send their children to those schools which will provide for their Catholic education". The State, according to Canon Law, must acknowledge this duty of parents and must provide them with the freedom to exercise their educational choice. "Parents must have a real freedom in their choice of schools" and they should be watchful "that the civil society acknowledges this freedom of parents".[12]

What is proposed here is very simple, and very divisive. A Church tells its members that their children must attend Catholic schools. A Catholic school is defined by Canon Law as follows:

"A Catholic School is understood to be one which is under the control of the competent ecclesiastical authority or of a public ecclesiastical juridical person, or one which in a written document is acknowledged as Catholic by the ecclesiastical authority. Formation and education in a Catholic school must be based on the principles of Catholic education, and the teachers must be outstanding in true doctrine and uprightness of life."[13]

---

[12] *The New Code of Canon Law in English Translation* (London, Collins, 1983), Canon 797.
[13] *Ibid.* at Canon 803.

These provisions are often summarised in the code word "ethos". The ownership or control of Catholic schools is not an end in itself; control is a means to insuring that the school curriculum communicates the Catholic version of Christian beliefs to students. This also requires teachers to be "outstanding in true doctrine and uprightness of life" so that the official teaching of the Church is not undermined or compromised by the teachers' failure to live as Catholics. In the words of the former Code of Canon Law, which informed policy discussions in 1937, the objection to Catholics attending schools other than those described above was "the danger of perversion" or, in less colourful language, the probability that citizens might cease to believe in the Catholic faith.[14]

The evangelical objectives of the various Churches are not objectionable as such. It is perfectly reasonable for each Church to try to persuade new members to join and to encourage current members to remain active. Freedom to pursue such objectives—on condition that the means used are unobjectionable—is exactly what is meant by freedom of thought and freedom of expression.[15] But, it is not the role of the State to co-operate in the evangelical missions of competing Churches. By adapting its educational policy to the theologies of competing Churches, the State reinforces the divisive and sectarian theologies of the churches in the civil life of citizens.

It should be acknowledged immediately that there is no reasonable basis for the claim that the state should have exclusive control of the management, curriculum, funding or philosophy of educational institutions, including schools. Therefore, the provisions of the Constitution which permit parents to arrange for the education of their children in a variety of different types of school are, in this respect, beyond reproach and are consistent with an enlightened philosophy of education. No State should establish one uniform style of school and attempt to force all children, by law or otherwise, to attend a "state school". The same applies to education at a more advanced level, when it is no longer a question of children and their parents but of the competence of the State to direct research and teaching at third level.

But it does not follow, just because the State should not coerce all young citizens into state schools, that parents have a right to demand that the State provide them with precisely the kind of schools that they prefer. In particular, there is no good reason why the State should provide parents, at public expense, with schools for their children from which other children are excluded simply because of their religion. Canon Law does not request merely

[14] The policy which informed the Constitution was inspired by the provisions of the Code of Canon Law (1918), which said: "Canon 1374: Catholic children may not attend non-Catholic, neutral, or mixed schools, that is, those which are open also to non-catholics. It pertains exclusively to the local bishop to decide . . . under what circumstances and with what precautions against the danger of perversion (*periculum perversionis*), attendance at such schools may be tolerated."

[15] See D. M. Clarke, "Freedom of Thought in the UN Declaration and Covenants" (1993–5) 28–30 *Ir. Jur.* 121.

that the State establish schools in which the religious beliefs of young Catholics are respected. That is a perfectly reasonable request. Instead it demands that the State finance schools from which children and teachers of other religious denominations are excluded because, by their presence in any given school in sufficiently large numbers, the ethos of the school is changed. The same kind of reasoning may be used by other religious traditions, including the Church of Ireland. Each in turn may argue that it has a right to have children of their church educated in a school from which pupils and teachers of different religious traditions are excluded so that the religious affiliation of students is not challenged by association with students or teachers of a different faith.

THE STATE'S ROLE IN EDUCATION

Education in its broadest sense is usually included among the goods which a State ought to provide for citizens. The extent to which it can provide them is always subject to economic constraints. Secondly, any distribution of such goods among citizens must be governed by principles of equality of access and of non-discrimination. In this sense, education is similar to healthcare. The ability of a modern democracy to provide healthcare to citizens is limited by the economic conditions of the State and by the public demand for healthcare at any particular time. Even in relatively affluent States where economic limitations are not very restrictive, there is a range of methods by which healthcare is provided; it varies from, on the one hand, those in which healthcare is almost completely privatised to, on the other hand, States in which most healthcare is provided from public funds. One could argue for the merits or otherwise of either system; economists often argue that the public provision of healthcare can never satisfy demand because the latter always increases more quickly than the supply available. Thus, there is a general background policy issue about whether most healthcare should be provided from public funds, or whether only a minimal healthcare should be provided publicly and individuals would then pay for as much or as little healthcare as they wish from private funds.

Whatever decision is made on that question, it is likely to vary from one generation to the next, from one economic situation to another and, especially, from one political philosophy to another. For this reason it is not the kind of policy which should be included in a country's constitution. If the State assumes an obligation to provide at least a minimal healthcare system from public funds, the question then arises about alternative systems of delivery. One could easily imagine the following type of argument, which is similar to the corresponding argument for exclusive schools. Roman Catholics wish to have healthcare provided in institutions (such as hospitals, clinics, etc.) in which their religious faith is supported and in which they have access to religious services when, for example, they are seriously ill. So far, no one could reasonably object. However, they might continue the analogy further and argue that, not only should hospitals respect their religious faith and facilitate the practice of their religion when they are sick, but they must be such as to exclude people of other religions from the same hospitals because of the fear of religious contamination. Since there are already in operation many hospitals which were founded by Roman Catholic religious orders, the State should channel its public healthcare funds through those private hospitals so that Roman Catholics may enjoy the kind of religiously exclusive healthcare that they want.

"Exclusive" here means that other citizens should be excluded from these publicly-funded Catholic hospitals, although of course they have a right to publicly-funded healthcare of their own—but in other hospitals. In simple English, the State should operate a system of "separate but equal" hospitals, in which the ethos of each religious sect, enforced by their respective ethics committees, would permeate the whole hospital environment. In towns or cities where there is no hospital for members of minority religions, such people may be admitted to a Catholic hospital in an emergency and even in non-emergency situations if the total number of admissions is small enough not to upset the balance of the hospital's ethos. The protection of a hospital's ethos could be guaranteed only as long as the hospital is officially owned and/or controlled by a legal person which is Roman Catholic. While Catholic hospitals may admit non-Catholics, they would not under any circumstances provide medical services which are judged by Roman Catholics to be immoral, even if they are legal in the jurisdiction which funds the healthcare services. Thus, unfortunately, the healthcare services that the State provides from public funds would be restricted by the religious or ethical views of the hospital owners.

Such a proposal is repugnant to our understanding of civil rights, of toleration and of equality of access of all citizens to publicly-funded healthcare services. It goes without saying that Catholics have a right to practise their religion while benefiting from healthcare services provided by the State, and that hospitals and clinics should be designed accordingly. It is equally obvious that Catholics (and anyone else for that matter!) may not be forced by law or regulation to undergo any healthcare procedure to which they do not consent. Finally, Catholics may obviously found, manage and finance private hospitals to which non-Catholics are not normally admitted. But the question here is: may they insist, because they are in a majority in a particular jurisdiction, that the State provide them from public funds with *exclusive* healthcare institutions from which non-Catholics are usually excluded?

EXCLUSIVE SCHOOLS

The argument in favour of exclusive denominational schools, or what I shall call *sectarian schools*, is similar to the argument for exclusive hospitals. There are differences, of course. A child is likely to be at school much longer than in hospital, and education is a much more value-laden enterprise than providing short-term healthcare. For these reasons and others, schools normally have a more important formative influence on young people than hospitals, and that has to be acknowledged in any policy adopted by the State. This explains why the Churches may settle for interdenominational *hospitals*, especially those which are so expensive that Churches cannot provide comparable healthcare services in an exclusively denominational manner, but still demand sectarian *schools* and even exclusive, sectarian correctional facilities for young offenders.[16]

The history of Roman Catholic educational policy in the nineteenth and twentieth centuries has been to extend the demand for sectarian education to the third level. In theory, the Catholic Church would prefer to have Catholic universities as it does in the United States and in various European countries, and to prevent Roman Catholics from attending universities (as it did in the case of Trinity College, Dublin) which are identified as a danger to the faith of its members. If this ideal cannot be sustained, mainly for financial reasons, then this strict educational policy is relaxed so that Catholics are allowed to attend universities or similar third-level institutes which are not officially Catholic. But they are required to attend Catholic schools at primary and secondary level. Given this theologically inspired educational policy, how should the State respond?

The State in Ireland, before 1921 and subsequent to the establishment of Saorstát Éireann, has conceded the educational demands of the main Christian churches but, in principle at least, has defended the constitutional ban on religious discrimination in the admission of students to publicly funded schools. The *Articles of Agreement for a Treaty between Great Britain and Ireland* (6 December 1921) stipulated in Article 16:

"Neither the Parliament of the Irish Free State nor the Parliament of Northern Ireland shall make any law so as either directly or indirectly to endow any religion or prohibit or restrict the free exercise thereof or give any preference or impose any disability on account of religious belief or religious status or affect prejudicially the right of any child to attend a school receiving public money without attending the

---

[16] S.133(18) of the Children Act 1908 stipulates that no Roman Catholic young offender may be sent to a school "which is not conducted in accordance with the doctrines of that church" and that no non-Catholic young offender may be admitted to a Catholic school. In *DPP (Houlihan) v. Gencer* [1977] ILRM 57, at 66, the Supreme Court decided: "What the court cannot do, because of the proviso, is send a Roman Catholic child to any school other than one conducted in accordance with the doctrines of the Roman Catholic church; or, conversely, send any child who is not a Roman Catholic to such a school."

religious instruction at the school or make any discrimination as respects state aid between schools under the management of different religious denominations or divert from any religious denomination or any educational institution any of its property except for public utility purposes and on payment of compensation."

The provisions of this Article are reflected in Article 8 of the Constitution of the Irish Free State. While Article 10 guaranteed the right of every citizen to "free elementary education", Article 8 was concerned primarily with freedom of conscience and provided, among other things, that:

"no law may be made . . . to affect prejudicially the right of any child to attend a school receiving public money without attending the religious instruction at the school . . . ".

Although the right to free elementary education was omitted in 1937, the provisions against discrimination in admission policy were retained in Article 44.2.4:

"Legislation providing State aid for schools shall not discriminate between schools under the management of different religious denominations, nor be such as to affect prejudicially the right of any child to attend a school receiving public money without attending religious instruction at that school."

In drafting the Constitution, its chief architects thought they could reconcile the demand of the Churches for sectarian schools and, at the same time, the requirement that publicly-funded schools may not discriminate on religious grounds in their admission policy. The key to implementing this compromise in practice, though obviously not in principle, was to assume that there would be relatively few applications to denominational schools from non-coreligionists and to tolerate their unwelcome presence as the price for public funding. A mechanism for implementing this was included in the *Rules for National Schools*, which required schools to identify clearly which periods were periods for religious instruction and thereby to facilitate any child whose parents decided to exempt them from religious instruction.[17] However, this distinction between different types of instruction has been eroded in time. The revised curriculum, approved by the Department of Education, has encouraged the integration of religious instruction into the whole school curriculum.[18] So while the provisions of the Constitution stand, in theory, it is currently impossible in practice to attend most publicly funded denominational schools without attending religious instruction.

The plight of a relatively few students, whose constitutional rights are not defended by the State, may not excite public interest. But the current situation is more serious than that; it is a glaring contradiction in public policy. The churches wish to make arrangements so that the ethos of denominational schools remains unchanged. That means that Roman Catholic schools would

---

[17] *Rules for National Schools* (1965), rr. 54 and 59(5).
[18] *Primary School Curriculum, Teacher's Handbook* (1971), pt 1, 19.

be such that, as far as possible, they would satisfy the requirements of Canon Law. That may require them to maintain a majority control of school boards, to discriminate against hiring teachers who are not Catholics or who, in the opinion of the schools, are not sufficiently supportive of Roman Catholic values in their semi-private lives (for example, those who live with a partner without being married in the Catholic church).[19] It also requires them to discriminate against non-Catholics in admission policy. As long as the number of non-Catholic applicants involved is very small, the provisions of Article 44.2.4 are easy to satisfy. But, if the number applying to a particular school were large, it is evident that the ethos of the school would quickly be changed. While this is unlikely for most large Catholic schools, it is already a real problem for much smaller Church of Ireland schools which are often expected to admit dissidents of any persuasion or none.

The constitutional provision which forbids discrimination on religious grounds in the admission of children to publicly funded schools is inconsistent, in principle and now in practice, with a public policy to finance sectarian schools which discriminate against student applicants on religious grounds and against qualified teachers on religious or life-style grounds. More fundamentally, an educational policy which supports, protects and finances the sectarian theological divisions of the churches is inconsistent with the constitutional requirement to treat all citizens equally and to provide publicly funded services, such as healthcare or education, through institutions which treat all citizens in a non-discriminatory manner. The State therefore should refuse to support from public funds educational institutions which discriminate against citizens on the basis of their religious or philosophical convictions.[20]

This proposal is sometimes caricatured as a proposal that education in schools should be value-free. It is also misdescribed as a suggestion that the State should impose a uniform system of secular schooling on all young people and coerce them to attend state schools in preference to the legitimate preferences of their parents. It is even understood by others as part of a conspiracy to disseminate a form of irreligious liberalism which is subversive of the religious values which many parents wish their children to acquire through education.[21] None of these claims stands up to scrutiny. There is no suggestion

---

[19] See *Flynn* v. *Power* [1975] IR 648.

[20] For a comparison with US civil rights legislation, including anti-discrimination provisions, and the public funding of private schools and colleges, see E. McGlynn Gaffney, Jr. (ed.), *Private Schools and the Public Good* (Notre Dame and London, University of Notre Dame Press, 1981) and E. McGlynn Gaffney, Jr. and P. R. Moots (eds.), *Government and Campus* (Notre Dame and London, University of Notre Dame Press, 1982).

[21] Fr Denis Faul, headmaster of St. Patrick's Academy in Co. Tyrone, wrote as follows in the *Irish Times* (12 July 1996): "Integrated schools were started by the British and given favoured legislative status as a 'dirty political trick' to undermine Catholic schools providing a specific religious ethos and moral training in family life as well as a distinctive Irish culture. . . . In Northern Ireland, in all Ireland, there is a battle for control of the minds of the young. The successes of the liberal agenda . . . have been damaging. The population has gone down; the individual can

here that education is, or ought to be, value-free, or that it should be exclusively secular. Nor is it suggested that the State should coerce young citizens into any particular type of school or education. The proposal is much simpler and narrower in scope: in providing educational services from public finances, the State should not discriminate, in principle or in practice, against any citizen on the basis of their religious or philosophical convictions.[22]

Irish educational policy is sometimes defended by claiming that it is democratic. It is argued that parents' choices are the ultimate criterion for government policy in the education of children and that, whatever type of school a democratic majority of parents want, that is what they should get. But, such simple majoritarianism is not what most people understand by a democracy. The reason is obvious. In a society in which some form of marxist communism is allegedly approved by the majority of parents, this concept of democracy would imply that the State should finance a system in which most schools are ideologically marxist. There should then be pictures of Marx and Lenin in the classrooms, and marxist ideology should be integrated into the whole school curriculum because, in the words of the *Primary School Curriculum*, the "separation of ideological and secular instruction into differentiated subject compartments serves only to throw the whole educational function out of focus".[23] Evidently, in such an arrangement the children of non-marxist parents would have a constitutional right to attend such schools without attending the ideological instruction provided. And if they happened to attend schools in which almost all the teachers and students were marxists and in which marxism was integrated into the whole school curriculum, it would be simply an unfortunate consequence of democratic control that they were taught marxism at school despite their parents' explicit objections.

If that example is too disturbing for religious believers, one could change the example to a predominantly Church of England society or a predominantly Buddhist society, and so on. The point is simple. In any jurisdiction in which the State finances a system of schools which are denominationally or ideologically affiliated in an exclusive way, parents of other children are deprived of their rights and the State becomes involved in supporting financially one particular religion or ideology rather than another. If Catholics would not accept a "democratic" arrangement in which 93 per cent of the publicly-funded primary schools are explicitly Marxist, Church of Ireland or

---

choose sex, drink, drugs and violence as he pleases; the sense of community welfare is gone. Our Catholic schools stand directly in the path of the monster, who recoils at the sight of loving communities directed to the love of God and their fellow men and women by prayer and penance." These loving communities demand schools from which Christians of other denominations are excluded.

[22] Compare the provisions of the European Convention on Human Rights, Protocol 1, Art. 2: "In the exercise of any functions which it assumes in relation to education and to teaching, the State shall respect the right of parents to ensure such education and teaching in conformity with their own religious and philosophical convictions."

[23] *Supra* n.18, substituting the word "ideological" for the word "religious".

Islamic, then they should have the same objection if non-Catholic citizens are offered a primary education by the State in schools of which 93 per cent have a guaranteed Catholic ethos.

The failure of the Constitution to protect the rights of citizens who belong to minority religions or to none suggests that the State should formulate a different policy by which to accommodate parents' rights in the education of their minor children, the rights of Churches to found and control private schools, and the constitutional imperative not to discriminate against students or teachers in publicly-funded schools on the basis of their religious beliefs. Parents must have a veto on the philosophical and religious instruction provided to their own minor children in schools, but they cannot demand that the State establish sectarian schools which coincide with their religious affiliation. In practice, the State can accommodate the rights of all by establishing and funding multi-denominational schools to which children of all religions or none are admitted, and in which the religious and philosophical beliefs of all children are respected equally. If some parents wish to educate their children at home, or in private schools in which they are protected from the danger of religious contamination, they should evidently have a right to do so. The State, for its part, should transcend the theological divisions between different churches and refuse to implement such sectarian divisions in its educational policy. Instead, while acknowledging that, in the private sphere, the churches are likely to compete for members and pursue their independent theological traditions, the State should provide educational services in the public sphere in a non-discriminatory manner, with equal access for all, independent of their religious or philosophical convictions.

7

The Family in the Constitution— Principle and Practice

FRANK MARTIN

INTRODUCTION

"There is nothing in the Article [Article 41, The Family] . . . it means nothing legislatively. . . . It may as a piece of guidance have some effect . . . it accomplishes nothing and compels the State to do nothing. It is exactly like Article 45. . . . Women have been rendered nervous by these Articles in the Constitution . . . great uneasiness has been excited in the minds of women . . . who have been exceedingly alarmed by the insertion of these Articles. . . . Merely writing down high principles in this Constitution is not going to see that these things are, in fact, achieved in practice. There is a lot of theory in this Constitution."[1]

ARTICLE 41—THE FAMILY

"1. The State recognises the Family as the natural primary and fundamental unit group of Society, and as a moral institution possessing inalienable and imprescriptible rights, antecedent and superior to all positive law.

1.2 The State, therefore, guarantees to protect the Family in its Constitution and authority, as the necessary basis of social order and as indispensable to the welfare of the Nation and the State.

2.1 In particular, the State recognises that by her life within the home, woman gives to the State a support without which the common good cannot be achieved.

2.2 The State shall, therefore, endeavour to ensure that mothers shall not be obliged by economic necessity to engage in labour to the neglect of their duties in the home.

3.1 The State pledges itself to guard with special care the institution of Marriage, on which the Family is founded, and to protect it against attack.

3.1 [No law shall be enacted providing for the grant of a dissolution of marriage: now deleted].

* The author would like to acknowledge the financial support received from the President's Research Fund in UCC in the Research and preparation of this chapter.

[1] *Dáil* Debates on the Draft Constitution, vol. 67, cols. 1850–9, 4 June 1937. Extracts from speeches by Professor O'Sullivan, Mr MacDermot and John A Costello.

3.2 A Court designated by law may grant a dissolution of marriage where, but only where, it is satisfied that—

i. at the date of the institution of the proceedings, the spouses have lived apart from one another for a period of, or periods amounting to, at least four years during the previous five years.

ii. there is no reasonable prospect of a reconciliation between the spouses.

iii. such provision as the Court considers proper having regard

to the circumstances, exists or will be made for the spouses, any children of either or both of them and any other person prescribed by law, and

iv. any further conditions prescribed by law are complied with.

3.3 No person whose marriage has been dissolved under the civil law of any other State but is a subsisting valid marriage under the law for the time being in force within the jurisdiction of the Government and Parliament established by this Constitution shall be capable of contracting a valid marriage within that jurisdiction during the lifetime of the other party to the marriage so dissolved."

The Article is located in the text as a distinct sub-heading under the major heading of "Fundamental Rights" and bears the distinctive hallmark of a typical liberal-democratic statement or directive.[2] J. H. Whyte, the distinguished scholar on Church and State relations, regarded Article 41 as "obviously marked by Catholic thought . . . with sonorous declarations."[3] It was a novel provision in 1937 since the Free State Constitution of 1922 contained no similar provisions dealing with either the Family or marriage formalities. In fact, the United States Constitution, generally regarded as the paradigm for written constitutions in liberal democracies, contains no specific reference to "the Family" as a social group requiring, or benefiting from, special explicit constitutional protection.[4] Since 1937, Article 41 has continued to generate a considerable degree of controversy for lawyers. Although this aspirational Article contains no comprehensive definition of "the family", it nevertheless has been primarily responsible for the evolution of a sophisticated body of family law jurisprudence, particularly since the mid-1970s.

An all-party informal *Oireachtas* Committee was set up in 1966 by the then Taoiseach, Mr Lemass, to review the Constitution and Article 41 obviously came within its ambit, but in particular Article 41.3.2, which deals with the absolute prohibition against civil divorce. The Committee contained no Protestant members (in contrast to the composition of the 1996 Constitution

---

[2] D. Keogh, "The Irish Constitutional Revolution: An Analysis of the Making of the Constitution" in F. Litton (ed.), *The Constitution of Ireland 1937–1987* (Dublin, Institute of Public Administration, 1988), 5 states that "[i]n the Catholic political world of the 1930s, the Constitution was exceptional in its commitment to liberal democracy".

[3] J. H. Whyte, *Church and State in Modern Ireland 1923–1979* (Dublin, Gill and MacMillan, 1980), 51–2.

[4] Art. 21 of the Constitution of Greece acknowledges the family as "the foundation of the preservation and the advancement of the Nation as well as marriage, motherhood and childhood and shall be under the protection of the State". Other contemporary examples of Constitutions referring to the Family are the Constitution of Portugal, Art. 68, and the Constitution of Italy, Arts. 29 and 31.

Review Group). In December 1967, the Committee issued its interim report which unanimously recommended, *inter alia*, the replacement of the absolute divorce prohibition. The Report suggested the following alternative text which, it was hoped, would be inoffensive and thus acceptable to all of the religions professed by the inhabitants of Ireland:

> "In the case of a person who was married in accordance with the rites of a religion, no law shall be enacted providing for the grant of a dissolution of that marriage on grounds other than those acceptable to that religion."[5]

Essentially, two reasons were advanced by the Committee for its proposed qualification of the absolute divorce law. First, since divorce was available in the North, the prohibition was believed to be a source of embarrassment to those seeking to bring about better relations between North and South. Secondly, and perhaps more significantly in the post-Second Vatican Council era of ecumenism, the Committee concluded that the prohibition:

> "ignored the wishes of a certain minority of the population who would wish to have divorce facilities and who are not prevented from securing divorce by the tenets of the religious denominations to which they belong."[6]

Condemnation by the Catholic hierarchy followed immediately on publication of the report. The bishops were somewhat peeved that their views had not even been canvassed by the "informal" Committee. The response of Dr McQuaid, Archbishop of Dublin, was that he regarded:

> "civil divorce . . . [as] contrary to the law of God. . . . The experience of other countries has proved that civil divorce produces the greatest of evils in society. . . . The effort, even if well-intentioned, to solve hardships within marriage by civil divorce has invariably resulted for society in a series of greater sufferings and deeper evils."[7]

Cardinal Conway, who feared the floodgate ramifications, suggested that if the prohibition were diluted, the result would be a "radical and far-reaching break with our national traditions".[8] Cardinal Conway's ignorance of the legal complexities of the civil law regulations governing the recognition of foreign divorces was manifestly evident in his simplistic statement suggesting that:

> "few of [our fellow] Christians believe in divorce, and still fewer of them want it. Even these few have little difficulty in securing a divorce elsewhere and many of them have done so."[9]

---

[5] *Report of the Committee on the Constitution* (Dublin, Stationery Office, 1967), 43–4. The Attorney-General, Mr Colm Condon, also convened a legal committee to review the Constitution in conjunction with, but independent of, the *Oireachtas* Committee. In 1968, it produced a draft Report and discontinued its review.

[6] *Ibid.*, at para. 123.

[7] *Irish Times*, 26 Feb. 1968.

[8] *Irish Times*, 15 Dec. 1967

[9] *Ibid.*

According to Chubb, the 1967 Committee on the Constitution was "remarkable both for the progressive views it expressed on a number of constitutional issues and for its complete misjudgment of what was politically possible at that time".[10] Its views on reform of the divorce laws were, in retrospect, pragmatic and its failure to undertake extensive consultations with the various religious denominations was a major error. Another difficulty regarding the divorce proposal was that it would have necessitated the courts, when making a determination on a divorce case, to scrutinise the complex tenets of the various non-Catholic denominations. Such a judicial exercise would have been practically impossible to implement. Also, the recommendation was too narrow in its focus, given that it examined divorce exclusively from a denominational perspective. The position of those, for example, who had married in a Registry Office was not addressed by the Committee.

For the next twenty years, politicians were remarkably reticent about advocating similar constitutional reform for fear of finding themselves "within the radiation zone of possible episcopal wrath".[11] Dr Garret Fitzgerald was to take valuable lessons from the 1967 Report for his 1980s constitutional crusade, in particular by consulting with the leaders of all religions, ascertaining their views on the civil law regulation of marriage. Dr Fitzgerald's consultation process confirmed the prevailing dichotomy of views: non-Catholic Churches expressed a reluctant preference for the removal of the absolute ban on divorce with the Catholic Church demanding the retention of the *status quo*.[12] Historically, these episcopal condemnations of the late 1960s were primarily responsible for maintaining the continued absolute rigidity of the Family Article, even though Article 41 was singularly "inconvenient and a legal hurdle for non-Catholics who had few, if any, religious difficulties regarding divorce".[13] The conservative ideology underpinning Article 41 would, for the next thirty years, continue to resemble the static qualities of Moses' tablets.

CONTEMPORARY CRITIQUES

Article 41 has not escaped academic and judicial textual and exegetical dissection and analysis. According to Professor Beytagh of Ohio State University: "[it] is one of the more innovative, interesting as well as controversial provisions of the 1937 document . . . with certain clauses in the Article providing textual support for the existence of natural rights jurisprudence".[14] Beytagh

---

· [10] B. Chubb, *The Politics of the Irish Constitution* (Dublin, Institute of Public Administration, 1991), 83.

[11] Michael O'Leary TD, *Irish Independent*, 4 Oct. 1985.

[12] Cardinal Ó Fiach declared that: "even a limited form of divorce law . . . would be harmful to society": quoted in J. Cooney, *The Crozier and the Dáil: Church and State in Ireland 1922–1986* (Cork, Mercier Press, 1986), 61.

[13] Cardinal Conway, *Irish Times*, 15 Dec. 1967.

[14] F. X. Beytagh, *Constitutionalism in Contemporary Ireland: An American Perspective* (Dublin, Round Hall: Sweet and Maxwell, 1997), 37.

goes on to note that, linguistically, the "language of the Family Article is sweeping" and can be given either a benign or an active reading.[15] This study also concludes that the family provisions are all the more commendable for their commitment to basic family values particularly in an era when the institution of the family is under threat.[16]

Writing extra-judicially, Costello J regarded Article 41 as "most efficacious and based on philosophical truths incorporating natural law tenets and not mere empty formulae safeguarding individualistic liberty".[17] The 1993 *Report of the Second Commission on the Status of Women* felt that Article 41 was outmoded, disadvantageous to women and the references in Article 41.2.2 to "mothers' duties in the home" seemed to give a misguided and inappropriate emphasis.[18] The Second Commission predictably recommended the deletion of Article 41.2.2 because:

> "A Constitution that reflects a paternalistic approach to women is no longer acceptable or appropriate to a modern democratic state . . . [it] should be brought into line with those of other democratic states and should cease to reflect a paternalistic view of women."[19]

Revisionist critiques of Article 41 have been advanced by some feminist lawyers. One study[20] has highlighted the obvious social "lag" of the Family text: first, for failing generally to keep pace with contemporary social change and, secondly, for referring explicitly and specifically to mother roles without concomitant, egalitarian or correlative references to father roles within the private domestic sphere of the family. As a consequence, it is argued that a dichotomy has emerged because the social values enunciated and endorsed in the Constitution in reality bear only an approximate resemblance to those evidenced in people's daily lives in the Ireland of the 1990s. The ramifications of this disparity bear heavily on the very legitimacy of those provisions and also have implications for our constitutional rule-of-law system. Prioritising and privileging female domestic roles and consigning them to the private altruistic domestic sphere of the home has probably been responsible for perpetuating the perceived dependent status of women.[21] Connolly's assessment of the dilemma is that:

---

[15] *Ibid.*, 130. Professor Beytagh, contextualises his review when he states that "[i]t is undoubtedly more than a bit presumptuous for a foreign commentator to suggest revisions, additions, deletions to the Constitution of a country other than his own."

[16] *Ibid.*, 118.

[17] D. Costello, "Legal and Social Studies" (1962) 50 *Studies* 201.

[18] *Second Commission on the Status of Women: Report to the Government* (Dublin, Stationery Office 1993), 27.

[19] *Ibid.*

[20] A. Connolly, "The Constitution" in A. Connolly (ed.), *Gender and the Law in Ireland* (Dublin, Oak Tree Press, 1993), 5, 13.

[21] Dr McQuaid stated in correspondence between himself and deValera that: "[n]othing will change the law and fact of nature that woman's natural sphere is the home. She is perfectly free not to marry or to marry, to choose this or that career. No Article of the Draft Constitution even

"The Family provisions of the Constitution with their gender and marital biases, need amendment. In particular, Article 41.2 should either be removed from the Constitution or balanced with another provision which recognises the role of men as fathers in the care of children and the role of women in the workplace."[22]

The Irish Constitution is regularly classified as a legal, political and social document containing overriding principles which perform the function of a social contract between the State and the people. However, many of the terms in this social contract, particularly in Article 41, no longer attract universal support. The desirable familial ideology as manifested in the 1930s is now clearly outdated.[23]

The issue of whether to amend or delete Article 41 was discussed in two further reports. The seven hundred and one page Report of the fifteen-member Constitution Review Group in 1996 comprehensively reviewed, *inter alia*, the provisions on the Family,[24] despite being somewhat constrained by the then prevailing legal uncertainty concerning the referendum result of the Fifteenth Amendment repealing the constitutional ban on divorce.[25] The Review Group's terms of reference limited it to merely "review the Constitution, not to rewrite or replace it" and "to establish those areas where constitutional change may be desirable or necessary". The Group was to regard the issue of divorce as a constitutional matter outside their brief as it was then "the subject of separate consideration".[26] Their critique of Article 41 bore all the hallmarks of their stated objective to examine constitutional provisions in a "clear and orderly manner with a résumé of relevant arguments". They also surveyed the compatibility of those provisions with the newly evolving pluralist society, which had undergone profound socio-economic and demographic changes since 1937, and which now, in their view, required a more responsive Constitution.[27] Some of the Review Group's recommendations have been criticised for their:

---

attempts to deny woman's fundamental right as a human being. Article 41.2.1 merely acknowledges a fact": quoted in A. Coughlan, "The Constitution and Social Policy" in F. Litton (ed.), *supra* n. 2, at p. 153.

[22] A. Connelly (ed.), *supra* n. 20, at p. 24.

[23] In the *Dáil* Debates on the Draft Constitution de Valera stated: "[t]he attempt in this Constitution is to state principles which are accurate, and to design it so that it will stand up to the practical test of rigid application—the test of life": *Dáil* Debates, vol. 67, col. 1607, 2 June 1937.

[24] *Report of the Constitution Review Group* (Dublin, Stationery Office, 1996), ch. 12, 319–37. Two of the Appendices to the Report dealt with Family issues; Appendix 22, W. Duncan, "The Constitutional Protection of Parental Rights", 612–26 and Appendix 23, K. Lynch, "Defining the Family and Protecting the Caring Functions of both Traditional and Non-traditional Families", 627–9. There were nine lawyers on the Review Group.

[25] See *Hanafin* v. *Minister for the Environment* [1996] 2 ILRM 161. Mr Hanafin was appealing the result of the 1995 referendum in the High Court and subsequently in the Supreme Court.

[26] *Review Report*, *supra* n. 24, Foreword, p. x. The Family Law (Divorce) Act, 1996 was going through both Houses of the Oireachtas at that time.

[27] *Ibid.*, at p. xi.

"[c]umulative secularisation . . . of a Christian document . . . and the radical shift in the direction of positivism as regards individual rights."[28]

The Review Group did recommend the deletion of phrases in Article 41.1.1 such as "inalienable" and "imprescriptible",[29] but such minor linguistic adjustments could not be regarded as tantamount to a radical ideological shift towards positivism *vis-à-vis* fundamental rights. Perhaps the Group was merely attempting to excise some of the excessive verbiage of the text with a view towards greater clarity of a provision which "would profit from rewriting".[30] At a more general level, the subsequent All-Party *Oireachtas* Committee on the Constitution of 1997 concurred with the Review Group's minimalist approach on the basis that:

"A constitution should deal with the perennial concerns of society. . . . A good constitution develops organically maintaining an overall . . . balance in its provisions between the rights of the community and the rights of the individual. . . . Those reviewing a constitution must engage in an Article by Article audit which will suggest amendments in the existing text and the addition of new Articles. Care must be taken lest such changes affect the overall balance of a constitution in unexpected ways. Tinkering with the constitutional mechanisms may also cause imbalance."[31]

Although the *Oireachtas* Committee concluded that there was an absence of popular demand for general constitutional change,[32] the Family Article in itself continues to be responsible for a deluge of academic criticism concerning its considerable detail about the various characteristics of the Family. The Irish judiciary has also been particularly vigilant in rigidly adhering to its constitutional duty of adopting a protective approach towards "the Family" to the extent of declaring some family-related statutes to be unconstitutional. A classic manifestation of this judicial protective function may be found in *Re Article 26 and The Matrimonial Home Bill, 1993*.[33] The primary objective underpinning this Bill was the vesting of an equitable interest in the matrimonial home in both spouses as joint tenants irrespective of when the home was first acquired by the couple and irrespective of the time at which a freely-reached decision between the spouses may have been made as to the nature of the ownership and in whom it should vest. The application of the legislation was to be automatic, mandatory and universal. The Supreme Court

---

[28] F. X. Beytagh, *supra* n. 13, at pp. 167, 189–90.

[29] *Review Group Report*, *supra* n. 23, at 330.

[30] The Review Group formulated about 100 recommendations for changes to the Constitution. It also made a trenchant request for greater gender sensitivity. The latter matter impacted substantially on its views of Art. 41. For its 11 recommendations on the Family provision see 336–7 of the *Review Report*.

[31] *All-Party Oireachtas Committee; First Progress Report* (Dublin, Stationery Office, 1997), 8. The Committee further noted that "the case-law that develops around a Constitution produces greater certainty for everyone. . . . Unnecessary changes in the Constitution jeopardise this evolved jurisprudence."

[32] *Ibid.*, 25.

[33] [1994] 1 ILRM 241.

regarded such statutory intervention as beyond the State's competence, repugnant to the provisions of Article 41 and an inappropriate violation of the constitutional authority of the Family. Finlay CJ delivering the judgment of the court stated:

> "[T]his Bill . . . constitutes a quite impermissible invasion into the authority of the family and a failure to protect that authority. [it] goes beyond the encouragement of joint ownership [and] constitutes a mandatory imposition of the State's decision on this family question. . . . [S]uch provisions do not constitute reasonably proportionate intervention by the State with the rights of the family and . . . [is] potentially indiscriminate".[34]

The decision highlights the potency of Article 41. The notion of partnership in marriage in the Ireland of the 1990s seems a laudable principle. But, the judgment confirmed the view that we still operate the doctrine of separate property, which disadvantages the economically weaker spouse to the detriment of the common good which the family might otherwise enjoy. Reasonable and proportionate interventions therefore by the State are only permissible once they do not infringe the authority of the family unit. This Supreme Court decision would probably also have surprised the drafters of the Constitution who had a much more limited view of family authority.

EVOLUTION OR STAGNATION?

A more detailed incremental evaluation of selective sections of Article 41 in the light of the various Reports, the body of family case law and especially the 1937 *Dáil* Debates on the Draft Constitution, makes it clear that there is ongoing controversy and debate, for example as to the definitional nature and scope of what is traditionally termed the constitutional family.[35] The orthodox model of the marital family unit in Ireland is declining with a corresponding evolution of a multiplicity of alternative non-traditional units.[36] The 1937 drafters probably assumed one paradigm of the family unit, i.e. family based on the so-called "institution" of marriage. Shatter concludes that the "constitutional family is the nuclear family, i.e. a husband, wife and their children, if any".[37] In *Murray* v. *Ireland* Costello J stated that:

---

[34] [1994] 1 ILRM 241, 253–4.

[35] According to the Council of Europe, Final Draft Report CDPS (1994), on the interaction between the Providers of Family Services, Strasbourg, 1994, 6 members (Ireland, Spain, Portugal, Italy, Greece and Germany) provide specific constitutional protection for the family founded on marriage.

[36] *The Review Report*, 321–2, identified 7 alternative family units: (i) a cohabiting heterosexual couple with no children; (ii) a cohabiting heterosexual couple looking after the children of either or both parents; (iii) a cohabiting heterosexual couple either of whom is already married; (iv) a cohabiting heterosexual couple either of whom is already married, whose children (all or some of them) are being looked after elsewhere; (v) unmarried lone parents and their children; (vi) homosexual couples; (vii) lesbian couples.

[37] A. Shatter, *Family Law* (4th edn. Dublin, Butterworths, 1997), at p. 12.

"The words used in the Article to describe the Family are therefore apt to describe both a married couple with children and a married couple without children."[38]

The 1996 Review Group favoured the retention of an express pledge by the State to protect the family based on marriage. However, it did not favour the retention of the words "on which the family is founded" on the basis that this phrase had "led to an exclusively marriage-based definition of the family which no longer accords with the social structure in Ireland".[39] One member of the Committee had reservations about the narrow and limited approach of the Constitution "protecting the institution of the marital family, *qua* institution".[40] Dr Lynch advocated a more substantive, activist Family Article which would include an express constitutional provision committing the State to provide protection for the core-caring and support related activities of family life, especially the caring of children and dependent persons".[41] Another related difficulty for the Review Group was the problem associated with defining cohabitation in either quantitative or qualitative terms in order to qualify for any constitutional protective treatment as a family:

"Questions will also arise such as what duration of cohabitation (one month? Six months? One year? Five years?) should qualify for treatment as a family."[42]

The Review Group was conscious that some cohabitees choose deliberately not to have a legal basis (either statutory or constitutional) for their relationships. Consequently, they feared that any blanket automatic conferring of family rights on those social units could be tantamount to an interference with cohabitees' personal rights, freely chosen.[43] The 1990s have witnessed some statutory rights being given to cohabitees. The Domestic Violence Act, 1996, for example, gives cohabitees limited statutory rights on application for a safety or barring order.[44]

During the 1937 *Dáil* Debates on the Draft Constitution, Article 41 did not attract much attention. Historians now acknowledge that "Dr McQuaid was very influential in the drafting process and in the actual formulation of

---

[38] [1985] IR 532, 536.

[39] *Review Group Report*, *supra* n. 24, 332: "[t]he Oireachtas should provide protection for the benefit of family units based on a relationship other than marriage".

[40] K. Lynch, *supra* n. 24, 628.

[41] *Ibid.*, 322, 628–9.

[42] *Ibid.*

[43] See Supreme Court judgment of Hamilton CJ in *W O'R* v. *EH and Bórd Uchtála*, unreported, Supreme Court, 23 July 1996, where he states: "[a] *de facto* family or any rights arising therefrom, is not recognised by the Constitution". The "*de facto*" family was also referred to in *Keegan* v. *Ireland* (1994) 18 EHRR 342.

[44] S. 2(1)(a)(ii) deals with cohabitees applying for Safety Orders: "[the applicant] is not the spouse of the respondent but has lived with the respondent as husband or wife for a period of at least six months in aggregate during the period of twelve months immediately prior to the application for the safety order." S. 3(1)(B) deals with cohabitees applying for Barring Orders: "[the applicant] is not the spouse of the respondent but has lived with the respondent as husband or wife for a period of at least six months during the period of nine months immediately prior to the applications for the barring order."

certain Articles, particularly . . . Articles 40 to 45".[45] W. T. Cosgrave indicated that the whole debate had been characterised by numerous abstentions by Deputies, and there was regularly no quorum during the eleven parliamentary days assigned to the Draft Constitution beginning on 30 April 1937 and ending on 14 June 1937. The substantive debates regarding the Family provision took place over three days—11 May, 4 June and 9 June 1937.[46] Many sections and sub-sections were not debated at all, whilst others received a disproportionate level of debate. Some *Dáil* deputies objected to de Valera's benevolent interference with the Family, and one deputy declared:

> "Hands off the [Family] home. The President's whole policy here means nothing more or less than nationalisation. His policy in effect means a policy symbolic of that which at the moment obtains in Soviet Russia. Take charge of the families, take charge of the mothers and with that done, of course, to use the words of the President, this little country of ours is going to be a paradise. I totally object to these sections being put into the Constitution."[47]

Questioned about the precise meaning of the word "authority" in Article 41.1.2, de Valera indicated in essence that it referred to the authority of the "heads over their children, their right to look after their education and not to be interfered with by another authority in the State. . . . Interference with this authority will have to be justified on certain grounds . . . authority is also the right to look after the maintenance and control of the children."[48] If the historical approach to constitutional adjudication—sometimes referred to by American legal scholars as Originalism—were adopted exclusively by the Irish courts, then the intention of the drafter would be the sole meaning given to the particular word or sentence. However, Irish constitutional case law to date indicates that an expansive definition of "authority" has been adopted by the courts, beyond that identified by de Valera, to include for example such matters as the "right to make a joint decision as to the ownership of a family home".[49] It would

---

[45] D. Keogh, *supra* n. 2, at pp. 19–20. De Valera stated that "[w]e had at our disposal in the forming of this Constitution experts far more experienced . . . than any of the experts who were called in to frame the original Constitution": *Dáil* Debates, vol. 68, col. 411, 14 June 1937.

[46] *Dáil* Debates, vols. 67–8, cols. 63–72, 1847–8 and 220–6.

[47] *Dáil* Debates, vol. 67, col. 1872, 4 June 1937, Mr Coburn. Introducing the debate on fundamental family rights, de Valera stated: "[i]n this part we set down what are the rights which the individual and the family have as against the operation of the otherwise all powerful Parliament. . . . You cannot make these statements in an absolute way . . . the most important group of the State is the family. We pledge the State to protect the Family in its constitution and in its right generally. This is not merely a question of religious teaching": *Dáil* Debates, vol. 67, cols. 61–62, 11 May 1937.

[48] *Dáil* Debates, vol. 67, cols. 1887–8, 4 June 1937. Dr Rowlette TD pointed out to deValera the problems of adherence to drafters' intentions by future interpreters: "[t]he President assumes that future generations will interpret the Constitution in exactly the same spirit as he has framed it . . . he assumes that the intentions will be the same in the minds of his successors. But that is an assumption which is not justified by our knowledge of the world."

[49] In *Article 26 and the Matrimonial Home Bill, 1993* [1994] 1 ILRM 241, 251. The Court further stated that the State, however, could intervene proportionately in the decision-making authority of the family in the interests of the common good.

also seem that the "family authority" aspect of the Article is given further support, with the ascription of absolutist, inalienable and imprescriptible rights to the family. The judiciary has interpreted those words to tilt the legal balance in favour of the autonomy of the family unit to the possible detriment of individual members.

Forceful opposition to the inclusion of Article 41 came from some *Dáil* deputies who felt that it contained "phrases that were directive rather than declaratory" and possessed "a vague indeterminate series of statements and sentences, almost [which were] contradictory".[50] The *Dáil* Debates on Article 41.2, sub-sections 1 and 2, provided ample opportunities for Opposition parties to find substantial grounds for attacking this aspect of the draft text. De Valera frequently refused to accept amendments even when presented with alternative sophisticated linguistic, philosophical or legal arguments favouring amendment. The two sub-sections were taken together for debate with each analysed and parsed in detail. Most contributors were male deputies[51] and the recurring themes of debate focused on "Women-Mothers-Wives", "life and functions within or for the home", the scope of "the State endeavouring", "divorce" and "parental roles". John A. Costello, a former Attorney General, highlighted the legal maxim of *expressio unius personae vel rei est exclusio alterius*[52] as applied to Article 41.2.1. The 1996 Review Group looked at these "much criticised and dated sub-sections which had not been of any particular assistance even to women working exclusively within the home".[53] On balance they recommended their retention but that they be slightly revised in gender-neutral form, where appropriate.[54] The 1997 *Oireachtas* Committee on the Constitution concurred with the general thrust of the 1996 Review Group's alternative wording for Article 41.2, probably in the knowledge that those particular sub-sections as originally drafted were merely aspirational, devoid of substantive effect and frequently the object of ridicule. De Valera's general thesis about those sub-sections was that they adhered to a general protective family law principle by expressly mentioning women to give them:

> "[p]rotection which is necessary as part of our social programme . . . and they ought not to go out and either supplement the father's wages or become the breadwinners themselves . . . is it not right that we should see then that the inadequate strength

[50] *Dáil* Debates, vol. 68, col. 387, 14 June 1937. Walsh J noted that "the Constitution was regarded as too family orientated": see B. Walsh, "Constitutional Rights" in F. Litton (ed.), *supra* n. 2, at p. 96.

[51] Mrs Redmond introduced one amendment on deleting the words "by her life within the home". She did not however speak on the amendment: *Dáil* Debates, vol. 67, col. 1847, 4 June 1937.

[52] The express mention of one person or thing is the exclusion of another, i.e. by expressly referring to "women within the home" you exclude constitutional protection to "women outside the home".

[53] *Supra* n. 24.

[54] *Ibid*. However, they did record that "the retention of Art. 41.2.3 might not be appropriate to a gender neutral form of the Article".

of women shall not be abused? . . . Mothers give to the State a support which is essential."[55]

From these extracts two key points are evident; first, the two sub-sections were discussed interchangeably, which tended to lead to some not inconsiderable confusion. Secondly, the concepts of "women" and "mother" were regarded as synonymous, although de Valera attempted to clarify this point when declaring that:

> "This has reference to mothers and there is no use in bringing into this context young girls and people who are not married . . . The greatest service she can render is to perform her duties in the due manner".[56]

Article 42.2.1 refers only to "women", yet during the *Dáil* Debates de Valera invariably used the word "mothers", rather than "women" as in the text. Exasperated with what he thought were unnecessary obstructive and hypercritical Opposition tactics, de Valera petulantly replied that:

> "There are mothers and wives too and not all wives happen to be mothers. I have made up my mind that this is accurate and I am not going to put in what is not here now."[57]

John A. Costello had reservations about the phrase, "her life within the home", because he felt it would be perceived as casting aspersions on those who opted to work outside the home either on a remuneration basis or otherwise.[58] Costello was also concerned that the "*expressio unius*" maxim when applied to the sub-sections meant that women's life outside the home was implicitly excluded and therefore attracted no constitutional protection. De Valera justified the absence of textually explicit references to "fathers in the home" on the basis that "that particular aspect did not demand attention from us and . . . this sub-section was not intended to be a catalogue of all the people who serve the home".[59]

It is now generally regarded that the two sub-sections here under review are probably not justiciable,[60] although if a literal reading were given to them by

---

[55] *Dáil* Debates, vol. 67, cols. 67–9, 11 May 1937. On 4 June 1937 he restated those principles: "[s]urely that is a praiseworthy object for the State to set before itself—that mothers . . . should not be compelled to abandon that fundamentally important work compelling them to neglect their duties in the home": *Dáil* Debates, vol. 68, col. 1848.

[56] *Ibid.*, at col. 1849. Ironically, in neither of these two sub-sections is the word "family" used.

[57] *Ibid.*, at col. 1868.

[58] *Ibid.*, at col. 1856. He also stated that "[i]t has given cause for uneasiness if not cause for offence", col. 1857; Dr Rowlette proposed an amendment deleting "within" on the basis that the sub-section "was too limited . . . suggesting that women's whole activity is exercised and should be exercised within the home": cols. 1875–6.

[59] *Ibid.*, at col. 1879.

[60] See, generally, G. Hogan and G. Whyte (eds.), J. Kelly, *The Irish Constitution* (3rd edn., Dublin, Butterworths, 1994), at pp. 1109–10. According to D. O'Sullivan, *The Irish Free State and its Senate* (London, Faber and Faber, 1940), at p. 495, "[l]arge sections of the new Constitution consist of declarations of a homiletic character concerning personal rights and the family. . . . Many of these are so vague that its difficult to see what purpose they serve in such a document."

the judiciary, the State could be under an obligation to fulfil its constitutional obligations in concrete socio-economic terms. The statement made in the debates that "they mean nothing legislatively" and that "they are a mere guidance" however remains true. Dr McQuaid's idealised notion that "nothing will change the law and fact of nature that woman's natural sphere is the home" now seems pathetically restrictive. In 1988, Walsh J, writing extrajudicially, recalled the McQuaid point of view where he observed that Article 41.2.1 "is a statement of fact . . . yet nobody has yet publicly challenged it as such. This protective guarantee has never been invoked in litigation."[61]

The proposal by the 1997 *Oireachtas* Committee to delete Article 41.2, subsections 1 and 2, replacing it with a gender-neutral provision is commendable. The new wording would read:

"The State recognises that [home and][62] family life gives to society a support without which the common good cannot be achieved. The State shall endeavour to support persons caring for others within the home."[63]

The Committee justified its desire for gender-inclusiveness on the basis that it was "a common courtesy the State should pay to more than half its citizens"![64] The elimination of such discriminatory features is more than a cosmetic ritual and could certainly be justified on more substantive grounds than on the basis of "mere common courtesy". However, even as revised, it may still not be justiciable in our courts.

DIVORCE—IRISH STYLE

The prohibition against civil divorce was abolished by the Fifteenth Amendment to the Constitution. Article 41.3.2 now prescribes in a detailed manner the constitutional legal conditions applicable to the granting of civil divorce decrees in certain limited circumstances.[65] Constitutional scholars had expressed doubts about the validity of putting the specific divorce grounds into the text of the Constitution, given that constitutions were supposed to be concerned with statements of fundamental principle and not matters of legislative detail. By international standards, the requirements specified by the Amendment are highly restrictive.[66] The constitutional conditions to be

[61] B. Walsh, *supra* n. 50, at p. 98.
[62] *The Review Group Report, supra* n. 24, proposed the same amendment but included the phrase "home and". This was rejected by the *Oireachtas Committee First Progress Report (1997)*, *supra* n. 30.
[63] *First Progress Report*, 85.
[64] *Ibid.*, 86.
[65] On 17 June 1996 it was incorporated into the text of the Constitution.
[66] *The Review Report, supra* n. 24, 335. F. X. Beytagh, *supra* n. 14, at p. 38, suggests that the conditions are "demanding . . . and unduly burdensome".

satisfied are replicated (with some minor variations) in section 5 of the Family Law (Divorce) Act 1996.[67] The requirements are:

"i) The spouses have lived apart from one another for at least four years during the previous five years, and
ii) There is no reasonable prospect of reconciliation, and
iii) Proper provision exists or will be made for spouses and dependent members of the family."

In essence, therefore, this complex, socially divisive area of family law is not only regulated by statutory law but is also rooted in specified express constitutional provisions. This makes Irish divorce procedures somewhat unique since the judiciary is under a specific obligation to uphold the provisions of the Constitution. It is therefore required to be much more vigilant in divorce cases.[68] What de Valera once termed "the obvious evil"[69] is now available as a legal remedy for marital breakdown. Among the arguments advanced against the introduction of divorce was that it was: (i) contrary to the religious views of the majority religion; (ii) it would open the floodgates; (iii) it would change the nature and perception of the marriage contract; (iv) it would dilute the overall constitutional protection of the family; and that it would result in increased financial hardship suffered by wives and children.[70]

The 1986 Divorce Referendum on the Tenth Amendment to the Constitution is now confined to the annals of history, but lessons were learned by the pro- and anti-divorce lobbies enabling a more reasoned, less trenchant, debate to take place during the 1995 Referendum. All the major political parties in the *Oireachtas* favoured the proposed constitutional changes. Also the Judicial Separation and Family Law Reform Act, 1989 had in a sense paved the way for a greater recognition of the uncomfortable and harsh reality of the increasing incidence of marital breakdown. The 1989 Act gave the courts a comprehensive array of powers to make the requisite and appropriate ancillary orders, but no decree of divorce was obtainable under this Act. By 1995, the Irish courts had developed a sophisticated body of family case law precedents, i.e. judicial separation cases, which could readily be adapted and applied, like a blueprint, to divorce cases. Empirical research of the reported and unreported judgments dealing with judicial separation cases reveals a gender-bias towards women in a preponderance of the decided cases with custody, maintenance, financial settlements and property adjustment orders disproportionately being made in women's favour.

[67] See SI 84 of 1997 for rules of Circuit Court for the Family Law (Divorce) Act 1996. The Act was enacted on 27 Nov. 1996 and became operational 12 weeks later on 27 Feb. 1997.
[68] See, generally, M. Walls and D. Bergin, *The Law of Divorce in Ireland* (Bristol, Jordans, 1997).
[69] *Dáil* Debates, vol. 67, col. 1886, 4 June 1937. See Dr Rowlette's *Dáil* speech for a Protestant view of the Divorce provision, at cols. 1884–6.
[70] See *Report of Joint Oireachtas Committee on Marriage Breakdown* (Dublin, Stationery Office, 1985), 81–2.

The "no-fault" type divorce under the Divorce Act 1996, with the attendant four years living apart requirement, avoids the requirement of apportioning blame for marital misconduct to either of the parties.[71] Although there is a solid body of authority available in other common law jurisdictions to direct our family courts, the unique constitutional gloss of Article 41.3.2 will necessitate a more vigilant and rigorous approach by the Irish judiciary in its pivotal role in divorce proceedings. Some legal interpretive problems have arisen in relation to the requirement that "proper provision be made for dependents/children". The formulation of Article 41.3.2(iii) differs from section 5(1)(c) of the Family Law (Divorce) Act, 1996. The latter refers to "any dependent members of the family", but the former refers to "any children of either or both of [the spouses]". Our rule of law in Ireland acknowledges that, in a clash between statutory laws and constitutional laws, constitutional laws are paramount. The definitional issue of dependent was addressed in the first High Court, constitutionally granted, divorce case in *RC* v. *CC*,[72] whereby Barron J, deriving his jurisdiction solely from the Constitution (the Divorce Act 1996 had not yet commenced), determined that it was proper that the two non-dependent adult children, i.e. two unmarried daughters in this particular case, should have provision made for them "in the interests of the family as a whole".[73] It would now seem that the constitutional formulation regarding "proper provision for children" is not confined merely to dependent children and has a wider sweep than section 5(1)(c) of the Divorce Act 1996 which requires the courts to consider the welfare of children only up to the age of twenty-three years.[74]

Barron J's assertion in *RC* v. *CC* that Article 41.3.2 was self-executing, as far as the High Court's jurisdiction was concerned, has caused some unease among constitutional lawyers. In Barron J's view, the Fifteenth Amendment created of itself a High Court divorce jurisdiction and, by extension, created a "right" for citizens to apply to the High Court for a divorce in the absence of any court having statutory jurisdiction. Michael McDowell SC has suggested that as a consequence of Barron J's judgment, it would now appear that:

---

[71] In 1920 New Zealand was one of the first common law countries to pioneer no-fault divorce, in its Divorce and Matrimonial Causes Amendment Act, 1920. See C. Archibald and H. Xanthaki, "Fault or Failure? Divorce in Other Jurisdictions" (1995) 13 *ILT* 275, at 277: "[t]here is not a consensus on the formulation of the no-fault ground; some jurisdictions choose to express it as pure consent, some by the broad ground of irretrievable breakdown' or 'rupture of communal life' . . . and some the neutral and ascertainable ground of a period of separation". The last ground is the Irish model for divorce.

[72] [1997] 1 FLR 1, [1997] 1 ILRM 410. The applicant husband was suffering from a terminal illness, and time was of the essence.

[73] *Ibid.*, at 6. The husband had already, to the Court's satisfaction, transferred considerable assets to the adult-dependents. See also M. Walls and D. Bergin, *supra* n. 68, at pp. 14–7.

[74] See s. 2(1)(a) and (b) of Family Law (Divorce) Act, 1996 for definitions of dependent member.

"the exercise of the legislature's right to specify pre-conditions for divorce or to specify persons whose interests must be protected in divorce proceedings, is not itself a legal precondition for the High Court exercising its new jurisdiction."[75]

The issue remains unsettled as the legal point was not argued in court, and it is a distinctive feature of common law jurisprudence that a point not argued is not necessarily a binding point of law.

The first divorce granted under the Family Law (Divorce) Act, 1996 was in Castlebar, County Mayo, two weeks after the legislation came into force. The irony of this fact was that Mayo had recorded one of the highest votes against the Fifteenth Amendment. Department of Justice statistics[76] indicate that a mere 244 divorce applications had been made by 27 June 1997 with a total of sixty-four granted. A majority of those applications were made in Dublin (141), and the second highest number of applications (twenty-two), was in Cork. During this period also, the Circuit Court in Tipperary, Kilkenny, Longford, Monaghan and Roscommon had not received a single application for civil divorce. The predicted stampede up the steps of the family courts did not happen.

CONCLUSION

The Family Article in the Irish Constitution has been one of the most controversial Articles, from its drafting in 1937 to its recent emendation in 1996 when the divorce provisions were incorporated into the text of Article 41. The intentions of the drafters have been overturned with the introduction of civil divorce. Linguistically, there is now a certain incongruity between the highly specific language of the divorce provision and some of the other sections, which continue to be regarded as patriarchal statements of outdated moral and social principles. Since 1937, our modern democratic State has undergone profound social and political changes, to the extent that the ideological rigidity of Article 41 envisaged by the drafters no longer reflects the social reality of present-day Ireland. Paternalism is no longer a dominant force and is gradually giving way to greater equality of the sexes, particularly with regard to parental roles. Gender roles within the private sphere of the family home are in a state of flux. The excessive emphasis given by the drafters to the family as a social unit, without ascribing express rights to children within that unit, is now under scrutiny in the "children's rights" era of the 1990s. Arguments are being advanced for a greater constitutional balance between parental autonomy and authority and individual rights of children within the family unit in a manner which would not threaten or devalue the family as an insti-

---

[75] "More than One Outcome as Man Wins Divorce", *Sunday Independent*, 19 Jan. 1997. The Attorney-General was not a notice party to the proceedings which was surprising, given the public law dimension of the case.

[76] *Irish Times*, 29 Aug. 1997.

tution. Any potential constitutional clash between parental and children's rights could then be resolved if the "best interests" principle were to be the paramount consideration in conflict situations. The lofty constitutional privileging of the marital family has created not insignificant legal difficulties for the family rights of unmarried mothers, unmarried fathers and children born of unmarried parents. Some statutory family law such as the Status of Children Act, 1987 may have alleviated some of the discriminatory aspects for the non-marital family, but the special position of the family based on marriage continues to enjoy substantial constitutional protection. It is because of this specified protective constitutional function that the judiciary and the *Oireachtas* continue to adopt a cautious and vigilant approach towards developments in Irish family law and family social policy. The essential potency of Article 41, according to Shatter, is that it has functioned as:

> "a catalyst to a creative judicial development of the law and as a brake on the State's and legislature's capacity to intervene in family life. Judicial interpretation and application of [Article 41] will for the foreseeable future continue to stir political, legal and social controversy and be a rich source for jurisprudential debate."[77]

A multiplicity of substantive family laws is now on the statute books and the family courts are "buckling under the pressure of business".[78] Structural reforms have been proposed by the Law Reform Commission regarding the processes and procedures of the Family Courts. Judicial activism regarding Article 41 will inevitably continue to generate debate. Moreover, the State will also, of necessity, remain involved in the regulation of the private and public spheres of the family, formalising and systematising any reform. In the final analysis, principles and practice of family life and marriage will continue to undergo change regardless of the formulation of Article 41 of the Constitution.

---

[77] A. Shatter, *supra* n. 37, at p. 95.
[78] *Law Reform Commission Report and Family Courts* (LRC 52–1996), p. *ii*. For a summary of its recommendations see ch.13.

8

The Irish Constitution, International Law and the Northern Question— The Need for Radical Thinking

ANTHONY CARTY

INTRODUCTION

There should be no more burning question for the Irish Constitution than the status and fortunes of the nationalist minority in Northern Ireland. Comprising about 600,000, virtually a sixth of the Irish nation, they have since 1920 been quite simply cut off from the rest of the nation without ever having been asked. This short essay will raise several points for discussion from an international law perspective. It will not repeat or elaborate upon internal southern Irish debates about Articles 2 and 3[1] of the Constitution which well-meaning liberally-minded politicians, including the last President of Ireland, would like to see modified so as to accommodate unionist wishes. Nor will it enter into fully technical debates concerning the Irish constitutional case, *McGimspey and McGimpsey* v. *Ireland*[2] concerning the nature of Articles 2 and 3 of the Constitution as either a political or a legal claim to jurisdiction over the whole island of Ireland. The claim is affirmed as legal by the Supreme Court, but since the Anglo-Irish Agreement of 1985,[3] at the latest, the Irish State's policy has been, *de facto*, if not *de jure*, to abandon the perspective of its 1937 constitution, and to accept that there are two parts of Ireland. The

---

[1] Art. 1 provides: "The national territory consists of the whole island of Ireland, its islands and the territorial seas" and Art. 2 that: "Pending the re-integration of the national territory, and without prejudice to the right of the Parliament and Government established by this Constitution to exercise jurisdiction over the whole of that territory, the laws enacted by that Parliament shall have the like area and extent of application as the laws of Soarstát Eireann and like extra-territorial effect." With regard to the revision of Arts. 2 and 3, see the discussion in J. A. Murphy, "The 1937 Constitution: Some Historical Reflections" in this volume.

[2] [1988] IR 567 (HC), [1990] ILRM 440 (SC). See C. R. Symmons, "International Treaty Obligations and the Irish Constitution: The McGimpsey Case" (1992) 41 *ICLQ* 311.

[3] See generally T. Hadden and K. Boyle, *The Anglo-Irish Agreement: Commentary, Text and Official Review* (London, Sweet and Maxwell, 1989).

consent of both parts, voting separately, to a unification of the island is regarded as essential. Indeed, the need is seen to have a three-part solution to the so-called Northern Ireland question since the adoption of the so-called "Framework Document"[4] of February 1995 by the Irish and British Governments—within Northern Ireland, between the North and the South, and between Ireland and the United Kingdom.

The argument of this essay is, instead, that there are two peoples within Northern Ireland, as within Ireland as a whole. This was recognised originally in the 1921 Treaty between the Provisional Irish Government (later Free State) and the British Government.[5] Article 12 of that Treaty attempted to implement a principle of respect for the wishes of the populations of the two nations of Ireland by providing for a regard for the wishes of the population of Northern Ireland with a view to substantial revisions to the boundary which were accepted as necessary by both sides during the negotiation of the Treaty. The problem of Northern Ireland, it is argued here, stems from a politically unrealistic *reification* of the geographical entity of Northern Ireland which occurred in the reasoning of the aborted Boundary Commission set up to give effect to Article 12 of the Treaty. That Commission had to have regard to two factors: respect for the wishes of the population as far as may be compatible with economic and geographical conditions. The former factor was subordinated completely to the latter by the Boundary Commission, with the effect that no alterations to the territory of Northern Ireland were to be allowed which affected its integrity as a territory. There could be only minimal alterations to a boundary line as such. This Commission's work was abandoned with the withdrawal of the member nominated by the Irish Free State.

The outcome was that the entity of Northern Ireland is a product of coercion in two respects. The Irish delegation to the negotiations for the 1921 Treaty was given assurances in writing that Article 12 was intended to give effect to a principle of respect for the wishes of the minority community in Northern Ireland, just as the very existence of a Northern entity was intended to give effect to the wishes of the unionist majority. Throughout, the British position was that the fullest expression should be given to the wishes of the two nations in Ireland. The Treaty was finally concluded with a threat of renewed conflict coming from the British delegation if the Treaty were not accepted. Afterwards, no implementation whatsoever of the terms of Article 12 took place.[6]

Hence, built into the entity that is Northern Ireland is an antagonism resulting from a history of conquest and subjugation, with all of the insecurity

---

[4] The text of the "Framework Document" is available at the *Irish Law* Home Page *http://nis.rtc-tallaght.ie/sig/law.home/irlaw/.html.*

[5] Articles of Agreement for a Treaty between Great Britain and Ireland (6 Dec. 1921).

[6] On Art. 12 of the 1921 Agreement see A. Carty, *Was Ireland Conquered: International Law and the Irish Question* (London, Pluto, 1996), ch. 7.

which this must imply also for the planter-settler unionist majority. Any attempt at negotiation within a framework beyond Northern Ireland can appear to the unionists only to threaten the uneven balance which at present gives this majority a precarious security. Given the exclusively negative nature of the inner Northern Irish relationship, it is impossible simply to treat Northern Ireland as an established regional identity which should be given, as an uncontested whole, a measure of regional autonomy.

THE PEACE PROCESS: MISTAKEN PARTNERS IN NEGOTIATION?

The so-called "two traditions" approach to the Northern question, with the consequent, supposedly legitimate, British and Irish dimensions to the identities of Northern Irish people, can serve only to extend the internal antagonism beyond the province to British–Irish relations generally. Britain and Ireland then function as antagonistic agents of the two communities. It is absurd to regard either agent as impartial in relation to its principal. Indeed, the more involved Ireland and Britain become the more they will revert to precisely the level of mutual antagonism which they felt for one another in 1921.

The sole foundation for the legitimacy of any political entity in international society at the present time is cultural. Self-determination of peoples is an expression of democracy, but it has to be more than formal democracy— which would ignore any principle of limitation of people's imaginations and experiences through time and space, and would therefore imply immediate world government. In fact, any people's consciousness is limited and determined by history, religion, race and language. Peoples invariable struggle to dominate one another, and relations between them are virtually never harmonious. Hence, the world community is divided, at present, into numerous nation states. The refusal of self-determination to stateless peoples who wish to have it is merely an illogical and irrational step-motherliness on the part of peoples who enjoy state structures.

Since the French Revolution the widespread and increasing democratisation of world society has found expression in the language of cultural self-determination. This concept undoubtedly expresses limitations of human consciousness and reproduces the endemic struggles for recognition and esteem which occur in international relations. So the concept of self-determination is contested as being forcibly exclusivist, pressing for homogenous States which are racist in all but name. However, such rhetorical arguments cannot cancel out a drive for such self-determination which is rooted in an experience of repression and denigration of the group to which one is attached, as a matter of perceived historical fact. The examples of such felt experience are too numerous to bother recounting.

Culture does not mean folklore or experience of language as an aesthetic enjoyment, but refers to the collective memory of a people who are defined for themselves from the outside and who are always engaged in an already ongoing process whereby they try to redefine definitions of themselves given to them by others. Physical separation of cultures will not end the memory of antagonism but, functioning as a divorce (or, more exactly, the ending of an arranged marriage), it will serve in time to reduce the pressures and tensions of an unwelcome, because forced, association. A full healing of relations would require repentance on the stronger side and forgiveness on the weaker, but such vocabulary does not have an obvious place in political life.

A part of the rhetoric used to defeat cultural nationalism is its supposed exclusiveness—that is, only victims may belong! Clearly, any conflict is accompanied by a closing of ranks. It is now, in addition, commonly argued against such nationalism that a post-modern era requires a recognition that so-called emancipatory discourses are henceforth "exploded narratives" which are no longer convincing in the era of multi-cultural global world villages. Anti-foundationalism is certainly a relevant criticism for any identity which is based upon cultural history. Its anti-essentialist argument as to the contingency of every claim to identity is metaphysical in its ambition to banish any pantheistic absolutism attaching to claims of nation, class, religion, and, maybe, eventually, gender. It is true that none of these entities have existed eternally and it may be desirable that antagonistic oppositions of identity be deconstructed. It can be easily conceded that two opposing collective identities are in fact a single identity which is internally motored by entirely negative forces. Unwind these negative forces and both so-called identities will disintegrate.

Thus, anti-foundationalism may set an ultimate goal. Indeed, it has been shown that members of either community within Northern Ireland, when transported (often literally) far afield (i.e. further than Scotland), do not carry their divisions with them, but dissolve into wider groups. However, the ethos of anti-foundationalism does not lead immediately to this conclusion. Instead, it also supposes the absence of a neutral, mediating, Archimedean point which can boast to undertake the worthy exercise of deconstruction of recalcitrant entities. Perspectivism is of little use in the face of open conflict. There has been no attempt to address the fact that the Northern Ireland conflict could have a mediator. Instead, anti-foundationalism, as a contemporary European political ethos, represents precisely the absence of a global, totalising moral perspective from which one might judge in firm moral terms gross human injustice—hence the indifference of "enlightened" European political society to the catastrophe of Bosnia.

In fact, post-modernist opposition to grand narratives should lead to a more modest close reading or thick description of conflicts. They should suppose that the would-be commentator is herself part of the process which she claims to observe. The southern Irish liberal-Europeanist may view her Northern poor relation with a step-motherly disdain which is just as disempowering as a British racial contempt. There is no credibility in any Irish State or British

State observation of Northern Ireland which makes any claim to distance or detachment. The boundaries are not simply fluid. They are non-existent.

This is the background offered to justify and explain the argument which follows for the reactivation of the idea of a Boundary Commission which would lead to a repartition of Northern Ireland. The arguments have been developed more fully in a recent study.[7]

LEGAL CONSIDERATION RELEVANT TO A BOUNDARY REVISION

The *McGimpsey* case decided that the Article 2 and 3 claims of Ireland to the Northern counties were legally binding upon the Irish State. Therefore, the Irish State did have to show that the Anglo-Irish Agreement of 1985, which gives the Northern Irish entity the right to decide separately, and as a whole, whether it does or does not want a united Ireland, was compatible with the Irish duty to respect the terms of its own Constitution in the two cited Articles. The terms of the 1985 Agreement seem to make it impossible to implement the idea of a united Ireland, given the clearly and repeatedly expressed wishes of the unionist majority. So, it might have been thought that the Supreme Court would have held the Agreement incompatible with the Irish Constitution. This is what the unionist plaintiffs in the case hoped. How did the Supreme Court avoid an obvious conclusion?

The Court argued that it was open to the Government of the State to use its political judgement as to how best to achieve another of its legal obligations, to observe international law. International law requires, under the United Nations Charter, that States settle their disputes peacefully. The Government was entitled to consider that a dispute with the United Kingdom could best be settled by submitting the future of the Northern counties to the democratic wishes of their majority, i.e. to deprive its own national minority in these counties, its poor relations, of anything approaching equal Irish citizenship, until their unionist protagonists saw fit to accord it to them by taking it upon themselves to opt as well for Irish citizenship, a politically inconceivable and therefore not a serious option. As the British Northern Irish Secretary said at the time, the Agreement makes Irish unification impossible.

It is important to understand the possible function of international law as an alibi. The State is fulfilling its international law duty to settle its disputes peacefully—inevitably a matter of political judgement which any judiciary had better leave to the politicians. In fact, statesmen acquiesce in international legal structures which are fatally flawed in the vital respect that they provide no procedural framework for the resolution of unresolved disputes. That is to say, international law has no convincing peaceful settlement procedures. This is as much as to say that, as a matter of any institutional theory of law,

---

[7] A. Carty, *supra* n. 6.

international law can provide no convincing reason why any State or non-State actor in contemporary international society should pay any deference to the United Nations Charter.

This weakness of international law was recognised at once by the supreme theorist of legal positivism of the twentieth century, Hans Kelsen, as soon as the United Nations Charter was elaborated in 1944–5.[8] Positivism is taken here to mean that any legal structures must provide a coherent response to the fact that law usually has its origin in the will of the modern State as the main concentration of political power. The latter is usually, but not necessarily, democratic. Kelsen argued that the United Nations failed to provide any framework for peaceful change. It prohibited the use of force by States to defend or promote what they considered to be their rights, for the pragmatic enough reason that the States would usually resort to a disproportionate measure of force to promote radically subjective conceptions of their rights. Nonetheless, in Kelsen's view, no constitutional legal order can coherently prohibit a right of self-help unless it provides an alternative judicial or legislative remedy for disputes. The General Assembly of the United Nations does not have authority to legislate for the international community. Given the improbability of an international legislative process ever arising, Kelsen favoured a system of compulsory judicial settlement of disputes as essential to the very existence of an international constitutional order. The body of international law was inadequate, but a court could, with time, through actual adjudication, build up a corpus of law. The Security Council of the United Nations was not a suitable alternative body to the court. It was undemocratic and political, inherently unlikely to reach either judicial or judicious solutions to disputes between States.[9]

This critique by Kelsen would suggest, from a legal perspective, that one should attempt a judicial-style solution to the Northern Ireland problem. There are two considerations which have to be stressed here. Some form of judicial solution is to be preferred to a legislative one, i.e. political solution left entirely to the hands of politicians, for the same reasons which Kelsen had for regarding any international political, legislative authority as improbable. The so-called international community lacks the moral coherence and cohesion to provide reasonable world government. This is why international mediation by politicians is extremely unlikely and has not in fact been forthcoming in any major international dispute, except perhaps the Norwegian intervention in the Palestinian–Israeli dispute. The interest of politicians of one national society in the troubles of another is simply not there. Hence the tedium with which most European politicians, and indeed intellectuals, regard the Northern Ireland question. The interest is not there. This is the bitter flip side of the fact that political legitimacy at present rests upon conceptions of

---

[8] See e.g. H. Kelsen, *The Law of the United Nations* (London, Stevens, 1964).

[9] See further the very illuminating recent study by C. Tournaye, *Kelsen et la sécurité collective* (Paris, LGDJ, 1995).

cultural national identity which do not rise above national horizons. There is simply not enough interest outside the British Isles for a solution and not enough impartiality within.

At the same time it would be pointless to rush into a standard international judicial settlement procedure which does exist for use on a voluntary basis. A decision by the International Court of Justice according to international law would simply reproduce the defects of the existing United Nations legal order. Even it were to decide that Article 12 of the 1921 Treaty between Britain and the Irish Free State was fraudulently induced and/or fraudulently disregarded, the Court would have no option but to call for a respect for existing boundaries and a duty of a majority and minority within these boundaries to settle their own disputes peacefully. This is what happened with the so-called Badinter Commission set up to advise the European Union on the debacle in Bosnia-Herzegovina. It held that a democratic majority of Bosnians within the former federal Yugoslav entity of Bosnia-Herzegovina had the right to independence if a majority chose it, and that the Serb minority had to accept minority status within Bosnia.[10] Just as Kelsen would have predicted, this solution, an insistence on the *status quo*, was not enforceable and not enforced. The actual outcome was violent ethnic conflict, with a hands-off policy from the European Union and an eventually forceful American intervention of uncertain political effect. The armistice line between so-called warring factions is set to become, effectively, the boundary between two States within former Bosnia-Herzegovina.

Instead, what the Northern Irish question requires is the re-establishment of a Boundary Commission to compensate for the one which failed in 1925. A Boundary Commission is never committed to applying international law as such. There is no exact international law with respect to frontiers. There are frequent territorial disputes which are conflicts between established States about the exact extent to which they have exercised sovereign jurisdiction in relation to one another. Such matters often exercise the International Court of Justice. It can resolve them by making a list of each State's assertions of sovereignty and by adding them up against one another. A Boundary Commission is set to find a just solution to a conflict of peoples' interest. So the constitution of such a Commission must not only have regard to the impartiality of its members, but also provide a specification of the principles which should guide the Commission.[11]

The first principle for the Boundary Commission, going back to the true intention of Article 12 of the 1921 Treaty, has to be to have full regard to the wishes of the inhabitants of Northern Ireland, in effect, cultural self-determi-

---

[10] Conference on Yugoslavia Arbitration Commission: Opinions Nos. 2 and 4, Jan. 1992, reported in 92 *Int Law Reps* (1993), at 167 and 173 respectively.

[11] A magisterial study of boundary arbitration in this sense is afforded by A. Munkmann in "Adjudication and adjustment: International Judicial Decision and Settlement of Territorial and Boundary Disputes", 46 *British Yearbook of Int. Law* (1972–3) 1.

nation. This is what democracy really means when translated into the world of competing territorially-based State sovereignties. The second principle, negatively stated, has to be explicitly to refuse to have regard to Northern Ireland as a geographical and economic entity which has to be maintained somehow separated from the wishes of its inhabitants—the mistake of the last Boundary Commission. This was to reify Northern Ireland as some essential, eternal—not at all post-modern—entity and to give it a legitimacy which does not attach to any non-living body in a supposedly democratic world community.

Neither of the above principles should exclude a third principle which gives a proper recognition to the complexity of boundary disputes. The third principle has a similar tendency to the excluded second. The latter is merely restated as a principle which has to be balanced against the others and not allowed to dominate and exclude them. It is fair that a measure of proportionality be introduced to decide how much territory should be allocated to a population. There should be some connection between the size of population and the size of territory. This is, once again, a reference to the economic and geographical needs of the unionist majority. The measure should not operate mathematically, as if it represented the only relevant principle, by dividing the entire island by the proportion of unionists to nationalists on the island. Such an idea sounds ridiculous, but then all divorces are sources of theatrical farce. Lawyers can only pick up the pieces. The principle should serve to exclude the transfer to the Irish Republic of entire counties or vast territories—vast in Northern Ireland terms—in which there is only a small nationalist majority. Opposed to this third principle should be a fourth principle, that the object of repartition is to separate as far as possible two politically incompatible communities. No redrawing of the boundary serves its purpose which leaves "unmanageable" minorities remaining on either side. The object is to minimise the size of recalcitrant minorities for purely security reasons.

It is obvious that no redrawing of the boundary will remove the "difficulty" of the large nationalist minority in Belfast, nor the large unionist community in South Fermanagh. Here a further principle should be taken into account which, while painful, has to be considered if the Northern Ireland problem is to be confronted once and for all. This is the principle of historical responsibility.[12] The Belfast nationalist community is historically largely an immigrant community which came to enjoy, however precariously, the benefits of the unionist industrial revolution. The Fermanagh unionists are, more than their Antrim and Down compatriots, the descendants of a plantation which was a dispossession. These principles cannot be mathematically applied. However, they should be taken into account in deciding whether particular pockets of minorities might be asked to settle indefinitely for the protected status of minorities rather than to claim full cultural self-determination *as a group*.

---

[12] *Supra* n. 6, at ch. 5.

Minority status in another political community means acceptance that its general ethos will be that of the very much dominant and now increased majority. There would be no right to group block representation in government or political committees. Instead, there would be merely a right to the absolute exclusion of discriminatory practices and to a full political participation *as an individual citizen* who accepts the permanence of the existing constitution and does not even aspire to its eventual disappearance. Mechanisms to guarantee group minority political representation serve only to accentuate ethnic divisions. They operate to ensure the eventual non-viability of any political community.

CONCLUSION

The manner in which the Boundary Commission should proceed is as follows. The wishes of the population should be ascertained at the smallest community level possible. A referendum should be called for this purpose on the question to which State does one wish to belong, with no place left for expressions of intensity of attachment. The result will, assuming most nationalists are not closet unionists, produce a mosaic, given the mixed location of the two nations. Hence, the second stage has to be a judicious application by the Boundary Commission of the above-outlined principles to accommodate the permanent establishment of a unionist political community, which is in a position to assure, above all, its own security needs.

This unpleasant and unpalatable, but none the less modest(!), proposal must have a jarring sound when presented to a sixtieth anniversary review of the Irish constitution. However, any proposal which confronts directly what is a tragic history of the Irish nation and of the island as a whole, including the unionist community, will inevitably have a disagreeable appearance. This is not a congenial proposal for a polished society. It recognises the harshness which attends even the renewed prospect of a peace-process. At the time of writing it is reported[13] that if Sinn Féin accepts the Mitchell Principles it will have to accept a "partitionist settlement". That is what is offered here, but with a twist!

[13] *The Observer*, 27 July 1997.

9

Judicial Activism— Too Much of a Good Thing

DAVID GWYNN MORGAN

INTRODUCTION

The innovative work of the Irish judiciary over the past three decades has been much praised, and indeed there is much to praise. Equally, however, as Dr Johnson remarked: "[t]he Irish are a fair people; they never speak well of each other" and elsewhere in this collection one will find a perspective which is less enthusiastic. I, too, prefer to line up with Cassandra rather than the chorus, for there are a number of criticisms which should be made of the performance of the judges in their significant intervention in the constitutional field. Their decisions have often been unmeasured and the consequences not fully thought through. As a result territory too rashly occupied has had to be evacuated in a way which establishes undesirable inconsistency. There has been a failure to consider—with a carefulness the question warrants—the proper place of the judiciary in the polity. There has also been a failure to follow a consistent doctrine of constitutional interpretation.

Non-lawyers may ask impatiently: does all this matter very much? The short answer, I believe, is that in the long run it does and that I shall return to discuss this kind of objection in the concluding section of this essay. For the moment, let us briefly consider three areas—international affairs, the demise of the Prerogative and the interpretation of the text of the Constitution—in order to see whether these strictures can be substantiated.

INTERNATIONAL AFFAIRS[1]

Of all subject areas, it is conventionally accepted that the one in which judges are least qualified to intervene is that relating to foreign affairs.[2] Indeed, this

---

[1] For a more refined, though broadly similar argument to that advanced here, see G. Hogan, "The Supreme Court and the Single European Act" (1987) 22 *Ir. Jur.* 55 at 68–9 and C. R. Symmons, "International Treaty Obligations and the Irish Constitution: The *McGimpsey* Case" (1992) 41 *ICLQ* 311, 316–17.

[2] See Barrington J's remark in *McGimpsey* v. *Ireland*, [1989] ILRM 209 at 220: "[the] onus is

field is one of the principal areas which fall within the judicial no-go area, embraced by the (originally US) doctrine of "the political question".[3] The notion of "the political question" was, however, not so much as mentioned in the significant case of *Crotty v. An Taoiseach*.[4] In *Crotty*, the plaintiff sought a declaration and injunction restraining the Government from ratifying the Single European Act, the critical parts of which provided for improved co-operation among EC Member States in the sphere of foreign policy. The plaintiff's successful argument was that since Article 29.4 of the Constitution vests the Government with the power to conduct foreign affairs, it is not open to the State to fetter the Government's authority by a Treaty (the SEA), which would oblige it to make foreign policy with a greater measure of co-operation with other nations of the EC. While the plaintiff's argument succeeded only by a majority of three to two, notice that the points of difference between the minority and majority judges were not related to the question of whether a judge should intervene in a foreign relations question. (The main ground of difference between the majority and minority in *Crotty* was that the minority held that the terms of the SEA were so loose that it imposed no significant obligation on Ireland on the international plane.) The sequel to *Crotty* was that Ireland had to hold a referendum in order to determine whether to amend the Constitution so as to authorise the Government to ratify the Single European Act. And, by analogy, *Crotty* has been taken to mean that all other major changes in the EU Treaty (for instance to enable Ireland to ratify the Maastricht and Amsterdam treaties) require a constitutional referendum.[5]

The second case, *McGimpsey v. Ireland*,[6] was equally politically charged. Here the plaintiff sought a declaration that the Anglo-Irish Agreement of 1985 was unconstitutional. There were two strings to his bow. In the first place, he relied on the *Crotty* argument just rehearsed, claiming that the Anglo-Irish Inter-Governmental Conference and Secretariat, constituted by the Agreement, provided fora through which the British and Irish Governments could seek to align their policies in relation to Northern Ireland. This, he submitted, was unconstitutional because, as in *Crotty*, there was a violation of the provision vesting authority in foreign affairs in the Government. However, *Crotty* was distinguished and the plaintiff's claim in *McGimpsey*

on the plaintiff clearly to establish that the Government has violated the Constitution in entering into the treaty. This onus necessarily must be a heavy one. The conduct of the foreign policy of the State is not a matter which readily lends itself to judicial review and if there is any area in which judicial restraint is appropriate, this is it."

[3] On which, see *Baker v. Carr* (1962) 369 US 186, 217; *McKenna v. Ireland* [1995] 2 IR 10, 18.

[4] [1987] IR 713; see also on *Crotty*, A. Whelan, "National Sovereignty in the European Union" in this volume.

[5] The referendum on the SEA and Maastricht amendments (the Tenth Amendment of the Constitution, 1987 and the Eleventh Amendment of the Constitution Act, 1992, respectively) resulted in "yes" votes of approximately 70% in each case. For details, see J. M. Kelly, G. Hogan and G. Whyte (eds.), *J. M. Kelly, The Irish Constitution* (3rd edn., Dublin, Butterworths, 1994) 281–5.

[6] [1988] IR 567 (HC), [1990] 1 IR 110, [1990] ILRM 440 (SC).

failed. In the High Court, Barrington J purported to distinguish the Anglo-Irish Agreement from the SEA, which was at issue in *Crotty*, on the ground that in *McGimpsey* the Court "was not dealing with a multilateral treaty conferring powers on supranational authorities" but with a "bilateral treaty between two sovereign governments".[7] Yet, as Dr Symmons observes: "[i]t is hard to see how in principle the fact of *bilaterality* in the case of the Anglo-Irish Agreement makes any substantive difference to the potential encroachment on Irish foreign policy discretion."[8] Nor does it matter whether the encroachment is from a supranational authority or a state:[9] the essential question, according to the interpretation of Article 29 of the Constitution adopted in *Crotty*, is whether there is an encroachment, irrespective of its source.

In the Supreme Court, Finlay CJ was equally unconvincing. He stated that "the Government of Ireland at any time carrying out the functions which have been agreed under the Anglo-Irish Agreement is entirely free to do so in a manner which it, and it alone, thinks is most conducive to the achieving of the aims which it is committed to".[10] This statement is, in fact, the basis of Finlay CJ's judgment in *Crotty* to the effect that just because the SEA used terms like "endeavour to avoid" and "as far as possible", it was too loose to impose any obligation to agree upon the Irish State. But, the striking point is that in *Crotty* Finlay CJ was in dissent and this argument (as we saw earlier) had been rejected by the members of the majority. Yet, in *McGimpsey*, all of his colleagues concurred with his judgment as well as his purported acceptance and distinguishing, of the majority in *Crotty*.

There was a second point in *McGimpsey*. As is well known, the Irish Constitution includes an irredentist claim on Northern Ireland (known, in the nationalist lexicon, as the "Six Counties"). In the Anglo-Irish Agreement, the main concession made by the Irish side (as a *quid pro quo* for the establishment of the Anglo-Irish Conference) was a declaration which went a substantial distance in the direction of renouncing Articles 2 and 3, which, so far as they are relevant, provide:

> "The national territory consists of the whole of the island of Ireland, its islands and the territorial seas.
> Pending the re-integration of the national territory, and without prejudice to the right of Parliament and Government established by this Constitution to exercise jurisdiction over the whole of that territory, the laws enacted by that Parliament shall [apply only in the Twenty-six Counties]."

Before coming to the second point which arose in *McGimpsey*, one ought to notice that a roughly analogous point had arisen before—in *Boland* v. *An*

---

[7] *Supra* n. 6, at 589.
[8] *Supra* n. 1, at 316.
[9] Or even a gang of international terrorists along the lines of SPECTRE, in the James Bond books.
[10] *Supra* n. 6, at 451.

Taoiseach,[11] which concerned the Sunningdale Treaty 1973 (which, for present purposes may be characterised as an early prototype of the Anglo-Irish Agreement). On that occasion, the argument had been made that Articles 2 and 3 sounded only in the political—and not in the legal—realm. However, this point was firmly rejected on the ground that the Constitution should be read literally, to mean what it says. Thus the two Articles are matters of law, which establish a constitutional mandate.

The relevant provision in *McGimpsey* was Article 1 of the Anglo-Irish Agreement, which provides as follows:

> "The two Governments;
> a. affirm that any change in the status of Northern Ireland would only come about with the consent of a majority of the people of Northern Ireland;
> b. recognise that the present wish of a majority of the people of Northern Ireland is for no change in the status of Northern Ireland;
> c. declare that, if in the future a majority of the people of Northern Ireland clearly wish for and formally consent to the establishment of a united Ireland, they will introduce and support in the respective Parliaments legislation to give effect to that wish."

Given that Articles 2 and 3 of the Constitution are matters of law, one might have expected the courts to hold Article 1 of the Agreement to be unconstitutional. However, Barrington J in the High Court avoided this result by a rather strained interpretation of Article 1 of the Agreement. He characterised it as saying that "the two governments merely recognise the situation on the ground in Northern Ireland (paragraph (b)), form a political judgment about the likely course of future events (paragraph (a)) and state what their policy will be should events evolve in a particular way (paragraph (c))".[12]

Likewise, in the Supreme Court, Finlay CJ held that

> "the only reasonable interpretation of Article 1 taken in conjunction with the denial of derogation from sovereignty contained in Article 2(b) of the Anglo-Irish Agreement is that it constitutes a recognition *of the de facto situation in Northern Ireland* but does so expressly without abandoning the claim to the reintegration of the national territory"[13] (author's italics).

Yet, surely, to acknowledge that a majority of people who live in Northern Ireland wish to remain outside Ireland undermines a substantial part of the moral basis on which Articles 2 and 3 rest.

Thus, it seems to the author that one could say of *McGimpsey* that the courts had second thoughts about trying to patrol areas of essentially political controversy, which they had rather rashly appropriated in *Crotty* and *Boland*.

Now, the question arises whether the courts' performance in *Boland*, *Crotty* and *McGimpsey* can be defended on some such result-orientated or *realpolitik*

---

[11] [1974] IR 338.
[12] *Supra* n. 6, at 224.
[13] *Supra* n. 6, at 450.

basis as the following. First, one may praise *Crotty* on the ground that it is appropriate for a free people to determine, by referendum, whether an intensification of a dominating supranational authority should be permitted. (In Britain, for instance, an entire political party—the Referendum Party—was set up by Sir James Goldsmith to champion this very issue.) On the other hand, in regard to *McGimpsey*, it might be argued, by way of justifying the decision, that given the delicate state of matters in Northern Ireland, it was not appropriate to risk opening further wounds there by a vigorous debate, even in the Republic, as to the merits of the Anglo-Irish Agreement. Yet, it seems to me that this line of justification has only to be stated for its implausibility to be exposed. One could easily—by assuming slightly different circumstances—turn the court's reasoning around so as to justify reverse decisions in both *Crotty* and *McGimpsey*. For instance, at the moment the EU is popular in Ireland— largely for economic reasons. This state of affairs could easily change, so that a situation might arise in which intensification of the EU would appear damaging to Ireland's short-term interest, though possibly likely to have beneficial effects in the long term. Wiser heads would then say that the People would not be far-sighted enough to take cognizance of the future and, thus, it would be better not to have a referendum. Equally, *McGimpsey* could easily be portrayed in a different light from that in which it seems to have appeared to the Supreme Court. It might be argued that the claim to Irish unity, laid down in Articles 2 and 3 of the Constitution, is the central issue in the Irish State. Accordingly, any interference with it could well be said (from a *realpolitik* perspective) to be the very issue on which the People ought to have been consulted. It seems, accordingly, that *realpolitik* is no help either.

THE DEMISE OF THE PREROGATIVE

Next, we must notice a particular and most individualistic piece of judicial interpretation, *Webb* v. *Ireland*,[14] which has had the effect of rendering unpredictable the law in an area which, on the occasions when it is called into use, can be very significant indeed. This concerns the compartment of the common law known as the Prerogative. Until the Supreme Court case of *Byrne* v. *Ireland*,[15] (the facts in which are not relevant at this point) it was assumed that, by virtue of two sets[16] of Constitutional Articles, the Prerogative

---

[14] [1988] IR 353. For criticism of this decision, see J. M. Kelly, "Hidden Treasure and the Constitution" (1988) 10 *DULJ* 5 and D. Gwynn Morgan, "Constitutional Interpretation" (1988) 10 *DULJ* 24.

[15] [1972] IR 241.

[16] To appreciate the reference to two sets of Arts., one should interpolate that there have been two Constitutions in independent Ireland: the present (1937) Constitution and the earlier (1922) Irish Free State Constitution. The two sets of provisions just mentioned are: Art. 50.1 (which may be equated fairly exactly with Art. 73 of the 1922 Constitution); and Art 49.1 (to be equated with Art. 51 of the 1922 Constitution).

continued to exist in independent Ireland. First, Article 49.1 of the present Constitution provides that:

> "All powers, functions, rights and prerogatives whatsoever exercisable in or in respect of, Saorstát Éireann [the Irish Free State], . . . by the authority in which the executive power of Saorstát Éireann was then vested [sc. the King] are hereby declared to belong to the people."

This provision makes the inquiry turn on the antecedent question of whether the Prerogative existed in the Irish Free State Constitution (which was the basic law of the State 1922–37). Prior to *Byrne*, it had been assumed that the presence of the King in the earlier Constitution drew with it the Prerogative. This argument was rejected by the majority in *Byrne*. It was said that the King's powers could be confined to those actually specified in the Free State Constitution: there was no necessary reason why they had to be identical with those which the Crown enjoyed in the United Kingdom or in pre-Independence Ireland. This may be so. There is, however, another and stronger argument for saying that the Prerogative came over into independent Ireland. This argument depends upon the second of the two sets of constitutional provisions adverted to earlier. It is that "[the prerogative] was part of the common law which was applied to the Irish Free State by Article 73 [and thence to the present polity by Article 50.1]".[17] The kernel of the court's argument, in response to this contention, is contained in the following extract from Walsh J's judgment:[18]

> " . . . the basis of the Crown prerogative(s) in English law was that the King was the personification of the State. Article 2 of the Constitution of the Irish Free State declared that all the powers of government and all authority, legislative, executive and judicial, in Ireland were derived from the people of Ireland and that the same should be exercised in the Irish Free State through the organisations established by or under and in accord with that Constitution. The basis of the prerogative of the English Crown was quite inconsistent with the declaration contained in that Article. The King enjoyed a personal pre-eminence; perfection was ascribed to him."[19]

It is proposed, now, to scrutinise this passage. In summary, Walsh J's argument is, first, that in Ireland all governmental authority flows from "the People" (author's capital letter) and, secondly, that the prerogative authority stems from the King. As a consequence of this difference the prerogative could not have come over into the polity established by the 1922 Constitution.

This argument merits this observation. It might have seemed more realistic to regard the constitutional provision to the effect that "all powers of government . . . derive . . . from the people" as a statement of political principle;

---

[17] *Cork County Council* v. *Commissioners of Public Works* [1945] IR 561, 578, *per* O'Byrne J.
[18] *Supra* n. 15, at 272.
[19] The passage refers to Art. 2 of the Free State Constitution. However, neither Art. 2 nor Art. 6—its almost identical equivalent in the 1937 Constitution—is reproduced separately here since it is quoted practically *verbatim* in this passage.

as a generalised warning to Irish governments that they held their power "on trust" for the People along the lines of the generally accepted Lockean, "Social Contract" theory of limited government; and also as a warning to the British Crown that, as governmental authority came ultimately from the People, it was not for the British to start trying to take power back from the Irish polity or to interfere with it in any way. To regard the provision in any other way seems to me to be a capital example of the judiciary fastening on to, and drawing exact legal consequences from, statements which were intended by their authors to have merely exhortatory political effect.[20]

At a broader level, Professor Kelly has criticised not so much the reasoning as the conclusion, in *Byrne*. He summarises his views, characteristically cogently, in the following passage:[21]

> " . . . the statutory usage of the Irish Free State, positive and negative, together with the opinions of judges who played a part in drafting its Constitution, together with the record of what actually was done in those years in such matters as pardons, passports, and the precedence of counsel, suggest that the Crown and its prerogative were understood to have survived into the newly independent Irish State, as part of common law, under Article 73, so far as such survival was not, in letter or in spirit, inconsistent with some specific dimension of the new Constitution. I think that for us today, 50 or 60 years later, to take the line that our fathers and grandfathers in legal and official life quite misunderstood the nature of the machine they were not only operating but had also in fact constructed is to adopt an unreal and intellectually unamiable position."

In any event, it might seem that, in the wake of *Byrne*, the Irish State as a result of being without the Prerogative, would be deprived of certain pockets of legitimate authority, the need for which is likely to arise unexpectedly or in an emergency, when there might be no time for the passage of legislation. Examples (drawn from English law) include the rules: permitting the seizure or destruction of private property in time of war or imminent danger (albeit on payment of compensation); affording a significant component of martial law; or enabling the State to create corporations without statutory authority.

The lame ducks released by *Byrne* soon came home to roost. In *Webb* v. *Ireland*,[22] the question of the continued existence of the prerogative of treasure trove was presented for consideration by the Supreme Court. The plaintiffs in this case were the finders (while trespassers on some farmland) of one of the most significant discoveries of early Christian art ever made, a hoard

---

[20] There is another criticism which might be made of the *Byrne* reasoning; the effect of Art. 2 is to stipulate (i) that all powers of government flow in some sense from the People, and (ii) that these powers may only be exercised by the independent Irish organs of government. But as to the content of the powers of government little is said. In view of this, Art. 2 could have been interpreted as not affecting the content of these powers, but rather as relocating the basis of State authority from the King to the people and as shifting the mode of its exercise from the King to the organs established by the Irish Constitution.

[21] J. M. Kelly, *supra* n. 14.

[22] [1988] IR 382.

of early Christian objects, valued at £5.5 million. The plaintiffs had handed over the artifacts to the National Museum for safe-keeping. They were dissatisfied with the £10,000 compensation offered to them by the State and commenced proceedings seeking the delivery up by the State of these objects. The State pleaded that it was not a mere bailee, but that by reason of the prerogative of treasure trove it had acquired a superior title to that of the plaintiffs.

The High Court, adopting the reasoning of Walsh J in *Byrne*, held that none of the prerogatives had survived the enactment of the Constitution and was, thus, driven to find for the plaintiff. The Supreme Court, however, was made of sterner stuff. Finlay CJ held that the State did enjoy a right to a modern form of the treasure trove prerogative by virtue of Article 5, which proclaims, without more, that: "Ireland is a sovereign, independent, democratic State". Finlay CJ stated:

> "[O]ne of the most important national assets belonging to the people is their heritage and knowledge of its true origins and the buildings and objects which constitute keys to their ancient history . . . [A] necessary ingredient of sovereignty in a modern state and certainly in this State, having regard to the terms of the Constitution, with an emphasis on its historical origins and a constant concern for the common good is, and should be, an ownership by the State of objects which constitute antiquities of importance and which have no known owner."[23]

The net effect of *Byrne* and *Webb* is that rights, privileges, etc., formerly inhering in the State by virtue of the Prerogative can do so now only if they can be rehabilitated by reference to the elusive basis of sovereignty bestowed by Article 5 (always assuming, of course, that the *content* of the particular prerogative does not conflict with the provisions of the Constitution, this *caveat* being eminently reasonable). While the hobgoblin of sovereignty did save the day in *Webb*, sovereignty is rather a wild card on which to rely. When the Prerogative was in place, there was at least a voluminous corpus of precedent to determine what rights the State did or did not have. The effect of *Byrne* and *Webb* is, at best, to render this area uncertain and unsettled, with no compensatory advantage, since sovereignty—it seems—embraces many features of the Prerogative, albeit under a more politically correct rubric.

INTERPRETING THE TEXT

The question of the approach(es) adopted to the interpretation of the Constitution is one of peculiar importance and peculiar difficulty. The reason, in each case, is that the Constitution was not drafted in quite the same way, or for the same purpose, as an ordinary statute. In the first place, it covers an unimaginably broader span than any statute: it deals with nothing less than the organs of government and, secondly, the fundamental rights, in other

---

[23] [1988] IR 382, at 395.

words the relationship between the individual and ordered society. Inevitably, the language and style will be different from the traditional approach to the drafting of a statute, which is thought to justify certain forensic and rather artificial assumptions (for example, that if a matter is not dealt with explicitly or by very necessary implication, it was not intended to be covered at all). Here, there is no space to address this large question in detail. However, as part of the theme of this essay—the inconsistency and lack of concern for the long term, too often shown by the judiciary—it seems appropriate to quote the judgment of Kelly, the leading text on the Constitution, and then to include some examples of the problems which inconsistencies in this area may cause. Kelly[24]—in passages unusually heart-felt for that austere text—deals first with some excessively literal decisions:

> "The minute word-by-word interpretation of the Constitution which the last decade has seen bears no relation to the realities of the process by which it was drafted and enacted. The principle of equality of citizens before the law was a shibboleth long before Article 40.1 put it in a constitutional text. But, did anyone in 1937 really intend that the phrase "as human persons" was to be used to whittle down its significance, rather than a piece of pious padding? 'Laws' is a word used in the Constitution in several contexts which require it to be understood *in those contexts* as statutes. Does it follow that the continuance provisions of Article 50 do not carry non-statutory law? or that such a conclusion is warranted by the use of the words 'repealed or amended', when the purpose of drawing such a distinction between these categories of law is not apparent? May we not simply say that the intent of the Article is plain, but its drafting awkward? The Irish text being the authoritative one (however absurd the background of this rule) it is used as an elucidatory aid in construing the English. But, does anyone believe that the nameless translators of 1937 (whose work was left virtually without debate in a Dáil most of whose members knew very little Irish anyway) deliberately used the Irish future tense rather than the Irish present (where English grammar would make no distinction) in order to convey that only post-1937 events were contemplated, or that the Government (let alone the Dáil or people) understood the results of such a technique? Such things have however been said or implied by the courts in recent times, and require from the observer an act of good faith of the kind which is normally accorded only to theological propositions."

Later,[25] Kelly surveys the various approaches adopted to constitutional interpretation (literal; broad; harmonious; historical; and natural law) and in this context remarks:

> "One needs to emphasise, however, that the courts have shown no consistency with regard to any particular approach and this gives rise to the suspicion that individual judges are willing to rely on any such approach as will offer adventitious support for a conclusion which they have already reached."

[24] *Supra* n. 5, at p. *xcii*.
[25] *Ibid.*, at p. *xcviii*.

The examples which I wish to take all come from Article 34.3 and 34.4—the part of the Constitution dealing with the jurisdictions of the various courts. The first line of authority concerns Article 34.3.1, by which "[t]he Supreme Court shall with such exceptions and subject to such regulations as may be presented by law, have appellate jurisdiction from all decisions of the High Court . . . ". In surprising decisions on this provision, it has been held that an appeal lies to the Supreme Court, from the High Court against: the grant of a habeas corpus;[26] a discretionary order as to costs in either civil or criminal matters;[27] and committal for civil contempt.[28]

A further consequence of Article 34.3.1 is even more surprising. The Supreme Court has applied the provision at its full, literal width to hold that the prosecutor may appeal to the Supreme Court *against* an acquittal in the Central Criminal Court. In the hotly-contested case of *The People (DPP)* v. *O'Shea*,[29] in which this rule was established, the two dissenting judges (Finlay P and Henchy J) appealed in vain to the argument that there is, inherently, no appeal from a jury acquittal and on the ancient tradition in the criminal justice system against double jeopardy.[30]

There is, for no apparent reason, a contrast between the judges' treatment of the provision regulating the jurisdiction assigned to the Supreme Court (just summarised) and the equivalent in the cases of the High Court and the lower courts. Let us take, first, the lower courts—namely the District and Circuit Courts. Their constitutional warrant is to be found in Article 34.3.4 which provides for "[c]ourts of local and limited jurisdiction". Without going into detail unnecessary in the present context, one can say that in almost all cases, the Circuit and District is, in general, local in that each judge's jurisdiction is

---

[26] *The State (Browne)* v. *Feran* [1967] IR 147.

[27] *Vella* v. *Morelli* [1968] IR 1; *The People (Attorney General)* v. *Bell* [1969] IR 24.

[28] *The State (H)* v. *Daly* [1977] IR 90.

[29] [1982] IR 384.

[30] The sequel to *O'Shea* came in another Supreme Court decision, *The People (DPP)* v. *Quilligan (No 2)* [1989] ILRM 245. In *Quilligan* the main question was whether the court's jurisdiction to hear an appeal against acquittal carried with it a concomitant jurisdiction to order a re-trial. According to Walsh J (at 247): "[t]he jurisdiction to set aside erroneous decisions in law must necessarily carry with it the necessary competence to ensure that the interrupted proceedings are brought to a conclusion in accordance with the law". However, Walsh J, who had been in the majority in *O'Shea*, was on this occasion one of two dissenting judges. The majority rejected this reasoning on the basis that in the case of statutory jurisdictions, authority to order a re-trial is always specifically conferred. But, this perhaps overlooks the fact that here it was the Constitution, and not a statute, which was being interpreted. In fact, to appreciate why the result in *Quilligan* was different from that which might seem to have been required by *O'Shea*, it is best to see the case as a continuation of the judicial differences in *O'Shea*. Many of the arguments rehearsed in the *Quilligan* judgments, on each side, were the same as those in *O'Shea*. More significant was the judicial line-up in the two cases. Henchy J, who dissented in *O'Shea* with Finlay P, was joined in *Quilligan* by Griffin J (in place of Finlay P). On the other side, Walsh J who concurred in *O'Shea* with O'Higgins CJ, was joined, in *Quilligan*, by McCarthy J. The reason for the contrasting results in such similar cases was that Hederman J acted, as it were, as "the swing vote", holding in *O'Shea* that the court had jurisdiction to hear an appeal against acquittal, and in *Quilligan* (in a half-page judgment) that, nevertheless, the court could not order a retrial.

confined to cases brought against defendants living in, or which arise out of, events happening or property located in the particular area. The question, however, arises whether the rare provisions which do purport to bestow nationwide jurisdiction upon the District or Circuit Courts are unconstitutional. This issue came up in *The State (Boyle)* v. *Neylon*.[31] The prosecutor had been charged with offences committed in County Wicklow and returned for trial to Wicklow Circuit Court. Then, however, the DPP had exercised his power under the Courts Act 1981 to have the prosecutor's trial transferred to the Dublin Circuit Court. The prosecutor argued that this provision was unconstitutional, in that the Circuit Court was a court of local and limited jurisdiction (in the language of Article 34.3.4) and accordingly Dublin Circuit Court could not be granted jurisdiction to try matters with no connection with Dublin Circuit. Walsh J met the prosecutor's argument by adopting a purposive interpretation of the Constitution. According to the learned judge:

"The purpose [of courts of first instance of local and limited jurisdiction] is . . . [to] provide local and cheaper and more convenient venues for litigants than would be the case if they had to go to the High Court. . . . It was left to the statute to decide how this would be achieved. . . . It is quite clear that the whole structure of the courts is based upon the exercise of its jurisdiction locally . . . It does not, however, follow that for a legitimate reason the Oireachtas may not provide that in certain cases another locality would be properly available for the trial of a case whether civil or criminal, as may be provided for by an Act of the Oireachtas. Experience has shown that justice itself would require a provision of this kind to avoid the risk of an injustice to one party or another by reason of local circumstances or conditions. The ability to transfer the trial of a case from one locality to another does not alter the essential local exercise of a jurisdiction of the Circuit Court."[32]

Here Walsh J (whose style of literal interpretation in regard to the Supreme Court has already been noted in *O'Shea*) was in effect holding—contrary to its literal wording—that all that the Constitution requires is that the Circuit Court's jurisdiction be *essentially* local.

A similar point arises in regard to the High Court, the jurisdiction of which extends—according to Article 34.3.1—to "all matters and questions whether of law or fact, civil or criminal". The point which arises here is whether "all" means all. In other words, does this provision bar the legislature from vesting a decision, in regard to a specified type of justiciable controversy, in some court other than the High Court—presumably in one of the lower courts, just mentioned. Perhaps surprisingly, an affirmative answer was given by the High Court in *R.* v. *R.*[33] One of the obvious dangers with this finding was that (in the criminal field) an accused might seek to frustrate a prosecution for, say, a parking offence by asserting a right to be tried in the High Court or that (in the civil field) an economically strong defendant might seek to deter the

[31] [1986] IR 511.
[32] *Ibid.*, at 556–7.
[33] [1984] IR 296.

plaintiff by insisting on having a minor claim tried before the High Court. However, this lapse into what the author regards as excessive literalism was corrected by the Supreme Court in *Tormey* v. *Attorney General*, in which it was held that Article 34.3.1 did not bear its full liberal meaning but merely meant that the legislature could not remove the High Court's "full jurisdiction [which] is there to be invoked—in proceedings such as habeas corpus, certiorari, prohibition . . . so as to ensure that the hearing and determination [of a lower court or tribunal] will be in accordance with law".[34]

To summarise this rather brief account of the case law relating to the constitutional provisions on the courts' jurisdictions, in the case of the Supreme Court literalism reigns; in the other two (the High Court and the lower courts, i.e. Circuit and District Courts) what appears to be common sense prevails. There seems to be no imperative justifying the divergence of treatment: the cases reviewed in this section all come from the same part of the Constitution. It is notable that in the Supreme Court jurisdiction cases a literal approach has been adopted which has had the effect of flying in the face of what might be called "civil liberties" values. Moreover, this line has been taken by a judiciary which has, on the whole, taken a very strong line in favour of civil liberties. Witness (among many examples of this)[35] the steady holding by the Supreme Court (in *The People (Attorney General)* v. *O'Callaghan*,[36] and *Ryan* v. *DPP*[37]) that bail cannot be refused on the ground that it is expected that the accused might commit another offence while out on bail. This view—which had made Ireland the most liberal state in Western Europe on this point and which had to be reversed by constitutional amendment (passed, by a ratio of three to one) in 1996—had been grounded on no provision of the Constitution, but merely on the holding that a refusal of bail amounted to preventive detention which was a violation of that elusive thing, "the Rule of Law".

CONCLUSION

We may summarise what has been said so far by two rather broad comments. In the first place, the Irish judges have, in many different contexts, adopted an approach which experience elsewhere would seem to show is likely, if followed consistently in later cases, to lead to undesirable results. Secondly, when the inevitable has happened and the awkward case materialised, the court has changed tack without much attempt to distinguish the earlier incon-

---

[34] [1985] IR 289, at 296–7.

[35] See, for instance, *Re Article 26 and the Emergency Powers Bill, 1976* [1977] IR 159; D. Gwynn Morgan, "The Emergency Powers Bill Reference—Part I" (1978) 13 *Ir. Jur.* 67; Part II (1979) 14 *Ir. Jur.* 252. (Parliamentary resolutions declaring that an emergency exists are possibly open to review, despite the subjective wording of Art. 28.3.3º.)

[36] [1966] IR 501.

[37] [1989] IR 399.

venient precedent, preferring to do this than to reach the undesirable result. This pattern has been demonstrated, in regard to foreign affairs, in the divergence between *Crotty* and *McGimpsey*; and, over the Prerogative, in the contradiction between *Byrne* and *Webb* above. And in regard to the interpretation of the Constitution we have seen—in case law on the jurisdiction of the lower courts (District and Circuit Courts), High Court and Supreme Court—how there has been an inconsistent approach to interpretation, for no apparent reason.

The reader who has come so far may well object: "Isn't all this rather precious? Surely a line of attack founded on an accusation of lack of respect for dogma or inconsistency is less than compelling, if the results achieved in the cases concerned are 'good', in some way." I have already discussed this line of thought in respect of foreign affairs above. Turning to the Prerogative, one could say that *Byrne* was not even result-orientated. For—to take a point which was not mentioned before—the particular prerogative involved in that case concerned State immunity against tort action (uprooted by the Crown Proceedings Act 1948 in Britain). This significant point is that this prerogative was—by its content—in conflict with the Constitution (Article 40.3.1, which includes the right to litigate a justiciable controversy). Accordingly, there was no need to haul out into the beguiling constitutional-theological waters to resolve this question. Choosing to do so led, rather predictably to the difficulty which became apparent in the *Webb* treasure trove case. Equally in the case of the interpretation of the text of the Constitution the case law seems to be open to the same kind of criticism, outlined in relation to the jurisprudence concerning foreign affairs and the prerogative.

Let me close by re-stating some conventional wisdom, something which it is sometimes no harm to do, especially since I believe that the precepts rehearsed here have remained conventional wisdom for some centuries just because they are useful in running a polity. The first verity is that it is important to have a strong judiciary. This will only continue if the judges are respected by the public and politicians, and even among those whose interests are not served by the results of particular cases. But, there is a major condition which is necessary for the continuance of this respect. It is that the judges' decisions are perceived as being derived from some clearly, articulated, consistently followed and rationally grounded principles. Some of the cases discussed above do not pass this test and, hence, in the long run risk losing respect for the judiciary. Whatever the possible gains, this means that there is an awful lot at risk.

10

Gendered Citizenship in the Irish Constitution

DOLORES DOOLEY

INTRODUCTION

Citizenship is alive and well in Ireland today as it has seldom been since the early twentieth-century suffragettes[1] or even earlier since 1825 when a radical Irish text on gendered citizenship, *Appeal of One Half the Human Race* was published.[2] The text, authored by the Cork political economist and feminist philosopher of the British Co-operative Movement, William Thompson, is a detailed discussion of the benefits of political rights in citizenship. The *Appeal* was damning in its indictment of women's categorical exclusion from citizenship in James Mill's treatise, *On Government*, published first in 1819. But the *Appeal* speaks to modern concerns about citizenship in unravelling the concept of political citizenship to show how skills of self-government and self-respect are best developed by exercising full rights of democratic participation. To the extent that women's citizenship became an issue, men, holding the power in institutions, were necessarily implicated. The text has been largely invisible in Irish history.

Today, there is a resurgence of writing on the concept of citizenship. Political theorists are aware that this renewed interest in citizenship is filtering down to grass-roots community projects where there is a growing awareness of a need to discover or define social and political identity. Multi-cultural groups within nation states, minority groups (religious, cultural, sexual), women and the economically oppressed question whether their citizenship has any meaning or power which might improve the quality of their lives.[3] Irish

---

[1] See L. Ryan, *Irish Feminism and the Vote* (Dublin, Folens, 1996), 15.

[2] The full title of William Thompson's text is *Appeal of one Half the Human Race, Women, against the Pretensions of the Other Half, Men, to Retain them in Political and thence in Civil and Domestic Slavery*. This text is abbreviated as *Appeal*. In an introductory letter in this text, William Thompson acknowledges the collaboration of Mrs Anna Doyle Wheeler from County Tipperary. She is the muse, the source of a woman's experience to clarify the arguments for women's inclusion in citizenship: D. Dooley (ed.), *W. Thompson, Appeal [1825]* (Cork, Cork University Press, 1997).

[3] W. Kymlicka and W. Norman, "Return of the Citizen: A Survey of Recent Work on Citizenship Theory", 104 *Ethics* (1994), 352–81. See further for radical reconceptualisations of

citizens have begun envisaging a European citizen identity which can both integrate and expand their sense of political participation.

> "In Western Europe the increasing economic, legal and political integration of the European Community is beginning to challenge national sovereignty and citizenship ... it is also beginning to involve the creation of a new transnational European level and sphere of citizens' rights, institutions and community."[4]

A scepticism among socially marginalised groups voices the suspicion that their citizenship is somehow subordinate to that of members of dominant social groups within Irish society.[5] Against this backdrop of history and current events, a review of the Constitutions of 1922 and 1937 as they pertain to women is overdue. Women's citizenship, as it is ideologically framed in the Constitution, is a case study of gender-differentiated and "second-class citizenship".[6] The Constitution of 1937 was a retrograde step from the non-gendered document of 1922. The question is whether women today can any longer give credence to the constitutional "social contract" endorsed in 1937?

FREE STATE CONSTITUTION: 1922

Liberal politics seems to have won the day when, in Article 3 of the Irish Free State Constitution of 1922, the following rights were conceded to women: to vote, to hold office on equal terms with men and to enjoy all the privileges of such citizenship. Unlike the successor Constitution of 1937, the Constitution of 1922 gives no code of behaviour for women in living out their citizenship. Nevertheless, if the Constitution of 1922 seemed distinctly liberal towards women's political participation, this

> "constitutional guarantee was almost immediately undermined by subsequent legislation that effectively denied a full political identity to Irish women. By 1937, women's political, economic, and reproductive rights had been so severely curtailed that women were explicitly barred from claiming for themselves a public identity."[7]

citizenship, P. Barry Clarke, *Deep Citizenship* (London, Pluto Press, 1996); A. Phillips, *Engendering Democracy* (Cambridge, Polity Press, 1991); S. Moller Okin, *Women in Western Political Thought* (Princeton, NJ, Princeton University Press, 1979); and C. Pateman's now classical studies of social contract theory in *The Sexual Contract* (Cambridge, Polity Press, 1988) and *The Disorder of Women* (Cambridge, Polity Press, 1989).

   [4] M. Roche, *Rethinking Citizenship* (Cambridge, Polity Press, 1992), 1.
   [5] See S. J. Healy and B. Reynolds, *Ireland Today* (Dublin, Justice Office of the Conference of Major Religious Superiors, 1985). See also G. Whyte, "Marginalised Groups Deserve Constitutional Protection", *Irish Times*, 8 July 1996.
   [6] I. M. Young, "Polity and Group Difference: A Critique of the Ideal of Universal Citizenship", 99 *Ethics* (1989), 250–74. Young defends the concept of "differentiated citizenship" as the best way to realize the inclusion, empowering and participation of everyone in full citizenship. My own analysis here agrees with her general point, but argues that the Constitution of a State is not the place for congealing citizenship debates.
   [7] M. G. Valiulis, "Power, Gender, and Identity in the Irish Free State" in J. Hoff and M. Coulter (eds.), *Irish Women's Voices Past and Present* (Bloomington, Ind., Indiana University

Gendered legislation between 1922 and 1937 prepared the way for the ideology of woman that would pervade the new Constitution. The Civil Service Act of 1924 restricted civil service examinations according to sex. While the Act was amended in 1925, the Civil Service (Amendment) Act still allowed the government to limit examinations for positions in the civil service on the basis of sex. During the civil service debate, the fact that determined the decision was that women married.[8] Given a presumption that women would leave work on marriage, positions appropriate to women, and not wasteful of too much training time, would be typists, stenographers and other lower grades in the civil service.[9] The operative assumption was that the highest civil service positions would be held by men. Accordingly, even though not all women would, in fact, marry, discrimination along the lines of sex was the admitted and unapologetic practice. The sanctity and indissolubility of marriage was reinforced, civil divorce being ruled out by a *Dáil* motion of 1925.

The Juries Bill 1927 was another legal marker that the 1922 Constitution's generous spirit of equality was under review. Concessions of equality might not guarantee the behaviour from citizens that is considered appropriate or necessary to achieve the social ideals and the common good of the State. The law on jury service was convoluted, but virtually excluded women from jury service since only citizens who were rate-payers or property owners could serve. Women had to apply for jury service. They would not be automatically invited.

Feminists saw the Juries Bill as discriminatory and subtly excluding women from the public forum. They were not far off the mark of the intent. In the Juries Bill debate, the Minister for Justice, Kevin O'Higgins, stated as if a matter of eternal truth: "It is the normal and natural function of women to have children. It still is the normal and natural function of women to have charge of households."[10] The statement makes transparent the Government's increasing reliance on a natural law philosophy which shows unwarranted confidence in reading from nature and the voice of inner reason what is "normal and natural" and, by implication, what is moral. This natural law philosophy becomes more overt in the constitutional Articles discussed below. O'Higgins defended himself and the Irish Government with unblushing paternalism for the provisions on jury service:

> "[we] . . . are preventing people getting something which they pretend they want, and which would not be good for them. . . . In this matter I am really the champion of women in the State, but I never expect to get any gratitude for that."[11]

Press, 1995), 117–36. See in this same volume, M. E. Daly, "Women in the Irish Free State, 1922–39: The Interaction between Economics and Ideology", 99–116. Daly has an alternative reading of the 1937 Constitution as it pertains to women to that offered here.

[8] M. G. Valiulis, *supra* n. 7, at p. 123.

[9] As documented in Valiulis, *supra* n. 7; *Seanad* Debates, 17 Dec. 1925, vol. 6, cols. 247–8 and *Dáil* Debates, 18 Nov. 1925, vol. 13, col. 504.

[10] *Dáil* Debates, 23 Feb. 1927, vol. 18, col. 766, as cited in Valiulis, *supra* n. 7, 134.

[11] *Seanade* Debates, 30 Mar. 1927, vol. 8, col. 691, as cited in Valiulis, *supra* n. 7, at p. 135.

It was not until 1975, in *De Búrca and Anderson* v. *Attorney General*,[12] that women were called to give service using the same criteria as applied to men, but, allowing opportunities for either sex to apply for exemption.[13]

By the early 1930s, the legal, philosophical and religious foundations were firmly in place for the ideology of women's citizenship that appears in the Constitution of 1937. A profoundly relevant yet predictable fact which makes one sceptical of the shared and equal "contractual character" of the Irish Constitution is that women had no part in framing *Bunreacht na hÈireann*. Not one woman took part in drafting it.[14] The plebiscite that approved the Irish Constitution on 1 July 1937 "agreed" to a number of rules and ideals contained in its Articles: rules which include the structures and offices of the emerging Government, stipulations defining the terms of citizenship and ideals spelling out goals to promote a state of equal civil freedom among Irish citizens. The margin of win was narrow enough: 685,105 votes to 526,945. The contract was conceptualised and written, in the main, by the then Head of State, Èamon de Valera, and Roman Catholic churchmen, most notably John Charles McQuaid and the Jesuit, Edward Cahill.[15] The shapers of the Constitution created a document that embodied the aspirations, ideals and social values of a Roman Catholic State. It was a constitution that pleased the Vatican.

WOMEN AND THE SOCIAL CONTRACT OF 1937

The Constitution of 1937 is complex in its ideological rendering of woman's identity, her proper nature and moral responsibilities to promote the stability of the Irish State. The discussion that follows is only one part of the story of women's citizen identity as interpreted from the Irish Constitution. The evolution of unenumerated rights in the Constitution has enabled women to progress in spite of the Articles analysed in this essay. Contemporary feminist theorising would have a field day with this Constitution. It embodies in a few explicit Articles the central disputed concepts in feminist theory: the false universal "woman", the public–private divide, family, mothering, reproductive rights for women. Similarly noted, is a radical asymmetry in only stipulating role assignments for women. The provision of particulars defining women's

---

[12] [1976] IR 38.

[13] This concern about taking women from their homes to serve on juries was not solely an Irish one. For the US debate on the issue of jury duty for women, see S. Moller Okin, *supra* n. 3, at pp. 260–4.

[14] Y. Scannell, "The Constitution and the Role of Women" in B. Farrell (ed.), *De Valera's Constitution and Ours* (Dublin, Gill & Macmillan, 1988), 123. See also A. Connelly, "The Constitution" in A. Connelly (ed.), *Gender and the Law in Ireland* (Dublin, Oak Tree Press, 1993), 4–27.

[15] D. Keogh, *Ireland and the Vatican, 1922–1960* (Cork, Cork University Press, 1995), especially 132–40. See also by the same author, "Church, State and Society" in B. Farrell, *supra* n. 14, at pp. 103–22.

role as citizens has no equivalent for male citizens, though there are implications for men in the provisions about women. An explanation of relevant Articles on marriage, family and reproduction gives a glimpse of aspirations for women's identity and duties that are still in place though vigorously under re-assessment by Irish women.

LEGAL AND "THICK" CITIZENSHIP

Article 9.1.3 in the 1937 Constitution insures that "no person may be excluded from Irish nationality and citizenship by reason of the sex of such person". What is conceded in Article 9.1.3 is the *legal status* of citizenship in the particular political community of the Irish State. This legal entitlement should be differentiated from citizenship-as-desirable-activity or "thick citizenship", where what is debated is the complex normative view of what is meant by a "good citizenship".[16] The normative view of "good citizen" remains deeply debated in political theory today. It is no less important that the understanding of "good woman citizen" in the Irish Constitution needs to be seriously contested. The equality of citizenship conferred in Article 40.1 of the Irish Constitution anticipates what looks like a surprisingly modern and feminist view of human persons as *equal but different*.

> "All citizens shall, as human persons, be held equal before the law. This shall not be held to mean that the State shall not in its enactments have due regard to differences of capacity, physical and moral, and of social function."

Article 40.1 combines the values of equality and affirmation of differences, an apparent move away from false universals of "human citizens" where "human" reads male. However, this liberality is only apparent. We are handed the proverbial two edged sword. To know how sharp the sword might be, one needs to ask what understanding of human persons supports the social contract ideal of equality with difference contained in Article 40.1.

Feminist theorists are divided in their analysis of contract theories.[17] Some are sharply critical, in that the traditional models of such theory are deeply patriarchal, in assuming the universal male as norm: the citizen is the worker in the public domain, the bread-winner, the politician and lawmaker and the economic head of households. Other feminists see greater potential in properly analysed contract theory, especially views in sympathy with the ideas of the German philosopher, Immanuel Kant, who sees a conception of human worth in citizen identity as non-negotiable.[18] The important insight in Kant's concept of person is that people have intrinsic, non-instrumental value.

---

[16] The distinction is clarified and expanded in W. Kymlicka and W. Norman, *supra* n. 3.

[17] See e.g. S. Mullally, "Equality Guarantees in Irish Constitutional Law: The Myth of Constitutionalism and the 'Neutral' State" in this volume.

[18] J. Hampton, "Feminist Contractarianism" in L. M. Antony and C. Witt (eds.), *A Mind of One's Own* (Boulder, Colo., Westview Press, 1993), 227–55.

Human persons should never be treated as means but always as ends in themselves. Respecting the worth of human persons cannot be essentially derivative of the functions they perform towards servicing the State or its institutions. If a concept of respect for human persons is not to be exploitative and is to value persons for their intrinsic worth, such respect needs to acknowledge the liberty of persons to explore, to learn and to choose their own defined interests and central concerns. The imaging of women in the Irish Constitution—the identity, ideals and moral norms given to women— betrays an underlying functionalist mode of thought which does not respect women for their choices of identity for themselves. Rather, this underlying instrumentalist philosophy permits rationalisations of inequality using the rhetoric of equality. A functionalist conceptualisation of women underlies the apparently benign affirmation of her "differences". Article 40.1 logically prepares the reader for the relevant sections defining woman's differences in her physical and moral capacities and her attributed social functions. The multiple "differences" of woman are ones she executes with superior skill within the presumed private sphere of the family. Her differences of reproductive capacity and domestic nurturing of others distinguish her by sex; such differences make her "other" and morally more responsible than men for promoting the prominent ideals of the State: the common good, public order and morality. The implications are negative for men who would see in their own identity qualities of nurturing, parenting and fathering. Nowhere in the Irish Constitution is parenting in the plural mentioned. Fathering is outside the conceptual framework of Natural Law's deliverance for women.

FAMILY: DEFINING WOMAN'S SPHERE

It is impossible to overstate the importance of the family as institution within the Constitution. Correlated with this pre-eminence of family is woman's prominent positioning within this social unit. Article 41.1.1 defines the family in the following terms:

> "The State recognises the Family as the natural primary and fundamental unit group of Society, and as a moral institution possessing inalienable and imprescriptible rights, antecedent and superior to all positive law."

Natural law theory is again implicit here in seeing family as "natural" and "fundamental" and as a "moral institution". The natural is deemed moral. The strength of commitment to the normal conceptualisation of family and the moral role it is to play is evident in its being given imprescriptible rights, "antecedent and superior to all positive law". It is the only correct understanding of family, as designed according to laws of nature. Thus, the implied description of this "natural" moral unit was clearly intended to be that of legalised heterosexual marriages. Today, these constricting terms of reference for the concept of family would be greatly contested. Many look for inclusion under the concept of family the reality of single-parent families (men or women) who never married, or who are now separated, the partnerships of gay or lesbian couples who choose means to have children which they then parent. Neither women's nor men's roles as citizen was ever envisaged in such "unnatural" units. The "unnaturalness" of such alternative family compositions made the experience of social ostracism and deviance a painful reality for persons with sexual orientations other than the heterosexual. Article 41.1.2 further emphasises the "naturally and properly ordained" parameters of "family":

> "The State, therefore, guarantees to protect the Family in its constitution and authority, as the necessary basis of social order and as indispensable to the welfare of the Nation and State."

It is the home which harbours the family woman's designated "proper" and "natural" place. An uncritical acceptance of Natural Law analyses and the certainty of insights derived from that philosophy determine the definitions and moral boundaries of family.[19] Conclusions are suited to the concern with control and sexual order in the ethos of the Constitution. With Article 41.2.1 there is little ambiguity about the ideal place for woman to live and develop her citizen identity:

> "In particular, the State recognises that by her life within the home, woman gives to the State a support without which the common good cannot be achieved."

In this Article, the Constitution adopts most explicitly a dualism of private and public spheres, with women's citizenship mandated for the realm of domestic management, nurturing, education of the young and a plethora of complex and demanding tasks. Woman's "life" is in her home and a strong implication can be drawn that this is where her primary citizen commitments should be contained. If the reality of women working caused distress to the politicians and husbands in early Ireland, the 1937 Constitution tries to consolidate an ideal for women to approximate. The life given to important realities of home and family may not be the choice of some women. Where is their diversity valued in the universalising thrust of the reference to "woman"? Are these diverse women who choose not to marry, not to mother, either legitimated or valued under the normative simplicity in the concept "woman"?

In a striking *non sequitur*, Article 41.2.2 conflates a false universal "woman" with the role of mother:

> "The State shall, therefore, endeavour to ensure that mothers shall not be obliged by economic necessity to engage in labour to the neglect of their duties in the home."

---

[19] See D. M. Clarke, *Church and State* (Cork, Cork University Press, 1984), especially ch. 2, "Natural Law".

This is the strongest statement of expectations that women will give their full energies in fulfilling duties in the home. It is seldom detailed what those duties are, though we are supposed to assume they are all, as duties, essential and praiseworthy. However, it is important to remember that one fundamental duty of women, often clarified by tradition in the Roman Catholic Church is woman's "sexual duty": making herself available for sexual relations virtually on demand. The reasoning is that this is inherent in the "constitution and authority" of marriage. It is a sexual imperative for women to help prevent male extra-marital liaisons.

While feminist theory critiques the implications of women's economic dependence on men, so defended by this Article, many women home-makers resent feminism's apparent under-valuing of the life of women in the home. It is a fair reminder of the need for vigilance in feminist theory so as to avoid undermining the importance of diversity of women's choice. A sympathetic reading of the Irish Constitution might see these Articles about women's duties in the home as implying that the private sphere has been validated and positively valued as women's contribution to the body politic. This reading has legitimacy—within limits. If the private sphere of domestic management, human nurturing and educational work is valued this is progressive. But, the role of home-maker is exclusive and defining of woman's citizen role. It includes praise, but, excludes provisions for her to be economically independent. The defining of woman's role in the home constitutionally endorses her radical dependency on the bread-winner who traditionally has been male. Two points need to be made to indicate that Article 41.2.2 was taken seriously by State legislators. Because work outside the home for married women was regarded as a selfish distraction from home duties, the Civil Service Regulation Act 1956 provided that women employed in the civil service, other than those employed in certain excluded non-pensionable posts, were required to resign on marriage.[20] If economic independence of women was valued, the State would have put money forward as economic endowments—indeed inducements to continue the valued work in the home. But, economic independence for women permits latent power to lose its grip. The power and the ultimate family "authority" often is vested in the income earner.[21] One is left with little evidence to believe the Government was committed to providing for economic independence for women, even by modest domestic endowment.

MARRIAGE AND THE SEXUAL CONTRACT

William Thompson and Anna Wheeler could have enlightened the prelates who accompanied Eamon de Valera to the Vatican and expanded their imag-

---

[20] Y. Scannell, *supra* n. 14, at p. 126.

[21] See G. Bock and S. James (eds.), *Beyond Equality & Difference: Citizenship, Feminist Politics and Female Subjectivity* (London, Routledge, 1992).

inations about lived marriages. Marriage is depicted in the *Appeal* of 1825 as too often little more than an opportunity for unrestrained exercise of power by husbands over women. Clearly the benign and flourishing relationships of marriage were evident, but, the opportunity for power in the marriage institution was little discussed, though clearly experienced, in 1937. Well-wrought Articles on marriage consolidated its legal indissolubility for almost sixty years to come. Article 41.3.1 gives the full backing of the State's institutions to insure family solidarity.

> "The State pledges itself to guard with special care the institution of Marriage, on which the Family is founded, and to protect it against attack."

The military metaphor of "attack" suggests that the Irish Government envisaged an onslaught of paganism from foreign shores reminiscent of the days of Brehon laws when women cohabited with more than one man. The pledge of special care is coupled with a legal ultimatum that would leave little discretion to subsequent judiciaries to alter the status of marriage. In the original Article 41.3.2. we read, "No law shall be enacted providing for the grant of a dissolution of marriage." The shapers of family and marriage ideology in the Constitution either failed to recognise the extent to which women's dependence and submission are encapsulated in the institution of marriage or, having recognised it, assumed that this dependence and submission are natural and so morally obligatory. The State has long refused to accept evidence which challenges the adequacy of their marriage proposals, the fact that marriage relationships irretrievably break down. If they do acknowledge this reality and still hold firm to the indissolubility of marriage then the metaphysical conception of idealised marriage exercises a tyranny over citizens' opportunities to build new relationships.

Increasing public awareness of domestic violence and family sexual abuse cannot be dismissed; it is a painful and not infrequent dimension of married, family life, especially for woman whose economic dependency is a major factor in restraining them from possible exits. The economically powerless homemaker was for years denied access to free legal aid, even though she was faithfully fulfilling the constitutional duties of upholding the stability of the State.

The Articles on family and marriage are clearly concessions to the teachings of social encyclicals of the Catholic Church. The universal abstractions of marriage and family are typical of metaphysical abstractions which one does not test against the concrete realities of people's lives. Women's voices have brought the metaphysics of these ideals down to earth with stories of lived realities within these rarefied social institutions.[22] The Articles on family and marriage are symptomatic of a State that has been fearful of the uncontrollable power that might be unleashed if the concession of sexual

---

[22] L. Connolly, "The Women"s Movement in Ireland 1970–1995: A Social Movements Analysis" in (1996) 1 *Irish J of Feminist Studies*, 43–77.

equality of citizenship were realised in action. Apprehensions of a "liberalism of fear" are not wide of the mark. The democratic order is vulnerable to the subversive dynamic of equality and the Irish Constitution's affirmation of women's difference, her designation as sexual "other" in the private sphere is:

> "an institutional fixation of sexual difference in the hierarchical marriage . . . to protect democratic society against an understanding of equality that would break down all distinctions and meaningful differences. . . . The task at hand is to construe a power that will secure the unity of marriage, as well as the tranquillity of civil society, against the adverse consequences of a wife's independence of will . . . and to ensure the sexual fidelity of a wife."[23]

A divorce referendum in 1986 was defeated by almost 66 per cent of the electorate. In 1996 a referendum to change the Constitution and allow the introduction of legislation for divorce was passed—but only barely. Contrary to the growing data on marriage breakdown, the specifically religious ideal of the Constitution, mandating permanence in marriage, seems still to be upheld by many citizens, though clearly for a diversity of complex reasons not the least of which are: adherence to one's Church beliefs on the matter *and* concern about the distribution of property in the event of divorce.

REPRODUCTION

No power of women has been more protected and constrained in Ireland than her capacity for reproduction. Choosing not to be a mother has never been a legitimate option under the cultural ideology of the Irish State. The containment of women's sexuality has been the single obsession of the Roman Catholic Church and successive Irish governments have refused to implement conditions for diverse women to have liberty of choice about reproduction.[24] Under the Criminal Law (Amendment) Act 1935, it was a criminal offence for any person to sell, or to import for sale, any contraceptive. It was not until *McGee* v. *Attorney General*[25] that the legal sale and use of contraceptives was permitted, and even then within the context of *bona fide* marriage relationships.

The Catholic Church has always taught that voluntary sterilisation of reproductive capacities is intrinsically wrong. Sterilisation is seen as the antithesis of the obligations within marriage to populate the State with new citizens or to abstain from sexual intercourse. This moral prohibition on sterilisation was clearly evident until the 1980s; there were no more than two hospitals in the State which freely provided female sterilisation. The control was effectively implemented through the religious control of hospitals in the State.

---

[23] U. Vogel, "Marriage and the Boundaries of Citizenship" in B. van Steenbergen (ed.), *The Condition of Citizenship* (London, Sage Publications, 1994), 76–89 at p. 84.

[24] See D. Dooley, "Expanding an Island Ethics" in J. Lee (ed.), *Ireland: Towards a Sense of Place* (Cork, Cork University Press, 1985), 47–65.

[25] [1974] IR 284.

Even public-run hospitals were effectively governed by the Catholic ethos pro-hibiting sterilisation. As a result, if a woman desired a tubal ligation, because a further pregnancy was either undesired or even risky to health, it was either flatly refused or a request had to be put by the consultant gynaecologist before an established ethics committee to hear the case. Because of the red tape the practice sometimes chosen was to recommend hysterectomy for women for contraceptive purposes. In giving reasons, one can always cite numerous rea-sons for hysterectomies and the contraceptive motivations need never be pub-licised.

Ethics committees with *ex officio* membership of Catholic and Protestant clergymen were standard for consultation on this issue. It was a moral tri-bunal to ensure as much as possible that the religious ethos would be a force in determining women's decisions about reproduction. The annoyance of medical consultants about the intrusion into their doctor–patient relationships has altered this situation to a great extent. There is an anomaly in the Irish State that proportionately many more men than women have been sterilised. The explanation is greatly in the institutional structures: women need to be in-patients in hospitals governed often by a denominational ethos; men can be sterilised as an out-patient procedure in family planning clinics after due coun-selling and necessary partner consent. Such constraints on reproductive choice are consistent with women's mandates in the Constitution. Such constraints are also partial evidence for my interpretation that fear of women's liberty, equality and sexuality has been an almost obsessive concern of the Irish State and has led to the adoption of severely controlling practises regarding women's reproductive choices.

Abortion has been an ethical hornet's nest for Irish citizens. The limits of patience in deliberative democracy have been sorely tested with emotive rhetoric and damning judgments about fascism surfacing on various sides of the debate.[26] This moral question has virtually dominated social and ethical debate since 1983, when a national referendum put in place the constitutional amendment, Article 40.3.3:

> "The State acknowledges the right to life of the unborn and, with due regard to the equal right to life of the mother, guarantees in its laws to respect, and, as far as practicable, by its laws to defend and vindicate that right."

This amendment is placed under the Articles on citizenship, thus making the unborn a citizen of the Irish State. The conceptual difficulties in attempt-ing to spell out the conceivable duties and responsibilities of the "unborn citizen" have not yet been faced. However, by inserting this Article in the Constitution, the citizens of the State declared that a human foetus is to be considered a constitutional person. In *Life's Dominion*, Ronald Dworkin

---

[26] See D. Dooley, "Abortion and the Law" in D. M. Clarke (ed.), *Morality and the Law* (Cork, Mercier Press, 1982), 31–47. For recent discussions relevant to the Irish abortion debate in the 1990s, see A. Smyth (ed.), *The Abortion Papers Ireland* (Dublin, Attic Press, 1992).

explains that the decision to make the human foetus a constitutional person is often anything but benign, especially to women and their liberty to make reproductive decisions. Such creation of the category of "unborn citizen" assumes that the Irish State:

"can curtail constitutional rights by adding new persons to the constitutional population, to the list of those whose constitutional rights are competitive with one another."[27]

This was, of course, the intent in seeking an amendment. But in the case of the Irish Constitution, where women's right to abortion was not clearly decided by any judicial decision, the creation of citizenship status for the unborn was pre-emptive curtailment of possible moves of the much feared "liberal" populus. Presently, abortion is legal in highly specified circumstances as determined in the Supreme Court decision in *Attorney General* v. *X and Others*.[28] But, the reality of Irish women's diverse choices reveals approximately 7,000 Irish women going to England each year to procure abortions. The efforts to contain and constrain women's powers in controlling their sexuality are most clearly demonstrated in the abortion debate. A strong pro-natal philosophy governs this debate, which simplifies to distortion the complex realities of women's lives that lead them to choose abortion. The respect for the unborn, voiced from all perspectives in the debate, is never thought compatible with the endorsement of abortion as essentially a woman's choice.

CONCLUSIONS

The Irish Constitution of 1937 purports to be a liberal social contract. To the extent that it is dependent on a liberal political philosophy it has also adopted the framework of dividing the State into the public and private domains where women are expected as citizen-actors dominantly in the latter. The implication is that women's fullest participation in *both private and public life* has been pre-empted. Only women's resistance and determination have made wider public participation a reality. Few women in 1937 would ever have envisaged a woman in the Presidency.

To the extent that the Constitution is meant to be a co-operative contract based on consent, the implied "respect" for the person inherent in legitimate contracts is lacking. Rather, a functionalist representation of women is provided. Her duties to the State are her reason for being. The "respect" for persons required for a legitimated social contract would call for liberties of choice and participation in the deliberative democracy—as much to encourage a development of women's person as to provide public contexts for diversity of women's voices and experience. Hearing these voices will help challenge the

[27] R. Dworkin, *Life's Dominion* (London, Harper Collins, 1995), at p. 113.
[28] [1992] 1 IR 1.

adequacy of both the public and private spaces of her society. Some writers might argue that the Articles examined in this essay are not circumscribing or stereotyping of women in Irish society, but rather that they positively and primarily credit women's special qualities.

"They [the Articles] should perhaps be seen as reflecting the lives of most Irish women in the 1930's. At that time the overwhelming majority of Irish women—married, widowed, and single—were based within the home. On this basis the Constitution can be viewed as acknowledging the importance of women's lives and work within the home giving status to many members of Irish society who were otherwise ignored."[29]

But, the document of a Constitution needs to be carefully wrought so that gender roles and norms are not specified today, only to become desperately outmoded tomorrow. Gender-norms in the Irish Constitution were not simply reflecting the way things were. Rather, the gender ideology achieved for many decades a containment and circumscription in women's citizenship; this ideology resulted in mechanisms to control the power of her sexuality. The Constitution's ideology of "woman" was perpetuated with a complex cultural dynamic with a history of its own. An understanding of the history and social origin of the Constitution cannot blind us to the profound underlying patriarchy of Church and State that determined the 1937 document. The document was a grand gesture of male political power. The citizen differentiation I have read from the Irish Constitution of 1937 is not a constructive and liberty-affirming endorsement of women's special qualities. We do not need to be suspicious or cynical about affirmations of special differences that women are credited with. We do need to be very cautious that the affirmation does not conceal an autocracy of intent in harbouring those differences for ends which women, in their diversity, might not choose for themselves.

The question which remains is how the Irish Constitution of 1937, with its Articles designating the sexual differences of woman, can continue to win consent from the diversity of women and men in Ireland. The radical changes in Irish society since 1937 must produce scepticism that this Constitution has anything of legitimacy in its presumed "contractual" features. The gendering of citizenship in the Irish Constitution provides a case study in what a Constitution should never aspire to: gender-differentiated citizenship premised on a socially precarious and uncritical ideology supporting, not the interests of women, but patriarchal interests of Church and State. The meanings of citizenship, what it means to develop skills for "good citizenship" need to be debated in the many local and national contexts of deliberative democracy. A State's constitution is not the place to copper-fasten sexual identities or attempt to determine constraints on women's diverse choices for full participation in the power dynamics of the closely inter-related private and public spheres of the State.

[29] M. E. Daly, *supra* n. 7, at pp. 111–12.

11

To *be an Irish Man—*
Constructions of Masculinity
within the Constitution

LEO FLYNN*

INTRODUCTION

When writing about the position of women within the Irish Constitution on the occasion of its fiftieth anniversary, one commentator remarked that the leading figure in its drafting process, Mr de Valera, was not a feminist.[1] This laconic observation was developed further in that essay, in which the point was made that while the Constitution did contain certain provisions which could be seen as operating to the advantage of women, other provisions, either when viewed on their own or when seen in light of their precursors in the Constitution of Saorstát Eireann, actively disempowered women as a group or else diminished their ability to press for changes in their social, economic or political positions. That essay is a good example of a vein of scholarship which has cast a critical eye over the Constitution of Ireland and the way that it affects women.[2] The focus of such enterprises is very much on case law of the Irish superior courts interpreting both the text of the Constitution and, increasingly, its gaps and shadows in which Irish judges have identified a corpus of unenumerated rights held by citizens and those appearing before the courts. These analyses and explorations have enriched our understanding of how women are treated in Irish law and offer an essential element in any critical understanding of the gendering dimension of Irish law. However, these studies have their own gaps and shadows, lacunae into which little, if any, study has been followed, chief amongst which are those which relate to masculinity. This essay is an attempt to outline why a closer study of the

---

* All views expressed are personal.
[1] Y. Scannell, "The Constitution and the Role of Women" in B. Farrell (ed.), *De Valera's Constitution and Ours* (Dublin, Gill and MacMillan, 1988) at p. 123.
[2] Other examples of this genre of scholarship include A. Connelly, *Gender and the Law in Ireland* (Dublin, Oak Tree Press, 1993) and D. Curtin, *Irish Employment Equality Law* (Dublin, Round Hall, 1988).

visions of masculinity within the Constitution of Ireland, as it has been interpreted by Irish courts, is worth undertaking, as well as an effort to outline
some lines of inquiry which might be pursued in that project.

THE ROLE OF LAW IN THE PRACTICE AND PERFORMANCE OF GENDER

One of the overriding concerns of those engaged in gender studies has been
to emphasise the diversity of experiences, aspirations and resources held by
that part of the population linked by the fact that they share the same sex.
Where women are concerned there is very little which links, for example, the
situations of a young, affluent, professional woman in Dublin with that of an
elderly, poor, retired woman living a few miles outside a small town in West
Cork. In some ways what feminists have been seeking to do is to highlight
this irrelevance of the sex of these individuals to a proper appreciation of their
positions and potentialities. However, that strategy has the paradoxical effect
of highlighting the many ways in which this irrelevant factor is, while merely
contingently significant in theory, often powerfully relevant to the ways in
which they are treated by individuals, by social structures and by the State.
To give one example, although anyone can be sexually assaulted, rape and
indecent assault remain largely crimes against women and so, irrespective of
their age, social status and location, this is a risk which is shared by women
to an extent that their male counterparts do not experience.

Thus one of the great challenges for feminist activists and scholars has been
to develop a sophisticated analysis which recognises the heterogeneity of
female experience without denying the social relevance of characteristics
which are shared by women as a group. For many purposes, this analysis need
not take a position on whether those shared experiences are somehow essentially linked with femininity or whether they are socially constructed and
imposed on women or adopted by them; so long as these shared traits, aspirations and social expectations are used as a basis for treatment which disadvantages women this common experience is a sufficient condition to allow
strategies for change and reform to be pursued. In developing such strategies,
many feminists have pointed out that a central feature of the social construction of relations between women, which both recognises and disguises diversity, is to construct a hierarchy of traits and of behaviours according to which
women are ranked. Various archetypes, from the Madonna to the whore, are
invoked in such a way that individual women can be graded against these
standards, and can be threatened with loss of status if they slip from their current position and be rewarded (or punished) with the degree of social appro-
bation that accompanies their present rank. In this way, the figures of "bad"
women are employed to discipline all women and to punish those who step
out of line. These mechanisms centre on the creation of "norms" which are
inculcated through various forms of education and training of individuals so

that individual women police themselves and others, watching for lapses in a process of self-surveillance. If this account of the power dynamics of identity were complete, it would seem quite fatalistic, offering no possibility for change and evolution, and denying any scope for agency or transformative potential to individuals. However, it should also be noted that for some individuals and some groups the failure to meet the standards promulgated for them is transformed into a positive or at least a defiant act. In this way the failure of the self to improve, to meet the socially ordained standards, is accepted, not merely endured, and may even constitute a deliberate act of resistance to that system of social norms.[3]

The role of law in this process of "normalization" and of resistance is, potentially, an important one. Law is one of the sites at which the self is formed and shaped, along with education, religion, medicine and the other constituents of culture. In this sense, law is a discourse which teaches us and trains us to be what we are and, while it is not the sole constitutive discourse, it is important in this process, partly because it provides certain formal limits within which other discourses operate, and partly because of the status with which it is invested in our society. In short, law has a role in telling us who we are and who we should be, and while law does rest on a coercive potential, legal subjects, when engaging with the law, are reacting to the identities which the law sets out for us. In this sense, law operates as a social contract in which identities are assumed, altered and traded. This process is particularly powerful in the realm of constitutional law because, in defining the boundaries of public power, the nature of the State and the role of the citizen, a constitution claims to be the base from which public power is constituted and, implicitly, on which key aspects of legal personhood are constructed.

These claims, as to the construction of identity through normalisation, the role of law, and of constitutional law in particular, in that process, and the value of scrutinising the claims made by law as a constitutive discourse, provide the underlying methodology for this essay. In their light it is possible to understand why it has been worthwhile looking at the emancipatory promises and coercive threats held out by law for women and men, exploring these to see where the promise is undercut by the threat and where the threat to those women and men at the margins of their sex is used as an inducement to reinforce the stability of gender categories which are inherently unstable. While much of this work that has been done to date has proceeded using the position of women as the focus of study, a similar exercise can and, it is submitted, should be conducted with regard to masculinity.

---

[3] This account of the politics of power in social relations draws heavily on the work of M. Foucault. For more detailed coverage of this theoretical framework, see M. Foucault, *Discipline and Punish: The Birth of the Prison* (transl. A. Sheridan, New York, Random House, 1977) and *History of Sexuality*, (transl. R. Hurley, New York, Random House, 1980).

GENDER AND THE IRISH CONSTITUTION

The text of the Constitution says less directly about men than it does about women. While the Articles which provide that rights relating to the franchise and to citizenship are to be extended without discrimination on grounds of sex apply equally to men and to women, there is no counterpart in the Constitution of the provisions which contain a vision of women's contribution to society or which specify certain categories of women, such as widows, who are to be the special objects of social protection. However, this silence does not mean that there is nothing being said by the Constitution about men. When the Constitution's text is read by the courts, it becomes apparent that a very definite paradigm of masculinity is at play within the Irish legal order. In some ways the contours of masculinity as imagined under the Constitution can be drawn in opposition to those of femininity. However, using the methodology described above, it is possible to discern how masculinity is identified with greater subtly and precision by specifying its proper type, using the core example to discover what is the ideal of Irish manhood under the Constitution.

The starting point for this investigation is the case of *The State (Nicolau) v. An Bord Uchtála*[4] which commenced before the High Court in 1964 and was finally decided by the Supreme Court in 1966. Leontis Nicolau, the applicant, unsuccessfully sought to challenge the making of an adoption order by the Adoption Board on the ground that the legislation under which the Board operated violated various provisions of the Constitution. Nicolau was the natural father of a child born in London in February 1960 to a woman of Irish parents who was an Irish citizen. She had taken the child with his consent to her parents' home in Ireland in June of that year and, while there, began to make preparations to have the child adopted. He was not initially aware of this plan, but when he learned of it he objected strongly to her. Notwithstanding his objections she went ahead, making an application for an adoption order in September 1960, and early the following year she completed the necessary adoption papers. The adoption order was made in September 1961. Nicolau had contacted the Adoption Board through his solicitor in October 1960 saying that it should not take any steps without informing him, but he took no subsequent action until November 1963 when he contacted his solicitor again, setting legal proceedings in motion.

The essence of Nicolau's action was that the Adoption Act 1952 violated rights to equality and to family life under the Constitution. The provisions of the statute which he claimed offended the Constitution were those which entitled the natural mother of a child born outside marriage to be heard prior to adoption and required her consent but which provided no role for the natural father of such a child. Neither the High Court nor the Supreme Court was

---

[4] [1966] IR 567.

prepared to accept any of the arguments made on Nicolau's behalf. The judgment of the Supreme Court was delivered by Walsh J who, having set out the facts of the case, dealt with an argument based on the Adoption Act itself before turning to Nicolau's challenge to its validity. His first argument, based on the guarantee of equality under Article 40.1 of the Constitution, was dismissed on the ground that "inequality may or must result from some special abilities or from some deficiency or from some special need and it is clear that the Article does not envisage or guarantee equal measure in all things to all citizens".[5] When this principle was applied to the Adoption Act it was clear to the court that those persons having rights under the Act could be regarded as having, or capable of having, a moral capacity or social function which differentiated them from persons who were not given any such rights. Walsh J continued:

"When it is considered that an illegitimate child may be begotten by an act of rape, by a callous seduction or by an act of casual commerce by a man with a woman, as well as by the association of a man with a woman in making a common home without marriage in circumstances approximating to those of married life, and that, except in the latter instance, it is rare for a natural father to take any interest in his offspring, it is not difficult to appreciate the difference in moral capacity and social function between the natural father and the several persons described in the subsections in question."[6]

It was accepted in the Supreme Court that Nicolau had lived with the mother of the child as man and wife without marriage for over a year before the birth of the child, that they had worked together in the cafe which he owned and that, while he had not proceeded with legal action in respect of the adoption for somewhat over two years after the adoption had occurred, his delay was largely due to his unwillingness to undermine the health of the mother by subjecting her to additional stress. Shortly after she had completed the adoption formalities she had undergone a significant period of treatment in Ireland following a nervous breakdown. In sum, while there were a number of categories of natural fathers who might not wish to have anything to do with their offspring, Nicolau did not fall within these categories. Nevertheless, by invoking variations on the theme of "bad father", the rhetoric of the court displaces the reality of Nicolau's situation and deprives him of the basis on which his equality challenge was premised. It is noticeable that there is no suggestion that a woman who gives her child for adoption is ever motivated by concerns other than altruism and a desire to further the welfare of the child. Nicolau is squeezed between the over-inclusive category of the uncaring, distant and unreliable natural father and the under-inclusive category of the natural mother who is always, first and foremost, a caring parent.

---

[5] *Ibid.*, at 639.
[6] *Ibid.*, at 641.

The judgments in the High Court are, it should be added, far less sympathetic to Nicolau's individual circumstances. Murnaghan J, in earlier proceedings, pointed out when considering whether Nicolau could make arguments based on the rights of his child that "it is more than probable that [Nicolau's] interests and those of the child conflict".[7] Teevan J added in the same proceedings that "[Nicolau's] attitude [in October 1960] and later appears to have been devoted to the assertion of authority with a coincidental absence of concern for the immediate condition or welfare of the child, hardly consistent with feelings of parental affection",[8] adding later that "it must be said that the prosecutor seems to establish rights [based on the interests of his child] for his 'own gratification or benefit'".[9] Similarly Henchy J found Nicolau an unappealing applicant, as he made clear when setting out why his tardy conduct disentitled him to the order of *certiorari* sought:

> "He knew the child to have been abandoned to a rescue society for adoption. . . .
> [H]e must have believed that the child was in a home run by the Rescue Society or
> in some such place. Yet he was prepared indefinitely to ignore the child—its health,
> its education, its religious upbringing, its welfare—until the mother should choose
> in her own time to return to him. Three years elapsed before she returned to him.
> During that time the prosecutor does not seem to have shown any interest in the
> child, which is all the more surprising when he now relies on the mother's nervous
> ill-health during that time."[10]

One of the most important background factors in the *Nicolau* case is that the mother of the child had left him initially, was unwilling to marry him as matters stood and had refused to leave the child in his custody, because she wished him to be admitted to the Catholic Church and wished to see the child raised in that faith as well. Although the Supreme Court did not exclude the possibility of Nicolau relying on constitutional rights guaranteed to citizens by reason of his non-Irish origin,[11] in contrast to the High Court,[12] Nicolau was an outsider and in many ways alien to what are seen as the standard Irish traditions. The figure of the non-Irish, non-Catholic man who claims rights over a Catholic Irish child is one which was not calculated to inspire sympathy, and there is a sense in which these traits overwhelm his desire to take an active interest in the child, which is expressed in the way that his situation is treated by the court as analogous to that of a man who fathered a child "in an act of casual commerce with a woman". The Irish courts in this case are overwhelmingly concerned with legitimacy but once the child born outside marriage has been adopted the focus of this concern is on the legitimacy of Nicolau's position. His inconvenient reality having been erased, the courts can

---

[7] [1966] IR 567, at 590–1.
[8] *Ibid.*, at 596.
[9] *Ibid.*, at 602.
[10] *Ibid.*, at 613.
[11] [1966] IR at 645.
[12] [1966] IR at 591–2, 599–600, 615–17.

send out the message that men are either fathers and married or else they should disappear, and that there will be no space for or recognition of those who do not conform to this model. These signals are amplified where their traditions are alien to Irish ways; their constitutional claims are difficult to reconcile with what Henchy J described as "a Constitution of the Irish people for the Irish people".[13]

One way in which the treatment of masculinity in this judgment might be analysed is as a form of performance. Gender roles are established as scripts to be played out by the individual subjects within a social system. The faithfulness with which they realise their task is constantly scrutinised both by themselves and by others, establishing multiple but largely coherent directorial voices. There are more than two gender roles, however, assigned on the basis of the apparent physical sex of the subject. Gender interacts with other variables such as social-economic origin and status, race, religion, nationality, age, degree of disability, to give examples of the variety of social norms and expectations we experience. In some circumstances gender will be a determining factor, but in other situations it may be overshadowed by the other variables which inform these performances. In this case Nicolau is penalised for being a man; it is clear that had he been the female parent he would have had a privileged voice in the adoption proceedings envisaged by the legislation under review. However, he is also penalised because of his social status—had he been married to the child's mother, his claims would have merited the constitutional protection they failed to attract in this case—and, to some extent, because of his failure to accord with the expectations associated with young, Irish Catholic men of the time. He did not display guilt in regard to his on-going liaison with the child's mother, nor did he disown her when the result of that relationship was pregnancy. His presence before the court produces two, contradictory strategies on the part of the members of the High Court and the Supreme Court, though it should be added that these operate to the same end. In the High Court his actions are transposed to the script that he should have played out, in that his failure to convert to Roman Catholicism, his reticence to pursue litigation while the child's mother was undergoing psychiatric treatment and his agreement to allow her to leave London for her parents' home in Ireland with the child are all seen as the uncaring and irresponsible acts which could be expected from an unmarried father. Indeed, the litigation which might appear to undermine the tenability of that thesis is re-cast as an attempt to exercise authority, conducted without any true parental concern for the welfare of his child. In the Supreme Court this reading is abandoned and the integrity of Nicolau is no longer called into question. However, the concerns which run through the judgments in the lower court surface here in a more abstract form, detached from Nicolau personally, but conspicuously linked to his suspect status, the man

---

[13] *Ibid.*, at 617.

who refused to play his part. And while he has confounded the expectations of the systems of social meaning within which the Supreme Court operates, the Constitution and the maintenance of true social order cannot allow for an admission of slippage between the role assigned and the script played out.

The same dynamic is evident in a later decision of the Irish superior courts concerning the constitutionality of legislation which supposedly penalised men in comparison with women. In the case of *Norris* v. *Attorney General*,[14] the Irish courts wrestled with the homosexual man, and in doing so they marked out, for constitutional purposes, the nature of his longings, and indeed a wider economy of masculine desire and identity. In this case the Supreme Court held by a majority that legislation criminalising same-sex sexual activities between men was constitutional. David Norris, the plaintiff in the case, had claimed rights to privacy and to bodily integrity, and asserted in addition that the relevant legislation failed to uphold equality before the law. Rather than analyse the doctrinal arguments used by the opposing sides in the Supreme Court, it is more useful for the purpose of this essay to study the homosexual constituted by the court because the nature of homosexuality was a crucial element in the complex of "facts" which underlie those doctrinal debates.

Writing for the majority of the court, O'Higgins CJ reviewed the moral and social status and the probable consequences of male homosexuality. He noted that Christian teaching regarded it as morally wrong, while society had for centuries viewed it as an offence against nature and a very serious crime. He stated that exclusive homosexuality, whether congenital or acquired, could result in great distress and unhappiness for the individual, leading to depression, despair and suicide. In addition, he observed that the homosexually inclined could be led into a homosexual lifestyle which could become habitual, and that male homosexual conduct had led elsewhere to a spread of all forms of venereal diseases and was currently a significant public health problem in England. Finally, he stated that homosexual conduct could be inimical to marriage and was *per se* harmful to it as an institution. He went on to hold that "on the ground of the Christian nature of our state and on the grounds that the deliberate practice of homosexuality is morally wrong, that it is damaging to health both of individuals and the public, and, finally, that it is potentially damaging to the institution of marriage, I can find no inconsistency with the Constitution in the laws which make such conduct criminal".[15] The minority of the Court dissented strongly on the ground that Norris had a right to privacy outside marriage, and McCarthy J went on to note the potential tension between purposive readings of the Constitution on the basis of Christian as opposed to democratic approaches.

In order to understand the homosexual, the members of the Court situated him within legal discourse, establishing the script which he must play out, by

---

[14] [1984] IR 36. See also observations on *Norris* by A. Hunt, "Evaluating Constitutions—The Irish Constitution and the Limits of Constitutionalism" in this volume.

[15] *Ibid.*, at 63.

placing him alongside various known figures, namely, the lesbian, the married couple, the adulterer and the fornicator. In addition, they interrogated him to determine if he was truly a homosexual or merely a simulacrum, one whose homosexuality was a pose or an affectation which had been acquired and had become habitual. The lesbian is invoked because Norris claimed that to criminalise sexual relations between men, while those of women were not criminal, violated the constitutional guarantee of equality. The Chief Justice dismissed this ground in relation to the crime of buggery on the ground that it can be committed only by men,[16] and while he admitted the possibility of comparison in relation to the crime of gross indecency, he found that the difference in treatment was permissible because it reflected a difference in capacity or social function based on the difference between the sexes and the fact that sexual conduct between females does not pose the social problems of such conduct between males.[17] This assertion reiterates common sense that male homosexuals, unlike lesbians, are promiscuous and sexually aggressive and that their acts directly attack social order. Lesbians are as invisible to the judiciary as they are to the legislature, while male homosexuality is a highly visible and monstrous sexuality.

When set alongside the married couple, the observations of the Chief Justice that homosexuality can be acquired by those inclined to it, though not congenitally homosexual, and that homosexuality is inimical to marriage become highly fruitful. The married state is the uniquely proper site for the expression of sexuality, and it is clear that no other form of expression of desire enjoys judicial blessing.[18] However, in *Norris* the court picks out male homosexuality as the antithesis of marriage, giving it a singular status not accorded to adultery or to fornication. The homosexual male entices weak but married men from "marriages which might have been successfully and happily consummated"[19] into individual and social sterility. The man who engages in homosexuality is driven by desire which cannot be satisfied in a productive fashion, undermining the basic unit of society. (There is no suggestion that the lesbian-inclined wife might leave her marriage in response to the temptations offered by the congenitally lesbian.) The dangerous and excessive nature of that desire is underlined by the fact that those men who are potentially happily married can be lured by the prospect of short-term and unstable liaisons which offer nothing other than the satiation of these desires.

---

[16] Giving the definition of the crime this fixed meaning overlooks both its history (e.g. buggery at one stage included intercourse between Christians and infidels, see A. Goldstein, "History, Homosexuality and Political Values" (1988) 97 *Yale Law J* 1073, 1083 at n. 61), and the fluidity subsequentially evidenced in another traditionally male-only crime, rape, by the Criminal Law (Rape Amendment) Act 1990, s. 4 of which makes statutory rape a gender-neutral crime.

[17] *Supra* n. 15, at 59.

[18] See L. Flynn, "Missing Mary McGee: The Narration of Woman in Constitutional Adjudication" in G. Quinn, A. Ingram, and S. Livingstone, (eds.), *Justice and Legal Theory in Ireland* (Dublin, Oak Tree Press, 1995), at pp. 99–101.

[19] *Supra* n. 15, at 69.

In fact, the formulae employed by the Chief Justice, suggesting, as they do, the possibility that the attractive qualities of sexual pleasures between men might wean many married men away from marital relations, imply an anxiety about the possibility that all men may carry within themselves some potential for homosexuality.

While the Chief Justice focuses on lesbians and married couples in comparison with homosexual males, Henchy J, one of the judges in the minority, examines the relative status of male homosexuals on the one hand and, on the other, adulterers and fornicators in relation to Norris' claims to a right of privacy. While both groups engage in sex outside marriage, only the former are subjected to a furtive and guilty lifestyle in which they endure ridicule and harassment while risking their careers and social lives generally.[20] O'Higgins CJ deals with this briefly, merely noting that the behaviour of the latter group creates different social problems and, indeed, no social problem which is similar to that of homosexual activity, so that there is no constitutionally prohibited discrimination here. Indeed, Henchy J takes this view when, having dealt with the privacy argument, he dismisses the claims based on equality for similar reasons to those of the Chief Justice.[21]

When reading *Norris* to identify the scripts of masculinity which are advanced within the judgment, it is worth observing initially that Norris as a person, a figure who rarely features within these texts, was at the time his action started a lecturer in English at Trinity College, Dublin, a noted Joycean scholar and a colourful public figure. His decision to commence litigation had been a difficult and a brave one to take[22] but, in a fashion similar to that of Nicolau, this was a plaintiff who carried a faint whiff of the exotic within a forum steeped in Irish and Catholic (notwithstanding the avowed Christian nature of the dogmas pronounced) common sense. Seen in this light, his portrayal in the judgments reveals as much about Irish masculinity as his own juxtaposition with other figures did about male homosexuality. Masculinity is linked to a focused, linear and conservative desire, in contrast to the wide-ranging and aggressive version of homosexuality which the Supreme Court deploys. This phallocentric vision of masculine desire is, of course, at odds with classical (and indeed feminist) representations of female sexuality as free-flowing. At the same time, there is a possibility of slippage, a weakness or a kink, which excites the anxiety of the court. The danger of men being enticed from marriage to the transient sexual pleasures of another man provokes a homosexual panic from within the court.

[20] *Supra* n. 15, at 69.
[21] *Ibid.*, at 70–1.
[22] V. Freedman, *Cities of David: The Life of David Norris* (Dublin, Basement Press, 1995).

CONCLUSION

What is important to appreciate at this point is that the differences drawn out by the court are not merely a social discourse, competing with others in a bid to claim veracity. The court, by invoking the founding law of the culture and the State, takes to itself a unique power to tell the truth of masculinity or, more precisely, of masculinities. From reading *Nicolau* and *Norris*, we have a better appreciation of what it is to be a proper Irish man and what the Constitution will recognise as such. There is no unique way in which masculinity will be played out against this backdrop—as noted earlier, there are a number of other variables which will interact with and influence the script of the individual's gender role—but boundaries are established whose transgression, even if it does not actively involve legal retribution, identifies male outlaws. In short, the Constitution must be actively invoked if we are to learn what it is, what it should be, to be an Irish man.

12

Equality Guarantees in Irish Constitutional Law—The Myth of Constitutionalism and the "Neutral" State

SIOBHÁN MULLALLY

INTRODUCTION

The idea of a constitution representing a social contract has ancient origins. In its various forms, it attempts to explain and justify power relations between rulers and the ruled. Society or the State, or both, are presented as being a product of binding mutual undertakings between individuals or groups. The terms of this agreement or contract establish obligations to obedience on the part of the subjects and may impose limits on the powers of government. For some theorists, the social contract is the product of an actual event—the coronation of a monarch, for instance. For others, the contract is a fictional device, either hypothetical (it is *as if* a contract was actually agreed upon) or ideal (the terms of the contract provide a normative ideal against which the legitimacy of government may be judged). It is in this last sense that the term is used in this essay. The question posed is whether or not Irish constitutional law and practice have served this normative ideal.

Contract theory has enjoyed a revival in recent years. Within law and legal theory, this revival is evident in jurisprudential debates on "constitutionalism".[1] Constitutionalism is usually used to describe a particular genus of constitutional system: the Constitution is viewed as a solemn covenant between the government and the people, and constitutional law and practice control and limit the powers of government. In addition, constitutionalism generally involves a declaration of individual rights. Of particular relevance to this essay are the liberal commitments to liberty and equality. These commitments frequently conflict.

---

[1] The influence of contract theory can be seen beyond academic writings and jurisprudential debates. The effective implementation of human rights law, for example has increasingly been linked with "good governance".

An acceptable "accommodation" between these two values has not yet been achieved in Irish constitutional law. The failure to reach this accommodation, I suggest, is exacerbated by the enduring public/private dichotomy within constitutional law and practice. The division between public and private spheres, central to liberal theory, still persists within this body of rules. As a result, there is a marked reluctance to limit private freedoms in the name of equality, despite the "absolute" nature of the constitutional guarantee of equality. Such are the contradictions and normative conflicts inherent within liberal theory and practice. If the normative ideals of constitutionalism are to be realised and the terms of the social contract fulfilled, it is clear that such conflicts must be avoided. It will be necessary, as Hutchinson and Petter argue, to replace the proclaimed "neutrality" of the liberal State with a substantive vision of social justice.[2]

LIBERALISM, NEUTRALITY AND PUBLIC/PRIVATE DICHOTOMIES

The liberal State is perceived as being a "neutral" State. Contemporary liberalism expresses its commitment to liberty by sharply separating the public power of the State from the private relationships of civil society, and by setting strict limits on the State's ability to intervene in private life.[3] These limitations on the power of the State to intervene in the exercise of "private liberty" provide "escape from the surveillance and interference of public officials", thereby "multiplying possibilities for private associations and combinations".[4] The priority accorded to the "right" over the "good"—the belief that individuals within "civil society" should be left "free" to pursue whatever ends they choose subject only to the proviso that they do not "harm" others—provides the justificatory basis for a number of the protected freedoms within liberal constitutional orders. This justificatory basis is not always made explicit; the idea of public and private spheres is often hived off from the freedom-based argument for the limited State and is applied in an apparently descriptive, yet ultimately question-begging, way to particular activities and institutions.[5] Once a sphere is labelled "private", normative conclusions that no intervention is appropriate are drawn, usually without the full argument for non-intervention being spelled out. The attribution of privacy which should be the conclusion of the argument is taken for the argument itself.[6] Difficulties arise, however, where the liberal commitment to equality comes

---

[2] A. C. Hutchinson and A. Petter, "Private Rights/Public Wrongs" 38 (1988) *University of Toronto Law Journal* 278.

[3] W. Kymlicka, *Contemporary Political Philosophy* (Oxford, Clarendon, 1990), at 251

[4] N. Rosenblum, *Another Liberalism: Romanticism and the Reconstruction of Liberal Thought* (Cambridge, Harvard University Press, 1987).

[5] See E. Fraser and N. Lacey, *The Politics of Community* (London, Harvester Wheatsheaf, 1993), at 73.

[6] *Ibid.*

into conflict with the exercise of "private liberty". The State's failure to "defend and vindicate" equality rights is frequently justified by appeals to the public/private divide and to the limited scope of constitutional norms. Thus, the distinction between public and private spheres has served to render invisible the "harms" suffered by women within the private sphere. Gender-neutral rights discourse fails to address this problem, because it is, itself, predicated on a public/private divide which is deeply gendered.

THE PUBLIC AND THE PRIVATE: GENDERED DIVISIONS

The dichotomy between the private and the public has been central to almost two centuries of feminist writing and political struggle. Carole Pateman argues that it is, ultimately, what the feminist movement is about.[7] As MacKinnon states:[8]

"For women the measure of the intimacy has been the measure of the oppression. This is why feminism has had to explode the private. This is why feminism has seen the personal as political. The private is public for those for whom the personal is political. In this sense, for women there is no private, either normatively or empirically."

Feminist writings on the public/private divide can be divided into what Gavison refers to as "internal" and "external" critiques.[9] Internal critiques purport that a given version of the public/private distinction is mistaken (it creates negative effects) and should be reconstructed (so as to avoid these negative effects). "Beyond this general criticism, however, this challenge acknowledges that the distinction can be used in beneficial ways."[10] For "internal" critics certain matters ought to remain private: it is assumed that within a private sphere, properly defined, women will be able to act autonomously and freely. The role of law is to protect women from undue pressure within this autonomous sphere and provide effective remedies where autonomy is infringed; consent is often seen as a key tool in defining autonomous action.

For external critics the personal is political (or public) and the label "private" merely a tool of oppression:

"When the law of privacy restricts intrusions into intimacy, it bars change in control over that intimacy. The existing distribution of power and resources within the private sphere will be precisely what the law of privacy exists to protect."[11]

---

[7] C. Pateman, "Feminist Critique of the Public/Private Dichotomy" in A. Phillips (ed.), *Feminism and Equality* (Oxford, Blackwell, 1987).

[8] C. A. MacKinnon, *Towards a Feminist Theory of the State* (Cambridge, Mass., Harvard University Press, 1989), at 191.

[9] R. Gavison, "Feminism and the Public/Private Distinction" (1993) 45 *Stanford L Rev.* 1.

[10] *Ibid.*, at 3.

[11] *Ibid.*

External critiques challenge the distinction itself, claiming "that there is no useful, helpful or valid way to draw the distinction".[12]

Some would argue that rights discourse serves only to perpetuate the idea of "separate spheres of justice". Certain matters are rendered private, either through silence (the failure of law to recognise particular rights-claims) or through the invocation of a "privatising" right (autonomy, freedom, privacy). Thus, some claims are protected at the expense of others—those others are rendered "invisible" to law. Feminists and liberals disagree about where and why the dividing line is to be drawn between the two spheres. The major difficulty confronting liberalism lies in identifying the line that separates the domain of individual liberty from the domain of "state action". Allan Hutchinson argues that this problem is less daunting for proponents of natural law who can at least claim that the boundary is a product of "the natural order of social life and justice". For positivists, however, the problem appears to be an intractable one:

> "While naturalists seek to 'find' that elusive line, positivists struggle over where to 'draw' the line. The line-drawers may be a more advanced and sophisticated lot than the line-finders, but they are part of the same intellectual heritage and political tradition. Moreover, the line-drawers tend to hide rather than dispense with their naturalist affiliations; they draw their lines in accordance with an undisclosed map of ideological commitments."[13]

Recently, the Constitution Review Group considered where that dividing line should be "drawn" or "found" within Irish constitutional law and, in particular, within the constitutional guarantee of equality. The narrow wording of the equality guarantee and its interpretation by the courts have been widely criticised by both academic and political commentators. Of particular concern here are the following questions addressed by the Review Group: (a) whether the obligation to respect equality should be directly enforceable against persons or bodies other than the State; and (b) whether the State's obligation should encompass a duty to ensure respect for equality by persons and bodies other than the State. These questions and the response of the Review Group serve to highlight the tensions that arise in a liberal State between equality protection and the preservation of "private liberty".

---

[12] R. Gavison, "Feminism and the Public/Private Distinction" (1993) 45 *Stanford L Rev.* 1., at 3.

[13] A. C. Hutchinson and A. Petter, *supra* n. 2, at 284.

EQUAL BEFORE THE LAW : A "CORE NORM"?

Article 40.1[14] is a general guarantee of equality for all citizens and is a free-standing equality norm. Equality before the law is guaranteed in itself, not merely in the context of a threat to other constitutional rights. Its scope of application is, therefore, potentially very broad. However, although Article 40.1 is phrased in absolute terms, equality is not identified within the Irish Constitution as being a "core norm". As a result, it is frequently in danger, as the Report of the Constitution Review Group notes, "of losing out in the inevitable boundary adjustment between it and other rights".[15]

A change in the status of the equality norm was considered by the Review Group. However, it was felt inappropriate to introduce into the Constitution a form of "ranking" of fundamental rights. Any reconciliation of conflicting rights-claims was more properly regarded as a matter for the courts.[16] At a later point, however, the Review Group argued against an extension of the equality guarantee, *inter alia*, on the ground that it would constitute an "unjustified intrusion" upon individual autonomy and might conflict with other fundamental rights, in particular the rights to freedom of expression and association. A tension can be seen here between the competing, and in this case conflicting, commitments to liberty and equality. Rather than leaving this conflict to resolution by the judiciary, the Group appears to have engaged in a form of ranking of fundamental rights. In doing so, it identified liberty, rather than equality, as being the "core" constitutional value.

MAINTAINING THE DIVIDE—REPORT OF
THE CONSTITUTION REVIEW GROUP

Jurisprudence on the question whether the obligation to respect equality should be directly enforceable against persons or bodies other than the State is not very well developed within the Irish legal system. It is generally presumed that constitutions regulate relations between the individual and the State. Traditional versions of social contract theory support this view. The Irish judiciary, however, has interpreted many of the fundamental rights provisions within the Constitution as being capable of "horizontal application".

---

[14] Art. 40.1 provides: "All citizens shall, as human persons, be held equal before the law. This shall not be held to mean that the State shall not in its enactments have due regard to differences of capacity, physical and moral, and of social function."

[15] *Report of the Constitution Review Group* (Dublin, Stationery Office, 1996), at 222. The recent decision of the Supreme Court in *In Re Article 26 and the Employment Equality Bill 1996*, is a good example of this (Supreme Court, 118/97, as is *In Re Article 26 and the Equal Status Bill 1996*, (Supreme Court, 156, 97)). An attempt to extend the scope of equality protection to persons with disabilities was held to be unconstitutional, *inter alia*, on the ground that it constituted an "unjust attack" on employers' rights to carry on a business and to earn a livelihood.

[16] *Ibid.*, at 223.

In a number of cases, the courts have imposed constitutional obligations on non-State actors and awarded damages for breach of constitutional rights against such actors. In *Meskell v. CIE*,[17] Walsh J remarked that constitutional rights could be protected or enforced by action, even though such action may not fit into any of the ordinary forms of action in either common law or equity. The courts have generally taken the view that the law of tort provides adequate protection for personal rights.[18] However, in the absence of a common law or statutory cause of action, an individual may sue directly for a breach of a constitutional right. The majority of these cases have revolved around the State's duty, under Article 40.3, "to defend and vindicate" the personal rights of its citizens.

The case of *Murtagh Properties Ltd v. Cleary*[19] could be identified as beginning the chain. The defendant, a trade union secretary, was found to have a duty to respect the constitutional rights of others, in particular the "unenumerated right" to earn a livelihood.[20] In *Meskell v. CIE*, the Supreme Court had no difficulty in imputing to trade unions a duty to respect constitutional rights. The particular right at issue in this case was the implied right of dissociation under Article 40.6. In *Glover v. BLN Ltd*,[21] it was held that the constitutional principles of natural justice were enforceable against a non-State entity. Article 40.3, the court stated, was a guarantee of fair procedures. The defendants, in exercising their powers of dismissal under a contract of employment, had a duty to act accordingly.[22] As Walsh J stated:

> " . . . public policy and the dictates of constitutional justice require that statutes, regulations or agreements setting up machinery for taking decisions which may affect rights or impose liabilities should be construed as providing for fair procedures."[23]

In *The State (Lynch) v. Cooney*,[24] Henchy J suggested, albeit *obiter*, that if Radio Telifís Éireann were to discriminate unfairly in the allotment of broadcasting time for party political broadcasts, it would be in breach of Article

---

[17] [1973] IR 121.

[18] In *O'Hanrahan v. Merck Sharp and Dohme* [1988] ILRM 629, the Supreme Court (*per* Henchy J) agreed that the tort of nuisance relied on by the plaintiffs was an implementation of the State's duties under Art. 40.3 to defend and vindicate their personal and property rights. See also *Murphy v. Ireland* [1996] 2 ILRM 461.

[19] [1972] IR 330.

[20] Although Art. 40.1 was also invoked by the plaintiffs, Kenny J concluded that it was not applicable in this case because of the constraints of the "human personality" doctrine.

[21] [1973] IR 388.

[22] The contract of employment in question contained a clause allowing for the plaintiff's employment to be terminated under certain circumstances, including where he was guilty of serious misconduct or serious neglect in the performance of his duties. For such dismissal to take effect, there had to be unanimous agreement on the part of the board of directors. The plaintiff was dismissed on the basis of this clause, but was not informed of the nature of the allegations against him. Walsh J concluded that it was necessarily an implied term of the contract that this enquiry and determination should be fairly conducted.

[23] *Supra* n. 21, at 425.

[24] [1982] IR 337.

40.1. In *Conway* v. *Irish National Teachers' Organisation and Others*,[25] it was held that exemplary damages could be awarded in the case of a breach of a constitutional right, even where the defendants were neither servants nor agents of the government or the executive. At issue in this case was the plaintiff's right to free primary education guaranteed by Article 42.4.

More recently, however, in *Carna Foods Ltd* v. *Eagle Star Insurance Co (Ireland) Ltd*,[26] McCracken J refused to apply constitutional norms to purely commercial relationships between private parties. It was submitted that the defendant had a constitutional duty to give reasons for its decisions regarding the non-renewal and cancellation of the plaintiff's insurance policies. Walsh J's dictum in *Glover* was invoked in support of this contention. McCracken J was not persuaded, however. The principles of natural or constitutional justice, he argued, do not apply to decisions taken in the context of a private contractual relationship. To decide otherwise would constitute a "serious interference in the contractual position of parties in a commercial contract". McCracken J was clearly of the opinion that the relationship between the parties in this case differed significantly from that in *Glover*. In fact, it differed so greatly that it came within a separate sphere of justice—one to which the ordinary principles of natural or constitutional justice did not apply. On appeal to the Supreme Court,[27] counsel for the defendants submitted that authorities in regard to "Public Law enquiries", such as *Glover*, were of no relevance to the case. Although the court did not discuss the constitutional issues, it was clear that the need to protect the autonomy of "freely contracting parties" was foremost in its mind.[28] The appeal was dismissed and separate spheres maintained.

Whether or not the equality guarantee is capable of horizontal application remains unclear. The possibility has not been ruled out. However, the Irish judiciary has displayed a marked reluctance to apply Article 40.1, preferring to rely on other substantive constitutional rights where possible. Questions as to the precise scope of the equality guarantee have thus been avoided.

The wording of Article 40.1 and its interpretation by the courts present a number of difficulties for any attempted application against a non-State actor. First, there is the "human personality" doctrine. The scope of the equality guarantee is severely restricted by the divisions and dichotomies that strike through the "citizen" protected by Article 40.1. The subject of the equality guarantee seems to be peculiarly devoid of a social context. It is certainly not the "embedded" self of communitarian philosophies. A distinction is made between "essential" rather than "contingent" features of a citizen's existence.

---

[25] [1991] ILRM 497. See also *Crowley* v. *Ireland* [1980] IR 102.

[26] [1995] 1 IR 526.

[27] Unreported, 28 May 1997.

[28] In his conclusions, Lynch J stated that one can imply a term into a contract only when the implied term gives effect to the "true intentions" of all the parties to the contract—an obvious deferral to the presumed consensual nature of contractual relationships.

It is the "essence" of the human person that is granted an entitlement to equality before law. The contingencies of daily existence are not deemed to be deserving of such protection. This narrow interpretation of Article 40.1 emerged for the first time in *Macauley* v. *Minister for Posts and Telegraphs*.[29] It was reiterated in *Quinn's Supermarket* v. *Attorney General* by Walsh J:

> " . . . this guarantee refers to human persons for what they are in themselves rather than to any lawful activities, trades or pursuits which they may engage in or follow."[30]

In the same case, Kenny J stated that the guarantee "does not relate to trading activities or to the hours during which persons may carry on business for neither of these is connected with the essentials of the concept of human personality".[31] Again we see the idea of "separate spheres of justice" serving to limit the scope of equality protection.

The "human personality" doctrine has been widely criticised and seems to be losing favour within judicial circles.[32] As is noted by Kelly, restricting the application of the equality guarantee, "to 'man' qualified only by race, religion, social position and not much else seems to put a constitutional premium on his remaining so far as possible in a state of nature".[33] The very word "citizen", it is argued, "carries within it the recognition that the subjects of the legal system exist within a society".[34] The Constitution Review Group recommended that the words "as human persons" should be removed from the equality guarantee. This restriction, they noted, is not found in other constitutional orders or in international instruments to which Ireland is a party.[35] It has served within the Irish jurisdiction to restrict unduly the effectiveness of equality protection.

Secondly difficulties arise from the wording of Article 40.1. The words "equal before the law" and the reference to "the State . . . in its enactments" suggest that Article 40.1 applies only to the State. Similarly, it is suggested that Article 44.2.3 (which opens with the words "The State") does not apply to private acts of religious discrimination.[36] In *Conway* damages were awarded against the defendants (non-State actors) for breach of the plaintiff's right to free primary education, despite the fact that the relevant constitutional provision (Article 42.4) is directly addressed to the State. In addition, as Casey points out (referring to the decision of the Supreme Court in *Meskell* v. *CIE*), it would seem just as legitimate to read Article 40.1 as implying a broad right

[29] [1966] IR 345.

[30] [1972] IR 1 at 14.

[31] *Ibid.*, at 31. See also *Murtagh Properties Ltd* v. *Cleary* [1972] IR 330 (*per* Kenny J).

[32] See generally G. Hogan and G. Whyte (eds.), *J. M. Kelly, The Irish Constitution* (3rd edn., Dublin, Butterworths, 1994), at 723.

[33] *Ibid.*, at 722.

[34] *Ibid.*, n. 53.

[35] *Supra* n. 15, at 224.

[36] Art. 44.2.3 provides: "The State shall not impose any disabilities or make any discrimination on the ground of religious profession, belief or status."

to equal treatment as to read Article 40.6.1. iii as implying a right of dissociation.

Whether or not Article 40.1 prohibits private acts of discrimination, it seems clear that the State could not lend its aid to private arrangements which worked on arbitrary discrimination.[37] The consensual nature of private relationships is frequently invoked to justify "non-intervention" on the part of the State. However, difficulties arise where an agreement is not voluntarily adhered to and can only be effected by judicial enforcement. If it is accepted that the State acts through its judicial arm, then Article 40.1 must be interpreted as precluding the courts from lending their weight to discriminatory practices.[38]

The existing institutional materials do not give decisive guidance on these questions. Whether the existing equality guarantee should be amended so as explicitly to allow for "horizontal applications" was considered by the Constitution Review Group. It was noted that discrimination is often practised by persons and bodies other than the State. Non-State actors such as trade unions, banks and insurance companies exercise enormous influence and control over individual lives. A more extensive obligation to respect equality would serve to afford constitutional protection to the victims of such discrimination. However, it was felt that an extended obligation of this kind would raise a number of difficulties—both conceptual and practical.

A Constitution, it was argued, regulates the relations between an individual and the State. Relations between private individuals do not raise issues of constitutional rights or wrongs. Indeed, it was felt that it would be difficult to identify to whom, other than the State, the obligation to respect equality should apply. It is hard to believe that this difficulty is insurmountable. Legislatures in many jurisdictions, albeit not yet the Irish legislature, have succeeded in identifying a wide sphere of activity within which individuals may claim a right to equal treatment. Perhaps if greater imagination were applied to the equality gaurantee we would not be without a comprehensive anti-discrimination law. No reference was made by the Review Group to the significant body of case law in which relations between non-State actors have been identified by the courts as raising constitutional issues. The influence of

---

[37] J. Casey, *Constitutional Law in Ireland* (2nd edn., London, Sweet & Maxwell, 1992), at 379 (invoking *McMahon* v. *Leahy* [1984] IR 525 in support of this argument).

[38] See e.g. the US case, *Shelley* v. *Kraemer*, 334 US 1. A similar issue arises with regard to Art. 44.2.3. Because it opens with the words "The State", it is argued that it does not outlaw discrimination by private individuals or bodies. In response to this, Casey argues that the State also acts through the courts. A court may not, therefore, ratify acts of religious discrimination by private parties. It is unlikely that a decision such as that in *Schlegel* v. *Corcoran and Gross* [1942] IR 19—upholding a refusal to sub-lease property for reasons of anti-semiticism—would be followed nowadays. See J. Casey *supra* n. 37, at 568. As Kelly commented of Gavan Duffy J's judgment in this case, "This is the dark side of a remarkable judge" (*supra* n. 32, at 1105, n. 16). It is arguable that judicial endorsement of *Schlegel* is contrary to Art. 44.2.3, if it is accepted that that provision precludes the State, acting through its judicial arm, from lending its weight to religious or racial discrimination between private parties.

classical social contract theory was clearly evident in the limited role accorded to the Constitution in the Report of the Review Group. This is particularly disappointing, given that the Irish judiciary has, on a number of occasions, displayed a willingness to transcend the public/private dichotomies of constitutional law and practice. The difficulty seems to lie, not in the ability of a constitutional text to regulate relations between non-State actors, but rather in a reluctance to recognise a general right to equal treatment. While a general right to equal treatment would be unworkable, it was open to the Review group to identify spheres of activity within which a right to equal treatment (and the corresponding duties) would exist.

A concern to protect against "unjustified intrusions" upon individual autonomy was evident. As was noted earlier, equality is not a core constitutional value. In this instance, liberty won out over equality and the Review Group eventually concluded against an extension of the existing guarantee. No reason was given for distinguishing between the degree of protection afforded by Article 40.1 and that afforded by other fundamental rights provisions which have been applied "horizontally".

A remaining question is whether the State may be held responsible for "inaction" in the face of private discrimination or, to put it another way, whether a failure to provide an effective remedy against private acts of discrimination attracts the responsibility of the State? This could only be the case, first, if it was accepted that Article 40.1 guaranteed all citizens a general right to equal treatment and, secondly, if the State has a duty to "defend and vindicate" this right against infringement by non-State actors.

The existing equality guarantee applies to any exercise of State authority. All arms of the State are bound by Article 40.1: the executive, the legislature and the judiciary. In addition, the state may impose an obligation on other persons and bodies to respect equality, as it has done, for example, in the field of employment. It is not clear, however, whether the State is *required* by the Constitution to do so. The existing jurisprudence does not provide decisive guidance on this point. The possibility of extending the scope of equality protection along these lines was considered by the Review Group.

As equality is a fundamental democratic value it was argued that the State should ensure that it is generally respected. Equality, it was noted, is not "solely a matter of individual effort". It involves "the development of strategies which would actively promote *a civil society* based on principles of social, economic and political inclusion".[39] An obvious strategy would be to bring private discriminatory practices within the scope of constitutional regulation. Again, however, the Review Group concluded against change. A concern not to interfere in the exercise of "private liberty" was evident in this decision. An additional point was also made: it would be undesirable and contrary to the separation of powers for the courts to *require* "State

---

[39] *Report of the Constitution Review Group, supra* n. 15, at 222, author's emphasis.

action", for example legislation, in order to ensure equality in private relations. Such matters, it was thought, are more properly regarded as policy issues to be determined by the Government and/or the Oireachtas. An obligation on the State to ensure general respect for equality would be more appropriately addressed in the Constitution as a non-justiciable directive of social policy. Thus, it seems that relations between non-State actors were perceived as raising policy issues only while relations between individuals and the State were presumed to raise questions of legal right. Again no reason was given for distinguishing the protection afforded by Article 40.1 from that of Article 40.3.

The question whether the State should have a duty to provide an effective remedy against private discrimination was not directly addressed. It was clear from the earlier discussion, however, that the Review Group was not in favour of recognising a general right to equal treatment. And, as can be seen from the above discussion, it was not in favour either of recognising a positive duty on the part of the State to take action. If, however, it is accepted that the correlative of a right is a duty, this implies the acceptance of duties on the part of the State, duties that may be either positive or negative. Thus, the social contract may be breached, by either action or inaction on the part of the State. This latter aspect of the social contract (a duty to act) is frequently neglected by constitutional lawyers and is clearly ignored here by the Review Group. While the State has a duty "to defend and vindicate" a wide range of personal rights, it does not seem to have any such duty with regard to equality rights. Equality seems very far, indeed, from being a core norm within the constitutional pecking order.

Applying Article 40.1 to relations between non-State actors would certainly pose a number of difficulties. However, to confine its scope to relations between the individual and the State is not to opt for a simpler solution. The Review Group failed to address a number of questions, not least the question of what constitutes "the State" or "State action". Both the US and Canadian courts have struggled with this question for a number of years without, as yet, arriving at a coherent answer.

NB!

COMPARATIVE PERSPECTIVES

The question whether or not the Canadian Charter of Rights and Freedoms applied to "private action" has been a troubling issue in Charter litigation. The Charter guarantees equality before the law, equality under the law, equal protection of the law and equal benefit of the law (section 15(1)). It also guarantees against "discrimination based on race, national or ethnic origin, colour, religion, sex, age or mental or physical disability". Section 32(1) limits the application of the Charter to the "Parliament and government of Canada" and to "the legislatures and government of each province". Peter Hogg argues that there is "no doubt" that this section excludes private action from the application of the Charter.[40] Others have argued, however, that this interpretation is unduly restrictive and has been "produced" by the Supreme Court of Canada's jurisprudence.[41] The oppressive potential of private power has been ignored. As Hutchinson and Petter argue, "in the Charter vision, the main enemy of freedom is not disparity in wealth or concentration of private power, but the state".[42]

In *RWDSU* v. *Dolphin Delivery*[43] the Supreme Court had to consider whether secondary picketing was a protected activity under the Charter's guarantee of freedom of expression. It concluded that the Charter did not apply to "private litigation divorced completely from any connection with Government".[44] In addition, it stated, the common law would be subject to the Charter only in so far as [it] is the basis of some "governmental action".[45] Thus, although concerned not to exclude the "whole body" of the common law, the court was content not to apply the Charter to that "great part" of the common law which regulates relationships among private actors. "Governmental action", it was agreed, would be difficult to define. A court order (in this case, an injunction) would not provide a sufficiently direct or precisely defined connection. To quote Hutchinson and Petter again, "[l]ike its marine namesake, *Dolphin* shows that, beneath the surface, there is a whole world of action and agony".[46]

In subsequent cases, the Supreme Court has developed an institutional test to determine whether or not the prerequisite of "governmental action" is present.[47] More recently, in *Hill* v. *Church of Scientology of Toronto*,[48] the

---

[40] P. W. Hogg, *Constitutional Law of Canada* (3rd edn., Toronto, Thomson Canada Ltd, 1992), at 1157. Although Hogg argues that this restriction is necessary, he recognises that it fails to identify the real problem for the pusuit of equality—private power. However, he argues that this gap is adequately filled by human rights codes. Ibid. "Constitutional conceits: The Coercive Authority of Courts (1991) 40 UTLJ 183, 190–1.

[41] See e.g. G. W. Anderson, "The Limits of Constitutional Law: The Canadian Charter of Rights and Freedoms and the Public-Private Divide" in C. Gearty and A. Tomkins (eds.), *Understanding Human Rights* (London, Mansell, 1996).

[42] A. C. Hutchinson and A. Petter, *supra* n. 2, at 283. See also A. C. Hutchinson *Waiting for Coraf: A Critique of Law and Rights* (Toronto, University Press, 1995).

[43] *Retail, Wholesale and Department Store Union, Local 580 et al.* v. *Dolphin Delivery Ltd* [1986] 2 SCR 573. *Dolphin* was applied recently in the case of *General Motors of Canada Ltd* v. *CAW-Canada* [1996] OLRB Rep. 409.

[44] *Ibid.*, at 593.

[45] *Ibid.*, at 599.

[46] *Supra* n. 2, at 283.

[47] In *McKinney* v. *University of Guelph* (1990) 76 DLR (4th) 545 and *Stoffman* v. *Vancouver General Hospital* (1990) 76 DLR (4th) 700, a university and a hospital, respectively, were held not to be part of the governmental fabric. In both cases, the institutions in question had been incorporated by statute and were in receipt of sizeable government funds. However, both enjoyed a considerable degree of autonomy such that the necessary "institutional link" could not be found. In *Lavigne* v. *OPSEU* (1991) 81 DLR (4th) 545, a faculty member of a community college challenged the payment of union dues. The payment was a term of his employment by virtue of an "agency-shop" collective agreement entered into by the college's Council of Regents. The Charter was found to be applicable because the Council of Regents was under the control of the provincial Minister of Education and, therefore, "part of the fabric of government".

[48] (1995) 25 CCLT (2d) 89.

Supreme Court again concluded that private litigants did not owe each other any constitutional duties and could not found their cases on Charter rights. Such rights, it was stated, "do not exist" in the absence of "state action".

As one commentator has noted, this jurisprudence has led to the creation of two categories of Charter violations: "those that are punished, and those that attract no official opprobrium".[49] A sort of private-sector immunity from Charter violations has developed.[50] Similar difficulties have arisen within the United States.

American political society, Louis Henkin believes,[51] was originally conceived as a social contract—an agreement among the people to form a polity as well as an agreement as to the kind of government to be created and the conditions that should govern it. Only the last part of that compact is reflected in the Constitution. Except for the amendment abolishing slavery, the Constitution protects individual rights only against invasion by government—against "State action"; the equality provisions of the Fourteenth Amendment,[52] "erect no shield against merely private conduct, however discriminatory or wrongful".[53] The State is required only to assume a neutral position with respect to such conduct. Inaction may attract the responsibility of the State if it amounts to "tacit ratification of a challenged private choice" or "delegation of a public responsibility to a private party". However, despite the existence of a significant body of case law,[54] the Supreme Court has not succeeded in developing a coherent body of rules to determine whether governmental or private actors are to be deemed responsible for an alleged constitutional violation.[55] According to Professor Charles Black, the "state action" cases, viewed doctrinally, are a "conceptual disaster area".[56]

[49] G. W. Anderson *supra* n. 41, at 535.

[50] See generally, D. Gibson, "The Deferential Trojan Horse: A Decade of Charter Decisions" (1993) 72 *Canadian Bar Review* 417.

[51] L. Henkin, "Constitutionalism and Human Rights" in L. Henkin and A. J. Rosenthal (eds.), *Constitutionalism and Rights: The Influence of the United States Constitution Abroad* (New York, Columbia University Press, 1990), at 390.

[52] "All persons born or naturalised in the United States, and subject to the jurisdiction thereof, are citizens of the United States and of the State wherein they reside. No State shall make or enforce any law which shall abridge the privileges or immunities of citizens of the United States; nor shall any State deprive any person of life, liberty, or property, without due process of law; nor deny to any person within its jurisdiction the equal protection of the laws."

[53] *Shelley* v. *Kraemer, supra* n. 38.

[54] A variety of tests and catch-phrases have been developed by the courts. "Public function" and "institutional nexus" are just two of those. The remedy sought by the litigants and the target of the relief have also been identified as relevant considerations.

[55] See L. Tribe, *American Constitutional Law* (2nd edn., New York, The Foundation Press, 1988), ch. 18 at 1690.

[56] C. Black, "The Supreme Court, 1966 Term—Foreword: 'State Action', Equal Protection, and California's Proposition 14" (1967) 81 *Harv.LRev.* 69, at 95. In *Shelley* v. *Kraemer, supra* n. 38, the litigant sought to prevent the judicial enforcement of a racially restrictive covenant. If the covenant in question had been voluntarily adhered to, the State could not have been implicated. However, because the covenant was secured by judicial enforcement in State courts, "State action" was present and the equality provisions were, therefore, applicable. However, numerous counter-examples can also be found. In *Moose Lodge No. 107* v. *Irvis*, 407 US 163 (1972), a litigant

Difficulties also arise concerning the validity of congressional legislation regulating private conduct. In a series of post-Civil War cases, most notably the *Civil Rights Cases*, the Supreme Court invalidated much civil rights legislation on the ground that, because this legislation purported to regulate the conduct of private citizens, it was not authorised by the Fourteenth Amendment, and hence was unconstitutional.[57] The result of this restrictive interpretation was that Congress was powerless to prevent what came to be referred to as "Jim Crow" discriminatory practices. It was necessary, therefore, to find other foundations—principally the power of Congress to regulate inter-state commerce—to support power for Congress to forbid private violations of rights.[58] (It should be noted, however, that neither Congress nor any State is constitutionally *required* to adopt such legislation.) Suggestions that Congress has less extensive powers to proscribe various forms of sex discrimination than to prohibit parallel instances of race discrimination have led to proposals for an Equal Rights Amendment (ERA), the purpose of which would be to foreclose any challenge to congressional competence in this field.[59]

Limiting the scope of constitutional protection must be seen, Henkin argues, in the context of the United States as a liberal State. Restrictions on the State are congenial to that concept. Restrictions on private persons are not. Two main justifications are advanced in support of the "State action"

sought to require a government agency to revoke the liquor licence of a racially discriminatory private club. The Supreme Court found no "State action", thus placing the discrimination in question beyond the reach of the equality guarantee. In *Burton* v. *Wilmington Parking Authority*, 365 US 715, 726 (1961), the named defendants included both a racially discriminatory private restaurant and the State agency that owned the building within which the restaurant operated. The Supreme Court found that "State action" was present and held that "the proscriptions of the Fourteenth Amendment must be complied with by the lessee as certainly as though they were binding covenants written into the agreement itself". See also *Medical Institute of Minnesota* v. *National Ass'n of Trade and Technical Schools*, CA 8 (Minn.), 817 F.2d 1310, in which the decision of an accrediting agency to deny reaccreditation to a school was not attributable to federal government and thus did not give rise to a claim for denial of equal protection, even though the Department of Education provides financial assistance only if the school remains accredited. In *Hartford Acc. and Indem. Co.* v. *Insurance Com'r of Com.*, 482 A 2d 542, the degree of governmental regulation of automobile insurance rates did not constitute "State action" sufficient to maintain an action. The basis of the action was an alleged violation of the equal protection clause by insurers who allegedly discriminated against males in setting automobile insurance rates.

[57] The situation under the 14th Amendment differs quite significantly from that under the 13th Amendment. The 13th Amendment's prohibitions of slavery encompass both governmental and private action. See *Civil Rights Cases*, 109 US 3, 20 (1883) and *Jones* v. *Alfred H. Mayer Co.*, 392 US 409 (1968)

[58] In the *United States* v. *Guest* 383 US 745, 782 (1966), the Supreme Court declared that Congress possessed the power under s. 5 of the 14th Amendment "to enact laws punishing all conspiracies to interfere with the exercise of Fourteenth Amendment rights, whether or not state officers or others acting under the color of state law are implicated in the conspiracy" (opinion of Brennan J, joined by Warren CJ, and Douglas J). In a subsequent case, *District of Columbia* v. *Carter*, a unanimous Supreme Court subsequently reaffirmed the proposition that to say that "the Fourteenth Amendment itself 'erects no shield against merely private conduct' . . . is not to say . . . that Congress may not proscribe purely private conduct under s. 5 of the Fourteenth Amendment": 409 US 418, 423, 424, n. 8 (1973). (S. 5. of the 14th Amendment provides "The Congress shall have power to enforce, by appropriate legislation, the provisions of this article.")

[59] See generally, L. Tribe, *supra* n. 56, especially 312–13 and 1585–8.

requirement.[60] First, it preserves a sphere of individual liberty, thereby protecting the values of freedom and autonomy. Secondly, it reinforces the two chief principles of division which organise the governmental structure that the Constitution creates: federalism and the separation of powers.[61] (These echo very closely the arguments put forward by the Constitution Review Group.)

A constant tension exists between these objectives.[62] Each differs with regard to the conception of individual liberty which it presupposes. The first presumes the existence of a developed conception of individual liberty which serves to limit the scope of possible government action. Liberty is defined without reference to government action and is thus capable of defining the proper limit of such action. The second treats liberty as being merely that range of choices left to the individual when government has not acted. Liberty is defined negatively, as simply "a residue of private choice left untouched by governmental regulation".[63] This second formulation cannot provide an adequate solution to the problem of government inaction. Government acquiescence in or tolerance of private discriminatory conduct is viewed merely as "inaction" and, therefore, not "State action". Under the first formulation, however, the State has a duty to preserve a sphere of individual autonomy free from both governmental and private infringement. Thus, a failure to protect individuals from private infringements may be defined as unconstitutional "State action" just as surely as if the government itself had acted directly. Equally, government inaction would not amount to "State action" where positive action would have usurped a "necessarily" private decision or choice.

Tribe rejects the critique that the "State action" requirement is an extraordinarily malleable formality, almost devoid of content. What is empty, he says, is the "State action doctrine". A unitary "State action" doctrine cannot coexist, he argues, with a pluralist jurisprudence of rights: "[c]ontemporary constitutional law recognizes and protects individual rights without reference to a single, necessarily procrustean, theory of liberty."[64] This does not mean, however, that the "State action" requirement cannot be explained. Constitutional rights define the characteristics of unconstitutional "State action". Government regulatory policy is always a mix of acts and omissions. A decision that the Constitution creates a zone, within which government should be free simply to leave the disputed choice in private hands, may be a defensible decision. However, the important point to note, as Tribe argues, is that this is a decision about the substantive reach of specific constitutional commands. It is not an example of "inaction".[65] Neither is it a manifestation of the "neutral" State.

---

[60] *Ibid.*, at 1691.
[61] *Ibid.*
[62] *Ibid.*
[63] *Ibid.*, at 1692.
[64] *Ibid.*, at 1699.
[65] *Ibid.*, at 1720.

A SOCIAL CONTRACT: RE-CONCEPTUALISING THE CONSTITUTION

Contrary to liberal legalist assumptions, the State's refusal to intervene in private matters does not necessarily expand individual autonomy. It has often simply substituted private for public power. Governmental "inaction" has frequently enlarged the liberties of men at the expense of women.[66] To date, Irish constitutional law and practice have failed adequately to address these questions. A coherent concept of individual liberty has not yet been developed. Neither have we faced up to the tensions between the constitutional values of liberty and equality. The Constitution Review Group had an opportunity to do so. However, instead of admitting to the complex substantive questions raised, they resorted to the rhetoric of liberalism, preferring to hide behind the facade of the "neutral State".

As Tribe notes, the decision to preserve a sphere of "private liberty" may be a defensible one. Critical feminism does not necessarily renounce the constraints on State power that liberalism has secured. What it does deny is that conventional public/private dichotomies can provide a useful conceptual scheme for "drawing" or "finding" lines. Rights discourse is frequently accused by feminism of perpetuating such dichotomies. By recognising "constitutional torts", Irish courts have already moved beyond the traditional confines of constitutionalism and social contract theory. The central problem with rights-based frameworks is not that they are "inherently limiting", but that they have operated within a "limited institutional, imaginative universe".[67] Perhaps the judicial imagination applied to the "defence and vindication" of "personal rights" will one day reach into the realm of equality.

[66] D. L. Rhode, "Feminist Critical Theories" in K. Bartlett and R. Kennedy (eds.), *Feminist Legal Theory: Readings in Law and Gender* (Boulder, Colo., Westview Press, 1991), at 340.
[67] D. L. Rhode, "Feminist Critical Theories" in K. Bartlett and R. Kennedy (eds.), *Feminist Legal Theory: Readings in Law and Gender* (Boulder, Colo., Westview Press, 1991), at 343.

13

Economic Inequality and the Constitution

TIM MURPHY

INTRODUCTION

Despite the strong influence of the Catholic Church in the Ireland of the 1930s, the Constitution of 1937 was based primarily on the political ideology of liberalism.[1] As Gerard Quinn has noted, political liberalism is constitutionally and legally expressed by the two aspects of "liberal legalism"—"constitutionalism" and the "rule of law".[2] In terms of the constitutional protection of rights within this model, the constitutionalist strand of liberal legalism traditionally affords this protection to civil and political rights rather than economic, social or cultural rights. In other words, the rights which are protected typically provide for a formal, universal equality amongst citizens in relation to the organisation and governance of the polity; and while they guarantee "private" individual citizens some degree of protection against the possibility of the abuse of "public" State power, they do not relate directly to the functioning of the economy or other "material" matters.[3] Thus, citizens of liberal

---

[1] "In the Catholic political world of the 1930s, the Constitution was exceptional in its commitment to liberal democracy": D. Keogh, "The Irish Constitutional Revolution: An Analysis of the Making of the Constitution" in F. Litton (ed.), *The Constitution of Ireland 1937–1987* (Dublin, Institute of Public Administration, 1988), 5.

[2] See G. Quinn, "The Nature and Significance of Critical Legal Studies" (1989) 7 *ILT* 282 at 283. Quinn describes constitutionalism as the fencing-in of public power mainly by the "separation of powers" doctrine and justiciable individual rights; he refers to the rule of law as rule through law rather than the arbitrary whim of persons and the requirement that law must have certain adjectival attributes—including generality, equality, clarity and certainty—before it can be labelled "good" law (*ibid.*).

[3] I am describing the "rights dichotomy" in a general way here and without reference to certain conceptual difficulties which undoubtedly exist. Geraldine Van Bueren has recently noted that "there is not any authoritative definition of the distinction between civil and political rights and economic, social and cultural rights" and that the right to education, for example, "embraces both civil and cultural aspects concerning rights of access to education and economic and social facets in the provision of the different levels of education." ("Deconstructing the Mythologies of International Human Rights Law" in C. Gearty and A. Tomkins, *Understanding Human Rights* (London, Mansell, 1996), 596 at 599). Despite this, the basic dichotomy does retain some expositional and analytical validity; as Van Bueren also remarks, "the demise of the distinction is hardly imminent" (*ibid.*, p.600).

states are normally granted the constitutional rights to vote, to liberty, to expression, to association, to assembly etc., but economic rights, such as the right of everyone to an adequate standard of living, including adequate food, clothing and housing, or the right to an adequate income, are usually not recognised at that level. The reason for this, of course, is that the political ideology of liberalism is historically associated with a particular economic system, a system where the capitalist mode of production is the dominant mode.[4] The movement during this century away from the *laissez-faire* capitalism of the last century has certainly involved the provision of economic rights at the statutory level, notably in the form of social welfare legislation, but generally not at the constitutional level. The main exception to this general dichotomy is the right to own private property: normally, this economic right—an essential prerequisite to the functioning of the capitalist mode of production—*is* protected by the constitutions of liberal-capitalist states.[5]

This essay explores the relationship between economic inequality and the Irish Constitution. More specifically, it examines and evaluates the manner in

[4] See G. H. Sabine and T. L. Thorson, *A History of Political Theory* (4th edn. Fort Worth, Texas, Harcourt Brace, 1973), 622–8. As Quinn puts it, "[L]iberal democracy provides a congenial backdrop to the rise and functioning of a market society": *supra* n. 2 282. The individualistic ethos required by capitalist economics is ensured by liberalism's failure to provide the same degree of protection and security to the material conditions of citizens as it provides to "political" and "civil" issues. The following historical conditions, taken together, describe succinctly the capitalist mode of production: "(1) the existence of the state; (2) the division of society into classes, defined by their relation to the means of production; (3) the development of wage labour as the main form of work; (4) the production of goods principally for exchange; and (5) the employment of wage labour in production so as to give rise to a profit, an amount (surplus value) in excess of the cost of the worker's subsistence, which is appropriated and then reinvested by the owner of the means of production" ("General Introduction" in Y. Ghai, R. Luckham and F. Snyder (eds.), *The Political Economy of Law: A Third World Reader* (Delhi and Oxford, Oxford University Press, 1987), p. xiii).

[5] Art. 43.1.1 of the Irish Constitution states: "[T]he State acknowledges that man, in virtue of his rational being, has the natural right, antecedent to positive law, to the private ownership of external goods". It should also be noted here that Art. 45 of the Constitution, the "Directive Principles of Social Policy", directly addresses socio-economic matters. It provides, for example, that the State shall direct its policy towards securing that "the citizens (all of whom, men and women equally, have the right to an adequate means of livelihood) may through their occupations find the means of making reasonable provision for their domestic needs" (Art. 45.2.i) and that "the ownership and control of the material resources of the community may be so distributed amongst private individuals and the various classes as best to subserve the common good" (Art. 45.2.ii). However, this Art. is "intended for the general guidance of the Oireachtas" and "shall not be cognisable by any Court under any of the provisions of this Constitution" (Art. 45). Although the Irish High Court have on occasion used Art. 45 as an interpretive tool, there has been no ruling on the question by the Supreme Court (but see the comments of McCarthy J in *Kerry Co-Operative Creameries Ltd* v. *An Bord Bainne* [1991] ILRM 851, where he stated that the doctrine of restraint of trade should be read in the light of Art. 45 and, more generally, that the courts could consider the Art. in the construction of the common law). See generally G. Hogan and G. Whyte, J. M. Kelly *The Irish Constitution* (3rd edn. Dublin, Butterworths, 1994), 1117–23. One final general point: while I have referred in the text to the right to vote, I have confined my brief discussion to political liberalism and capitalist economics, without reference to democracy. As Quinn comments, "[T]he Anglo-American legal tradition owes much more to the political philosophy of liberalism than it does to that of democracy. Indeed the liberal-democratic variant of democratic theory turns out to be more liberal than democratic." *Supra* n. 2, 283.

which the Constitution fails to protect individual citizens from poverty and its consequences. The first substantive section of the essay will briefly outline the extent of economic inequality and poverty in the State. The following two sections then discuss the possibility of the constitutional recognition of economic rights in Ireland. [Under the present Constitution, such recognition could come about either by amendment or by a decision of the courts to add such rights to the existing range of unenumerated rights] The discussion of the possibility of amendment in the 1996 *Report of the Constitution Review Group*[6] will be analysed first. I will then examine the possibility of judicial recognition of economic rights, a possibility that was addressed during a recent academic debate about the unenumerated rights doctrine in Irish constitutional law. I will argue that the reasons typically advanced against the recognition of economic rights from within the liberal-legal tradition, and also the explanations offered as to judicial non-recognition of these rights, are conceptually confused and question-begging and I will refer, in a brief conclusion, to the potential sources of future demands for constitutional economic rights: the traditions of Christian democracy and socialism.

ECONOMIC INEQUALITY IN THE REPUBLIC OF IRELAND

"Economic inequalities", as Kathleen Lynch and Alpha Connelly have stated, "are fundamental realities of Irish life . . . Not only do they have a direct impact on low income groups and individuals, they also interface and greatly compound other inequalities such as those arising from gender, disability or age."[7] In 1995, the Inter-departmental Policy Committee on the National Anti-poverty Strategy, while acknowledging that there is no one single definition that has been fully accepted as defining poverty and social exclusion in a comprehensive way, provided the following working definition:

> "People are living in poverty, if their income and resources (material, cultural and social) are so inadequate as to preclude them from having a standard of living which is regarded as acceptable by Irish society generally. As a result of inadequate income and resources people may be excluded and marginalised from participating in activities which are considered the norm for other people in society."[8]

The Committee identified the following groups as those at greatest risk of poverty: the unemployed, particularly the long-term unemployed; children, particularly those living in large families; small farmers; some groups of

---

[6] *Report of the Constitution Review Group* (Dublin, Stationery Office, 1996).

[7] K. Lynch and A. Connelly, "Equality Before the Law", *ibid.* Appendix 18, 589–90.

[8] Discussion Paper by the Inter-departmental Policy Committee on the National Anti-Poverty Strategy, *Poverty, Social Exclusion and Inequality in Ireland: An Overview Statement* (Dublin, Department of *An Taoiseach*, 1995), 3.

women, particularly lone mothers; people with disabilities; Travellers; and people out of home.[9]

There are a variety of approaches to the measurement of the risk and incidence of poverty.[10] In Ireland, it is usually done by using "relative income lines" or by combining these with "deprivation indicators".[11] Relative income lines are based on average household disposable income and the relative approach to constructing a poverty line involves calculating a line as a proportion of that income, taking differences in household size and composition into account. "Income poverty lines" are usually drawn at 40 per cent, 50 per cent or 60 per cent of average household disposable income. Deprivation refers to the extent to which someone is denied the opportunity to have or to do something. In Ireland, the deprivation index of the Economic and Social Research Institute (ESRI) includes indicators such as enforced debt to cover ordinary living expenses or the enforced lack of adequate heating.

Whichever indicator is chosen, the number of Irish citizens living below the "poverty lines" is extremely large. In setting out the background to its discussion of economic rights, the 1996 *Report of the Constitution Review Group* refers to information about poverty in Ireland derived from the 1987 Household Budget Survey. The results of this survey, which was carried out by the ESRI, comprised the most recent available data of their kind. On the basis of these figures, the report of the Review Group explicitly acknowledged the extent of both poverty and economic inequality in Irish society:

> "An estimated 30.4% live below the 'poverty line', defined as having an income 60% or less of the average industrial wage . . . It has been estimated that, within Ireland, the richest 10% (measured in terms of disposable income) receive 25% of total income while the bottom 10% receive 2.5%. The only countries within the twenty-five OECD countries with a more uneven distribution of income are the US and the UK."[12]

The 1994 Living in Ireland Survey, which was also carried out by the ESRI and the results of which only became available after the compilation of the Review Group's report, confirms the high levels of economic inequality and poverty identified in the household survey of 1987:[13]

> "Compared with 1987, the proportion of persons below the 40 per cent relative line had fallen or was stable by 1994, but the proportion below the 50 per cent line and even more so the 60 per cent line had increased. The percentage of persons

[9] *Poverty, Social Exclusion and Inequality in Ireland: An Overview Statement* (Dublin, Department of *An Taoiseach*, 1995), 6. The Committee also stated: "[o]ther, less easily identifiable groups may also be at risk of poverty, particularly through discrimination, but evidence on their levels of poverty is difficult to obtain."

[10] See T. Callan, B. Nolan, B. J. Whelan, C. T. Whelan and J. Williams, *Poverty in the 1990s: Evidence from the 1994 Living in Ireland Survey* (Dublin, Oak Tree Press, 1996), 5–30.

[11] Discussion Paper, *supra* n. 8, 4–5.

[12] *Report of the Constitution Review Group*, *supra* n. 6, 234.

[13] See T. Callan, B. Nolan, B. J. Whelan, C. T. Whelan and J. Williams, *supra* n. 10.

below the highest 60 per cent line was 3–4 percentage points higher in 1994 than in 1987."[14]

The statistics from the 1994 survey also indicate that economic disadvantage in the State is not the result of a scarcity of resources but rather of the concentrations of the wealth which does exist in the State.[15] Economic inequality and poverty continue as major social problems despite the contemporary rhetoric of the "economic boom".[16]

At another level, of course, the references to "poverty percentage points" and other statistics tend to obscure the true nature and extent of the "social problem". In addition to the individual human suffering and hardship associated with the fact of poverty,[17] there are also several broader social consequences, such as certain forms of crime and drug misuse, as well as a general inefficiency in the use of talents and resources in the State. These broader consequences were referred to in more detail in the arguments for constitutional economic rights in the 1996 report and will be referred to in the next section of this essay.

THE CONSIDERATION OF ECONOMIC RIGHTS BY THE CONSTITUTION REVIEW GROUP

The Constitutional Review Group addressed the question of "whether there should be provision for specific economic rights as a counterweight to economic inequality" in the context of the equality guarantee in Article 40.1.[18] A minority of the Group, after noting the desirability of an expression of State concern about the material needs of citizens, identifies political instability and

[14] *Ibid.* 124. See also C. Curtin, T. Haase and H. Tovey, *Poverty in Rural Ireland* (Dublin, Oak Tree Press, 1996).

[15] One of the most recent indications of this results from the calculations of the Justice Commission of the Conference of Religious of Ireland (CORI) in their response to the first budget of 1997: "[s]ufficient resources were available to Government as it planned Budget '97 to ensure that everybody received at least the '*minimally adequate*' level of income recommended by the Government's Commission on Social Welfare eleven years ago. Instead of allocating it to achieve this end and eliminate income poverty, *Government has again taken decisions which result in the better off getting more, while the poverty gap widens.*" *Budget Response 1997: Analysis, Critique, Comment* (Dublin, CORI, 1997), 18 (emphases in original).

[16] Martin Loughlin described "the post-industrial era of the 1980s" as one "in which growth occurs without a significant proportion of the population being at all involved": *Public Law and Political Theory* (Oxford, Clarendon Press, 1992), 222. See, further, F. O'Toole, "In the Land of the Emerald Tiger", *Irish Times*, 28 Dec. 1996 and "Poverty in the Land of the Emerald Tiger", *Irish Times*, 3 Jan. 1997; and A. Johnson and M. Gallagher, "The Paradox of Irish Economic Development" (1994) 22 *Class Struggle* 14.

[17] See, e.g., the discussion of the effect of poverty on health and levels of stress in Discussion Paper, *supra* n. 8, 26–7.

[18] *Report of the Constitution Review Group, supra* n. 6, 234–6. Art. 40.1 states: "[A]ll citizens shall, as human persons, be held equal before the law. This shall not be held to mean that the State shall not in its enactments have due regard to differences of capacity, physical and moral, and of social function."

social and economic dysfunctionality as two key aspects of economic inequality in Ireland. Stating that "[a] society strongly polarised in economic terms is fundamentally unstable", the minority note two sources of this instability: "political alienation from the democratic process and the development of alternative 'economies' based on crime or illegal trading".[19] Although no more detail is given by the minority concerning political alienation, there is clear evidence that socio-economic factors exert a very strong influence on voting patterns.[20] In relation to the development of alternative "economies", it is argued convincingly in the Report that this:

> "is particularly likely to happen in societies which encourage high levels of consumption through advertising, media images etc, and thereby create high levels of aspiration for a wide range of goods and services. The message of pervasive consumption is universal, and is not confined to any one sector of society. The frustration arising from the inability to match aspiration and realisation is a fountain of political instability."[21]

More directly, it is clear that the incidence of certain criminal behaviour and forms of problematic drug use can be traced to economic conditions in Irish society. For example, as a recent government report on drugs stated, "drug misuse is closely associated with social and economic disadvantage, characterised by unemployment, poor living conditions, low educational attainment, high levels of family breakdown and a lack of recreational facilities and other supports".[22] The minority also point out that economic inequality and poverty are "socially and economically dysfunctional" as they result in:

> "inefficient use of talents and resources and substantial costs to the State (and this means the members of society generally) both directly via welfare, housing, health and other costs, and indirectly through the alienation and detachment which develops among those economically excluded from equal participation in society".[23]

---

[19] *Report of the Constitution Review Group*, supra n. 6, 235.

[20] As Richard Sinnott writes, "[a]reas of low voting in Dublin are characterised [most of all] by . . . a pattern of social disadvantage, i.e. low levels of education, high unemployment and higher numbers of people in lower status occupations . . . [This] has disquieting implications when viewed from the perspective of the democratic criterion . . . 'that every individual, whatever his social or economic circumstances, should have an equal say' ". *Irish Voters Decide: Voting Behaviour in Elections and Referendums since 1918* (Manchester, Manchester University Press, 1995), 142.

[21] *Report of the Constitution Review Group*, supra n. 6, 235. For a discussion of how the same conditions are relevant to the assessment of State responses to drug use and misuse, see T. Murphy, *Rethinking the War on Drugs in Ireland* (Cork, Cork University Press, 1996), 32–48.

[22] *First Report of the Ministerial Task Force on Measures to Reduce the Demand for Drugs* (Dublin, Stationery Office, 1996), 22. See also S. Butler, "Drug Problems and Drug Policies: A Quarter of a Century Reviewed" (1991) 39 *Administration* 213 and T. Murphy, *Rethinking the War on Drugs in Ireland*, supra n. 21. For discussions of the connections between socio-economic conditions and crime, see P. O'Mahony, *Crime and Punishment in Ireland* (Dublin, Round Hall, 1993), 57–72 and C Mc Cullagh, *Crime in Ireland: A Sociological Introduction* (Cork, Cork University Press, 1996), 30–58 and 117–44. Also see, generally, J. Hagan and R. D. Peterson (eds.), *Crime and Inequality* (Stanford, Cal., Stanford University Press, 1995).

[23] *Report of the Constitution Review Group*, supra n.6 p.235.

These minority arguments for the inclusion in the Constitution of economic rights were obviously authored, at least in part, by two particular members of the Review Group, Kathleen Lynch and Alpha Connelly. These two members co-authored a briefing document appended to the report which concludes as follows:

> "The Constitutional Review Group cannot ignore economic inequalities even if traditional constitutional jurisprudence has ignored them to date. To ignore them is to do a grave injustice to a large sector of the Irish population. There is no logical reason why the Constitution does not have an Article committing us to a democracy based on principles of social solidarity with the aim of eliminating poverty and promoting economic equality through a system of taxation based on principles of equality and progressiveness."[24]

As Gerry Whyte has remarked, it is difficult to find words to improve on this basic demand for a high (constitutional) priority to be attached to the problem of tackling social exclusion.[25] However, a majority of the Review Group were against the idea of specific enumeration of economic rights in the Constitution. In a key passage, it states:

> "The main reason . . . why the Constitution should not confer [such rights] is that these are essentially political matters which, in a democracy, it should be the responsibility of the elected representatives of the people to address and determine. It would be a distortion of democracy to transfer decisions on major issues of policy and practicality from the Government and the Oireachtas, elected to represent the people and do their will, to an unelected judiciary".[26]

This line of reasoning—which represents the classic liberal objection to the rights in question—raises a wide range of constitutional issues. The most significant of these relate to the issue of what precisely constitute "law" and "politics". There is an assumption in the argument that a logical basis exists for distinguishing social or economic rights from political or civil rights on the basis of what is "political" or an "issue of policy and practicality". However, it cannot be coherently proposed that the rights, for example, to freedom of expression or to freedom of association are inherently more "legal" or "constitutional" than "political" (and this is apart altogether from the irony that it is decisions as to civil and *political* rights such as these that, according to the majority view in the Report, are *not* "essentially political" and therefore acceptably transferred to "an unelected judiciary").

The problem is essentially one of the majority regarding that which is historically contingent as "given". Although the two sets of rights are recognised in international human rights law by the Universal Declaration of Human Rights, two separate International Covenants—the International Covenant on

---

[24] K. Lynch and A. Connelly, *supra* n. 7, 590.
[25] G. Whyte, "Marginalised Groups Deserve Constitutional Protection", *Irish Times*, 8 July 1996.
[26] *Report of the Constitution Review Group*, *supra* n. 6, 235.

Civil and Political Rights and the International Covenant on Economic, Social and Cultural Rights—were adopted by the United Nations in 1966 to transform the Declaration's provisions into legally binding obligations. While the existence of these formally similar Covenants—which "constitute the bedrock of the international normative regime in relation to human rights"[27]—suggests a parity of esteem in relation to all rights, this parity exists only at a superficial level. The cracks begin to appear when one realises that the obligation placed on signatory States in relation to each Covenant are markedly different: the Covenant dealing with civil and political rights requires State parties to "respect and ensure" its rights, whereas the Covenant governing economic, social and cultural rights only requires that they should "take steps individually and through international assistance and cooperation . . . to the maximum of its available resources with a view to achieving progressively the full realisation of the rights . . . ". This distinction in international law means that economic, social and cultural rights are only regarded as "aspirational goals to be achieved progressively" with relatively weak forms of implementation and "low priority" in terms of state expenditure.[28] The significant point in terms of the present discussion is that this distinction arose not because of the intrinsic nature of the various rights—whether they were "political matters" or not—but rather because of specific historical circumstances. As Henry Steiner and Philip Alston write:

> "Even before the final adoption of the UDHR, the debate over the relationship between the two sets of rights had become a casualty of the Cold War: the Communist countries abstained from voting on its adoption in the General Assembly on the grounds that the economic and social rights provisions were inadequate. Moreover, at least since the 1970s, it has taken on an important North–South dimension."[29]

Despite these geopolitical influences on how these rights are perceived, most commentators acknowledge that both sets of rights are both "legal-constitutional" *and* "political". In his discussion of what he terms "the liberal normativist constitutional project" in the United Kingdom, Martin Loughlin cites the ten-point statement of the Charter 88 group as a typical example, and goes on to question the precise meaning of the citizenship rights envisioned in the reference to "universal citizenship" in the Charter.[30] Noting that "the *principle* of civil and political rights . . . is relatively uncontested", Loughlin remarks that the "contemporary challenge concerns social and economic entitlements".[31] *The key political question, in other words, is the way in which these*

---

[27] H. J. Steiner and P. Alston, *International Human Rights in Context: Law, Politics, Morals* (Oxford, Clarendon Press, 1996), 256.

[28] G. Van Beuren, *supra* n. 3, 598–9.

[29] *Supra* n. 27, 257; see also G. Van Beuren, *supra* n. 3, 599.

[30] M. Loughlin, *supra* n. 16.

[31] *Ibid*, 222 (emphasis in original).

entitlements will be adressed by legal and constitutional means.[32] Indeed, returning to the Review Group, the "political issue" argument of the majority seems to be totally undermined when they themselves suggest that judicial vindication of the right to life and the right to bodily integrity under the present Constitution offers the ultimate safeguard against the risk of anyone being allowed to fall below the minimum level of subsistence.[33]

Another issue arising from the above statement of the Review Group majority is its view of the "transfer" of these socio-economic issues from the *Oireachtas* to an "unelected judiciary". In saying that economic rights (because of their "political" nature) are essentially matters which are the preserve of

---

[32] Loughlin argues that the boundary lines between law (particularly constitutional law) and politics are, at the very least, blurred. See his discussion of "public law" (of which "constitutional law" is an undisputed subset) in *Public Law and Political Theory*, *supra* n. 16, 1–4, where he refers to public law as "[dealing] with the legal arrangements which establish the institutions of the state and regulate the exercise of political power". The traditional view of the subject in the United Kingdom is that there is no distinctive system of public law, i.e. that it merely comprises a particular set of institutional arrangements which may be treated as forming a discrete object of analysis. This tradition, according to Loughlin, "is based on the idea that legality is a singular and universal concept and the state and its officers are subject to the ordinary processes of law in much the same manner as all other persons are governed by law. Public authorities, therefore, hold no special status in the legal ordering of our society and there is nothing peculiar in the application of legal method to disputes involving public bodies." Given the conceptual distinction that is now made by courts (and European Union law) between matters of public law and private law, and given the special procedure (application for judicial review) that is used to process disputes concerning public law issues, Loughlin states that "the ideas on which [the traditional view] is founded seem to hold little plausibility". In addressing the question of what is distinctive about public law, Loughlin rejects the notion of proceeding by examining the claim "that somehow, because of the subject-matter [the political nature of the relationships which public law regulates] and the demands which that imposes on method [where those called upon to exercise legal judgment must understand the broader framework within which decision-making takes place], public law is categorically different from private law". The difficulty with such an approach, he argues, is that it begins with the implicit assumption that law in general is a discrete discipline and only then proceeds to examine the case for the distinctiveness of public law. Instead, Loughlin begins with the following assumption: "that public law is simply a sophisticated form of political discourse; that controversies within the subject are simply extended political disputes". These broad understandings of the "legal" and the "political" find support in the following classic description of political theory: "quite simply, [it is] man's attempts to consciously understand and solve the problems of his group life and organization." G. H. Sabine and T. L. Thorson, *supra* n. 4, 3. Consider also John Kelly's view of the "general politico-economic ideology" of the "average Western liberal democracy"—that "[its] entire structure is given life and force by the legal system . . . In fact when an economist or a political scientist talks about our system, although he is focusing only on its economic effects or on its political inspiration, he is talking about a structure not only embedded in law, but actually consisting of law." "Property, Ireland and Marxism" *Business and Finance*, 18 Sept. 1986. Of course, as Wayne Morrison has recently remarked, "[although] the question ['what is law?'] has been posed from at least the time of the classical Greeks, some 2,500 years ago, [. . .] no settled answer to the question has been arrived at": *Jurisprudence: From the Greeks to Postmodernism* (London, Cavendish, 1997), 1. Roger Brownsword and John Adams note that the basic questions as to what constitutes "law" relate to whether it is to be characterised in formal or functional terms, and in morally neutral or moral terms, and also that there are other conceptions of law which insist on viewing it in relation to the exercise of various forms of power—social, political and economic as well as "legal" power. *Understanding Law* (London, Sweet and Maxwell, 1996), 1–25.

[33] For this point, and the point that the Review Group's subsequent endorsement of the right to free primary education also undermines their basic argument, see G. Whyte, *supra* n. 25.

those two branches of government—the executive and the legislature—which are associated with the "democratic" representational process, several questions regarding the judicial branch of the tripartite "separation of powers" are raised. However, I will leave discussion of this aspect of the role of the judiciary until the next section, where the prospect of judicial recognition (as opposed to mere interpretation) of these rights will be analysed.

The other major argument put forward by the majority against economic rights is made "by reference to the implications of conferring a constitutional right on everybody to freedom from poverty were conferred".[34] They claim that poverty is "a condition not susceptible to objective determination" and that it would fall to the judiciary to determine, in particular cases, what constitutes poverty and what remedies would be required, thus leaving "no discretion" to the Government and *Oireachtas* as regards the amount of revenue required to fund the remedial requirement. As Mark Tushnet has written, "[m]any critics of [economic rights] provisions, and some supporters, argue that no government can actually implement such a right, considering the fiscal constraints that governments are under."[35]

There are several problems with the view that these rights are unenforceable. The idea that the measurement of poverty is difficult is negated, first, by the fact that this is ultimately the case with all rights (how, for example, can the right to freedom of expression be "objectively determined"?)[36] and, secondly, that measuring methods for various "poverty lines" already exist.[37] Further, as Gerard Hogan has observed, while the rights protected by Article 40.3 of the Constitution are explicitly qualified by considerations of practicability, "it could scarcely be suggested that it would not be practicable for the State to commit adequate resources to house the (relatively small) number of homeless, were it minded so to do, or, indeed, where it was judicially ordered to provide such resources".[38] When the majority continues to point to the question of resources, it overlooks the fact that the 1987 household survey (on which its economic analysis was based) indicates, as I have already mentioned, that poverty in Ireland is not the result of a scarcity of resources but rather of the concentration of the wealth which does exist in the State.[39]

---

[34] *Report of the Constitution Review Group, supra* n. 6, 235.

[35] M. Tushnet, "Living with a Bill of Rights" in C. Gearty and A. Tomkins (eds.), *supra* n. 3, 13.

[36] As Loughlin states, "there will always be disputes about [the application of civil and political rights]" *supra* n. 16, 222.

[37] See reference at n. 10 above.

[38] G. Hogan, "Unenumerated Personal Rights: *Ryan's* Case Re-evaluated" (1990–1992) 25–27 *Ir. Jur.* 95 at 107. Tushnet has expressed his scepticism about the problems of "affirmative rights" as follows: "I believe that it is just as much within the capacity of judges to enforce affirmative rights as negative liberties. I find it interesting, for example, that some who object to constitutional guarantees of minimum subsistence or of jobs or housing are much less troubled by constitutional guarantees of environmental protection, which seems to me to raise the same problems of enforceability": *Supra* n. 35, 19 (n. 27).

[39] In addition, this view of available resources fails to address the inefficiency of severe economic inequality such as exists in Ireland. See the comments of the minority *supra* at n. 23. It

Ultimately, it is difficult to agree with Francis Beytagh's observation, in his brief discussion of this recommendation of the Review Group, that the reasoning is "sound and sensible".[40] Beytagh does go on to point out that "the result might be a harsher one than the Committee intended, especially where there is an interconnection between economic status and the inability of a person to exercise a fundamental substantive right",[41] but this very interconnection is explicitly referred to by the minority of the Review Group when it acknowledges a general "interdependence between the resources which people own and control and their access to justice and other aspects of equality".[42] The majority of the Review Group cannot be said to have been unaware of either the nature or extent of one of the most obvious consequences of its recommendation. As another constitutional commentator wrote in the immediate aftermath of the Report's publication, "For those concerned about the increasing social and economic exclusion of a significant section of our population, the approach of the Constitution Review Group . . . is ultimately disappointing."[43]

ECONOMIC RIGHTS AS UNENUMERATED RIGHTS?

The prospect of economic rights arising as unenumerated rights was discussed in a recent academic debate, between Gerard Hogan and Richard Humphreys, on the subject of interpretation in Irish constitutional jurisprudence.[44] In general terms, the debate addresses the question of the proper basis for the recognition of unenumerated rights under Article 40.3.1[45] Hogan's main concern is

should also be noted that the majority view that it "would not accord with democratic principles to confer absolute rights in the Constitution in relation to economic or social objectives" (*Report of the Constitution Review Group*, supra n. 6, 236) seems to deny the weight of constitutional jurisprudence which holds that there are no absolute rights *of any kind* in the Constitution (see G. Hogan and G. Whyte (eds.), J. M. Kelly, *The Irish Constitution* (3rd edn. Dublin, Butterworths, 1994), 686–7).

[40] F. X. Beytagh, *Constitutionalism in Contemporary Ireland: An American Perspective* (Dublin, Round Hall Sweet and Maxwell, 1997), 179.

[41] *Ibid.*

[42] *Report of the Constitution Review Group*, supra n. 6, 235. See also text *supra* at n. 7.

[43] G. Whyte, *supra* n. 25.

[44] The "debate" in question spans four separate pieces: G. Hogan, "Constitutional Interpretation" in F. Litton (ed.), *supra* n. 1; R. Humphreys, "Constitutional Interpretation" (1993) 15 *DULJ* 59; G Hogan, "Unenumerated Personal Rights: *Ryan's* Case Re-evaluated", *supra* n. 38; and R. Humphreys, "Interpreting Natural Rights" (1993–95) 28–30 *Ir. Jur.* 221.

[45] Art. 40.3 states: "1. The State guarantees in its laws to respect, and, as far as practicable, by its laws to defend and vindicate the personal rights of the citizen. 2. The State shall, in particular, by its laws protect as best it may from unjust attack and, in the case of injustice done, vindicate the life, person, good name and property rights of every citizen." The broad clause in this Art.—"personal rights"—has been the textual source of numerous unenumerated rights. The decision that originally opened up this possibility was that of the High Court in *Ryan v. Attorney General* [1965] IR 294. Kenny J's decision that there was a constitutional right to bodily integrity was based in part on his view that there is a whole range of unenumerated rights which "flow from the Christian and democratic" nature of the State. This reasoning—albeit often with

with the legitimacy of the judicial activism of Irish courts in using Article 40.3.1 in this way. He argues that there is no objective means of ascertaining the provenance of the personal rights referred to in Article 40.3.1.[46] but rejects the notion that the function of ascertaining the unenumerated rights should be reserved to the *Oireachtas*. He expresses his dissatisfaction with the present situation as follows:

"while the language of Article 40.3.1 would seem to compel the courts to arrive at the analysis approved in Ryan, this is not necessarily a result which should meet with our unqualified approval, since the lack of objectivity in the method whereby such unenumerated rights are arrived at, coupled with the attendant uncertainty thereby entailed, all seriously undermine the important legal values of objectivity and certainty. In other words, the gist of the objection is that the rather loose language of Article 40.3.1 has resulted in a vast—and, it must be said, unprincipled— expansion of the power of judicial review."[47]

Objecting, ultimately, to any "politicisation" of constitutional adjudication, Hogan supports the suggestion of John Kelly, who wrote in the wake of the decision in *Ryan* that one solution would be:

"to amend the Constitution by incorporating in Article 40 an expanded recital of specific personal rights, laying down in each case the standards upon which the

---

several modifications—has spawned a whole series of decisions which identify such rights. For a list of rights "identified by the courts as being amongst the latent or unenumerated rights constitutionally protected by Article 40.3.1", see the *Report of the Constitution Review Group*, *supra* n. 6 at, 246 (in all, 18 such rights are listed).

[46] Hogan argues that three possible bases for the unenumerated "personal rights" of Art. 40.3.1 have been relied on by the Irish courts: *supra* n. 38, 104–11. First, there is the approach taken by Kenny J in *Ryan*—that the rights stem from the "Christian and democratic" nature of the state. Hogan demonstrates that the two "limbs" of this test are unpersuasive guides to ascertaining which rights are protected. There is only one recognised unenumerated right—the right to travel—that could be said to derive from the "democratic" nature of the State. As for the "Christian" nature of the state (leaving aside the fact that some of the text of the Constitution, for example Art. 44.2, which prevents the State from endowing any religion or from imposing disabilities or making any discrimination "on the grounds of religious profession, belief or status", suggests that the State does not in fact have this character), Hogan shows that the "practical utility" of this standard in determining the rights of citizens is also highly questionable he refers to the use in the *Ryan* case of the papal encyclical, *Pacem in Terris*, where the reference therein to a right to bodily integrity was invoked by Kenny J, and points out that the use of this encyclical to interpret the 1937 Constitution, given that it was only published during the course of argument in the *Ryan* case, "seems remarkable", and also that the later decision in the case of *McGee v. Attorney General*—[1974] IR 284—directly contradicts another papal encyclical, *Humanae Vitae*. This latter contradiction, as Hogan notes, was originally pointed out by Desmond Clarke ("The Role of Natural Law in Irish Constitutional Law" (1982) 17 *Ir. Jur.* 203–4). Hogan also dismisses the argument that the natural law approach provides anything like an objective standard for the identification of unenumerated personal rights. "There is an express judicial acknowledgment that the nature or extent of natural law is a matter of considerable dispute, but that it falls to the judiciary to determine its extent and application." (G. Hogan, *supra* n. 38, 110). Finally, Hogan dismisses the "human personality test" as "a secular version of earlier natural law theories" (*ibid.*, 111).

[47] G. Hogan, *supra* n. 38, 114.

Oireachtas may delimit such rights. We would then be back to the simple principle of testing black-and-white constitutional norms."[48]

Richard Humphreys rejects Hogan's argument that natural law does not provide adequately precise guidelines for the task of ascertaining unenumerated rights and favours a constitutional jurisprudence that would draw on natural rights theory and "the international experience":

"This task involves an attempt to determine the extent to which the international community has recognised the right sought to be protected, and the result of that enquiry goes directly to the question of whether the right concerned, or the aspect of it that is at issue, deserves protection as a natural right under the Constitution of Ireland."[49]

Of more direct relevance to the present discussion, this general debate between Hogan and Humphreys also includes reference to the specific question of economic rights. In relation to these rights, Hogan refers to the quotation from *Pacem in Terris* that was employed in the *Ryan* case:[50]

"Beginning our discussion of the rights of man, we see that every man has the right to life, to bodily integrity and to the means which are necessary and suitable for the

---

[48] J M Kelly, *Fundamental Rights in the Irish Law and Constitution* (2nd edn, Dublin, Jurist Publishing, 1984), 47.

[49] R Humphreys (1993–95), *supra* n. 44 at 227. It should be noted here that, at a superficial level at least, the role of natural law in the context of *Bunreacht na hEireann* would appear to be greatly diminished since Humphrey's article was written. In *In re Article 26 and the Regulation of Information (Services outside the State for Termination of Pregnancies) Bill 1995* [1995] 2 ILRM 81, the Supreme Court declared that, "[f]rom a consideration of all the cases which recognised the existence of a personal right which was not specifically enumerated in the Constitution, it is manifest that the Court in each such case had satisfied itself that such personal right was one which could be reasonably implied from and was guaranteed by the provisions of the Constitution, interpreted in accordance with its ideas of prudence, justice and charity. The Courts, as they were and are bound to, recognised the Constitution as the fundamental law of the State to which the organs of the State were subject and at no stage recognised the provisions of the natural law as superior to the Constitution" at p. 107. But for a discussion of the extremely poor reasoning of the Supreme Court in this case, see G. Whyte, "Natural Law and the Constitution" (1996) 14 *ILT* 8. While it may be true that theocracy "long recognised the social responsibility of property and historically retarded the early introduction of market economies throughout feudal Europe" (G. Quinn, *supra* n. 2, 282), it is interesting that natural law ideology, when it was "in force", was never applied in relation to the substantive economic inequality with which this chapter is concerned. The *Report of the Constitution Review Group* recommends the amendment of Art. 40.3.1 to provide a comprehensive list of fundamental rights along the lines of the Kelly–Hogan suggestion (Hogan was himself a member of the 15-person Review Group). Since it is recommended that this list "might also include those set out in the European Convention on Human Rights and the International Covenant on Civil and Political Rights" (*Report, supra* n. 6, 259), John Morison draws a conclusion that seems to take on board Humphreys' deference to "the international experience": "[t]his recommendation, building upon the outward-looking approach that characterises some of the more progressive aspects of modern Irish society and which seeks to locate itself within best practice internationally, surely provides the basis for the future development of Bunreacht na hEireann towards the realisation of its early potential as a liberal rights based document" ("'A disposition to preserve and an ability to improve': The Report of the Constitution Review Group in the Republic of Ireland" [1997] *Public Law* 55 at 62).

[50] See *supra* n. 45.

proper development of life: these are primarily food, clothing, shelter, rest, medical care and finally the necessary social services."

Hogan states that since the right to life is expressly referred to in the text of the Constitution (Article 40.3.2), and the right to bodily integrity was acknowledged in *Ryan*, the question remains as to why rights to adequate food, clothing, shelter, rest and medical care have not been recognised. He suggests that the main reason is a class bias on the part of the judiciary and quotes John Hart Ely:

> "Experience suggests that there will be a systematic bias in judicial choice of fundamental values, unsurprisingly in favor of the values of the upper-middle professional class from which most lawyers and judges, and for that matter, most moral philosophers, are drawn . . . [W]atch when most fundamental-rights theorists start edging towards the door when someone mentions jobs, food or housing: those are important, sure, but they aren't fundamental."[51]

Hogan also notes two further reasons behind the Irish courts' non-recognition of such rights: first, there is the view of John Kelly that the ideals of *Pacem in Terris* are similar to those in Article 45, the Directive Principles of Social Policy, and that if encyclicals such as that one are used as interpretative tools in the present context, "the situation will have been reached that the general ideas of Article 45 will have been introduced into the machinery of judicial review by the back door";[52] and secondly, Hogan himself feels that if the courts were to recognise constitutional economic rights, "then they would be acting as little more than a third House of the Oireachtas."[53]

On this question of economic rights, Humphreys is again in strong disagreement with Hogan. As regards Kelly's fears about the "back door", for example, Humphreys points out that "if the result is so awful, the back door should not have been left wide open by the explicit recognition of natural rights".[54] Humphreys also rejects the idea of Ely that protected rights tend not to be socio-economic rights: he points to the International Covenant on Economic, Social and Cultural Rights as part of a "formidable body of binding international law reinforcing these . . . rights".[55] This seems completely to overlook the fact, noted above, that the wording of this Covenant allows for weak forms of implementation and a low priority status as compared with the Covenant on civil and political rights. More to the point, however, is the issue of the role of the judiciary in both of their analyses (and indeed in that of the majority of the Review Group).

In response to Hogan's view that for the courts to recognise rights in this field would be to "act as little more than a Third House of the Oireachtas",

---

[51] J. H. Ely, *Democracy and Distrust: A Theory of Judicial Review* (Cambridge, Mass., Harvard University Press, 1980), 58–9.
[52] J. M. Kelly, *supra* n. 48, 45.
[53] G. Hogan, *supra* n. 38 at 108.
[54] R. Humphreys (1993–95), *supra* n. 44 at 230.
[55] *Ibid* at 229.

Humphreys suggests—correctly, in my view—that this argument seems itself to fall into "the fetishism about economic rights which Hogan earlier implicitly condemns". In other words: if, as he appears to do at one point, Hogan agrees with Ely in the view that the distinction made between the two sets of rights is essentially a question of judicial class bias, why does he then imply that recognition of socio-economic rights, but, not other kinds of rights, would amount to judicial law-making?. On the other hand Humphreys rejects the notion of any judicial class-bias against socio-economic rights and claims that "there is no reason why rights in this category should not be recognised by the Irish courts in an appropriate case".[56] The reality, as Hogan clarifies, is that Ely's observations are borne out by the Irish jurisprudence: "[t]here has been no question at all of the courts taking the view [that economic rights be recognised]".[57] To hint, as Humphreys does, that it is a question of "an appropriate case" is unfounded speculation.

Hogan's anxiety about the role of the courts here is very surprising. As Edward Rubin and Malcolm Feeley have observed, "[t]he old, self-justificatory bromide that judges do not make the law, but only find it, is generally rejected—even scorned—these days".[58] Hogan's reference to a "third House of the Oireachtas" seems akin to the "whispers [. . .] from the dark corners of legal formalism that there is no such thing as judicial lawmaking and that, if there is, it is a violation of the rule of law".[59] At another point in his argument Humphreys also falls into the same outmoded way of thinking on this matter when he implies that "the natural rights technique" is a matter of "reading law" rather than "making law".[60]

Indeed it would appear that both authors are rooted ultimately in a quasi-formalist conception of law and legal systems. They do not approach the extreme version of Langdell's academic science, the notion that "law and legal decision-making are to be understood as taking place within a hermetic logical universe of clear-cut rules and deductive inferences",[61] but neither do they allow for any substantial political role for judges in their normative constitu-

---

[56] R. Humphreys (1993–95), *supra* n. 49, 230. Humphreys does recognise the point noted above (*supra* n. 3) that the right to education cannot simply be classified as based on the values of the "upper-middle professional class", as Ely seems to claim. He also points out that the conclusions of the 1994 Cairo Conference on Population and Development refute the suggestion that privacy of the home and personal autonomy are "the values of the wealthy" (*ibid*).

[57] G. Hogan, *supra* n. 38, 107.

[58] E. Rubin and M. Feeley, "Creating Legal Doctrine" (1990) 69 *Southern California Law Review* 1989 at 1989.

[59] *Ibid.*

[60] As regards Hogan's preference for an explicit catalogue of all the rights which the Constitution would protect, Humphreys responds: "[T]his is a separate and effectively political project of reform, and is clearly distinct from any suggestion as to how the Constitution which we actually have should be interpreted. It is not an exercise in 'reading law' but rather in 'making law'": (1993–95) *supra* n. 44, 223.

[61] B. Leiter, "Is There An American Jurisprudence?" (1997) 17 *Oxford Journal of Legal Studies* 367 at 372.

tional theories.[62] It would seem that neither writer would have much time for the basic realist assumption "that judges—stimulated, primarily, by the facts before them rather than by the rules to which those facts might be fitted—work backwards, 'from a desirable conclusion to one or another of a stock of logical premises' ".[63] As to what actually determines the responses of judges to particular facts, Brian Leiter has recently pointed out that the most influential realist view has been that it is "common sociological facts about judges (e.g. their background, their professional socialization experiences, and the like)" (rather than Jerome Frank's view that it is idiosyncratic facts about each judge's personality which counted).[64] Interestingly, realist jurisprudence does find some expression in an Appendix to the 1996 report entitled "The independence of the judiciary". The author, Kathleen Lynch, writes:

> "While it may not have been the remit of the Constitution Review Group to engage in a class and gender analysis of the judiciary (although I retain my view that such an analysis would have been of great public interest), they remain matters which impact directly on how the Constitution and the laws operating under it will be, and have been, interpreted. For it is a sociological fact that the perspectives of all persons are profoundly influenced by their own biographical experience, including their gender and social class-related socialisation. Judges (and other persons exercising judicial functions), being human, are subject to the same biases and prejudices as other persons"[65]

Generally, however, it would seem that there has been little of a swing in the realist direction in Irish constitutional discourse.[66] The absence of a work in Ireland akin to, for example, the monumental study of the British judiciary by Professor Griffith[67]—assessing the *politics* of the Irish judiciary—goes some way to explaining this state of affairs. I wish to conclude here by suggesting

---

[62] Obviously and somewhat ironically Hogan comes closest to doing this. Apart from his references to Ely's ideas, he remains conscious of the problem with the Kelly proposal of a return to "black-and-white constitutional norms": there is still indeterminacy and significant room for interpretation, and therefore the possibility of legal-political bias on the part of the judges. He acknowledges this, to some limited extent at least, when he refers to the express protection of rights in the European Convention of Human Rights: "[t]his, of course, is not to pretend that the wording of the Convention is not very 'open-textured' and leaves much to individual judicial discretion" (*supra* n. 61, 116).

[63] N. Duxbury, *Patterns of American Jurisprudence* (Oxford, Clarendon Press, 1995), 123 (quoting Max Radin) Although this assumption is most often associated with statutory interpretation and the use of precedent by courts of first-instance, it is generally applicable to all forms and levels of adjudication.

[64] B Leiter, *supra* n. 58 at 375.

[65] K. Lynch, "The Independence of the Judiciary", Appendix 17, *Report of the Constitution Review Group, supra* n. 6, 584.

[66] As Tushnet remarks, while noting that the USA and the UK share a common law culture: "[t]he contemporary legal culture in the UK appears to me more formalist, less affected by legal realist jurisprudence, than the US legal culture, however" (*supra* n. 35, 18 (n. 2)). Irish legal culture is similarly "less affected" by realist jurisprudence than that of the USA.

[67] J. A. G. Griffith, *The Politics of the Judiciary* (4th edn., London, Fontana, 1991). For another example, see G. H. Gadbois, "Indian Supreme Court Judges: A. Portrait" (1968–69) 3 *Law and Society Review* 317.

that only when such work is undertaken by Irish legal academic scholars will it be possible to have a truly informed debate on the much discussed topic of constitutional interpretation.

CONCLUSION

While the evidence presented here would seem to suggest that the protection of economic rights in Irish constitutional jurisprudence is not a likely prospect in the foreseeable future, I have argued that the explanations for this that are commonly offered from within the tradition of "liberal legalism" are, to say the least, highly questionable. The essential reason, why economic rights are not afforded constitutional recognition in Ireland is because the state and its institutions (including the judiciary and virtually all of the political parties) are committed to a form of liberal-capitalist economic system which tacitly incorporates the inequalities and the poverty which have been the subject of this essay. Any movement to a situation where substantive economic rights were recognised and protected would have at least the *potential* to undermine, ideolgically and perhaps practically as well, that mode of production.

Nevertheless there remain two (by no means mutually exclusive) strands of thought that could argue for constitutional economic rights in Ireland, and I will conclude with reference to these. Gerry Whyte has placed his call for such rights in the context of the philosophy of "Christian democracy", a philosophy he sees as the other (along with liberal-democracy) central feature of the Constitution. Stating that this tradition "currently provides constitutional legitimation for a political system based on . . . transformative politics, where the question of human good has a central place", Whyte argues that "if the political system has failed a marginalised group, it should be permitted to have recourse to the courts to vindicate its basic socio-economic rights".[68] However, while it would certainly be difficult to deny the strain of Christian democracy in the Constitution, this has never, in the text or through its interpretation, extended to the recognition of economic rights. On the contrary, Quinn has argued that the trend of "economic development" means that theocratic ideology "will either become marginalised or even positively expurgated from the constitution",[69] an argument that has gained increased force since the Supreme Court decision in *In re Article 26 and the Regulation of Information (Services Outside the State for Termination of Pregnancies) Bill 1995*.[70] At the same time, it is worth noting that even if such expurgation were

---

[68] *Supra* n. 25. See also G. Whyte, "Some Reflections on the Role of Religion in the Constitutional Order" in this volume.

[69] *Supra* n. 2, 286.

[70] See *supra* n. 49.

to take place, the tradition of Christian democracy could still be relied on by a non-interpretivist reading of the Constitution.[71]

The other possible "line of attack" would also be essentially non-interpretivist: it would base the argument for economic rights on a political tradition that finds no express approval in the Constitution itself, that is, on the tradition of socialist political thought.[72] I would suggest that the option of demanding these rights will become increasingly attractive to a political tradition that is undergoing a process of renegotiation with itself.[73] When discussing the sense of displacement brought about by the shifts in left thinking over the past fifteen years, Anne Phillips refers not only to "the cultural displacing the material" and "identity politics displacing class", but also "the politics of constitutional reform displacing the economics of equality".[74] Implicit in this latter perspective is the assumption that constitutional reform is in some way incapable of addressing "the economics of equality". The possibility of economic rights challenges that assumption, albeit more by their ability to address the extent of poverty and *in*equality as distinct from being a potential guarantee of economic equality. The advocacy of economic rights, in other words, allows "left thinking" some scope to address the problems of economic inequality within present constitutional structures. The difficulty with this is the traditional socialist antipathy to individual rights. This perspective has been represented in jurisprudence by the Critical Legal Studies

[71] For a typology of interpretivist and non-interpretivist methods of constitutional interpretation, as suggested by Quinn and others, see A. F. Twomey, "Bork's Originalism: Reconciling Judicial Constitutional Interpretation with the Rule of Law" (1996) 14 *ILT* 278 at 278. It strikes me that the whole project of "reconciling" Irish judicial activism with the rule of law (which is also a basic purpose of the contributions of Hogan and Humphreys which were discussed in the preceding section) is a project that is again at the naïve end of the formalist-realist spectrum and, as such, doomed to failure from the outset. For a critique of, for example, the originalist approach, see G. Whyte, "Constitutional Adjudication, Ideology and Access to the Courts" in A. Whelan (ed.) Law and Liberty in Ireland (Dublin, Oak Tree Press, 1993), 156; as for natural law approaches, see the comment of G. Hogan *supra* at n. 46 and also D. M. Clarke, "Natural Law and Constitutional Consistency" in G. Quinn, A. Ingram and S. Livingstone (eds.), *Justice and Legal Theory in Ireland* (Dublin, Oak Tree Press, 1995), 22.

[72] However, it could be argued that some of the provisions of Art. 45 are close, in their basic philosophy, to socialist ideas on wealth distribution.

[73] While there are strong arguments to the effect that the general collapse of "actually existing socialism" does not in any way theoretically refute the basic principles of the socialist tradition (see, e.g., J. Petras and C. Polychroniou, "Nature of Capitalist Transformation: Continuing Relevance of Marxism", *Economic and Political Weekly*, 28 Jan. 1995 and A. Callinicos, "Whither Marxism?" *Economic and Political Weekly*, 27 Jan. 1996), it cannot be denied that a "renegotiation" is taking place on the left. See, e.g., the comments of Anne Philips *infra*. In my view, and despite the tendency of some commentators to see the two traditions as polarised, the influence of postmodern thought on socialism will be central to the ultimate outcomes of the renegotiation. In relation to the present subject, it may be noted that Costas Douzinas has suggested that respect for human rights "seems to be the only regulative principle of state organization which unites every country, race and creed in the world" and argues that, "in their paradoxical linkage of symbolic openness and ethical determinacy, human rights can become the postmodern formulation of the principle of justice." "Justice and Human Rights in Postmodernity" in C .Gearty and A. Tomkins, *supra* n. 3, 115–17.

[74] A. Phillips, "From Inequality to Difference: A Severe Case of Displacement?" (1997) 224 *New Left Review* 143 at 143.

movement (CLS). CLS pointed to an ideology of "possessive individualism" associated, in their view, with rights and also suggested that rights could not properly insulate the individual from public power since the logic of rights-based argumentation was circular.[75] According to Duncan Kennedy:

> "Rights are by their nature 'formal', meaning that they secure to individuals legal protection for as well as from arbitrariness—to speak of rights is precisely not to speak of justice between social classes, races, or sexes."[76]

However, these CLS views of rights have to some extent been superseded by the more recent Critical Race Theory movement (also known as "outsider jurisprudence"). One of the leading exponents of this movement, Patricia Williams, has argued as follows:

> "For the historically disempowered, the conferring of rights is symbolic of all the denied aspects of their humanity: rights imply a respect that places one in a referential range of self and others, that elevates one's status from human body to social being."[77]

Developments such as these mean that it is becoming increasingly accepted by the left, as Tom Campbell argued over a decade ago, that "[t]he concept of rights . . . is not inherently biased against socialist ideals and aspirations".[78] The traditional antipathy is basically a consequence of the fact that the rights protected by liberal states have not been socio-economic rights. CLS scholars were of the view that, "even if rights did function to effectively insulate individuals against public power then they are still open to the charge that they effectively expose individuals to the full brutalities of private power where such is left unregulated by positive law".[79] Economic rights, particularly at the constitutional level, have the potential to confront these "brutalities" in no uncertain terms.

[75] See G. Quinn, *supra* n. 2, 284–5.

[76] D. Kennedy, "Legal Education as Training for Hierarchy" in D Kairys (ed.), *The Politics of Law* (New York, Pantheon Books, 1990), 46.

[77] P. Williams, *The Alchemy of Race and Rights* (Cambridge, Mass., Harvard University Press, 1991), 153.

[78] T. Campbell, *The Left and Rights: A Conceptual Analysis of the Idea of Socialist Rights* (London, Routledge and Kegan Paul, 1983), 214. At a more general level still, as Michael Perry has demonstrated, "rights-talk is a derivative and even dispensable feature of political-moral discourse". *Morality, Politics, and Law* (New York and Oxford, Oxford University Press, 1988), 188–9.

[79] G. Quinn, *supra* n. 2, 284.

14

The Constitution and Criminal Justice

PAUL O'MAHONY

INTRODUCTION

The primary function and the chief achievement of any Constitution is the fashioning of the institutional infrastructure for the administration of government and the law. There are two other vital tasks. First, there is the issue of the character and quality of the society envisioned by the Constitution. A Constitution will explicitly and implicitly embody a set of fundamental principles and ideals that express an ordering of values for society and are intended to shape the type of society that emerges. Secondly, there is the more immediately practical issue of the relationship between the State and its powers, vested in its officers and institutions, and the citizen.

The Constitution of a modern parliamentary democracy must be concerned to curb the potentially immense coercive powers of the State and make them subject to the law in a manner that both promotes the liberties of the individual citizen and protects him, or her, from possible abuses and injustices. This essay will briefly examine some aspects of the role of the Constitution in shaping criminal justice procedures, controlling the exercise of the State's coercive powers, and defining, realising, and protecting the civil liberties of the citizen.

The essential task of the 1937 Constitution was to define the organisational structures and the basic ground rules for the exercise of political and legal power in the State. Few would argue with the proposition that it succeeds admirably in this task. Many might question the quality, utility, and even the rationality of much of the political and judicial activity in this country, but few harbour serious dissatisfaction with the actual structures of government or of the legal system as laid down by the Constitution. In particular, the separation of the powers of the executive, the legislature and the judiciary and the critically important function of the Supreme Court in interpreting the Constitution itself and in testing the constitutionality of legislation have proven to be enduring and, arguably, effective mechanisms for the creation and maintenance of democracy.[1]

---

[1] J. M. Kelly in the introduction to his first edition of *The Irish Constitution*, reproduced in G. Hogan and G. Whyte (eds.), *The Irish Constitution* (3rd edn., Dublin, Butterworths, 1994)

It is likely that the Constitution of the United States was an important model for de Valera and the other framers of the Irish Constitution,[2] and both Constitutions are most obviously successful at the work of fashioning governmental structures. The most obvious flaws in both Constitutions, on the other hand, relate to the value-ordering function and the manner in which the Constitutions were partially shaped by unresolved political and ethical dilemmas arising directly from the political and cultural context at the time of drafting.

Just as it is possible to discern in the US Constitution the influence of specific historical imperatives, most obviously the need to win over some reluctant States which were fearful of the strength of federal government and concerned to protect their slave-owning traditions, the Irish Constitution can be seen to have been written from a particular political, historical and religious perspective with an anxious weather eye on Westminster and the unionists in the six counties and with a deferential, indeed in places subservient, nod to the Roman Catholic Church.[3]

The original US Constitution of 1787 was concerned to create a federal nation which could survive the fact that some States permitted, while others strongly disapproved and were moving towards prohibition of, slavery. Article 4ii stated that "[n]o Person held to Service or Labour in one State, under the Laws thereof, escaping into another, shall, in consequence of any Law or Regulation therein be discharged from such Service or Labour, but shall be delivered up on Claim of the Party to whom such Service or Labour may be due." This Article, which would later allow for the infamous fugitive slave laws, was from the beginning considered by many to be inconsistent with the Declaration of Independence and inimical to the core values of the United States, but was also considered necessary to gain the compliance of the Southern slave-owning States. It represented compromise and troublesome, unfinished business that was not finally resolved until the American Civil War and the inclusion in the Constitution in 1866 of the Thirteenth, Fourteenth and Fifteenth Amendments which, among other things, abolished slavery and conferred citizenship on former slaves.

There is, clearly, also much compromise and unfinished business lurking menacingly in the Articles of the Irish Constitution. The territorial claim of

p. *xcii*, expressed the view that the average liberal observer "would probably say the overall impact of the courts on modern Irish life, in their handling of constitutional issues, had been beneficial, rational, progressive, and fair . . . ".

[2] The US Constitution of 1787, according to J. M. Kelly, *A Short History of Western Legal Theory* (Oxford, Clarendon Press, 1992), at 278, was "virtually a world novelty" and as a successful model in English undoubtedly exerted some influence over the framers of the Irish Constitution, particularly with respect to the central doctrine of the separation of powers, which finds clear expression in the US Constitution, although as B. Chubb states in *The Government and Politics of Ireland* (London, Longman, 1970), Britain was the chief model for governmental structures.

[3] See N. Browne, "Church and State in Modern Ireland"; G. Whyte, "Some reflections on the Role of Religion in the Constitutional Order"; and D. M. Clarke, "Education, the State and Sectarian Schools" in this volume.

Articles 2 and 3, ever more anomalous and anachronistic, remains to taunt unionist opinion in Northern Ireland and Britain and to reinforce aggressive nationalism in the whole of Ireland.[4] The Constitution's patronising view of women[5] and its increasingly irrelevant endorsement of religiously inspired values regarding the family, marriage and other aspects of personal morality have been challenged and undercut by amendment, as in the case of the Fifteenth Amendment permitting divorce, and even more obviously by social evolution and by developments in national and international law. But for the fact that the Irish people are generally so satisfied with the form of government defined by the Constitution, it is likely that the deficiencies of the Constitution in its value-ordering function would have by now led to its demise and replacement by a more modern, realistic and pluralist alternative.

THE CONSTITUTION AND THE CRIMINAL JUSTICE SYSTEM

The general satisfaction, or absence of dissatisfaction, with Constitution provisions governing criminal justice procedures can hardly be fully justified by reference to the explicit enumeration of rights within the text itself, since these are relatively few and sometimes far from unequivocal.

The important Articles are the following: Article 13.6 which endows the President with the power to commute or remit punishments imposed by the courts (significantly, some of these powers can be conferred by law on executive authorities, in particular the Minister for Justice); Article 15.5 which prohibits retrospective criminalisation; Article 34.1 which provides that justice be administered in public by courts; Article 35.2 which provides that judges are independent and subject only to the law and the Constitution; Article 38.1 which provides that no person shall be tried on any criminal charge except "in due course of law"; Article 40.4.1 which provides that no person shall be deprived of personal liberty except in accordance with law—with further subsections setting out specific procedures for taking a habeas corpus case to the High Court; Article 40.1 which provides that every person should be held as equal before the law; Article 38.5 which provides that, except for certain specified exceptions, no person should be tried on a criminal charge without a jury; and Article 40.5 which provides that a person's home is inviolable and shall not be forcibly entered except in accordance with the law.

Even before taking account of the qualifications that have been built into the Constitution severely to constrain some of these rights and of the Offences Against the State Act, 1939, which is a part of permanent legislation and provides mechanisms for the suspension of normal constitutional rights, it must be admitted that the Constitution is a disappointingly vague legal framework on which to

---

[4] See A. Carty, "The Irish Constitution, International Law and the Northern Question—The Need for Radical thinking" in this volume.

[5] See D. Dooley, "Gendered Citizenship in the Irish Constitution" in this volume.

base the protection of individual liberty from State power and on which to construct fair and just criminal procedures. Compared to the Bill of Rights in the American Constitution and more recent European Constitutions, such as the Spanish, the Irish criminal justice provisions appear to be spare and minimalist. There is little of a concrete or definitively affirmative nature apart from the right to a jury trial, the openness of the process, the independence of the judiciary and the more general principle of equality before the law, and all of these have been subjected to certain unfortunate limitations by the Constitution itself.

By contrast, the American Bill of Rights enunciates quite specific liberties (e.g. in the Fourth Amendment, from searches and seizures without probable cause) and procedural rights (e.g. in the Sixth, the right of an accused to a speedy trial and to "have compulsory process for obtaining witnesses in his favor" or in the Fifth, the right not to be "compelled in any criminal case to be a witness against himself"). The Spanish Constitution, as a modern European example, is also more explicit than the Irish Constitution and stipulates the abolition of the death penalty and the principle of proportionality of punishment, as well as actively supporting the principle of rehabilitation of offenders.

The focus of the criminal justice provisions that do appear in the Irish Constitution is firmly on the criminal process itself, and the areas of law enforcement and police powers are not covered in any detail. Most especially, the crucial area of punishment is almost completely ignored. In contrast, the Eighth Amendment to the US Constitution addresses this area directly, declaring that "[e]xcessive bail shall not be required, nor excessive fines imposed, nor cruel and unusual punishments inflicted".

THE RULE OF LAW AND THE EMERGENCE OF A "META-CONSTITUTION"

The most obvious general point to make about the criminal justice provisions in the Irish Constitution is that several of the Articles simply invoke the concept of "the Law", allowing certain state interventions in individuals' lives only "in accordance with the law". In this manner the Constitution establishes, as it were, the rule of law. Two things flow from the minimalist approach of the Constitution and its reliance on the concept of the rule of law. First, it is clear that the actual quality of justice and of protection of individual rights must be determined more by the statute laws already in place and to be developed in the future, by the tradition of the common law and all the principles on which it is based, and increasingly by international conventions to which Ireland is a signatory, such as the European Convention on Human Rights,[6] than by the Constitution itself. All of these three sources of

---

[6] The Supreme Court has repeated that, with regard to international agreements, Art. 29.6 means that in the absence of incorporation the Convention is not part of domestic law: *In Re ó Láighléis* [1960] IR 93. Nevertheless, the Convention and other international agreements have an indirect effect in domestic law: see generally G. Hogan and G. Whyte, *supra* n. 1, at 295–301.

law are influential so long as they do not contradict the Constitution. Secondly, the approach implicitly, but perhaps unwittingly, recognises the contingent, evolutionary and fluid nature of the law and, consequently, advances and ensures the critical role of the judiciary in interpreting the Constitution and the law and in, effectively, creating a "meta-Constitution" based on judge-made law that arises out of the actual Constitution like the genie out of Aladdin's lamp.

In practice this has meant that the High and Supreme Courts, in exercising their interpretative powers, have fleshed out the Constitution and plugged many of its obvious gaps, particularly in the area of criminal justice procedures. The judiciary have "read into" the Constitution a whole set of safeguards, which come close to the American Bill of Rights, not just in content, but also in comprehensiveness and effectiveness. One Article in the Constitution has played a vital and positive role in the discovery, definition and protection of rights. This is Article 40.3, in which the "State guarantees in its laws to respect, and, as far as practicable, by its laws to defend and vindicate the personal rights of the citizen" (in particular, the life, person, good name and property rights of every citizen). Article 45 has also played an auxiliary, if more indirect, role in the process of constructing a "meta-Constitution". Article 45—the "Directive Principles of Social Policy"—is intended exclusively for the guidance of the *Oireachtas* in its law-making function—especially at 45.1 which provides that "[t]he State shall strive to promote the welfare of the whole people by securing and protecting as effectively as it may a social order in which justice and charity shall inform all the institutions of the national life." Nevertheless, judicial interpretation has inevitably been influenced by this high-minded aspiration.

Judicial interpretation and argument, leaning on these and other Articles and sometimes deriving principles from them, have led to the doctrine of unenumerated rights through which certain rights, such as of access to the courts, to privacy, to bail, to legal counsel and to fair procedures in decision-making, have been granted constitutional status. In this way the framework of constitutional safeguards has been extended and reinforced to an extent that might make the minimalist and often equivocal provisions in the actual Constitution appear irrelevant or, some might argue, even beneficial, since they have given rise to such an efflorescence of important civil rights.

However, this is not the case. The vagueness and the deficiencies of the Constitution in the area of criminal justice have had a very definite negative impact at both the theoretical and practical levels. The special exemptions built into the Constitution, which in certain circumstances allow for the suspension or curtailment of the rights which the Constitution simultaneously brings to life, have been a major and growing problem through the years. The judiciary has extended the Constitution in many positive ways, delineating individual rights, but this process has coexisted with an acquiescence in the way in which successive governments have chosen to use the special and emergency powers, allowed to them by the Constitution, and with a tendency to interpret the law and the Constitution in certain key areas relating to special and emergency powers in a manner that appears to undercut rather than bolster civil liberties. In recent years, this has meant that the Constitution has not provided the kind of clear, unambiguous guidance that has been needed to temper the growing momentum of the political hardline agenda on criminal justice, an agenda which seems irrevocably wedded to a programme of increasing "toughness on crime" and ever more repressive measures.

THE RHETORIC–REALITY GAP

Before looking at some of the key areas more closely, it is worth making two general points. First, the vagueness of the Constitution on criminal justice and its reliance on the concept of the rule of law and the consequent need for extensive judicial interpretation have meant that this crucial area of law has become almost impossibly complex and arcane. For example, the low level of public and political debate prior to the 1996 bail referendum[7] can be related to the inherent legal complexity of the issue, which manages to baffle many lawyers as well as the general public. The convoluted ramifications of the law in many areas of the "meta-Constitution" on civil liberties ensures that these matters remain the preserve of a handful of specialists. Because of this, there is a lack of information and understanding amongst citizens about their constitutional rights and, even more crucially, no sense of personal ownership of the Constitution. In some countries like the United States the guarantees of the Constitution are widely known and have a significant psychological impact on the general population and the way they relate to the State and civic authorities. The remoteness of Irish people from their Constitution in this critical area is a real loss.

Secondly, it is worth emphasising that, in the final analysis, what counts is the day-to-day practice within the courts and the wider criminal justice system. The most eloquent declaration of rights and the noblest of ethical principles, even when embodied in a Constitution, mean little, if in practice the police harrass the innocent and guilty alike, the courts punish disproportionately and the prisons oppress, degrade and alienate the convicted. The important questions are how well on a day-to-day basis is the liberty of the ordinary citizen protected from unwarranted interference by the State and how effective are the controls on the authorities as they go about their crime prevention, investigation, prosecution, judicial, and penal business. Are suspects, detainees, and convicts treated with justice and charity? To what extent can a citizen expect equality of treatment before the law?

---

[7] See e.g. the editorials "Bail Reform: Expediency before Principle" (1995) 13 *ILT* 233 and "Bail Reform: Might We Think Before We Leap?" (1996) 14 *ILT* 29; also C. Mc Cullagh, "Asking the Wrong Questions: A Note on the Use of Bail in Irish Courts" (1990) 38 *Administration* 271–79.

A substantial degree of discretion, in the courts, the prosecution service, the prisons and police operations is inevitable in the process of translating the principles of any Constitution into daily practice. It is also inevitable that vested interests within the system, such as the police, will employ the full latitude of their discretionary powers and will exploit legal grey areas and constitutional ambiguities to advance their own activities. Even perfectly explicit and unambiguous constitutional guarantees require a panoply of practical measures and mechanisms to ensure that rights are not infringed or at least not infringed regularly and with impunity.

In this regard, the American experience is a salutary lesson. The American Bill of Rights is undoubtedly a far superior instrument for the governing of criminal justice procedures than the Irish Constitution. However, the reality of the US criminal justice system is an object lesson in the yawning gulf between the rhetoric of the law and the reality of law enforcement.

Despite the impressive constitutional safeguards, many Americans today experience their society as little better than a police state. As the Rodney King case[8] demonstrated, in some areas of the United States the illegal use of violence by officers of the law has become institutionalised and widespread.[9] The justice system was in this case shown to be so skewed that, even when a savage and unwarranted beating was captured on video and seen throughout the world, the police perpetrators were found innocent in a criminal trial. This disaster for American civil liberties was made possible mainly by moving the jury trial to an outlying suburb, which, it so happened, was home to many Los Angeles policemen but to very few Afro-Americans.

The fact that, by comparison with the United States, there is relatively little systematic abuse of civil liberties in Ireland and few clear-cut cases of miscarriage of justice should not blind us to the deficiencies in our system and the potential for a substantial escalation of problems in this area. There is at present in Ireland a serious lack of effective and adequate control mechanisms within the criminal justice system. For example, we allow an accused to be convicted on the basis of a retracted, uncorroborated confession, yet, despite the lessons of the Sallins Train Robbery,[10] the "Kerry Babies" case[11] and the more recent *Pringle* and *Connell*[12] cases, we still have not implemented the

---

[8] *Koon v. United States*, 116 SC 2035; 1996 US LEXIS 3877; 135 L Ed. 2d 392.

[9] See e.g. C. Pope and L. Ross, "Race, Crime and Justice: The Aftermath of Rodney King" (1992) 17 *The Criminologist* 1–10 and R. McNeely and C. Pope (eds.), *Race, Crime and Criminal Justice* (Beverly Hills, Cal., Sage, 1981).

[10] *Kelly v. Ireland* [1986] IR 757.

[11] See *Report of the Tribunal of Inquiry into the Kerry Babies Case* (Dublin, Stationery Office, 1995), and for a discussion of the inadequacies of the official response to the implications of the case regarding police interrogation see P. O'Mahony, "The Kerry Babies Case: Towards a Social Psychological Analysis" (1992) 13 *Irish J of Psychology* 223–38.

[12] For a brief overview of both the *Pringle* and *Connell* cases and for an examination of their implications with respect to Gárda interrogation methods see P. O'Mahony, "The Gárda Siochana and the Ethics of Police Interrogation" (1996) 6 *Irish Crim. Law J* 46–54.

Martin Committee's recommendations of 1990[13] to have all interrogations video-taped. Neither have we acted on the recommendation of the European Committee for the Prevention of Torture, which has expressed concern about the possibility of frequent physical abuse of suspects during detention in Dublin police stations, to reform the Gárda Complaints Board in order to make it more independent of the Gárda Siochana. Neither have we acted on the 12-year-old recommendation of the Whitaker Committee[14] to establish an independent inspectorate of prisons to monitor one of the most secret and neglected areas of State criminal justice activity. In these and other areas the Irish criminal justice system is weak and ineffectual at the vital work of practical vindication of undisputed constitutional rights.

Turning, then, to some of the key areas of concern arising from the ambiguities of the Constitution itself and judicial interpretation of it, I will briefly discuss emergency powers, the system of petitions, and the question of the refusal of bail as a form of preventive detention as defined by the amendment to the Constitution, passed by referendum in November 1996.

THE OFFENCES AGAINST THE STATE ACT 1939

Broadly speaking it is the area of emergency powers, special criminal courts and special criminal procedures that gives most direct cause for concern with respect to civil liberties today in Ireland.[15] In 1937, Ireland was a young nation led by Eamon de Valera, the chief framer of the Constitution, who was himself a former rebel against the "legitimate" government of the country and a former active protagonist in a bitter and bloody civil war. It is perhaps not surprising that de Valera would have been sensitive to the dangers of armed rebellion and would, in his Constitution, have made provision for the suspension of normal civil rights in the event of active attempts to subvert the Irish government. In any event, such emergency provisions for the suspension of normal constitutional safeguards in a time of war or armed rebellion are normal features of most Constitutions. However, the relative ease with which the normal safeguards can be set aside under the 1937 Constitution is, to put it mildly, unfortunate and the way that these special provisions have been used in Ireland gives cause for real concern.

---

[13] *Report of the Committee to Enquire into Certain Aspects of Criminal Procedure* (Dublin, Stationery Office, 1990). This report recommended routine taping of interrogations but, while there have been small-scale experiments with audio- and video-taping in a few Gárda Stations, the recommendation has yet to be implemented.

[14] *Report of the Committee of Inquiry into the Penal System* (Dublin, Stationery Office, 1985). More recently, a recommendation for a part-time, independent Inspector of Prisons was made in the Department of Justice paper, *Towards an Independent Prisons Board* (Dublin, Stationery Office, 1997).

[15] See generally J. Casey, *Constitutional Law in Ireland* (London, Sweet and Maxwell, 1992), at 149–56; G. Hogan and G. Whyte (eds.), *supra* n. 1, at 236–48.

Indeed, there is, in Article 28.3.3 of the Constitution, a power bestowed on the *Oireachtas* to, in effect, suspend the Constitution itself in a time of national emergency. Such powers were used in 1976 to introduce seven-day detention.[16] However, this legislation was only implemented for a year, and in practice the most obviously problematical Article has been 38.3.1, which allows for the establishment of non-jury special criminal courts, whenever the government deems that the "ordinary courts are inadequate to secure the effective administration of justice, and the preservation of public peace and order".[17]

The present Special Criminal Court was established in 1972 by way of a Governmental proclamation under Section 35 of the Offences Against the State Act 1939 and as envisaged by the Constitution. The Offences Against the State Act is part of permanent legislation and has been referred to the Supreme Court under Article 26 and found by it to be consistent with the Constitution.[18] It is, therefore, highly significant that as well as providing an instrument for the setting up of the Special Criminal Court, it provides for the suspension of certain normal legal safeguards in the area of police detention and admissible evidence.

The High Court has struck down as unconstitutional one section of the Act, which provided that anyone convicted before the Special Criminal Court could be barred from public service employment for a seven-year period.[19] However, Section 52 of the Offences Against the State Act, which requires a person to account for their movements, and so is a clear infringement on the right to silence, and Section 12, which permits possession of a pro-IRA poster to be used along with the word of a senior police officer to convict a person of IRA membership, and so breaches the normal precepts of admissible evidence, have both received the seal of approval of the Supreme Court.[20] Challenges to the constitutionality of the Special Criminal Court itself and of the powers of the Director of Public Prosecutions to refer non-subversive offenders to it have failed.

Of the special police powers, conferred by the Offences Against the State Act, Section 30, which allows a person to be detained without charge for up to 48 hours, is the most important partly because it is so frequently used. Significantly, this section was upheld by the Supreme Court in 1992 in a case that involved clearly "non-subversive" type offences. Section 30 has come to be used routinely by the Gárdai to investigate serious crime generally.[21] It is

---

[16] See D. Clarke, "Emergency Legislation, Fundamental Rights and Articles 28.3.3" (1977) 12 *Ir. Jur.* 217.

[17] See M. Robinson, *The Special Criminal Court* (Dublin, Dublin University Press, 1974).

[18] *In re Article 26 and the Emergency Powers Bill, 1976* [1977] IR 159; D. Gwynn Morgan, "The Emergency Powers Bill Reference—Part I" (1978) 13 *Ir. Jur.* 67 and "The Emergency Powers Bill Reference—Part II" (1979) 14 *Ir. Jur.* 253.

[19] *Cox v. Ireland* [1992] 12 IR 167.

[20] *Heaney and McGuinness v. Ireland and The Attorney General*, unreported, 23 July 1996 and *O'Leary v. The Attorney General*, unreported, 24 May 1995 respectively.

[21] *The People (Director of Public Prosecutions) v. Quilligan* [1986] IR 495.

used in preference to the normal powers of detention for the period subsequent to arrest but before charge, under the Criminal Justice Act, 1984, which permits detention for only up to twelve hours and only of persons suspected of having committed an offence that carries a sentence of at least five years imprisonment.

Normal civil rights are clearly curtailed for anyone detained under Section 30 and it is a matter of concern that only a small minority of those detained are actually charged with offences. This suggests that the Gárdai may be using these special legal powers routinely in an intimidatory fashion and as a questionable means of collecting criminal intelligence. Between 1975 and 1985, 14,000 people were arrested under Section 30, but only 500 of these were charged and less than 300 were eventually convicted under the Act.

Although the annual number of cases dealt with by the Special Criminal Court has declined dramatically from 286 in 1974 to 29 in 1994, more than two thousand non-scheduled offences cases have come before the Court and non-subversive cases continue to be tried there. For example, in 1993, Fr Patrick Ryan was tried on charges of receiving a stolen caravan and its contents and, in 1994, Rossi Walsh was convicted for arson, despite no evidence of a paramilitary dimension to the crime. In the High Court in 1995, Joseph Kavanagh, apparently an "ordinary, common or garden criminal", who was alleged to have kidnapped Jim Lacey, the chief executive of the Northern Bank, sought an order prohibiting his trial before the Special Criminal Court.[22] This was in effect an attempt to ensure he be granted his constitutional right to trial by jury. This was refused. Laffoy J in the High Court held that the proclamation setting up the Special Criminal Court was not unconstitutional and that the certification by the Director of Public Prosecutions stands even if "the true factual situation is that the alleged offences . . . have no subversive or paramilitary connection".

There are three important points to be made here. First, while some provision for special arrangements in a time of war or rebellion is probably necessary and sensible, in Ireland, the use of special powers, most especially the Offences Against the State Act (which does not rely on a state of emergency), has crossed the line between the suspension of normal rights when warranted by extraordinary circumstances and the expedient use of special provisions to establish a quasi-permanent, alternative and, potentially, more repressive criminal justice system. A complacent judiciary, political establishment, and general public have become habituated to the presence of the Special Criminal Court and there appears to be no will to abolish it and no sense of urgency about subjecting the rationale for its existence (i.e. that the ordinary courts are inadequate to secure the effective administration of justice and the preservation of public peace and order) to any form of reality-testing. Indeed, there is some political pressure to extend its operations to cover organised crime

---

[22] *Kavanagh* v. *Ireland* [1996] 1 ILRM 133.

and drug dealing and, alarmingly, a majority of the Constitution Review Group, reporting in 1996, supported this view.[23]

However, looking at the level of crime and terrorism in Ireland in recent years, many countries would be astonished at the continued existence of the Special Criminal Court and at the public tolerance of, or indifference to, the suspension of the fundamental constitutional right to a jury trial (for other than a minor offence). Similarly, the normalisation of special police powers is to be decried, even though it should be noted that many European countries allow similar forty-eight-hour detention as a matter of normal police powers. It is to be decried most of all because it compromises the Supreme Court, setting up a system of double standards, whereby the Supreme Court both continues to maintain that the constitutional guarantee of personal liberty means that a person should not be detained for questioning for more than 12 hours and, simultaneously, allows the routine use of 48 hour detention at the wide discretion of the police.

Second, while the Special Criminal Court and special powers under the Offences Against the State Act have become a normal, unremarkable part of the criminal justice system, it is clear that the remit of the Court has also been broadened by judicial rulings and practice, to include non-scheduled offences and non-subversive offenders. This creeping net-widening is most regrettable and further attenuates the basic constitutional principle of equality before the law.

Third, the continued reliance on special powers has served as a negative model and a kind of bridgehead for the introduction of more repressive "ordinary" legislation. The widespread insensitivity to the seriousness of suspending normal rights on spurious or weak grounds creates an ethos, which is conducive to the extension of such alternative arrangements to cover more and more cases. In particular, recent legislation targeting drug dealers has resurrected the concepts of seven-day detention for interrogation and restrictions on the right to silence and made them applicable to a specific group of non-subversive suspects, thereby severely eroding the principles of equality before the law and of the presumption of innocence.[24] Judicial rulings in cases relating to similar provisions in the Offences Against the State Act have meant that this can be done without change to the Constitution and with little fear of legal challenge.

---

[23] *Report of the Constitutional Review Group* May (Dublin, Stationery Office, 1997), at 283. The Group recommended that Art. 38.3 be amended to provide that special courts may be established only for a fixed period but they argued that, because of the existence of organised crime in Ireland, changes were appropriate which would allow the use of special courts where it appeared that ordinary courts, with trial by jury, were "inadequate to secure the administration of justice".

[24] Criminal Justice (Drug Trafficking) Act 1996.

THE PETITIONS SYSTEM

Even the apparently straightforward and reasonable provision in Article 13.6 of the Constitution to grant the right of pardon to the President and to extend it to the Minister for Justice has had highly regrettable consequences for justice in Ireland. This area is a graphic illustration of how the intentions of the Constitution can be distorted when translated into actual practice and how a measure directed at leniency rather than at repression can become a source of inequity and injustice in the system.

Over the years, until the 1994 High Court challenge in *Brennan* v. *Minister for Justice*,[25] the questionable system of petitions to the Minister for Justice had expanded to such an extent that over 6000 people per annum were petitioning the Minister. The majority of these convicted people were successful in having their fines or even sentences of imprisonment commuted. This clearly amounted to an alternative system of justice firmly under political control. It had become a system for second-guessing and sometimes overturning the legitimate, supposedly independent, judicial process of sentencing. As such it was clearly open to abuse and a potential source of inequity and unfair advantage in a criminal justice system which, according to its own traditional and constitutional principles, should always be totally fair and even-handed. The very fact that some citizens do not know that you can have your fine reduced by petitioning the Minister for Justice and that others would not demean themselves to make such a petition means that the system must operate unfairly.

The system was also essentially secret. In the District Court, Judge Brennan cited the response to a recent Dáil question on the reduction of fines, in which the Minister for Justice conveyed no information whatsoever except to say, in effect, that no details would be given. The Judge said of this: "In other words, a Minister for Justice can do what the Minister likes with fines and is not accountable to anyone, not even the Dáil".[26] Because of this secrecy it is impossible to judge the extent to which the system has become not only a source of inequality before the law but a politically motivated system of favouritism. For example, two highly pertinent but unanswered questions are: do the constituents of Ministers for Justice petition more frequently than other citizens?; and are the constituents of Ministers more frequently successful in their petitions than other people?

In *Brennan*, the High Court expressed considerable disquiet at the petitions system as then operated and held that it should be used more sparingly and only for clear-cut humanitarian reasons. However, it felt constrained by the Constitution itself, at Article 13.6, to conclude that the system was not unconstitutional. As a consequence, the system has continued, though at a much

---

[25] Unreported, 28 Apr. 1995.
[26] District Judge Patrick Brennan quoted in an article in *The Sunday Press*, 16 May 1993.

reduced level. Recent figures suggest that petitions are currently running at about a quarter of their former level.[27] This is an improvement but the system remains shrouded in secrecy and to an extent open to abuse.

The bail issue has recently taken on immense importance with respect to the role of the Constitution in civil liberties in Ireland. The referendum of November 1996, passed an amendment allowing for preventative detention. The amendment, which read "Provision may be made by law for the refusal of bail by a court to a person charged with a serious offence where it is reasonably considered necessary to prevent the commission of a serious offence by that person", was passed by a 3 to 1 majority. However, there was a very low turnout at the poll, of around 30 per cent, and so the Constitution was in fact amended by the pro-amendment votes of only 22 per cent of the electorate.

The origins of this referendum can be traced to the genuine disquiet about the failings of the bail system, but its motive force was a political belief that it was a surefire proposal that would gain overwhelming popular support and would triumphantly demonstrate the then Government's determination to be "tough on crime".

The proposed amendment was specifically designed to counteract Supreme Court judgements in *The People (Attorney General)* v. *O'Callaghan*[29] and *Director of Public Prosecutions* v. *Ryan*,[30] relating to the Articles in the Constitution which protect the personal freedom of the individual. These judgements concluded that there is an essential and crucial difference between depriving suspects of freedom by denying them bail in order to ensure that they face justice and depriving them of freedom in order to prevent them from committing crimes while on bail. The latter was seen by the Supreme Court as unacceptable because, in effect, it punishes people for a future offence, of which, in reality, they could never be guilty. In *O'Callaghan*, Chief Justice O'Dalaigh ruled that "The courts owe more than verbal respect to the principle that punishment begins after conviction, and that everyone is deemed to be innocent until tried and duly found guilty".[31] More recently, in *Ryan*, Chief Justice Brian Walsh stated that "The criminalising of mere intention has been usually a badge of an oppressive or unjust system".[32]

---

[27] Minister of Justice Nora Owen in response to a Dáil Question on the petitions system, 30 Apr. 1997.
[28] See Law Reform Commission, *An Examination of the Law of Bail* (Dublin, Stationery Office, 1994) and P. O'Mahony, "The Proposed Constitutional Referendum on Bail: An Unholy Grail?" (1995) 13 *ILT* 234–39.
[29] [1966] IR 501.
[30] [1989] IR 399.
[31] *Supra* n. 29, at 509.
[32] *Supra* n. 30, at 407.

This amounts to a vigorous reiteration and defence of the concept of the presumption of innocence. The Supreme Court have, through their rulings, firmly established a right to bail within the "meta-Constitution" and placed severe limits on the grounds on which bail can be refused. In contrast to other countries where preventative refusal of bail of the type envisaged by the Amendment has long been in place and also in contrast to the Supreme Court's more tentative positions on other civil liberties issues like the right to silence, this approach represents a highly principled and even purist vindication of the citizen's right to liberty.

In this context the political decision to seek to amend the Constitution must be seen as an extraordinary attack not just on the formerly very liberal Irish bail laws but also on the system by which the Supreme Court act as the ultimate guardians of our civil liberties. Of course, it is right that the will of the people, expressed in a referendum, should override even the deeply considered opinion of the Supreme Court, but it is extremely disquieting that this can happen on foot of an inadequate and ill-informed public debate fuelled by exaggerated perceptions of the crime problem, by unwarranted expectations of benefit from the proposed changes, and by politicians vying with each other to appear the toughest on crime. The Supreme Court in their rulings were alert to the fact that the presumption of innocence is an essential protection for all citizens, but it is likely that many of the voters for the amendment thought that the question of bail is rarely, if ever, of any relevance to the innocent and that refusal of bail will only ever impact on the guilty. The public were certainly encouraged in such a narrow and misguided view by the campaigns of the political parties, who resorted to simplistic slogans like "Jail not bail" and "Tougher bail for safer streets".

The Supreme Court, having taken perhaps their most principled civil libertarian stance on the bail issue, now find themselves forced to interpret, as best they can, a Constitution which allows preventative detention in a potentially wide range of circumstances, yet which, according to their former scrupulously considered view, disallows it as a matter of fundamental principle. The less than harmonious end result must be both an erosion of the fundamental principle of the presumption of innocence and a diminution of the Supreme Court's ability to uphold such fundamental principles. There also results an unfortunate increase in the uncertainty and vagueness surrounding the constitutional provisions for civil liberties and in the general level of tolerance for double-thinking and for parallel standards of justice characterised by ever greater use of discretion. In short, the bail referendum represents a triumph of populist, pragmatic politics and sloganising hardline rhetoric over principled concern for fairness and civil liberties.

There are many other key issues, which have hardly been touched upon, such as police interrogation, tacit forms of plea-bargaining, prisoners' rights and prison conditions, and—perhaps most significant of all—the manifest tendency of the criminal justice system to target certain types of crime (property theft) and certain types of offender (those from socially, educationally, and economically disadvantaged backgrounds) and to largely ignore the undoubtedly fairly widespread crimes of dishonesty and exploitation committed by the privileged and powerful classes. However, the issues that have been discussed do clearly indicate that the 1937 Constitution has been a mixed blessing. It has not always afforded the clear and definitive guidance that one might wish for in this sensitive and vital area. While there has been much progress in terms of the construction of a "meta-Constitution", vindicating important civil rights, the bail amendment and Supreme Court rulings in recent years have muddied the waters and to an extent justify a sense of disillusionment about the role of the Constitution in upholding "just and charitable" criminal justice procedures and institutions.

Professor Ralph Steinhardt of George Washington University has argued[33] that a slow revolution was proceeding by which the distinction between domestic constitutional law and international law, as exemplified in the Universal Declaration of Human Rights and the European Convention on Human Rights, was increasingly perceived as unworkable and irrelevant. Perhaps the time is now ripe in Ireland to give serious consideration to the incorporation within Irish domestic law of the European Convention on Human Rights[34] insofar as it relates to the operation of the criminal justice system. This would provide a lucid, coherent, and easily comprehended set of basic minimum standards, which could be harmonised with the more stringent protections that already exist in certain areas in Irish law.

[33] Speaking at a conference entitled "The Role of the Judiciary in Liberal Democracies" at University College, Galway in October 1995.

[34] For some discussion of the issues see L. Heffernan (ed.), *Human Rights: a European Perspective* (Dublin, Round Hall Press, 1994) and for an interesting application of European and international instruments to the Irish prison situation, see Irish Commission for Justice and Peace, *Human Rights in Prison* (Dublin, Irish Bishops' Commission for Justice and Peace, 1994).

15

Freedom of Expression— Talking About "the Troubles"

PATRICK TWOMEY

INTRODUCTION

The formulation of the liberty of expression guarantee in the 1937 Constitution raises a series of questions. Some of these are posed in this collection in relation to the Constitution generally, but others relate specifically to this particular right, variously identified as the touchstone of constitutional democracy:[1] at the core of individual dignity:[2] "the matrix, the indispensable condition of nearly every other form of freedom".[3]

Article 40.6.1.i provides:

"The State guarantees liberty for the exercise of the following rights, subject to public order and morality:

(1) The right of the citizens to express freely their convictions and opinions. The education of public opinion being however a matter of such grave import to the common good the State shall endeavour to ensure that organs of public opinion such as the radio, the press, the cinema while preserving their rightful liberty of expression including criticism of Government policy shall not be used to undermine public order or morality or the authority of the State. The publication or utterance of blasphemous, seditious or indecent matter is an offence which shall be punishable in accordance with the law."

Sub-paragraphs ii and iii of the Article respectively set out, though in noticeably less circumscribed terms, the related rights of free assembly and free association.[4] The collection of these rights together offers at least one possible

---

[1] For the prioritisation of political expression, see A. Meiklejohn, "Free Speech and its Relation to Self-Government" in *Political Freedom: The Constitutional Powers of the People* (New York, Oxford University Press, 1965).

[2] See, e.g., C. E. Baker, *Human Liberty and Freedom of Speech* (New York, Oxford University Press, 1989) and F. Schauer, *Free Speech: A Philosophical Enquiry* (Cambridge, Cambridge University Press, 1982). For reasoning linking the two rationales by stressing the individual dignity aspect of having one's say in governmental decision-making, see *Downing* v. *Williams*, 624 F 2d 612, 618 (5th Cir. 1980).

[3] Cordoza J, *Palko* v. *Connecticut*, 302 (1927) US 319 at 327.

[4] On the right of association, see I. Lynch, "Lawyers and Unions—The Right to Freedom of Association in the Irish Constitution" in this volume.

conception of the Constitution's free speech guarantee. A conception supported by the fact that the right is specifically guaranteed to "citizens",[5] its reference to "convictions and opinions", "the education of public opinion" and "criticism of Government policy", as well as some judicial misgivings regarding the inclusion of the right to communicate *information*[6] within the Article.

The most recent judicial analysis of Article 40.6.1.i tends to confirm that the Article is concerned with preserving democratic debate and ensuring good governance. In *Murphy* v. *IRTC and Attorney General*[7] Geoghegan J elaborated on the Article 40.3/Article 40.6.1.i distinction in the context of the refusal by the Independent Radio and Television Commission (IRTC) to permit the broadcasting of an advertisement for the screening of a religious video at a public meeting.[8] While declining to define the precise ambit of the enumerated expression guarantee, the judgment refined the distinction between the right to "communicate" and the Article 40.6.1.i right to express one's "convictions and opinions", by regarding the latter as "mainly directed at protecting expression of opinions . . . with a view to influencing public opinion". In support of this view, reference was made to "convictions and opinions" in Article 40.6.1.i and the accompanying paragraphs on assembly and association. Furthermore, the reference to "citizens", in the plural, was taken as further evidence of the drafters' intention to protect something other than advertisements. Geoghegan J did acknowledge that an advertisement designed to attract people to a political, as opposed to religious, gathering might be treated differently, but was, nevertheless, convinced that the Article, a specific aspect of the wider unenumerated right of expression in Article 40.3, only protected expression targeting the collective, as opposed to individuals.

---

[5] The trend has been towards allowing challenges by non-citizens where their rights are affected. See, e.g., the judgment of Gannon J in *Rederij Kennemerland BV* v. *Attorney General* [1989] ILRM 821. In the context of expression, *Attorney General for England and Wales* v. *Brandon Book Publishers* [1986] IR 597, saw the right successfully invoked by an artificial legal person.

[6] See *Brandon Books, ibid.*, where Carroll J took the view that the Article encompassed factual "information". Cf. *Attorney General* v. *Paper Link* [1984] ILRM 373, where Costello J took a contrary line on the breadth of Art. 40.6.1.i resorting to the unenumerated rights of Art.40.3 to find a right to communicate information. This latter view was endorsed most recently by Keane J in *SPUC* v. *Grogan and Others*, unreported, Supreme Court, 6 Mar. 1997, but a majority of the Court regarded the right to receive and impart information as arising from Art. 40.6.1.i as an ancillary right to the right to express convictions and opinions. Implicit support for the thesis that the expression guarantee has an individual liberty rationale is offered in *Heaney and McGuinness* v. *Ireland and the Attorney General* [1997] 1 ILRM 117, where the right to silence was regarded as a corollary of the Art. 40.6.1.i expression guarantee. See *Frank* v. *Maryland*, 359 US 360 (1959) where Douglas J linked the First, Fourth and Fifth Amendments and the prohibition of the "prying open the lips of an accused to make incriminating statements against his will" to "conscience, human dignity and freedom of expression". The special position of abortion information resulted in its explicit inclusion in Art. 40.3.3 by the 14th Amendment to the Constitution.

[7] Unreported, High Court, 25 Apr. 1997.

[8] On the ground that it would be contrary to s. 10(3) of the Radio and Television Act, 1988 which prohibits religious or political advertising.

Further clues regarding the conceptual basis of the Article are offered by the *Dáil* debates on the draft Constitution, which reveal de Valera's conception of permissible speech as being premised on the "public good", to the exclusion of "expression of such opinions . . . inconsistent with man's nature that he should be governed at all".[9] Moreover, while recognising that the press had a "rightful liberty of expression, including the criticism of Government policy", this too was seen as falling within strict constraints of "right" and "wrong" on the basis that one "should not give to the propagation of what is wrong and unnatural the same liberty as would be accorded to the propagation of what is right".[10] Thus, while it appears that the promotion of democratic governance lies at the heart of Article 40.6.1.i, this democratic underpinning does not envisage an open-access market-place[11] for good and evil, popular and unpopular, speech. In the decades that followed, "wrong and unnatural" ideas and information would be identified by an alliance of Church and State, rather than informed scrutiny by the citizenry. This paternalism led de Valera to equate his conception of the development of the State with that of children.

> "Just as there are stages in the life of a nation in which different sides of capacity have to be trained, so there are stages in the life of the pupil. . . . In the earlier stages the memory is the strongest faculty, the reasoning power the weakest. Common sense dictates that at this stage we should not try to appeal to reasoning power".[12]

Whatever its conceptual base, the formulation of the Article, with the limitation set out prior to what is cumbersomely a *liberty* to exercise a *right*,[13] offers so little that it is perhaps less than surprising that it has, over sixty years, never been the basis for the Supreme Court deeming a statute unconstitutional. The result is that, even taking account of the developing personal rights jurisprudence, triggered by the *Ryan*[14] revolution, there remains a considerable lacuna regarding the theoretical basis of the Constitution's expression guarantee.[15] Indeed, the 1996 Constitutional Review Group, commenting on the paucity of case law in the area, in particular direct challenges to the constitutionality of legislation, was of the view that "not much would be lost if Article 40.6.1.i were to be replaced".[16]

---

[9] *Dáil Éireann* Debates, vol. 67, cols. 1634–5.

[10] *Ibid.*

[11] Classically espoused in 1859 by John Stuart Mill, *On Liberty* (London, David Campbell, 1992).

[12] M. Moynihan, *Speeches and Statements by Eamon de Valera, 1917–1973* (Dublin, Gill and Macmillan, 1990), 431.

[13] In stark contrast is the blunt edict of the First Amendment of the US Constitution that "Congress shall make no law abridging the freedom of speech, or of the press, . . .".

[14] *Ryan v. Attorney General* [1965] IR 294.

[15] Nevertheless, several critical trends and principles have emerged to offer some guidance regarding constitutional rights generally including, the move away from a positivist interpretative approach; their extension beyond citizens; the notion of a hierarchy of rights; the permissibility of limitation; the requirement that waiver of rights be informed and consensual; the extension of *locus standi*, etc.

[16] *Report of the Constitutional Review Group* (Dublin, Stationery Office, 1996), 292.

This essay explores one aspect of the failure of the constitutional guarantee: the specific context of the Northern Ireland "troubles". It suggests that a combination of the weak formulation of the enumerated guarantee in Article 40.6.1.i, combined with a timid judicial approach[17] to the principle of free speech, fostered a culture of silence that prevented the free flow of information, debate and education on one of the most important of the State's ongoing political concerns.

A STATE OF EMERGENCY

The potential of the expression guarantee has been retarded in particular by the ill-defined notion of the "authority of the State" and the almost ever-present state of emergency on the island of Ireland.[18] These emergencies can be traced from when the Irish people were *given*[19] their first Constitution, when the very survival of the fledgling democracy was threatened, through the Second World War, until the 1990s. Indeed, it was not until February 1995, some months after the paramilitary cease-fires in Northern Ireland, that, for the first time in the lives of most of its citizens, the State was not in an "emergency".[20]

In many respects the 1937 expression guarantee follows its predecessor, Article 9 of the 1922 Constitution, which guaranteed the "right of free expression of opinion . . . for purposes not opposed to public morality", in its concern for State and societal preservation. Article 9 co-existed with military censorship,[21] under which newspapers, including the *Irish Independent*, which took an anti-treaty stance were banned. The regime remained in place, unchallenged, until well after the end of the civil war. As late as 1927, following the assassination of the Minister for Justice, Kevin O'Higgins, the Free State Government introduced the Public Safety Act, section 9 of which made it an offence to "print, publish, distribute, sell, or offer, or expose for sale, without the previous permission of the Minister for Justice, any book, newspaper, magazine, periodical, pamphlet, leaflet, circular or other document, containing any statement by, or on behalf of, or emanating from, or purporting to emanate from, an unlawful organisation, or any statement aiding or abetting or calculated to aid or abet an unlawful association". Subsequent

[17] For a critique of the "dangers" of innovative judicial activism in other contexts, see D. G. Morgan, "Judicial Activism: Too Much of a Good Thing?" in this volume.

[18] See further D. Keogh, "Ireland and 'Emergency' Culture, Between Civil War and Normalcy, 1922–1961" (1995) 1 *Ireland: A Journal of History and Society* 4–43. Since its inception, Northern Ireland has had emergency legislation of some form or another.

[19] "Given" is perhaps the most appropriate verb as the 1922 Free State Constitution, which was a direct bye-product of, and to be interpreted in accordance with, the Anglo-Irish Treaty, was never put to the people in a referendum.

[20] F. O'Toole, "Our Second World War Finally Comes to an End", *Irish Times*, 10 Feb. 1995.

[21] *Official Notice of Military Censorship of Newspapers and Publications* and *Official Notice of Military Censorship of Reports of Military Operations*, 2 July 1922.

to the Public Safety Act, the Government introduced the Constitution (Amendment No. 17) Act, 1931,[22] section 9 of which prohibited newspapers from publishing statements "by, or on behalf of, or emanating from, an unlawful organisation", making such publication a breach of the Constitution. Thus, in somewhat understated terms, did the Constitutional Review Group observe that "the unsettled political conditions prevailing in the aftermath of the Civil War and the perceived need for decisive executive and legislative action did not assist in the creation of a 'rights' culture".[23]

One result of a culture of emergency was a certain acclimatisation on the part of the legislature, courts and other institutions. Rather than assessing, at each point in time, the need for a particular measure, the State succumbed to the lure of efficiency and convenience, with ill-defined notions of "interests of the State" requiring unquestioning obeisance.[24] Intrinsic to this culture is the pressure on individuals to ignore the excesses of the State's efforts to confront its "enemies" and "preserve" itself.[25] It also meant that the press in the new State and, in particular, the embryonic broadcast media, were frequently reduced to engaging in publishing and broadcasting that bore little relation to the political life of the State and sometimes acting as little more than uncritical conduits for the Government line. But, this conspiracy of silence was even wider. As Joe Lee has observed "it was not censorship that obliged the university to make so modest a contribution to the quality of social, economic or political thought in the free State".[26] Similarly, the Irish Film Society, despite its private status, succumbed to the sometimes farcical control of the Censor's Office during the Second World War. Indeed, the accusation has been levelled at the population at large, that it was:

"prepared, in the interests of a 'sacred egoism' and the 'nightmarish satisfaction of looking on in comparative safety at horrors we can do nothing to prevent,' to forego some of the basic rights accorded to them by the constitution".[27]

---

[22] By contrast with Art. 46 of the 1937 Constitution, amendment of the 1922 Constitution, provided for by Art. 50, was possible by ordinary legislation without a popular referendum, for 8 years after the Constitution initially entered into force. In 1929 the period in Art. 50 was extended to 16 years.

[23] *Supra* n. 18, at p. 213.

[24] Despite the Supreme Court decision in *The State (Hoey)* v. *Garvey* [1978] IR 1 holding that while emergency law is removed from challenge by virtue of Art. 28.3.3, an individual may nevertheless challenge the constitutionality of acts done under that legislation.

[25] In the introduction to its consideration of the Constitution's fundamental rights provisions, the 1996 Constitution Review Group observed, with regard to the 1922 Constitution, that "most members of the new judiciary had been schooled in the British tradition of parliamentary sovereignty and were not at ease with concepts of fundamental rights and powers of judicial review of legislation": *supra* n. 16, 213.

[26] J. J. Lee, *Ireland 1912–1985: Politics and Society* (Cambridge, Cambridge University Press, 1989), p. 160.

[27] K. Woodman, *Media Control in Ireland: 1923–1983* (Carbondale and Edwardsville, Ill., Southern Illinois Press, 1984), p. 17, citing M. Tierney, "Ireland and the Anglo-Saxon Heresy" (1940) 30 *Studies* 2. This pervasive silence made isolated voices of sanity against censorship, including publications such as *The Bell* and *Ireland To-Day*, all the more important as vehicles for the country's leading writers, many of whom were victims of the censorship regime.

The reasons of this are complex. In part, a period of peace was necessary to stabilise the new State, to purge memories of the war of independence and civil war and to recover after the 1930s trade war with Britain. People were both tired of confrontational politics and scared by the ferocity it could unleash. Thus, did the "solution" of not talking about matters take root, with the result that many decades would pass before the national school history curriculum would address the civil war and, despite the constitutional imperative, there evolved a desire in the South for Northern Ireland to "go away". In such a climate there is little need to control the flow of information, but the nature of the constraints imposed on the organs charged with generating and facilitating informed debate meant that control was easily guaranteed.

While the threat of civil war faded with the peaceful transfer of power between its protagonists in 1932, prior to the Second World War, increased IRA activity and the fascist mimicry of the Blueshirt movement raised fears once more of old divisions being reopened. The drafting of a replacement for the 1922 Constitution coincided with unresolved tension regarding Northern Ireland and the threat of war on the Continent. Yet, when the latter became a reality, neutrality necessitated an amendment to the new Constitution in the form of the First Amendment extending the Article 28.3 definition of "time of war" (during which legislation is withdrawn from normal judicial control) to include conflicts in which the State is not a participant but which affected the "vital interests of the State".[28] Subsequently, in 1941, the Second Amendment to the Constitution extended the definition, to include such time after the termination of such war or conflict until the *Oireachtas* deems the national emergency to have passed. Thus, the 1939 emergency continued in place until it was overtaken in September 1976 by a new national emergency, this time arising out of the conflict in Northern Ireland.

The specific concerns of the Second World War[29] saw the legislative mechanism for controlling expression expanded by the Emergency Powers Act, 1939, which, renewed annually until 1946, provided for governmental orders for the "censorship, control, or partial or complete suspension of communications"[30] and prohibited the "publication or spreading of subversive statements and propaganda".[31] More generally, the Offences Against the State Act,

---

[28] Leading this period of Irish history to become known, euphemistically, as "The Emergency".

[29] For an in-depth assessment of the censorship regime during the emergency, see O'Drisceoil, *Censorship in Ireland: 1939–1945* (Cork, Cork University Press, 1996) and R. Fisk, *In Time of War: Ireland, Ulster and the Price of Neutrality 1939–45* (London, Paladin, 1985), 162–71.

[30] Building upon pre-existing controls in the Wireless Telegraphy Act, 1926 and Post Office Act, 1908, these included the Emergency Powers (Censorship of Postal Packets) Order, 1939; Emergency Powers (Censorship of Postal Packets) (No 1) Order, 1939; Emergency Powers (Restriction on the Conveyance of Informative Articles) Order, 1939; Emergency Powers (Telegraph Cable Companies) Order, 1939; Emergency Powers (Wireless Telegraphy Apparatus) Order, 1939.

[31] S. 2(2) of the Emergency Powers Act, 1939. A range of Orders governing press censorship included the Emergency Powers (No 5) Order, 1939; Emergency Powers (No 36) Order, 1942; Emergency Powers (No 67) Order, 1941; and Emergency Powers (No 151) Order, 1942.

1939, which survives to this day, contains a wide range of offences and penalties with respect to seditious matter and incriminating and treasonable documents, targeting the creator, possessor, disseminator and publisher of such materials as tend to undermine public order or the authority of the State or which challenged, explicitly or otherwise, the legitimacy of the Government.[32]

The existing regulation of cinema, the Censorship of Films Acts of 1923 and 1930 aimed at obscene and blasphemous material,[33] was bolstered by Article 52 of the Emergency Powers (No. 6) Order of 1939 which provided for the prohibition of film, which the Film Censor's Office was of the opinion was "prejudicial to the maintenance of law and order or the preservation of the state or would be likely to lead to a breach of the peace or to cause offence to the people of a friendly nation". The combined result of this broadsweeping mandate and a suspicion of the special characteristics of the medium meant that the bulk of newsreel war news and films, including Charlie Chaplin's *The Great Dictator*, was considered a potential threat. The "threat", however, was not simply to the neutrality of the State: nor was the censorship simply designed to pre-empt the belligerent sides from being given an excuse to invade the island, but was rationalised in the broader terms of preventing popular passions being inflamed.[34] Central to this caution was the threat posed by the activities of the IRA.[35] Thus press and telegram references to the IRA, however indirect, were deleted, whatever the context.

THE SPECIAL POSITION OF BROADCASTING[36]

Historically, the broadcast media have been recognised, for the purposes of regulation, as a special case.[37] This stems from the capital investment needed

---

[32] Ss.10, 11, 12. In 1972 the Act provided the basis for the destruction of the printing press type-set used to publish *Freedom Struggle of the Provisional IRA* and all copies of the book. The breadth of the "incriminating document" concept was illustrated in 1988 when a conviction for IRA membership was based on possession of posters with the slogan "The IRA Call the Shots": *The People (DPP)* v. *O'Leary* (1988) 3 Frewen 163.

[33] The Obscene Publications Act, 1857 and Customs Consolidation Act, 1876 were carried over into Irish law after independence and followed by the Censorship of Publications Act, 1929. See generally, M. Adams, *Censorship: The Irish Experience* (Dublin, Scepter Books, 1968).

[34] For a detailed exposition of the Government's rationale for war-time censorship, see the memorandum of the Minister responsible for Defense, Frank Aiken, "Neutrality, Censorship and Democracy", S 11586a (Dublin, State Paper Office, 1940), quoted in R. Fisk *supra* n. 29, Appendix I, 560.

[35] Both in terms of the internal threat posed, and indirectly, by its bombing campaign in the UK and attempts at collaboration with Germany, as providing a justification for British intervention in Ireland. Though selective coverage of Northern Ireland was permitted, allowing de Valera to maintain his claim to be the true inheritor of the republican mantle.

[36] For the most recent detailed consideration of broadcasting in Ireland, including consideration of the issue of governmental interference, see the Green Paper, *Active or Passive? Broadcasting in the Future Tense*, Pn 1540, 1995.

[37] Persuasive, though not binding, in the Irish constitutional context, Art. 10(1) of the European Convention for the Protection of Human Rights and Fundamental Freedoms, for example, provides that the right of free expression "shall not prevent States from requiring the

for its establishment, its origins in most states as a public service, the result-ing need to ensure impartiality, its immediacy and pervasive nature and the limited availability of airwaves.[38] This is reflected in the history of broad-casting in Ireland, with the national radio service, *2RN*, established in 1926 and run initially within the Ministry of Posts and Telegraphs, and subse-quently with the establishment of *Radio Éireann*[39] in 1960. Throughout the Second World War, a combination of scarcity of resources (including batter-ies) and regular Ministerial interference stunted the development of *2RN*. Not only news bulletins, which were forwarded to the Censorship Office prior to broadcast, but weather forecasts, religious sermons, court reports and state-ments by *Dáil* members[40] were the subject of censorship. As in the case of the printed press, the IRA were effectively "airbrushed" from broadcast news, so that attacks, trials, hunger-strike deaths and executions all went unreported or were sanitised.[41]

Despite John Kelly's assertion[42] that Article 40.6.1.i precludes a State monopoly of broadcasting,[43] practical and policy considerations meant that government control of radio was to be extended with the advent of television. The Broadcasting Authority Act of 1960 provided that members of the newly formed Authority were to be appointed, and initially removable, by the Government.[44] Furthermore, the Act reinforced the notion of governmental control, providing, as it did, untrammelled scope for ministerial interference by way of a direction not to broadcast any particular matter or matter of a particular class.[45] Nevertheless, there was little disquiet during the passage of the bill through the *Oireachtas* as it appeared to be accepted that the power would be exercised only in cases of emergency.[46] At odds with this, ministers were later, in defending informal interference, to express views that suggested

---

licensing of broadcasting, television or cinema enterprises". Cf. Art. 19 of the International Covenant on Civil and Political Rights which affords the individual freedom of expression "through any . . . media of his choice".

[38] For a more modern perspective, see the decision of the European Court of Human Rights in *Informationsverein Lentia* v. *Austria*, Series A, No. 276 (1993).

[39] Renamed *Radio Telefís Éireann* (RTÉ) in 1966.

[40] Notably, James Dillon, the principle advocate of Ireland's entry to the war on the Allied side.

[41] One famous incident in 1942, recounted in M. Gorham, *Forty Years of Irish Radio Broadcasting* (Dublin, Talbot Press, 1967), 132, highlighted both the "danger" of live broadcast-ing and the scope of ministerial war-time sensitivities. A participant on the "Question Time" radio programme, broadcast from Belfast, on being asked to name the world's most famous story-teller replied, to appreciative applause from the nationalist audience present, "Winston Churchill!". Subsequent reporting of the incident was quickly quashed.

[42] J. M. Kelly, "The Constitutional Position of RTÉ" (1967) 15 *Administration* 205.

[43] Which survived until the advent of commercial broadcasting with the Radio and Television Act, 1988.

[44] This power, exercised in Nov. 1972 to dismiss the Authority, was replaced by s. 2 of the Broadcasting Authority (Amendment) Act, 1976, which provided for removal, accompanied with stated reasons, only by resolution of both Houses of the *Oireachtas*.

[45] S. 31 of the Broadcasting Authority Act, 1960. See further below.

[46] *Seanad Éireann* Debates, vol. 52, cols. 20–22, 20 Jan. 1960.

they saw the national broadcaster as something more akin to a government public relations organ.[47] The dangers of such interference, information on which is largely anecdotal, have long been evident.[48] In no small part the scope for such interference and the culture that it generated, delayed for over a decade the need to resort to the section 31 power. Such forms of interference do not give rise to recourse to Article 40.6.1.i, and in that respect were even more invidious than legislative interference. In this context, John Kelly's view[49] that the absence of judicial consideration of Article 40.6.1.i between 1937 and 1967 was evidence of the success of the Article understates the wider role of a constitutional rights guarantee.

THE STORY OF SECTION 31

One of the bleakest chapters in the history of Article 40.6.1.i is also part of one of the darkest periods for rights protection generally in the State's history. Dublin's response to the outbreak of violence in Northern Ireland in 1969 was to declare a state of emergency[50] and to reactivate or adopt a range of special measures. These included the Offences Against the State Act, 1939, the Emergency Powers Act, 1976 and the Criminal Law Act, 1976. In parallel with this, the Coalition Government of 1974–7 turned a blind eye to the excesses of an element, known as the "heavy gang", operating within the ranks of the *Garda Siochana*. As in the past, control of information and debate was a central plank of the Government's response to the situation.

It was in this context that Conor Cruise O'Brien, the Minister responsible for broadcasting, is alleged to have toasted a group of political journalists with the words "to our democratic institutions, and the restrictions on the

---

[47] That politicians saw RTÉ as "an instrument of public policy" was famously confirmed as late as 1966, when the *Taoiseach*, Seán Lemass, told the *Dáil* that "[RTÉ] should [not] be, either generally or, in regard to its current affairs and news programmes, completely independent of Government supervision. As a public institution supported by public funds and operating under statute [RTÉ] has the duty . . . to sustain public respect for the institutions of Government", *Dáil Éireann* Debates, vol. 224, col. 1045. One of the criticisms of the 1960 Act raised by John Kelly was that, in addition to providing for unlimited Ministerial interference via s. 31, it failed to prohibit all other forms of ministerial interference: *supra* n. 42.

[48] John Kelly refers to several incidents of such interference regarding programmes on planning decisions and the activities of the Garda Special Branch in "Are our Broadcasting Structures Out of Date" (1978) 2 *Irish Broadcasting Review* 5. See also D. G. Morgan, "Section 31: The Broadcasting Ban" (1990–92) 25–27 *Ir. Jur.* 117 at 123, recounting Governmental interference with plans by RTÉ to send reporters to Vietnam and Biafra and a telephone call that led to comments critical of the Agriculture Minister being dropped from a news bulletin.

[49] J. M. Kelly, *Fundamental Rights in the Irish Law and Constitution* (Dublin, Allen Figgis and Co, 1967), 124.

[50] On the challenge to this Emergency Powers Bill and the Supreme Court reserving the right to scrutinise the validity of an *Oireachtas* conclusion that a emergency actually exists, see *Re Article 26 and the Emergency Powers Bill, 1976* [1977] IR 159; D. G. Morgan, "The Emergency Powers Bill Reference—Part I" (1978) 13 *Ir. Jur.* 67; "Part II" (1979) 14 *Ir. Jur.* 252.

freedom of the press which may become necessary to preserve them".[51] He was not alone, either as a democratic politician or journalist, in holding such views.[52] The Irish State would neither have been the first to eviscerate those very democratic institutions in the name of defending them, nor the first to do so against the backdrop of constitutional rights guarantees. As time passed the arguments for such censorship were refined to include: denying a morale boost for IRA supporters; preventing the targeting of potential sympathisers on the left, protecting susceptible teenagers and preventing the decriminalising of the organisations in the minds of the public.[53]

The mechanism for putting this into practice was the sweeping power of section 31 of the Broadcasting Authority Act, 1960,[54] by which the Minister could prohibit the broadcasting of "any particular matter or matter of any particular class". It was not until October 1971, after the RTÉ current affairs programme, "Seven Days", had interviewed IRA members, that the first ministerial Order was signed, with the support of the main opposition party. The Order prohibited RTÉ from broadcasting any matter:

> "that could be calculated to promote the aims or activities of any organisation which engages in, promotes, encourages or advocates the attaining of any particular objective by violent means."

The justification given at the time, echoing that offered for informal interference in the past, was that:

> "we do not wish to exercise undue control over the national network, but we are nevertheless determined that *a service provided by the government and paid for by the public* should not be used against them and especially in a way that threatens the security of the state."[55]

Despite complaints from RTÉ regarding the indeterminacy of the Order—it was, for example, not confined to the Northern Irish situation—guidance

---

[51] Quoted in "Conor Cruise O'Brien and the Media" (1981) 9 *Belfast Bulletin* 1.

[52] This represented a shift in stance for Cruise O'Brien. As an opposition TD, he had favoured allowing interviews of paramilitaries and their supporters for the purpose of exposing the flaws in their cause and campaign. Offering the same view, John A. Murphy urged the lifting of the ban so as to let the "godfathers of violence be cross-examined on radio and television, to have their pseudo-historical mythology exposed, the hear them justify sectarian terrorism": "Tackling the Crisis" (1983) 16 *Irish Broadcasting Review* 26.

[53] C. Cruise O'Brien, "Freedom to Peddle Murder", *The Times*, 16 Sept. 1989, mirroring in part the justifications outlined by the Home Secretary, Douglas Hurd, on the introduction of the UK ban, *Hansard*, vol. 138, cols. 893–903, 19 Oct. 1988.

[54] See generally, D. G. Morgan, *supra* n. 48, and G. Hogan, "The Demise of the Broadcasting Ban" (1994) 1 *Euro. Public L* 458.

[55] *Dáil Éireann* Debates, vol. 224, cols. 1045–6, author's italics. At the same time the press was in receipt of informal "encouragement" to restrict the coverage given to paramilitaries and their supporters. See account in *Hibernia*, 8 Oct. 1971, referred to in K. Woodman, *supra* n. 27, 179. Even an Amnesty International report criticising the Special Criminal Court was to fall foul of the Government, though the excised section was immediately published in the *Irish Times*, 15 Oct. 1977: see M. Robinson, "The Special Criminal Court—Eight Years On", 125 *Fortnight*, Mar. 1980.

on the interpretation was not forthcoming.[56] It was only a matter of time before the uncertainty produced a crisis. In November 1971, RTÉ broadcast an interview with the Chief of Staff of the IRA, Seán MacStiofain. In the early hours of the morning police arrested MacStiofain at the home of the interviewing journalist, Kevin O'Kelly, and seized a tape-recording of the interview. The saga that followed began with a letter from the Minister expressing his dissatisfaction with the interview and, in light of the perceived inadequacy of the RTÉ Authority's response,[57] saw its peremptory dismissal announced within the week.[58] Once more, it appeared that the public interest was being confused with what the Government of the day considered to be in *its* interest.[59]

The newly-appointed Authority issued internal guidelines for the implementation of the Order. Doubts about their compatibility with the Ministerial Order lasted until the insertion of the 1976 Amendment to the 1960 Act by the Minister for Posts and Telegraphs, Conor Cruise O'Brien. In addition to providing increased security of tenure to the Broadcasting Authority,[60] and introducing obligations to "be mindful of the need for understanding and peace within the whole island of Ireland", to "reflect the varied elements which make up the culture of the people of the whole island", to uphold "rightful liberty of expression" and "have regard to the need for the formation of public awareness and understanding of the values and traditions of countries other than the state",[61] the Amendment narrowed, in terms of form,[62] duration,[63] and scope, the existing section 31 Order. The Minister now had to be of the opinion that the matter prohibited "would be likely to promote, or incite to, crime or would tend to undermine the authority of the State".

The 1976 Order prohibited interviews and "report of interviews" with a list of named organisations including the IRA, Sinn Féin, Republican Sinn Féin,

---

[56] One issue was the relationship between the s. 31 Order and s. 18(1A) of the Act of 1960 (inserted by s. 3 of the 1976 Amendment Act) which prohibits the broadcasting authority from including in any of its broadcasts "anything which may reasonably be regarded as being likely to promote or incite to crime or as tending to undermine the authority of the State".

[57] Which, while identifying the newsworthiness of a visit by the British Prime Minister to Northern Ireland and the resulting coverage that included interviews with a cross-section of views, included an admission that the interview should not have been broadcast,.

[58] The incident also produced the first judicial pronouncement on the status of journalistic privilege as a corollary of the "rightful liberty of expression" of the press, recognised by Art. 40.1.6.i. In balancing the journalist's right not to divulge his sources, in the particular case not to be forced to identify MacStiofain as the interviewee, with the State's desire to prosecute, the Special Criminal Court refused to recognise that any special privilege attached to members of the press. On appeal, the Court of Criminal Appeal, while acknowledging the journalist's constitutional right to gather news, endorsed this view: *In Re Kevin O'Kelly* (1974) 108 ILTR 97.

[59] P. O'Higgins, "The Irish TV Sackings" (1973) 3 *Index* 24.

[60] See *supra* n. 44.

[61] S. 17(a)–(c).

[62] As an "Order", as opposed to a "Direction", it fell within the publication requirements applicable to Statutory Instruments.

[63] S. 31(1A) provided for duration up to a maximum of 12 months, though the reality was that its annual renewal occurred without parliamentary debate.

the UDA, the INLA and "any organisation which in Northern Ireland is a proscribed organisation for the purposes of section 21 of the Act of the British Parliament entitled the Northern Ireland (Emergency Provisions) Act, 1978".[64]

Describing the amended section 31 Order as "a minimum power which no Irish Government could do without",[65] John Kelly set out the establishment thinking on the need to "allow nothing to weaken [the consensus about murder] or dilute people's natural abhorrence of cruelty by presenting its perpetrators as excusable. I think the values of full public enlightenment must take second place to this."[66] The argument convinces only so far as one assumes that the consensus about murder *would* be weakened, the natural abhorrence *would* be diluted, the perpetrators *would* have been presented as excusable. Apparently, de Valera's children, broadcaster and citizen alike, still had some growing up to do.

THE BAN IN THE COURTS

The first challenge to the constitutionality of a section 31 Order, *The State (Lynch)* v. *Cooney*,[67] arose when RTÉ's decision to allow party political broadcasts by Sinn Féin during the 1982 General Election Campaign prompted the Minister to extend the ban.[68] Lynch, a Sinn Féin election candidate, challenged the constitutionality of the Order, arguing in the alternative that the Minister's action was *ultra vires* the statute.

Having raised the difficulty in balancing the "encroachment on liberty of expression . . . and the maintenance of public order, morality, and the authority of the State", Hanlon J, in the High Court, considered two Privy Council decisions[69] (from jurisdictions with written Bills of Rights)[70] to elucidate on the interpretation of constitutional, as distinct from statutory, provisions. The former is to be the subject of more lenient interpretation. While referring to "the very limited qualifications to which the exercise of this right [freedom of expression] may be subjected"[71] an essentially administrative law, as opposed to a rights approach, is evident when attention was turned to the constitu-

---

[64] This meant that the scope of the Order and the resulting limitation of Art. 40.6.1.i were determined in part by Westminster.

[65] *Supra* n. 48, at 6.

[66] *Ibid.*

[67] [1982] IR 337.

[68] To include broadcasts, "whether purporting to be a party political broadcast or not, made by, or on behalf of, or advocating, offering or inviting support for" Sinn Féin or Republican Sinn Féin and broadcasts "by any person or persons representing, or purporting to represent" them.

[69] *Minister of Home Affairs* v. *Fisher* [1980] AC 319 and *Attorney General* v. *Reynolds* [1980] AC 637.

[70] However, while Hanlon J noted that the Bermudan Constitution was influenced by both the European Convention on Human Rights and the Universal Declaration of Human Rights, he chose not to consider the relevant Arts. of these instruments in assessing the conflicting claims.

[71] *Supra* n. 67, 354.

tional guarantee. Instead of assessing the Act and the Order made under it, for compliance with Article 40.6.1.i, the decision appears to suggest an equality of merit between the Statute and the constitutional guarantee:

> "It is necessary to place s.6, sub-s.1, of Article 40 side by side with the provisions of s.31 of the Act of 1960 for the purpose of examining *their compatibility with each other*".[72]

Hanlon J held that the scope of the 1960 Act, excluding, as it did, judicial review, allowed the Minister to "cut down" the individual's expression rights on grounds of public order and morality. The fact that the Minister's opinion could be formed on wholly unreasonable grounds meant that the Act contained "insufficient safeguards for the right of constitutionally guaranteed rights of freedom of expression for the expression of convictions and opinions—with particular reference to the protection of freedom of the press and the radio" and was therefore unconstitutional.[73]

The Supreme Court arrived at a different conclusion. In considering the permissible breadth of State interference with the expression guarantee, the Chief Justice, speaking for the Court, chose to rely on the lower threshold offered by administrative law principles, that the interference be merely not "irrational or capricious".[74] Applying the presumption of constitutionality, he reasoned that the section did not confer "wide, unfettered and sweeping powers" and was in fact subject to the review jurisdiction of the courts. Thus, by extending the Court's judicial review powers and circumventing the strict wording of the statute, O'Higgins CJ saved the statute from falling foul of Article 40.6.1.i. He went on to accept the Minister's assessment of the need for the Order,[75] on the basis that the broadcasts would invite support for an organisation that, on the evidence, which was not denied by the prosecutor, was committed to overthrowing the State and its democratic processes. In a separate assenting judgment, Henchy J makes no reference to Article 40.6.1.i, confining himself to comment that the prosecutor had no right to *broadcast*. Equally, only a passing reference is made to the European Convention on Human Rights (ECHR)[76] and then only in the context of the prosecutor's *locus standi*.

It was not until 1993, in *O'Toole* v. *Radio Telefís Éireann (No. 2)*,[77] that the Supreme Court finally offered a rights-based analysis of the constitutionality of section 31. The case arose from one example of a wider practice of "chill" censorship prevalent throughout the life-time of the Order.[78]

---

[72] *Ibid.*, 355, author's italics.
[73] *Ibid.*
[74] *Ibid.*, 361.
[75] Despite the Order having been made before the text of the proposed broadcast was submitted to the Authority.
[76] By Walsh J at 368.
[77] [1993] ILRM 458.
[78] Known as the "rose-grower's syndrome" after apocryphal stories of the exclusion of Sinn Féin members from broadcasts on even the most innocuous subjects. In one incident a caller to

O'Toole was a trade union representative and chairman of a strike committee during industrial action in a Dublin factory. He was interviewed by RTÉ on several occasions regarding the dispute. One of these interviews was broadcast, but RTÉ refused to broadcast further recorded interviews on discovering that he was a member of Sinn Féin. No reference was made to the party, or his membership of it, in the interviews. O'Toole instituted judicial review proceedings seeking a declaration to the effect that the section 31 Order did not prohibit broadcasting of statements by an individual solely because they were a member of Sinn Féin. In its defence the Authority argued that Sinn Féin's policy of infiltrating organisations so as to promote their political agenda, meant that the only option open to RTÉ was to apply a blanket ban. In the High Court, O'Hanlon J granted the declaration sought, on the ground that the Broadcasting Authority had, by its breadth of application, misinterpreted the Ministerial Order and breached its statutory duty to observe rules of "fairness and impartiality" in its coverage of current affairs.[79]

Despite criticism,[80] RTÉ appealed against the decision. Rejecting the appeal, the judgment of Finlay CJ[81] hinged essentially on the matter of RTÉ competence. The Chief Justice choose not to engage in any analysis of the constitutional expression guarantee. Indeed, the only references to freedom of expression in the Court were *obiter* comments by O'Flaherty J, observing that it was:

> "not necessary to engage in any extensive analysis of the liberty of expression clause in the Constitution except to point out that the liberty of expression guarantee is obviously not such that can be invoked to undermine public order or morality or the authority of the State. However, someone speaking on an innocuous subject on the airwaves, even though he is a member of an organisation which includes in its objects a desire to undermine public order or the authority of the State, is *neither outside the constitutional guarantee nor is he within the ministerial order.*"[82]

Once again, the decision suggests an administrative solution to a constitutional problem. Ironically, the Irish Government later sought, unsuccessfully, to rely[83] on the narrowness of the Court's approach, when, in *Purcell,*[84] it

a phone-in radio programme spoke on the topic of mushrooms before identifying himself, falsely, as a Member of Sinn Féin. For details regarding other incidents of "chill" censorship, see the account by Betty Purcell. (RTÉ journalist and first named applicant in the application to the Strasbourg Commission challenging s. 31), "The Silence in Irish Broadcasting" in B. Rollston, *The Media and Northern Ireland: Covering the Troubles* (London, Macmillan, 1991), pp. 51–68.

[79] S. 18 of the Broadcasting Authority Act, 1960.

[80] "RTÉ's professionalism as an impartial purveyor of news and opinions is questioned by this affair, in relation to the manner in which it improperly interpreted the ministerial order and the manner in which it so zealously argued before the courts that more rather than less censorship was appropriate": Editorial, *Sunday Tribune*, 4 Apr. 1993. The Authority also choose to continue to apply its interpretation of the Order until after the Supreme Court decision.

[81] Hederman, Egan and Blaney JJ concurring.

[82] *Supra* n. 77, at 462, author's italics.

[83] For the purpose of claiming that the applicants had not exhausted local remedies by challenging the constitutionality of the ban in the Irish courts.

[84] *Purcell v. Ireland*, App. (No. 15) 40/89, 70 D&R 262 (1989).

argued that *Lynch* had not addressed the ban in the context of the constitutional guarantee of freedom of expression.

Despite their limited nature, *Lynch* and *O'Toole* sent important signals to the Government and Broadcasting Authority, respectively. They also opened the important issue of editorial judgement with respect to Northern Ireland that had largely lain dormant during the years of the blanket ban. Between 1988[85] and 1994 similar, thought not identical, broadcasting restrictions existed in the United Kingdom.[86] However, despite being wider in one respect,[87] the UK ban cannot be said to have had as detrimental an effect on the coverage of Northern Irish matters as the section 31 Order had in the Republic. In part this was due to the fact that the UK ban was lifted during elections and only covered "direct speech", thus allowing voice-overs and reports of interviews.

Also, in contrast to the situation in the Republic, the UK ban was the subject of more concerted attempts by British broadcasters to function at the outer limits of its restrictions, to discredit its operation and to highlight to viewers, through the use of "health warnings", and voice-overs poorly synchronised, that what they were viewing was subject to constraints. Most famously, a *Real Lives* documentary entitled "Enemies Within" was broadcast with direct speech of an IRA prisoner in the Maze voicing his reasons for becoming an IRA volunteer, while scenes of the "Officer Commanding" the IRA prisoners complaining to a prison warder about the size of the sausage rolls was subtitled. There was also a wider debate on the censorship issue itself.[88]

But even this strategy is not without its dangers. Northern Ireland, as any prolonged conflict situation, has seen a refinement of propaganda strategies and resulting difficulties for broadcasters. In October 1979, before the ban was

[85] For almost two decades before the introduction of the UK ban in 1988, a large section of the population along the border and the East coast or with cable television could receive the forbidden television broadcasts by switching to UK channels. British radio signals are received over the whole of the country.

[86] On the operation of the UK ban, see *Art. 19, No Comment: Censorship, Secrecy and the Irish Troubles* (London, Article 19, 1989); L. Curtis and M. Jempson, *Interference on the Airwaves: Ireland, the Media and the Broadcasting Ban* (London, CPBF, 1993); E. Barendt, "Broadcasting Censorship" (1990) 106 *LQR* 354; B. Thompson, "Broadcasting and Terrorism" [1989] *Public Law* 527 and "Broadcasting and Terrorism in the House of Lords" [1991] *Public Law* 346. A challenge to the Home Secretary's Order failed in the House of Lords: *R. v. Secretary of State for the Home Department, ex part Brind* [1991] 1 All ER 720.

[87] It applied e.g. to historical material including much of Robert Kee's acclaimed series, *Ireland: A Television History* and Kenneth Griffith's biographical film of the life of Michael Collins, *Hang Up Your Brightest Colours*.

[88] Including the screening of the "Banned" series on Channel 4 in 1991. The series was accompanied by a joint Channel 4, British Film Institute and *New Statesman and Society* publication, *New Statesman*, 4 Apr. 1991. Though, even in this laudable exercise an element of self-censorship crept in. In showing the documentary, *Mother Ireland*, pulled from the schedule after one of the interviewees, Mairéad Farrell, was shot at Gibraltar, Channel 4 chose to cut scenes of masked individuals preparing molotov cocktails and, inexplicably, Christy Moore and Sinéad O'Connor singing the ballad, "Irish Ways and Irish Laws".

introduced in the UK, one such incident took place in the village of Carrickmore. BBC *Panorama* journalists were tipped off to go to the village for a staged IRA show of arms. At one and the same time, it was newsworthy that an illegal organisation could parade armed, in public, for several hours, and yet, the journalists were clearly producing footage that would be used to magnify the strength of the organisation and provide it with a propaganda victory.[89] Equally, throughout the period of the ban, Sinn Féin press conferences were regularly conducted with a banner backdrop featuring the word "censored". As potent as any broadcast to its American supporters.

Within RTÉ, opposition was muted. While a small number of journalists and producers, some of whom were later named applicants in the *Purcell* application, lobbied against the ban, coverage of Northern Ireland was generally carried out in quiet acquiescence to it. Apart from protests in 1972, when journalists staged a strike in opposition to the jailing of Kevin O'Kelly, and again in August 1985, in opposition to a management decision not to interview Martin Galvin of NORAID (an organisation not covered by the section 31 Order), opposition to the ban itself was largely confined to RTÉ's Belfast office until the late 1980s, which saw strike action against the renewal of the Order.[90] The absence of wider opposition may be explained by, in addition to career worries,[91] a concerted campaign to smear journalists that challenged the ban as IRA "fellow-travellers" or "hush puppies".[92] In some minds, when national security is raised there is, it appears, no room for objective journalism and a desire to present the full picture or to credit viewers with the ability to hear, and consider, the argument and opinions feared, was to be equalled with naïveté, ambivalence or, worse, support. Even to question the misapplication of the section 31 ban was to risk such opprobrium.

The advance made on O'Toole was short-lived. Four months after the Supreme Court decision, Carney J in the High Court[93] signalled a retreat, in upholding RTÉ's refusal to broadcast a radio advertisement for a collection of short stories by Gerry Adams.[94] The refusal was based on the view that by

---

[89] The fall-out of the affair also highlighted the perils of provoking government reaction, as the documentary featuring the Carrickmore incident was subsequently withdrawn by BBC management, and only after NUJ protests was the dismissed *Panorama* editor, Roger Bolton, reinstated.

[90] In 1993, a year before the lapse of the order, the NUJ and the trade union, SIPTU, launched the "Let in the Light" campaign in opposition to the ban.

[91] Jenny McGeever was dismissed in 1988 by RTÉ, having included the voices of Sinn Féin's Martin McGuinness and Gerry Adams attempting to calm crowds at the funeral cortege of the IRA members shot in Gibraltar. The response of the broadcasting community to the episode was in stark contrast to that of the O'Kelly affair and an out-of-court settlement of £5,000 ended the matter.

[92] One of the most trenchant attacks on opponents of s. 31 was made in an internal RTÉ document, *Television and Terrorism*, produced by Eoghan Harris, then an RTÉ editor. Cruise O'Brien is attributed with engaging in similar invective, describing senior *Irish Times* journalist, Dick Walsh, as "a provo mouthpiece": see *Belfast Bulletin, supra* n. 51.

[93] *Brandon Books* v. *RTE* [1993] ILRM 806.

[94] In a letter to the publisher RTÉ expressed its willingness to broadcast the advertisement provided it was by way of a voice-over by a member of the actor's union, Equity.

showing his "human" side it would somehow lead to support for his political views and party. A similar prohibition was instituted by the IRTC on the different ground that some of the stories presented a favourable perspective of the IRA and might thereby encourage support for the organisation. Without considering the actual content of the book, which, apart from one story from the perspective of an fictional IRA volunteer, were largely childhood reminiscences, the High Court upheld the ban. It accepted the argument put forward by RTÉ that Adams' "public persona is such that he cannot be divorced in the public mind from advancing the cause of Sinn Féin".[95] Carney J concluding by saying:

> "it seems to me that greater expertise in relation to making a judgment on these matters must lie with the national broadcasting authority than the courts. Secondly, it must be asked whether the exercise of such a judgment by the broadcasting authority is reviewable by the courts. On the facts of the case as established on affidavit with cross-examination of two of the deponents . . . I do not see that it is proper for the court to interfere."

Once again, the judgment makes no reference to the constitutional expression guarantee, except in so far as it quotes Flaherty J in *Lynch* to the effect that an examination of Article 40.6.1.i was in that case not necessary. Had such an examination been offered, the nature of the advertisement would have come in for consideration. It could hardly be described as "political", otherwise one assumes that section 10(3) of the 1988 Act would have been relied upon, and yet the argument raised to justify the application of the section 31 Order effectively amounts to saying that all of Gerry Adams' expression is "political".

Ultimately, Strasbourg appeared to offer the only possibility of a proper rights examination of section 31. However, despite developed and strict scrutiny employed by the Human Rights Commission and Court with regard to the right to free expression in Article 10, *Purcell v. Ireland* was to fail at the initial hurdle of admissibility.[96] The decision was both surprising and, in light of the 1996 Constitution Review Group's[97] recommendation that Article 10 ECHR be the model for the replacement of Article 40.6.1.i, instructive. It is surprising for the ease with which the Commission majority arrived at the conclusion that the ban constituted an interference "necessary in a democratic society" as permitted by Article 10(2). In part, the decision stems from a generous application of the margin of appreciation doctrine, that allows States scope to determine what is "necessary" interference, the Commission

---

[95] Hogan and Whyte opine that a distinction is hereby introduced between prominent members of Sinn Féin and the rank and file, with only the former being properly subject to blanket exclusion from the airwaves: G. Hogan and G. Whyte (eds.), J. M. Kelly, *The Irish Constitution* (Dublin, Butterworths, 1994), p. 956.

[96] *Supra* n. 84. The application to Strasbourg challenging the UK ban was to suffer the same fate: see *Brind & McLaughlin v. United Kingdom*, App. Nos. 18714/91 and 18759/91, 77–A D&R 42 (1994).

[97] *Supra* n. 16, 292.

deeming the Government's reasons for the ban "relevant and sufficient".[98] It also stressed the *dangers* of the broadcast media, but not their importance as a vehicle for people to receive and exchange opinions and ideas.[99] Fundamentally, the Commission failed to apply any real proportionality test, focusing on the live broadcast scenario, even talking of the risk of coded messages being conveyed, without asking whether other, less restrictive, measures would achieve the aim of denying terrorists legitimacy. The decision is instructive in highlighting the weakness of even the strongest rights formulation in the face of State assertions of terrorist threat and the prevalence of a view regarding the ease with which viewers might be led to support violence.[100]

AFTER THE BAN

In January 1994 the Minister responsible for broadcasting, Michael D. Higgins, announced the Government's decision not to renew the Order. This had been on the agenda since an undertaking by the Minister[101] a year earlier to conduct a review of the ban and propelled by UN criticism and the expectation that all-party talks on Northern Ireland would follow the Downing Street Declaration.[102] Within days of the Order lapsing, RTÉ issued new guidelines.[103] Based on section 18 of the 1960 Act, they took a cautionary line, stipulating that interviews with Sinn Féin members be pre-recorded and under the "strict control" of management, and that interviews with members of proscribed organisations would only take place in "exceptional circumstances". From the outset difficulties were reported, with the first request by current affairs producers to management for permission to interview Gerry Adams being refused.[104]

In contrast the IRTC[105] interim guidelines[106] (initially for six months, they

[98] Which suggest a lower threshold than other pronouncements regarding the idea of "necessary in a democratic society": see, e.g., *Handyside* v. *UK*, Series A, No. 24 (1976).

[99] The ban is, for example, described as an "inconvenience" to the journalists' duties at p. 16 of the Commission's decision.

[100] In contrast, the UN Human Rights Committee, in its Response to the Irish Report on 28 July 1993, deemed the s. 31 ban to be in breach of Art. 19 of the International Covenant on Civil and Political Rights.

[101] Higgins, a writer, was a long-time opponent of the ban. It was also suggested that a combination of ss. 17 and 18 of the Broadcasting Act, 1960 and the Prohibition of Incitement to Hatred Act, 1989 would provide adequate safeguards in the absence of a s. 31 order: *Irish Times*, 31 Dec. 1993.

[102] Though the Minister denied that the move was a "sop" to the IRA following the Downing Street Declaration: *Irish Times*, 12 Jan. 1994.

[103] *Broadcasting Authority Act 1960 to 1993. Guidance for Staff on Observance of S.18(1) of the Broadcasting Authority Act, 1960.*

[104] "RTE Turns Down Request for Adams", *Irish Times*, 29 Jan. 1994.

[105] Established by the Radio and Television Act, 1988 and responsible for the broadcasting activities of national and local independent broadcasters.

[106] These supplemented ss. 9(1)(a), (b) and (d) of the Radio and Television Act, 1988, the equivalent of s. 18 of the 1960 Act.

have been renewed until the present) are significantly more pro-freedom of expression than their RTÉ equivalent. An accompanying IRTC statement of principles stressed the importance of freedom of communication in a democracy, a flexible interpretation of section 9 of the 1988 Act, a strong presumption against prior restraint of subject matter and for *ex post facto* rebuttal or correction to be favoured over a policy of prior restraint. Fundamentally, the statement of principles noted that in a democracy viewers and listeners should be presumed to be capable of responsible decision-making in relation to their response to material broadcasts.

The guidelines themselves require "careful examination" with respect to interviews with Sinn Féin and Republican Sinn Féin, "extreme caution" with regard to broadcasts of illegal organisations which are to take place only in "exceptional situations", and that "form, style and content" be such as to meet section 9 of the 1988 Act, OAS, 1939, Defamation Act, 1961, Prohibition of Incitement to Hatred Act, 1989, contempt of court law and the criminal law generally. The also express a preference for pre-recording in relation to "sensitive matters" and prior management approval of party political broadcast scripts of Sinn Féin.

In its consideration of Article 40.6.1.i.[107] the *Report of the Constitutional Review Group* did not engage in any detailed consideration of the section 31 saga. It did, however, profess to seek to balance submissions offered to it, which it described as ranging from: "if it ain't broken, don't fix it" to "ensure its [the Constitution's] responsiveness to the ethos of 21st Century Ireland".[108] That Article 40.6.1.i. is in need of "fixing" is recognised by the Review Group's recommendation of the adoption of a formula along the lines of Article 10 of the ECHR. This has the appeal of bringing with it a relatively coherent rights theory, with the right and limitation in proper perspective. Such a revision would also serve to provide coherence in place of diverse development of expression under Articles 40.3 and 40.6.1.i.

CONCLUSION

A revived peace process gives rise to hopes that the smothering of uncomfortable voices and important debate in pursuit of some ill-defined "public good" will not recur. Equally, the growth of media outlets and technologies makes the revisiting of such control difficult. The democratic institutions of the State did not quake when the population was first exposed to the sound of Gerry Adams' voice. If any tremor was felt, it was perhaps a realisation of the weakness of our bedrock law. A constitutional rights provision that permits a coalition of government, judiciary and broadcaster to assume some sort

---

[107] *Supra* n. 16, 291–304.
[108] *Ibid.*, at p. *xi*.

of child-like naïveté on the part of the citizenry might well prove a useful starting point for a revision exercise.

The test for a constitutional rights guarantee is not how it functions when skies are blue, but whether it actually protects rights when dark clouds gather. In the lifetime of the 1937 Constitution the ongoing conflict in Northern Ireland has been, perhaps, our greatest political storm. Yet, when the Constitution, the "the trouble-maker from Thebes",[109] proved most difficult, the solution by Government, courts and in some cases broadcaster, was to seek to prevent it corrupting the siblings. Slowly the "not in front of the children" mindset is abating and, while the damage done is not easily gauged, one lesson has hopefully been learnt, that "it's as true to say that no democracy should negate the principle of free speech as to say that no democracy can tolerate terrorism".[110]

[109] C. Cruise O'Brien, "View", *The Listener*, 24 Oct. 1968.
[110] J. Dougal, "The Media and the Troubles" (1982) 13 *Irish Broadcasting Review* 7.

16

Lawyers and Unions—The right to Freedom of Association in the Irish Constitution

IRENE LYNCH

INTRODUCTION

"One of the eternal conflicts out of which life is made up is that between the effort of every man to get the most he can for his services, and that of society disguised under the name of capital, to get his services for the least possible return. Combination on the one side is patent and powerful. Combination on the other is the necessary and desirable counterpart, if the battle is to be carried on in a fair and equal way . . . "[1]

The establishment and growth of the Irish trade union movement predates the Irish Constitution of 1937. In that sense the right to freedom of association guaranteed in Article 40.6.1.iii of the Irish Constitution[2] cannot be regarded as part of the original theoretical or legal foundation of trade unionism in Ireland. However, since the enactment of the Constitution into Irish law, a number of cases have been considered by the courts concerning the activities of trade unions and the rights of individuals against the backdrop of the constitutional provisions. Fundamental tensions have arisen in these cases between the emphasis on individual rights in this part of the Constitution, having its roots in liberal political theory, and the demands of the collective group. It is argued that the conflict emerging within constitutional law analysis of trade unionism is a fundamental aspect of the historically difficult relationship between the law and the trade union movement.[3] Similar conflict has

---

[1] Holmes J (dissenting), *Vegalahn* v. *Guntner*, Supreme Judicial Court of Massachusetts (1896) 44 NE 1077.

[2] Art. 40.6.1.iii states: "The State guarantees liberty for the exercise of the following rights, subject to public order and morality: . . . The right of the citizen to form associations and unions. Laws, however, may be enacted for the regulation and control, in the public interest of the exercise of the foregoing right." Art. 40.6.2 states in part: "Laws regulating the manner in which the right of forming associations and unions . . . may be exercised shall contain no political, religious or class discrimination."

[3] Today a very significant feature of this legal tension is found in the system of immunities from liability under common law principles which is granted to trade unionists in respect of

taken place in the United States legal system and some comparisons will be made.

The tensions which exist between attempts by union leaders and trade unionists to organise and to pursue their goals on the one hand, and the response of the legislature and judiciary on the other, can certainly be couched in terms of competing legal principles. At the outset the fundamental common law ethos of freedom of contract posed a substantial obstacle to the acceptance of trade unions. Historically trade unions were considered to be acting in restraint of trade as a combination, in the same way that businessmen and tradesmen would have been considered to be acting in restraint of trade when they agreed to fix prices for their goods. Under this legal paradigm trade unionists were considered to be fixing the price of their labour amongst themselves and accordingly were acting illegally. In Ireland we have some early examples of both social and legal hostility to trade unions. In 1824 an Act had been passed repealing pre-existing laws against combinations of workers.[4] Following that, increased union activity had led to tensions which culminated in the murder of Thomas Hanlon, a Dublin sawyer in 1824. In the following year a report from the Divisional Justices of the Peace in Dublin pleaded with the legislature to return to the common law position which outlawed combinations of workers.[5] Part of the report referred to the "wisdom of the law in abstaining from any interference as to the rates of wages" and referred to "ignorant and injudicious persons" who sought "to coerce the conduct of others and by fixing unattainable rates of wages, to put a stop to employment altogether".[6] The interesting point here is that even at this early stage the legal response was to view labour as a commodity which was being disposed of by the worker and in turn bought by the employer, who was thus the owner of that labour. Any interference in this contract arising from industrial action such as strike, boycott or other concerted action was exactly the same as interference in commercial contractual relations. Thus the employer was assisted by the courts in protecting his property rights in the worker's labour. This intellectual conception is evident as a theoretical basis to many much more recent industrial relations cases.[7] It has been argued by a number of notable

industrial action. This is a notoriously difficult area of the law which serves to confound and confuse. In this respect the Irish situation closely reflects the position in Britain. See further the Industrial Relations Act 1990.

[4] 5 Geo. IV c. 95.

[5] Referring to the unrest described the report stated: "should therefore the examples now made not succeed in arresting distinctive progress, we trust that they may have the effect of directing the attention of the legislature to the consideration of the laws on the subject of combination, and to the expediency of reverting to the principle of the Common Law by repressing the proceedings of combinators in the early stages, before they shall have manifested themselves in threats and violence": F. A. D'Arcy and K. Hannigan (eds.), *Workers in Union: Documents and Commentaries in the History of Irish Labour Law* (Dublin, Stationery Office, 1988), 63.

[6] *Ibid.*, at n. 5.

[7] E.g. in *South Wales Miners Federation* v. *Glamorgan Coal Company Ltd* [1904–7] All ER 211, where the court declared illegal a number of "stop days" implemented by the union, and *Morgan* v. *Fry* [1968] 2 QB 710, where the courts held that strike action amounted to a breach of

labour theorists in the United States that this commodification of human labour is pivotal to the development of the legal response to trade unionism, both in terms of legislative and judicial analysis. Moreover the argument continues that this view adversely affected the legal position of trade unionism:

> "The labor black hole is traceable to the commodity theory of labor dominant during the 'Lochner' era. For decades the labor movement argued passionately that human labor is not a commodity. This philosophical debate neatly coincided with the proper place of labor in the constitutional order. If labor is a commodity then the constitutional principles that govern the commercial marketplace also govern labor. For the past century judicial acceptance of the commodity conception has cut against the constitutional protection of labor protest . . . "[8]

The purpose of this essay is not to provide an in-depth analysis of particular industrial relations cases but to present the argument that judicial misconception in particular, as distinct from the legislative conception, of the appropriate place of the collective trade union organisation within the legal order has led the courts to undermine trade unionism and the goals of trade unionism. This has been a consequence of the emphasis which the legal order has traditionally placed on the individual and individual rights. This has in turn, emanated from a particular political philosophy which it is argued usually gives rise to a better fit between the issues at stake and the legal response. The same pattern has emerged in both Britain and American labour history and has been analysed in considerable detail by some American commentators.

In describing the development of the American labour movement, Forbath comments on the US case law of the late nineteenth and early twentieth centuries:

> " 'Treating unions' 'interferences' with employers' labor supplies as invasions of property rights may have been hard to reconcile with the liberal individualist zeitgeist. However the goodwill cases in equity, the enticement action at common law, as well as the centuries-old habit of treating servants' labor as masters' property, meant that there were many familiar mental grooves into which the new notions of property could comfortably fit."[9]

In the following paragraph Forbath goes on to observe that at this point in American labour history the judges also turned to the Constitution to provide additional force to the proposition that a business or enterprise is property,

---

contract. In Ireland the contractual paradigm was also adopted in cases such as *Becton Dickinson & Co Ltd* v. *Lee* [1973] IR 1, where the court held however that the effect of strike action was to suspend the contract in relation to certain terms.

[8] J. G. Pope, "Labor and the Constitution: From Abolition to Deindustrialisation" (1987) 65 *Tex. L Rev.* 1076. See also P. Forbath, "The Shaping of the American Labor Movement" (1989) 102 *Harv. L Rev.* 1111 and C. K. Hurvitz, "American Labor Law and the Doctrine of Entrepreneurial Property Rights: Boycotts, Courts and Juridical Reorientation of 1886–1895" (1986) 8 *Industrial Relations J* 307.

[9] P. Forbath, *supra* n. 8, at 1170.

and furthermore that a business-person's or worker's right to pursue his own trade or vocation was a constitutional property right to be protected by the courts.[10] Interestingly the hostile approach of the courts to organised labour was arrested in the United States by the passing of the "Norris-La Guardia" Act in 1932[11] and the National Labor Relations Act (the "Wagner" Act) in 1935.[12] Similarly in Ireland the Trade Disputes Act of 1906 arrested the legally hostile environment facing Irish Trade Unions.

THE RIGHT TO FREEDOM OF ASSOCIATION AND ITS MEANING UNDER THE 1937 CONSTITUTION

This essay will explore these themes as a backdrop to the examination of the right to freedom of association provided for in Article 40.6.1. iii of the 1937 Constitution and the growth and organisation of the trade union movement. The emphasis on the individual rights-bearing, rational free bargaining agent which is central to the development of our legal culture has not served the collective organisation well. Furthermore I would argue that the reason for this is that there is, to borrow Forbath's phrase, a "pre-existing mental groove" for the courts to avail themselves of, which limits in some cases an understanding of the overall industrial relations issues. To illustrate this thesis the decisions of the High Court and the Supreme Court in *National Union of Railwaymen* v. *Sullivan*[13] will be considered.

Apart from the industrial relations issues raised by this case it is also significant in that it was the first case where the Supreme Court struck down a piece of legislation which had been enacted by the *Oireachtas*.[14] In outlining the court's jurisdiction to exercise this power of judicial review the Supreme Court judgment in this case differs significantly from that of the High Court and outlines the jurisdiction of the court in clear and unambiguous terms.

However, from an industrial relations perspective the decision in *NUR* v. *Sullivan* excluded a method of dealing with trade union bargaining rights and recognition issues which arguably presented a far better alternative to the present system. This system had been conceived of and passed by the legislature

---

[10] P. Forbath, *supra* n. 8, at 1171. Here Forbath refers to cases such as *In re Jacobs*, 98 NY 98 (1885); *Barr* v. *United Essex Trades Council* 53 NJ Eq. 101, 30 A 881 (1894), *Brace Bros.* v. *Evans*, 5 Pa. C 163 (1888) and *Pierce* v. *Stableman's Union*, 156 Cal. 70, 103 P 324 (1909).

[11] Forbath refers to the fact that at that time "Senator Norris enlisted the help of Felix Frankfurter and a number of other progressive legal reformers to draft a substitute bill. Their draft made no mention of the 'definition' of property but it was a thorough and well-crafted set of hedges against labor injunctions." This bill was presented as a substitute to an AFL sponsored bill and was passed in 1932 as the Norris-La Guardia Act.

[12] See below.

[13] [1947] IR 77.

[14] Although the Court had previously advised the President that the School Attendance Bill of 1942 was unconstitutional. See further G. Hogan and G. Whyte (eds.), *J. M. Kelly, The Irish Constitution* (3rd edn., Dublin, Butterworths, 1994), at 976.

in consultation with certain trade unionists but was struck down by the Supreme Court by reference to the right to freedom of association. For this reason it represents a pivotal point in the development of modern industrial relations in Ireland.

Part III of the Trade Union Act of 1941 provided for the establishment of a Trade Union Tribunal which would decide on the rights of representation of particular unions organising workers of particular classes within particular employments. So where unions were competing with each other Section 26(1) of the Act allowed a trade union to apply to the Tribunal for determination that that union alone had the right to organise "workmen of that class" where the union could show that it had organised "a majority of workmen of any particular class". Section 26 provided that on foot of such an application the Tribunal could:

"(a) grant such determination, or
(b) refuse to grant such determination, or
(c) determine that two or more specified trade unions alone shall have the right to so organise workmen of that class."

Under Section 34(3), once such a determination has been made, that union had sole organisation and representation rights for workers of that class in that employment. Thus the ability of an individual employed in that class to choose an alternative union to represent him was restricted under the Act. Other sections in the Act provided for the arrangement and supervision of ballots by the Trade Union Tribunal for the purposes of establishing the question of support of the union within the particular class of workers in question[15] and also provided that the determination of the Tribunal in favour of the union would remain in place for five years.[16]

NUR v. *Sullivan* arose because the plaintiffs brought an action against the Irish Transport and General Workers' Union (ITGWU) which had applied for a determination under the Act in relation to employees of Córas Iompair Éireann (CIE) who worked in the road passenger service of CIE (Tramways). NUR argued that Part III infringed the rights of the individual to form associations and to join the union of one's choice and that therefore this part of the Trade Union Act 1941 was unconstitutional.

THE DECISION OF JUSTICE GAVAN DUFFY IN THE HIGH COURT

In giving his judgment against the plaintiffs in the High Court, thus upholding the scheme introduced by the Trade Union Act, Gavan Duffy J held that the right to freedom of association contained in the Constitution was subject to the "regulation and control in the public interest" of the exercise of that

---

[15] S. 27 of the Trade Union Act 1941.
[16] See below Part III of the Act.

right. In considering the plaintiff's case, that the restrictions in Part III of the Trade Union Act were too restrictive to be covered, Gavan Duffy J stated "The claim is that regulations or control in the context cannot as a matter of law, extend to prohibition . . . ". He referred to a United States case *US* v. *Hill*[17] where a statute passed by Congress which prohibited the bringing of alcoholic beverage across State lines was upheld, and observed that he "found impressive authority in the *United States* v. *Hill* . . . for the opinion that a constitutional power of regulation may be broad enough in law to carry a veto . . . ". He went on to hold that to strike down the legislation "would be to narrow a term ('regulation and control') of very wide connotation in the organic law, and to do so after the need for the measure has been declared by the appropriate organ of government, far better equipped than the judiciary to know the need."

Gavan Duffy J's judgment in this regard allows a broad area of discretion to the legislature under the "regulation and control" exemption provided for in the guarantee of the right to free association. Furthermore his willingness to defer to the judgment of the legislature can also be contrasted with the much more assertive stance of the Supreme Court in relation to legislation challenged constitutionally.

More centrally to this essay Gavan Duffy J seemed to appreciate the significance of the Trade Union Tribunal system in the context of trade unionism, in particular the situation of Irish trade unionism which suffered particularly from fragmented membership and inter-union competitiveness:

> "one need not be a trade union expert to see that a powerful union is more likely than a weaker one to achieve results. The Act seeks to strengthen the stronger bodies and in the fortifying process includes a restriction on competitive organisation within a class."[18]

THE SUPREME COURT DECISION

The judgment of the court given by Murnaghan J first asserts the jurisdiction of the court to review legislation in this manner and for that reason alone is historically significant:

> "Constitutions frequently embody within their framework important principles of polity expressed in general language. In some Constitutions it is left to the Legislature to interpret the meaning of these principles, but in other types of Constitution, of which ours is one, an authority is chosen which is clothed with power and burdened with the duty of seeing that the Legislature shall not transgress the limits set on its powers."[19]

---

[17] 248 US 420.
[18] *Supra* n. 13, at 88.
[19] *Ibid.*, at 99.

He then goes on to use very strong language to describe both the effect of the impugned part of the Act and the issue that:

"[the Act] does not prohibit all association but it purports to limit the right of the citizen to join one or more prescribed associations i.e. the union or unions in respect of which a determination has been made. Any such limitation does undoubtedly deprive the citizen of a free choice of the persons with whom he shall associate. Both logically and practically, to deprive a person of the choice of the persons with whom he shall associate, is not a control of the exercise of the right of association, but a denial of that right altogether."[20]

The court then went on to strike down the entire Trade Union Tribunal system as contained in Part III of the Act on the grounds that it was unconstitutional.

THE NATIONAL LABOR RELATIONS ACT 1935 IN THE UNITED STATES

In 1935 the United States Congress passed the National Labor Relations Act (the "Wagner" Act) which established a system similar to that provided for by the Irish Trade Union Act of 1941. Described as the exclusivity rule, this legislation is generally regarded by Labour law commentators in the United States as being pro-union.[21] Following as they did on the heels of the "Norris-La Guardia" Act 1932 these two pieces of legislation are generally viewed as heralding the start of a more pro-union era in the history of American trade unionism.[22] The Wagner Act established a National Labor Relations Board which was designed to perform, among other functions, the functions which Part III of the Trade Union Act of 1941 had assigned to the Trade Union Tribunal. The machinery for designating the trade union with sole representation rights is similar to that described in Part III of the Irish Act. The legislation also imposes an obligation on the employer to recognise and bargain with the properly elected trade union. This system is still in place in the United States and is still operated in much the same manner as it originally was by the National Labor Relations Board. It is considered to be a very important part of the process leading to union organisation and recognition. It is clear that instead of the Irish system which does nothing to prevent inter-union competitiveness and where the individual may choose to be a member of any union of his choice, the US system regulates the operation of the trade union within the workplace. However, the system also grants to the union in

---

[20] *Ibid.,* at 102.

[21] See e.g. J. G. Pope, *supra* n. 8, P. Forbath, *supra* n. 8; and generally, B. D. Melzer and S. D. Henderson, *Labor Law: Cases and Materials* (Boston, Mass., Little, Brown and Company, 1985), ch. 1.

[22] "Such measures reflected the growing acceptance of the legitimacy of unions, their increased political power, the costs of repressive policies, the validity of labor's historic grievances, and legislative responsibility for the basic policy issues": B. D. Melzer and S. D. Henderson, *supra* n. 21, at 25.

question recognition rights which are not accessible to Irish trade unions through any legal mechanism. Recognition therefore in the Irish context is solely a matter for negotiation between the trade union and the employer.

No specific reference is made in any of the sections in Part III of the Act to a correlative duty or obligation on the employer to recognise or bargain with the trade union in favour of which a determination is made. However, it is important to realise that such a trade union would have the benefit of the endorsement of the Trade Union Tribunal and that therefore there would certainly be at least an implied correlative obligation on the employer to recognise that particular union.

JUDICIAL APPROACHES TO RECOGNITION RIGHTS AFTER *NUR* V. *SULLIVAN*

In decisions after *NUR* v. *Sullivan* and in more recent cases before the courts, the robustly individualist approach to the right to freedom of association has been consistently followed by the courts. This has been very significant in relation to the protection of non-unionised employees, again reiterating the point that the right to freedom of association has often served to work against the collective organisation.[23]

However, in the context of the system which would have operated under the legislation declared unconstitutional in *NUR* v. *Sullivan*, the courts have also consistently refused to impose any obligation on the employer to bargain or recognise a union. The courts have never assisted individual members or unions to insist that the employer bargain with them. Thus, for example, in cases such as *Dublin College ASA* v. *City of Dublin VEC*[24] and in *Abbott and Whelan* v. *ITGWU and the Southern Health Board*[25] the courts have consistently reiterated their view that although the Constitution guarantees the right of an individual to join the union of his or her choice there is no corresponding obligation on the employer to recognise or bargain with that union. Or, to put the proposition in the converse, there is no enforceable right to have one's union recognised as a party to collective negotiations despite one's exercise of the right to join such a union. Thus in *Abbott and Whelan* v. *ITGWU and the Southern Health Board*, McWilliam J noted that there was no constitutional right to be represented by the union of one's choice, although of course the courts are clear that there is freedom to choose a union. The difficulty identified by McWilliam J was that in his view:

> "The suggestion . . . that there is a constitutional right to be *represented* by a union in the conduct of negotiations with employers . . . in my opinion could not be sus-

---

[23] See e.g. *Meskell* v. *CIE* [1970] IR 121 and *Educational Company of Ireland* v. *Fitzpatrick (No. 2)* [1961] IR 345.

[24] Unreported, High Court, 31 July 1981.

[25] (1982) 1 JISLL 56.

tained. There is no duty placed on any employer to negotiate with any particular citizen or body of citizens."[26]

It is argued here that joining a union which does not have any right to assert recognition as against an employer renders the exercise of asserting one's right to choose meaningless. By contrast, in the United States the choice of union is restricted, or perhaps regulated is a better description, and the *quid pro quo* has been that there is a right to have that union recognised by the employer. Furthermore there is a corresponding legal mechanism to enforce the obligation to bargain as against the employer.

The loss of the exclusive majority representation system as described by Part III of the Trade Union Act 1941 also meant the loss of any rights to be recognised by the employer. So, although every individual now has a broad ranging right to join the union of his choice it is argued here that this judicially protected right is meaningless where there are no recognition rights.

A very interesting issue is that whilst the decision in *NUR* v. *Sullivan* was extremely significant in its impact on the development of the industrial relations structure in Ireland, and it is argued here that the impact was a negative one, the decision has been distinguished or not followed in subsequent cases which raise a similar point. In *Aughey* v. *Ireland*[27] the High Court upheld the Gárda Siochana Act 1977 which restricted the associations which could seek to negotiate on pay and conditions in the police force. It could be argued therefore that the decision of the Supreme Court represents an overly aggressive exercise of the court's jurisdiction. This point is supported by Hogan and Whyte who express the view that the court may have unduly restricted the power to regulate the exercise of freedom of association conferred on the Oireachtas by Article 40.6.1.iii and support this view by referring to the fact that the decision was not followed in the *Aughey* or *PMPS* cases.[28]

From the industrial relations standpoint this sort of regulation of the trade union was excluded. Most importantly, while losing the exclusivity rule the trade union movement also lost recognition rights in any strong form and this was the greatest casualty of the decision.

CONCLUSION

Not all trade unionists would agree that this sort of exclusivity rule would have been a good thing and it is interesting and important to note that the litigation in *NUR* v. *Sullivan* was brought by one trade union against another. However, the preparation of the legislative scheme and the Trade Union Act

---

[26] *Ibid.*, at 57.
[27] [1989] ILRM 87. See further *PMPS* v. *Attorney General* [1983] IR 339.
[28] G. Hogan and G. Whyte, *supra* n. 14, at 976.

1941 as a whole was very much contributed to by William O'Brien, General Secretary of the ITGWU, and was supported by a considerable number of trade unionists.[29] In *Workers in Union*, D'Arcy and Hannigan discuss the preparation of the Trade Union Act 1941. They describe how the Trade Union Act of 1941 reflected the personal contribution of both Seán MacEntee, the Minister for Industry and Commerce, and William O'Brien, the General Secretary of the ITGWU. The drafting of the Bill moved from an initial desire to reform trade unions, in the context of a public sense that trade unions in the 1930s had become too militant, to a close examination of the need to regulate trade unions. This development in the progress of the Bill coincided with the invitation to O'Brien to make an input on a more formalised basis through a series of meetings held between officials in the Department of Industry and Commerce and O'Brien and the President of the ITGWU, Tom Kennedy.

> "In accordance with O'Brien's suggestions the Bill now shed its original and oldest sections and became a measure dealing solely with regulation of the trade union movement. O'Brien had argued strongly in favour of a tribunal which would have the power to confer on certain unions exclusive rights of organisation in respect of certain categories of workers. The establishment of such a tribunal now became central to Part III of the new Bill. Ironically it was this section which was later held by the Supreme Court to be unconstitutional."[30]

Referring back to the US experience, Melzer and Henderson in their text on US labour law note that the passing of the "Wagner" Act was followed by a sharp increase in trade union membership, and note that the Act gave "affirmative legal protection against the exercise of employer power to frustrate the organisation of employees for collective bargaining".[31]

Recently, in a collection of essays on the further development of labour law in Britain and Europe, Lord Wedderburn identified a number of weaknesses in the British industrial relations system.[32] These weaknesses are mirrored in Ireland. A distinction is made by Wedderburn in these essays between the legal immunities approach to industrial relations common to both Ireland and Britain and a system of affirmative rights. This distinction has been made before, but here Wedderburn puts forward strong arguments in favour of the introduction of affirmative rights to Britain. One of the most significant of these rights is the right to recognition which imposes a correlative duty on the employer to recognise the union and a duty to meet and negotiate with the union. Lord Wedderburn points out that increasingly in Britain large companies "refuse a union presence" and in addition "attempt to displace the recog-

---

[29] F. A. D'Arcy and K. Hannigan (eds.), *supra* n. 5.

[30] *Ibid.*, at 202.

[31] *Supra* n. 21, at 20.

[32] K. W. Wedderburn, *Employment Rights in Britain and Europe: Selected Papers in Labour Law* (London, Lawrence and Wishart and the Institute of Employment Rights, 1991). See a commentary on these essays by C. Summers, "Lord Wedderburn's New Labour Law: An American Perspective" (1992) 21 *ILJ* 157.

nition of established unions". As Summers points out Lord Wedderburn argues that such difficulties facing British trade unions are at crisis point. Solutions are not obvious but Summers observes that:

> "Although there is no general legal duty to recognise and bargain in many countries, there is in almost every country an accepted practise of recognition and bargaining, and in countries as diverse as Japan, Sweden and the United States, there is a general legal duty to bargain."

Solutions to the crisis facing British trade unions could be fashioned from such examples. Similar difficulties facing Irish trade unions may not have arisen if the decision in *NUR* v. *Sullivan* had taken a different turn.

As regards the role of the courts, Hogan and Whyte, in their discussion of the guarantee of right to freedom of association in the Irish constitution, make the following observation:

> "While one could reasonably regard the guarantee as having been intended in the context of industrial relations, for the protection of trade unionism and the right of workers to organise against potentially hostile employers and/or State policy, it has never been applied by the courts in this way. Instead litigation on the guarantee has almost invariably been directed against trade unions."[33]

However, from a labour lawyer's point of view the outcome of judicial consideration of industrial relations issues in the context of legal rules and principles is less surprising. It is argued here that there has always been considerable tension between legal rules and the goals and policies of the trade union movement. Furthermore this tension has existed in other legal jurisdictions. The conflict presents itself most acutely in relation to judicial decisions which have on occasion, in relation to certain issues such as immunity for industrial action, been resolved by legislative enactments. However, this was not the case in relation to Part III of the Trade Union Act 1941 where the courts acted as the final arbiter of good industrial relations practice. The observations of Hoxie seem particularly apt:

> "[T]he union problem is neither simple nor unitary. It is not a mere question of wages and hours, of shop conditions and the narrow economic rights of employer and employee, and it cannot be resolved by a mere resort to economic theory. . . . It is a complex of economic, legal, ethical and social problems which can be understood and met only by knowing the facts and the genesis of the viewpoint of organized labor in all its reach, diversity, contradictions and shifting character, and by considering this viewpoint in relation to developing social conditions and social standards."[34]

---

[33] *Supra* n. 14, at 977.
[34] R. Hoxie, "Trade Unionism in the United States: General Character and Types" (1914) 22 *J Pol. Econ.* 207, referred to by B. D. Melzer and S. D. Henderson, *supra* n. 21, at 35.

17

Information, Justice and Power

BRENDAN RYAN

INTRODUCTION

Constitutional issues are too much the preserve of lawyers. Legal analysis and understanding of our Constitution is undoubtedly valuable, but it can also be excessively narrow. A broader view can come from a practical involvement with the Constitution. Politics is one such means of practical involvement and, in my own case, this has concerned an endless list of campaigns and agitations. Of their nature, these force one to confront the law (at least intellectually) and, in particular, the Constitution, our most basic law. It is in many ways a process of learning by doing. One learns very early on, for instance, of the need to observe due process in even the smallest sports or social club, learning as one goes that no one, however grand or however insignificant, can assume they are not bound by constitutional provisions. One learns even more perhaps by observing, as I did, the Committee on Privileges and Procedure of *Seanad Eireann* attempting to act, in a case involving the then *Cathaoirleach* Sean Doherty and Senator David Norris, apparently oblivious to such provisions and being forced to reconsider by the courts.[1] One cannot but wonder why something that should be obvious to an official of a social club could come as such a surprise to members of *Seanad Eireann*.

Reflection on such incidents leads one to a deeper conception of what our Constitution does and fails to do. One is better able to perceive where it has been successful, sometimes perhaps inadvertently, and where it has, sometimes equally inadvertently, been unsuccessful. It also leads one to consider popular assumptions about these successes and failures.

In my view, there are a number of areas where popular consensus seems at variance with the facts, particularly where the Constitution has been successful but without this being popularly recognised. I am referring here to the relatively common allegations that the Constitution is sectarian in nature and that its defence of private property reflects an antiquity that we have long left behind us. This essay begins with some observations on these allegations.

Conversely, it is also possible to identify areas where the Constitution is seriously deficient and an inhibition to progress, and two such areas will also

[1] See *The Irish Times*, 17 March 1990.

be considered: the absence of any explicit guarantee of access to information and the absence of any socio-economic guarantees other than that of free primary education.

The essay concludes that while many amendments would be possible which would extend the usefulness of the Constitution, any attempt to provide us with a "modernised" Constitution would give exponents of the present dominant ideology a dangerous opportunity to reduce or restrict individual rights on the pretext that such rights inhibit executive action. The occasionally irritating forms of words of a religious nature might disappear, but they would probably be replaced by an even more rigid version of the current dominant ideology.[2]

PRIVATE PROPERTY

There is often considerable unease about what are sometimes inaccurately referred to as the rights of property in the Constitution. In fact, there are no rights "of" property referred to in the Constitution, although there are plentiful references to the right "to" property. These rights, even as elaborated by the courts, are far from absolute. As I understand it, judicial decisions based on the right to property are invariably premised on what the courts perceive to be fair or equitable. Neither the Constitution nor the courts inhibit either regulation or acquisition by the State of private property. The courts have simply attempted to ensure that procedures and practices are fair. This was the basis, for instance, on which agricultural rates were struck down.[3] It was pointed out that rateable valuations of agricultural land were not based on any universal yard-stick of property valuation, but rather were arbitrary in the extreme. The State did not apply logical criteria for such valuation, so the Supreme Court ruled that such a system based on arbitrariness was unfair. Such a decision, far from being an assertion of property rights, was in fact no more than a vindication of the rights of citizens in the face of arbitrary and abusive State power.

Indeed, in the area of property rights, there can be few other constitutions which envisage the expropriation under any circumstances, without compensation, of private property, as the Irish one does. In fact, the application of the planning laws to prevent the commercial exploitation of areas of great natural beauty clearly involves the expropriation by the State (without compensation) of the value (or at least the potential value) of private property.

---

[2] Constitutions and treaties are documents of their time. For example, the Maastricht Treaty's convergence criteria are seen by many as an insertion into the constitutional order of more 1980s ideological fashions.

[3] *Brennan* v. *Attorney General* [1984] ILRM 355.

SECTARIANISM

Not so long ago a British commentator described Ireland as "the most theo-cratic [state] outside of Iran" and it is not difficult to identify elements of the Constitution, or indeed its subsequent interpretation by the courts, which at first glance appear to confirm that view. The invocation of God is clearly one such characteristic,[4] the relatively recent "pro-life" Amendment is another,[5] and of course the recently removed prohibition on divorce[6] had previously copper-fastened this perception. The invocation of the Christian nature of the Constitution by the Supreme Court when it rejected attempts to have anti-gay legislation overturned appeared to give further weight to the "sectarian" image.[7]

However, the suggestion of sectarian bias, like the criticism of property rights, is only superficially plausible. Certainly, politics were sometimes delib-erately denominational in Ireland, but more often this was unintentional. This was perhaps not surprising, given the preponderance of a single denomination and obviously the absolutism of Roman Catholicism also encouraged denom-inationalism. However, it was never as all-pervasive as some assert. In legis-lation it was ignored to a considerable extent in matters such as licensing laws, while it was also considerably diluted by decisions (in the face of hos-tility from some Roman Catholic circles) to proceed with large-scale public housing, and a degree of socialised health care which one bishop said reminded him "of the claims put forward by Hitler and Stalin".[8] Only in the area of sexuality and the family was there a clear denominational character to Irish legislation.

Such a character was even less apparent concerning the Constitution. For a Constitution drafted in the 1930s, the inclusion of a guarantee of the right of children to be withdrawn from religious education in national schools is remarkable. That right may yet have dramatic consequences for the national school system in Ireland. This is because, while it is common practice to excuse children who are not Roman Catholics from formal religious instruc-tion, the actual rules under which national schools operate insist that a reli-gious spirit should be all-pervasive. In the past, this was probably tolerable

[4] See, e.g., Art. 6: "All powers of government, legislative, executive and judicial derive, under God, from the People . . .".

[5] The Eighth Amendment to the Constitution (1983) inserted Art. 40.3.3: "The State acknowl-edges the right to life of the unborn and, with due regard to the life of the mother, guarantees in its laws to respect, and as far as practicable, by its laws to defend and vindicate that right."

[6] Until 1995, Art. 41.3.2 read as follows: "No law shall be enacted providing for the grant of a dissolution of marriage." This was replaced with a provision allowing for divorce legislation in certain circumstances. See further F. Martin, "The Family and the Constitution" in this volume.

[7] *Norris* v. *Attorney General* [1984] IR 36. For criticism of this decision see C. Gearty, "Constitutional Law, Homosexuals and the Criminal Law—The Right to Privacy" (1983) 5 *DULJ* 264, and also the essays by A. Hunt and L. Flynn in this volume.

[8] Bishop Browne of Galway, quoted in J. H. White, Church and State in Modern Ireland 1923–70 (Dublin, Gill and Macmillan, 1974), 257.

for many religious, but non-Roman Catholic, parents. However, it is increasingly intolerable for the growing minority of parents who describe themselves as having no religion, or who wish to be exclusively responsible for their children's religious education. How can they exercise their right to withdraw their children from an all-pervasive religious ethos?

Even in the area of sexual behaviour, the Constitution, in particular as interpreted in the *McGee* case,[9] which initiated the liberalisation of access to contraceptives, has been a powerful force in the struggle against sectarianism. The Supreme Court in this case ruled that prohibition of access to contraceptives breached personal rights to privacy. This achieved an objective which would surely have been contrary to the objectives of a truly sectarian Constitution. Not unrelated to this is the Supreme Court's interpretation which resulted in married women being guaranteed equal status with their husbands under tax law.[10] It is a pity that the spirit of that decision is still missing from the practice of the Revenue Commissioners, who still insist on putting only one name on tax returns when dealing with a couple under joint assessment. Indeed, they appear to insist that where joint assessment is in force the husband must make the returns. This is further evidence that whatever produces manifestations of conservatism and sectarianism in Irish society, it is rarely the Constitution.[11]

ACCESS TO OFFICIAL INFORMATION

The whole question of access to official information, on the other hand, is a cause for grave concern. Here, the Irish political system claims a range of unfettered rights for "itself". For example, section 1(4)(a) of the Data Protection Act excludes from the provisions of the Act any information which "in the opinion" of either the Minister for Justice, or the Minister for Defence "is or was" assembled for reasons of national security. Mere opinion, unprovable and therefore unchallengable, is the basis for exclusion. This legislation emanated from the Department of Justice and it therefore came as no surprise to discover that the same Department carried out a resolute and tedious rearguard action in an attempt to dilute the provisions of what is now the Freedom of Information Act 1997. When I attempted to introduce such an Act over ten years ago, Justice was the first Department to seek a copy of the draft legislation. Naïve people thought they wanted to prepare their own legislation![12]

---

[9] *McGee* v. *Attorney General* [1974] IR 284.

[10] *Murphy* v. *Attorney General* [1982] IR 241.

[11] This is not to deny the significance of the former prohibition on divorce. But, it is possible to argue that prohibition was exceptional and not typical of either the letter or the spirit of the Constitution, or, indeed, of its interpretation.

[12] See, generally, B. Ryan, *Keeping Us in the Dark: Censorship and Freedom of Information in Ireland* (Dublin, Gill and Macmillan, 1995).

The Constitution has been less than completely successful in the area of citizens' rights of access to information from the State. The courts have been diligent in preserving their own right to access and evaluate information in the hands of the State and have insisted on the right to inspect all records prior to adjudication. This right of the courts has been upheld in spite of vigorous opposition from the executive, in particular in relation to planning matters. The courts still claim the right to examine all records and all documents related to an issue which comes before them, up to and including cabinet papers. This right was not, contrary to some popular and legal opinion, diluted by the decision on cabinet confidentiality.[13] That decision was essentially a determination of the relation between the executive and a tribunal established by the *Oireachtas*. It did not purport to involve judicial consideration of executive decisions.

The decision on cabinet confidentiality was regrettable not so much for its impact as for the arguments used by judges of the Supreme Court to sustain it. These essentially said that government members would be inhibited and unwilling to engage in frank discussion if the nation were to get even a hint of what was said. Such a dull, staid understanding of the nature of democracy is both disappointing and a negation of the dynamism on which democracy depends. It is also a considerable, though no doubt unintended, insult to the character and capacity of members of government.

It is difficult to exaggerate the negative implications of that decision for the right to information. It is as if the Supreme Court is suggesting that only the courts can be trusted with much of the information that is in the hands of the State. This is not, of course, explicit in the majority judgments, but it is clearly implied in their reasoning. Great weight is given to the doctrine of collective responsibility and the need to avoid inhibiting free debate within government. Disclosure, it is argued by the Supreme Court, would inhibit such free debate. Disclosure of vigorous debate is therefore understood to be at least regrettable—if not destabilising. According to this reasoning such arguments could be used by local authorities, health boards, educational institutions and bodies such as *An Bord Pleanála* and the Environmental Protection Agency to maintain as much secrecy as they desire. If the right to information of the *Oireachtas* (and of a tribunal established by it) is so heavily qualified then clearly the citizen is even more constrained.[14]

SOCIAL JUSTICE

The Constitution has also been a major inhibition to social progress in the general struggle to build a just and equal society. There is no explicit

[13] *Attorney General* v. *Hamilton* [1993] 2 IR 250.
[14] See, further, G. Hogan, "The Cabinet Confidentiality Case of 1992" (1993) 8 *Irish Political Studies* 131.

guarantee of health care, shelter or basic income in the Constitution. Perhaps the guarantee of free association has deterred any forceful attack on trade union rights, but not much else. One would have hoped that sixty years of judicial reflection might by now have found some such rights, however limited, in implicit fashion at least. Indeed, notwithstanding frequent references by members of the Supreme Court to the Christian nature of the Constitution, little evidence exists that it grasps the Christian moral obligation to justice.

In general, marginalised groups and vulnerable individuals have received a fair hearing from the courts. To an extent all courts, and in particular the Supreme Court, have tolerated self-representation by individuals pursuing worthy social causes. Nevertheless, these cases have produced no fundamental extension of rights. Indeed, they have in some cases been the inadvertent cause of delay in achieving reforms. This was clearly the case in the area of social welfare appeals. A judicial decision that social welfare deciding officers were not obliged to make known all the information on which decisions were based allowed the Department of Social Welfare to ignore the need for reform for many years.

Equally absent has been any deep commitment to issues such as shelter or health care. Anomalies have, admittedly, been dealt with, but rarely have fundamental rights in the social and economic sphere been asserted.[15] In that context the decision of the Constitution Review Group to raise, and dismiss, the possibility of constitutionally guaranteed socio-economic rights is potentially extremely dangerous.[16] It is dangerous first of all because it makes even more difficult the struggle of those who are outside the circle of growing prosperity—those excluded are at least 25 per cent of citizens. To explicitly exclude guarantees of rights which are the most fundamental for a vast minority is to invite contempt for the Constitution—a potentially even more dangerous consequence. To people without shelter, food or income the rights to free speech, habeas corpus and property are close to irrelevant. The latter rights are not seen by the socially marginalised as "fundamental" rights, and a Constitution *should* be about fundamental rights. The rights sought for poor people are no more than a logical extension of the existing guarantee of free primary education for all our children. One cannot identify a reason why a child should have a constitutional guarantee of a basic education but no such guarantee of basic nutrition, health and shelter.

A recent invocation of the primary education guarantee illustrates well the conservative mind-set which dominates our society. When this guarantee was first invoked in the courts on behalf of a profoundly handicapped young person,[17] the State produced two lines of argument. The first argument, so

---

[15] See, further, T. Murphy, "Economic Inequality and The Constitution" in this volume.

[16] *Report of the Constitution Review Group* (Dublin, Stationery Office, 1996), 234–6.

[17] See *O'Donoghue* v. *Minister for Health*, unreported, High Court, 27 May 1993. The decision of O'Hanlon J supported the right of severely or profoundly retarded children to appropriate education facilities provided by the State. The State withdrew its appeal to the Supreme Court on 6 Feb. 1997.

offensive to ordinary decency as to be beneath contempt, was that such a young person was incapable of being educated. The second was that it would be constitutionally improper for the courts to compel the executive to spend public money in a particular way. In typical fashion, such decisions were said to be matters for the *Oireachtas*, not the courts. This is strikingly similar to the argument used by the Constitution Review Group to exclude socio-economic rights from the Constitution:

> "these are essentially political matters which, in a democracy, should be the responsibility of the elected representatives of the people to address and determine."[18]

Together, the arguments employed by the State give an insight into what is best described as the "establishment" mind after sixty years of the present Constitution.

None of this is very reassuring. Our society has become dangerously unequal; we are more unequal than ever in income and in property ownership and we are more unequal in access to work. Most have increasing choice—the rest have none. We are also unequal before the State. Power can buy access both to the justice system and to information—excluded people have neither. It is through our Constitution that the concept of equality is worked out. Where it can be used, it works very well. But it is limited, and it is based on assumptions which, to many in our society, are as dated as the religious phraseology. One of these assumptions is that there is a common good in the light of which the operation of individual rights must be exercised. The Constitution asserts that there is such a thing as society but would require amendment to make that assertion more explicit and to emphasise that membership of that society involves commitments as well as rights. Both rights and obligations should be elaborated in the Constitution. Understanding and effectively exercising these rights and obligations presupposes a sufficient level of information being available to citizens. However, there is widespread concern that, in the absence of such information, full participation in a democratic society is in fact diminishing.

CONCLUSION

It is a commonplace assumption among Irish liberals that the Constitution is in great need of modernisation. This modernisation, it is assumed, will eliminate supposed sectarianism and other anachronisms. For many in Ireland, an economic and cultural conservatism was identified as overlaying, and indeed flowing from, the sectarian character of the Constitution. Of course, the association of the Constitution with Eamon de Valera and with the 1930s is readily interpreted as further confirmation, if such be needed, of anachronism and sectarianism. As a result, a large section of liberal Ireland now appears

---

[18] *Report of the Constitution Review Group, supra* n. 18, 235.

to subscribe to the view that we need a "new" or "modern" or "simplified" Constitution. By this method, the embarrassment of sectarianism and the overtones of 1930s' corporatism which some identify could be expunged.

Never, it seems to me, have so many been so misled. I am convinced that any new Constitution drawn up by the present generation of politicians would be more illiberal than that which we currently have, and would tilt the balance of power decisively in favour of the State and against the citizen. As it stands, the Constitution is a major inhibitor of the abuse of political power. All through its lifetime, and particularly in the last thirty years, it has been the major, and sometimes the only, inhibition to the extension of State power. This was clear as recently as 1997, when only an express constitutional guarantee of free primary education was able to compel a hostile State to provide proper education for severely mentally handicapped children. A State which resisted such an explicit constitutional prescription would readily ignore these and other groups, if constitutional guarantees were either diluted, removed or indeed modernised.

Those of us who were adults in Ireland in the 1970s and at the receiving end of reduced Garda sensitivity to the rights of the innocent also have good reason to be grateful. The Gardai, or elements among them, would have been many times more oppressive but for the assertion by the Supreme Court that certain rights are implicit in the Constitution and therefore cannot be removed by legislative action. For the accused, these included the right to contact, and be visited by, a lawyer, to make a telephone call, and to contact one's family. Through that means was afforded at least the possibility of a successful constitutional challenge to measures such as those in the UK Prevention of Terrorism Act, which provides for detention incommunicado for up to seven days. In the absence of similar constitutional guarantees in the UK, attempts to challenge that legislation before the European Court of Human Rights led ultimately to a pyrrhic victory. After a successful challenge to elements of the Act's detention provisions,[19] the UK Government simply filed a derogation to Article 5(3) of the European Convention on Human Rights—and the validity of this derogation was subsequently upheld by the Strasbourg Court.[20] There, no remedy was available as the European Court deferred to the UK's own assessment of its security needs. In contrast, judicial interpretation by Irish courts of constitutional guarantees remains of the utmost practical importance. For example, the recently adopted constitutional Amendment to restrict the right to bail will come in for judicial scrutiny and hopefully will receive restrictive interpretation.[21]

More generally, if both the current fashion of glorious individualism and the views of the State regarding access to information and socio-economic

[19] *Brogan* v. *United Kingdom*, Series A, No 44 (1981).
[20] *Brannigan and McBride* v. *United Kingdom*, Series A, vol. 258–B (1993).
[21] For further perspectives on the bail amendment see P. O'Mahony, "The Constitution and Criminal Justice" and G. Fitzgerald, "The Constitution in its Historical Context" in this volume.

rights, were to form the basis for a new and modernised Constitution—what a disaster we would face. It would mean a Constitution diminished in compassion, which strengthened the powers of the executive and perhaps even the *Oireachtas*, and which diminished us as citizens—converting us instead to mere subjects of the State. Inequality would flourish, participation would decline further and a moderately benign oligarchy would rule.

However, it is not too late to take a different path. We could accept the value of what we have inherited and build on it. We could assert the right of the citizen to sufficient information on all the activities of the executive, the *Oireachtas*, public bodies and agencies. We could recognise the success of a constitutional guarantee of free primary education and extend that guarantee at least to cover the nutritional, health and shelter needs of our children. Changes like these would build on what has worked—and what has worked has not been the fashion of a particular time but the deepening of our understanding of eternal values, values of compassion and democracy, values worthy of a republican Constitution.

18

Bunreacht na hÉireann *and the* Polish *"April Constitution"*

BOZENA CIERLIK

INTRODUCTION

"The State is what it is, not what I say or think it is. How a particular State is to be classified politically is a matter not to be settled by the *ipse dixit* of any person but by observation of the State's institutions and an examination of its fundamental laws. Our one fundamental law is the Constitution."[1]

While some features of national legal systems have a universal flavour, with legal concepts that are shared with other States, other features are more unique, reflecting the distinctive traditions, beliefs, customs, heritage, and frequently the religion, of the society concerned. The comparison of legal systems and traditions has a long history that incorporates the investigation of how similar nations independently developed legal institutions, how they inherit legal institutions from other, generally colonising, nations and developed them according to their own needs, and how the legal systems of various nations developed along parallel lines under the influence of common "laws" of development. The relationship between the law, and more fundamentally the Constitution, and the national identity of a State has been one of the fundamental issues of political science and political philosophy since Aristotle. It is obviously true that institutional structures and legal norms can have important, even determinative, influences on political behaviour, social structures and historical outcomes. The nature of the interaction between State, society and the individual is at the heart of the matter. Equally central is the question whether constitutions can be seen as "creators" of national identity, either as normative symbols or as actual determinants of power, in ways historically crucial to the emergence of a particular State, or whether they must be seen as expressions or reflections of a particular given social and cultural reality, rooted in a particular "national genius". The French philosopher, Montesquieu, emphasised the

---

[1] De Valera, *Dáil Éireann* Debates, vol. 97, cols. 2569–74, 17 July 1945.

intimate connection between law and the culture of the nation in which it is in force.[2] The Historical School of Law claimed that the transplantation of foreign legal rules on a system developed under different conditions invariably involves undesirable consequences.[3]

This essay draws some comparisons between the bedrock law that was central to the shaping of political life and the development of the legal systems of Poland and Ireland. Not only did the two States gain independence at the same time, after the First World War, but their immediate subsequent constitutional history is chronologically similar: independent Poland adopted Constitutions in 1921 (the "March Constitution") and 1935 (the "April Constitution") and independent Ireland's Constitutions were adopted in 1922 and 1937.

More fundamentally, their experiences leading up to the adoption of these Constitutions are replete with similarities. The denial of statehood, the struggle to retain identity in the face of imperial pressures created a shared historical experience, even if it might be said that "if the Irish were faced with one imperial 'enemy' the Poles were faced with three",[4] and, following independence, the need to heal national divisions.

A constitution is an important source of information about the political culture of its drafters and those whose mandate they operated under at the time of its drafting. Questions continually arise as to the extent to which it reflects, or is capable of reflecting, the political culture of the people as a whole at various points in time. In this sense it is more than a legal document; it is also a political and social one, reflecting the "aspirations and aims and . . . the political theories on which the people acted when they first enacted" [it].[5] Commonly, a constitution marks the coming into being of a new State following independence and frequently stems from a radical upheaval or revolution. In that respect it is an instrument crafted from hard lessons of the past and shaped by an optimism for the future. As the basic document of government, it is both a point of reference and an instrument by which the government itself can be controlled. Generally, it cannot be changed in the manner of ordinary legislation[6] and supersedes all other legal rules. It is these features, a combination of the symbolic and the concrete, that make them a fertile

---

[2] For an analysis of Montesquieu's ideas on comparative law, as set out in his *Esprit des Lois*, see O. Kahn-Freund, "On the Uses and Misuses of Comparative Law" (1974) 37 *MLR* 1.

[3] See R. Zimmermann, "Savigny's Legacy: Legal History, Comparative Law, and the Emergence of a European Legal Science" (1996) 112 *LQR* 576.

[4] N. Davies, *God's Playground: A History of Poland* (Oxford, Clarendon Press, 1981), II, 18.

[5] As expressed by the Supreme Court decision in *In re Article 26 and the Criminal Law (Jurisdiction) Bill 1975* [1977] IR 129.

[6] In this respect the 1922 Free State Constitution was the exception amongst the Constitutions under consideration here in that Art. 50 permitted amendment by ordinary legislation for a period of 8 years. In 1929 this period was extended to 16 years by the Constitution (Amendment No 16) Act, 1929.

source of analysis as a means to understanding the government and politics of Ireland and Poland.[7]

In addition to recalling the recent national history that provided the backdrop for the early Irish and Polish Constitutions, the wider political scene is also critical. The first exercise in constitution-making in Ireland and Poland coincided with the European-wide commitment to democracy and the freedom of small nations that followed the First World War. It was the time for the establishment of many new constitutions (most of which were to prove short-lived) for the successor nations of the old European empires. However, the short period that would intervene before both States were to revise their constitutional frameworks also witnessed the appearance of Fascist clouds over Europe as well as internal disorder that was to play a critical part in the minds of both sets of drafters. Yet, despite these shared concerns, the Constitutions that resulted in Poland and Ireland in 1935 and 1937 respectively, were to prove profoundly different from each other.

THE IRISH CONSTITUTIONS OF 1922 AND 1937

The Irish struggle for independence has been described as "less a demand for a new economic and social order than an expression of the frustrated urge of Irishmen to manage Ireland's affairs in Ireland's interests".[8] Thus, in 1922, not only was much of the pre-existing British system adopted at the parliamentary level, but the civil service, with its attendant cultural and institutional norms, enjoyed almost perfect continuity from the pre- to the post-imperial period. The relationship between Ireland and Britain was to remain a very special one influenced by the long history of Anglo-Irish relations, British constitutional ideas and the requirements of the Anglo-Irish Treaty. And yet, determined efforts were made to stress the State's new-found independence. Thus, the incorporation of a reference to the Monarch in the new Constitution sat uncomfortably with the declaration in Article 2 that all powers of government derived from the People. The document reflects a combination of two tensions: the momentum to establish something distinct after the independence struggle (in no small part motivated by the need to persuade discordant voices that the struggle had not been in vain) and the continued historical, legal and economic connections between the protagonist nations, which were to have profound consequences. Decision-making might shift from Westminster to Dublin but the same sources of legitimacy were claimed,

---

[7] For a specific contemporary comparison between the two countries, see L. Garlicki, "Some Comparisons Inspired by Professor Hogan's Remarks: Campaign Regulation in Poland" (1992) 21 *Capital University Law Review* 555 (responding to G. W. Hogan, "Federal Republic of Germany, Ireland, and the United Kingdom: Three European Approaches to Political Campaign Regulation", at 501 in the same volume).

[8] B. Farrell, *The Founding of Dail Eireann: Parliament and Nation Building* (Dublin, Gill and Macmillan, 1971), 78.

the same representative functions exercised and the same model of cabinet government with its conventions of parliamentary responsibility and accountability adopted.[9]

Change might well have been expected when some of the arch-enemies of the 1922 Treaty and Constitution (or at least key symbolic elements of that document) assumed power in 1932. However, just as the events leading up to the 1922 Constitution took place without any real ideological opposition to the form of government, neither did the 1937 Constitution (*Bunreacht na hÉireann*) represent an ideological shift. In many respects it sought simply to dilute the existing links with Britain. The object was to weaken, not sever, the umbilical cord connecting the two States, lest it hampered eventual reunification of the island. Thus, the Constitution stopped short of declaring a republic. In many respects it did little more than recognise the many amendments and *de facto* changes to the existing 1922 constitutional regime. With regard to the legal structure of government, it was very much a successor to two previous constitutions—the Constitution of *Dáil Éireann* (1919) and the Constitution of the Irish Free State (1922). The 1937 document incorporated the principle of the tripartite separation of powers (executive–legislature–judicature), the principle of the primacy of Parliament and the principle of the sovereignty of the People. Much like the independence movement's opposition to British rule, the dissatisfaction of de Valera and Fianna Fáil with the Irish Free State Constitution did not extend to the system by which the country was governed, but rather with its despised origins in the Anglo-Irish Treaty.

The 1937 Constitution declares that all powers of government derive under God from the People, whose right it is to nominate the rulers of the State and, finally, to decide all questions of national policy. The people, the first and primary authority, created the State, the organs of the government, and declared fundamental freedoms. The State is defined as a self-governing political community, sovereign, independent and democratic. The legislative power is reserved to the *Oireachtas* consisting of the President and the two Houses (*Dáil Éireann* and *Seanad Éireann*). The executive power is vested in the government and judicial power is reserved to the courts. The government consists of between seven and fifteen members who are nominated by the *Taoiseach*, approved by the *Dáil* and appointed by the President. The *Taoiseach* is Head of Government and is appointed by the President on the nomination of the *Dáil*. He has to resign on ceasing to retain the support of a majority of the *Dáil*. The *Taoiseach* nominates a member of the government to be *Tánaiste*, or deputy Prime Minister. He acts in place of the *Taoiseach* in the latter's absence. The government is responsible to the *Dáil* but not to the *Seanad*. The powers of government under the doctrine of the separation of powers are divided into three: the government's power to legislate; the executive power; and judicial power. It meant that the government could create subordinate

[9] B. Farrell, *The Founding of Dail Eireann: Parliament and Nation Building* (Dublin, Gill and Macmillan, 1971), 78.

executive legislation, carry laws into effect and interpret the law and its application by rule or discretion in disputes which arose between the State and an
individual, and between an individual and another individual. Strange-
sounding titles aside, these arrangements would have met with nods of recognition from any British constitutional lawyer.

On the other hand, if the new Constitution reflected the English legal heritage of the State, it was also the vehicle through which distinctively Irish features of the State (as identified by de Valera) were to be encapsulated. Thus,
for example, there is an explicit acknowledgment of the supremacy of moral
law founded upon Christian doctrine. The 1937 Constitution drew heavily on
Catholic social teaching of the time, as expressed in the Encyclicals of Leo
XIII and Pius XI, from the recently formulated Code of Social Principles and
Code Sociale as well as from contemporary Irish Catholic luminaries.[10] In
addition to an absolute ban on divorce, the Constitution also included special
emphasis on the position of the family, the domestic role of women (Article
41) and private property rights (Article 43). These were capped by a guarantee of religious freedom to all which afforded special recognition to the Holy
Catholic Apostolic and Roman Church (Article 44). In addition, Article 45
laid down Directive Principles of Social Policy, unexceptional in themselves,
but scarcely enforceable, subsequently little-observed and recently dubbed the
"codification of collective national hypocrisy".[11] All these were thought necessary if Church approval, so vital in the original constitutional referendum,
was to be obtained, though it is only fair to point out that more far-reaching
Church demands were not met.[12]

All in all, the 1937 Constitution reflected the predominant political culture
of the twenty-six counties. One can clearly detect major features of that culture: the great legacy of the British that both geography and history made
inevitable, nationalism (Article 2) and the Catholic social teaching of the inter-
war period which a 93 per cent Catholic population was conditioned to accept
without question.

THE POLISH CONSTITUTIONS OF 1921 AND 1935

In the case of Polish constitutional history, historical experience, past political connections and geographical location were also to prove decisive. The

---

[10] See discussion in J. H. Whyte, *Church and State in Modern Ireland 1923–1979* (2nd edn.,
Dublin, Gill and Macmillan, 1980), 24–61. See also, on the relationship between the Catholic
Church and faith and the 1937 Constitution, N. Browne, "Church and State in Modern Ireland"
and G. Whyte, "Some Reflections on the Role of Religion in the Constitutional Order" in this
volume.

[11] J. J. Lee and G. O'Tuathaigh, *The Age of de Valera* (Dublin, Ward River Press, 1982), 154.

[12] See, generally, D. Keogh, "The Irish Constitutional Revolution: An Analysis of the Making
of the Constitution" in F. Litton (ed.), *The Constitution of Ireland 1937–1987* (Dublin, Institute
of Public Administration, 1988).

end results reflect the involvement of the neighbouring great powers of Austria, Germany and Russia during the period between 1795 and 1918—known as the "Period of the Partitions".[13] It was not until the end of the First World War that the modern State of Poland came into existence when the military leader, Marshal Joseph Pilsudski, assumed power in Warsaw.[14] As in the Irish context, despite the adoption of the 1921 Polish Constitution, the separate legal systems in force during the three-way partition prevailed. There was a certain similarity between the systems of former German and Austrian Poland, but little between them and that of former Russian Poland. A civil service had developed only in the provinces ruled by Austria—whereas in Russian and Prussian provinces Poles were not permitted to pursue administrative careers. It was only natural that, when entrusted with the task of preparing new unified laws and regulations, they usually looked for models in Austrian law, much of which had developed under the strong influence of German legal doctrines. It would be rather difficult to find in Polish administrative law any corresponding evidence of a Russian law influence, which was completely inadequate to the needs of the new Republic.[15] There were also quite a number of enactments which were products of original Polish juridical thought.[16]

As with many of the European constitutions promulgated in the wake of the First World War, including those of Germany and Austria, the Polish Constitution of 1921 was a product of the complementary effect of two forces: the predominance of a hesitant left in the constitutional conventions or cabinets of that almost revolutionary era and the teachings of legal theorists who identified themselves with this political faction. The primary constitutional objective of these forces was to ensure the obedience of the executive to the parliament. Theoretically, it resulted in the concentration of almost unlimited power in the parliament and was influential in the use of mechanisms—the "popular initiative" and the "referendum"—which operated alongside electoral representation.

Within a matter of decades the pendulum shifted, with the collapse of many European democracies of the inter-war period and the resulting revision of many national constitutions. Most of these revisions had two immediate causes: the change in the balance of political forces, from left to right, and the desire to give the executive flexibility of decision-making designed to enable it to respond to domestic and international insecurity of the time.

---

[13] See, generally, N. Davies, *God's Playground: A History of Poland* (Oxford, Clarendon Press, 1981), II, 3–392.

[14] See M. M. Drozdowski, "At the Birth of an Independent Polish Republic" in A. Chruszczewski, E. Fiala, B. Pietrasiewicz and J. Skarbek (eds.), *Nation, Church, Culture: Essays on Polish History* (Lublin, Catholic University of Lublin, 1990), II, 136.

[15] See W. Wagner (ed.), *Polish Law Throughout the Ages* (Stanford, Cal., Stanford University Press, 1970).

[16] See, e.g., the discussion of the Codification Commission in *ibid.*

The Polish Constitutions, therefore, reflected the continental constitutional trend of their times: first parliamentary democracy and later authoritarian elements in European political and constitutional history. Principally, they differed from each other as regards the concept of the State and its role in the social and political life of the country. The 1921 Constitution created the model of parliamentary government based on the following principles: (i) the tripartite division of power: legislative—*Sejm* (lower House) and *Senat* (upper House); executive—the government and the President; judicature—independent courts; (ii) the predominance of legislative power; (iii) the principle of the sovereignty of the people[17] (from which stems the predominance of the *Sejm*, which had the power of legislative initiative); and (iv) a largely powerless head of State (prompted by fears of Pilsudski's designs on this office).

Compared to the historic Polish Constitution of 3 May 1791, which was advanced for its time,[18] the Constitution of 1921, like most other European constitutions of recent date, reflected the enormous progress towards democracy that was characteristic of political opinion after the First World War. The French Constitution of 1875 was taken as a model, and traces of that Constitution appeared in the bicameral system and in the provisions governing the election of the President. Echoes of the German Constitution were to be found in the formulation of the principles of the parliamentary regime and in its provisions regarding the rights and duties of citizens.[19] Like the Irish Constitution of 1937, the 1921 Constitution of the Second Polish Republic combined liberal democratic principles with a home-grown Catholic flavour and opened with the lines; "In the Name of Almighty God! We the People of Poland, thanking Providence for freeing us from one and a half centuries of servitude, remembering with gratitude the bravery, endurance, and selfless struggles of past generations . . .". Equally, both the Polish Constitutions 1921 and 1935 and Irish 1937 Constitution afforded a special status to the Catholic Church as having "the leading place among other religious denominations enjoying equal rights" in the case of the former[20] and a "special position . . . as the guardian of the Faith professed by the great majority of the citizens" in the case of the latter.[21]

---

[17] "All powers of the State derive from the people . . . who govern themselves through their representatives" (Art. 2).

[18] See J. Lojek, "The Constitution of May 3, 1791, and the American and French Revolutions" in *Nation, Church, Culture: Essays on Polish History, supra* n. 10, II, 91 and R. Ludwikowski and W. Fox, *The Beginning of the Constitutional Era: A Bicentennial Comparative Analysis of the First Modern Constitutions* (Washington, Catholic University of America Press, 1993), 131–7 and 147–62.

[19] See: A Ainenkiel, *Polskie Konstytuije [Polish Constitutions]* (PWN, Warsaw, 1982).

[20] Arts. 109–120 governing the status of the Catholic Church and other denominations were taken directly from the March Constitution of 1921. Art. 114 stated: "The Roman Catholic faith, being the religion of the great majority of the nation, occupies a leading position in the State among other religions which however, enjoy equal rights. The Roman Catholic Church is governed by its own laws. The relation of the State to the Church shall be determined on the basis of agreement with the Holy See which shall be subject to ratification by the *Sejm*."

[21] Art. 44.1.2 and 3.

The April Constitution of 1935 was drafted with the principal goal of securing strong government so that "Poland . . . passed from partial democracy in the first period of dictatorship to 'incomplete fascism'".[22] It legitimised the situation that had existed in Polish politics since Pilsudski orchestrated a *coup d'état* in 1926 (the beginning of the *Sanacja* regime). The new State structure was designed to evolve around Marshal Pilsudski's forceful personality. Pilsudski's death the following month denied the drafters their obvious President, but the personality cult built around him provided the basis for a cult of the State: "[. . .] the state has to be a natural and necessary institution based on solidarity and the relationship between it and all citizens. Its main goal is the organization of the cooperation between citizens for a better legal order and the improvement of social conditions."[23]

Apart from prevalent anti-liberal theories and the presidential model, the most decisive influence on the 1935 Constitution was Carr's "Six Power Doctrine",[24] which, rather that adopting Montesquieu's classic tripartite division of power, aimed instead at dividing authority between the President, the government, the military high command, the *Sejm*, the *Senat* and the judiciary. The principle of governmental responsibility to the Parliament was preserved but the balance of power was shifted dramatically. The President was released from the obligation of having his decrees countersigned by the Prime Minister. The legislative powers of the *Sejm* were restricted by the creation of a strong *Senat* (upper House). Thus, the dominant feature was the relegation of the parliament to a secondary sphere of importance, while power was retained in the hands of the executive branch. The government was answerable to the President instead of the parliament and the chief executive was declared to be responsible for the State's fortune solely to "God and History" (Article 2). As the supreme head of State, the President, apart from partial controls (Articles 12, 13, 15), enjoyed a broad range of powers. The President was authorised to appoint his replacement in time of war (Article 24). He appointed, at his discretion, the Prime Minister and on his recommendation the other Ministers were appointed. He summoned and dissolved the Parliament (*Sejm* and *Senat*), and also opened, adjourned and closed its sessions and was invested with the power to call referenda (Article 16). He was the supreme head of the armed forces, deciding on war and peace with sole responsibility for the appointment and dismissal of the Commander-in-Chief and the Inspector General of the Armed Forces. His prerogatives also included; the appointment of the First President of the Supreme Court and the President of the Supreme Board of Control as well as the nomination of the judges to the Tribunal of State. Although his official acts required the coun-

---

[22] A. Gieysztor *et al.*, *History of Poland* (Warsaw, Polish Scientific Publishers, 1968), 693. In 1967, the Polish Government-in-exile in London published a dual English–Polish text of the document.

[23] W. Rostworowski in *Senat* Debates, 11 Dec. 1934.

[24] S. Carr—the main ideologist of Pilsudski's *Sanacja* movement.

tersignature of both the Prime Minister and the responsible Minister, any acts arising from his prerogative powers did not require such countersignature. Nor was he personally responsible for his official acts (Article 14).

In effect, the organs of the State, the government, *Sejm*, *Senat*, armed forces and courts of justice were all subordinate to the President. The legislative body, whose disorganisation made it a target for the *Sanacja* camp, was reduced to the role of reminding ministers or the Premier of their constitutional responsibilities, to calling the government to order on a particular matter, and to enacting, though without any power of amendment, the budget. The Constitution declared explicitly that "the functions of governing the State do not belong to the *Sejm*" (Article 31).

According to the Constitution the Polish State was the "common weal"[25] (*rzeczypospolita*, *respublica*) of all citizens. Each generation had a duty to increase the power and authority of the State by its own efforts and was responsible for the fulfilment of this duty by all means compatible with its honour and good name. An authoritarian State was to be the vehicle for the attainment of these goals. Article 4 declared that "the activities of the community are based upon and developed within the framework of the State" which was charged with assuring that it grew by "directing and co-ordinating its conditions according to the requirements of public welfare". The creative talents of individuals were identified as "the lever of collective living" and the State guaranteed its citizens "the possibility of developing their personal capabilities along with the liberty of conscience, speech and assembly"; however, "the limit of these liberties is the common good" (Article 5). Thus, the ultimate aim of this State was to unite all its citizens "in harmonious co-operation for the common good" and no activity could be permitted to oppose "the aims of the State, as expressed in its laws" (Articles 9 and 10). The provision dealing with the political participation of the citizenry clearly favoured élitist principles over the traditional liberal egalitarianism of the earlier Constitution. Article 7 stated explicitly that "the rights of a citizen to influence public affairs will be respected according to the value of his efforts and services for the common good". The 1935 Polish Constitution in Article 7 introduced the idea of an élite, by which it meant the domination of quality not quantity, but the word "nation" was abandoned.[26] As one observer commented:

"The former Constitution stated that 'The supreme authority in the Polish Republic belongs to the Nation'. The President with his ministers was one of its organs, along with the *Sejm* and the courts; he was merely the spokesman for the will of the Nation. But according to the new Constitution, the President 'stands at the head of

---

[25] Art. 1.
[26] By contrast, the incomplete national project meant that "the nation" would take on a primary significance in the 1937 Constitution, featuring in the very first Art. a signifier that "the State" did not yet encompass all of "the nation".

the state' and combines in his person supreme and total power. With few exceptions it does not even mention the Nation."[27]

Nevertheless, this concentration of power was not unlimited. Power had to be exercised "according to the requirements of the common good" with "the rights of a citizen to influence public affairs [to] be estimated according to the value of his efforts and services for the common good" and was subject to a final spiritual sanction.

CONCLUSION

The Constitutions of Ireland and Poland give a picture of the formal organisation of the government and limits within which the government operated. In the case of Ireland, the Constitutions were the products of the same general movement, and each succeeding version reflected another stage in the evolution of the Irish State with constitutional symbols and structures being refined, as opposed to fundamentally altered, so that they found general acceptance. By contrast, the two Polish Constitutions were markedly different. They did not exhibit any evolutionary process, but rather two contrasting, indeed diametrically opposed, conceptions of the State. The resulting divergence between the two 1930s Constitutions is primarily in terms of the primacy afforded to the State, with important signals to be found in the importance given to the various State organs. The Irish Constitution of 1937 identifies the Nation, the State, the President, Parliament and Government— in that order. The Polish Constitution of 1935 is concerned *primarily* with the State. The first ten Articles are concerned with the structure of the State, indicating the the Polish Constitution's ambition to ensure a stable and strong State.[28] But, while de Valera's paternalist thinking was to be equally influential in the drafting of the 1937 Irish Constitution, fears regarding possible ambitions for the newly-created Presidency were misplaced. Far from being established with a Pilsudski in mind, the occupant of the Irish post was charged with responsibility to "guard the people's rights and mainly to guard the Constitution" and "in exercising his power he is acting on behalf of the people who have put him there for that special purpose".[29] The Polish Presidency was to have an altogether different purpose. He not only guarded, but "[stood] at the head of the state", thus was "the authority of the state. . . united in his person".[30]

Despite having so much in common during their first years of independence,

[27] (1935) 14 *Przewodnik Katolicki* 223.
[28] See E. Gdulewicz, "Niektore koncepcje ustroju politycznego w Konstytucji Rzeczypospolitej Polskiej z 23 kwietnia 1935" (Political Concepts in the 1935 Constitution of the Polish Republic), *Panstwo I Prawo* 1975, 71–82.
[29] De Valera, *Dáil* Debates, 11 May 1937.
[30] Art. 3.

both in terms of historical baggage, as well as internal and external instability, the Irish and Polish States chose two radically different constitutional paths in the 1930s. This divergence of fortunes of the two States may be traced to many sources, but in no small part credit ought to go to those who resisted the temptation of "strong government" to which so many States succumbed at that time. If the different formulae chosen for their bedrock law were influential, as it is suggested here, then so too credit is owed to the drafters of the time. In this regard, Brian Farrell has observed:

> "In the wrong hands, Ireland could have gone the way of other European states in the dangerous Europe of the mid-thirties. De Valera by now had abolished the Senate, had an overall majority in the *Dáil* and a totally flexible Constitution with neither effective judicial review nor the requirements of a popular referendum to restrain his will. He could, by simple act of the single parliamentary chamber dominated by his party, make whatever constitutional changes he wished. It was a classic opportunity to establish a dictatorship. Instead his mind had already turned to writing a new Constitution for modern Ireland."

Antiquated and inappropriate as it may be in parts, it is only when de Valera's project, of which he was so proud, is viewed in the wider political circumstances prevailing at its genesis, that its contribution to Irish constitutionalism and democracy can be truly appreciated.

19

The Constitution, the Courts and the Irish Language

NIAMH NIC SHUIBHNE*

INTRODUCTION

A reawakening of cultural consciousness profoundly affected Irish political revolutionaries in the late nineteenth and early twentieth centuries, thus accelerating the intricate interaction between the cultural and the political that overturned the course of Irish history. With the foundation of the Irish Free State, the Irish language enthusiasts had at their disposal an entire state apparatus in order to realise their dream of an independent, Irish-speaking Ireland. The constitutional declaration that the Irish language was both the national and an official language of the Free State (Article 4)[1] could, therefore, be described as the repayment of a national linguistic debt. Despite growing scepticism of both the validity and methods of implementation of Irish language policy, the position of the language was somewhat strengthened in Article 8 of the 1937 Constitution:

"1. The Irish language as the national language is the first official language.

2. The English language is recognised as a second official language.

3. Provision may, however, be made by law for the exclusive use of either of the said languages for any one or more official purposes, either throughout the State or in any part thereof."

Since 1922, successive governments have pledged their commitment to the revival and promotion of the Irish language. The Free State was tormented by intense political, economic and social problems, which necessarily set its pri-

---

* The author would like to thank Ms Marie McGonagle, Faculty of Law, University College, Galway, for her advice on an earlier draft of this piece: *míle buíochas*.

[1] Art. 4 of the Free State Constitution (1922) provided: "The national language of the Irish Free State (Saorstát Éireann) is the Irish language, but the English language shall be equally recognised as an official language. Nothing in this Article shall prevent special provisions being made by the parliament of the Irish Free State . . . for districts or areas in which only one language is in general use." Kohn describes the enactment of Art. 4 as marking the "consummation of the process of national emancipation"—L Kohn, *The Constitution of the Irish Free State* (London, G. Allen and Unwin Ltd, 1932) at 123—while O'Callaghan refers to the Art. as a "debt of honour to the wounded national psyche"—M. O'Callaghan, "Language, Nationality and Cultural Identity in the Irish Free State 1922–1927" (1924) 24 *Studies* 226, at 230.

orities in practical terms. The language issue was not going to be one of those priorities. And yet the State continued to adopt an approach engineered in times of chaos and upheaval. At the outset of Irish language policy-formulation, it was generally assumed that since the Irish language had largely been destroyed by the imposition of English in the classroom, strategy for revival should focus on the schools. Notwithstanding the crucial role of education in the development of any language, the policy-makers seemed to neglect the fact that very few domains in which Irish could be used *outside* the classroom were promoted or even considered. The absence of Irish in legal and administrative functions or in commercial life did not, therefore, generate any particular interest. But while co-ordinated language planning, as a science, may be a relatively recent phenomenon, the application of common sense is not. Forcing the language revival burden on Irish schoolchildren was a double-edged sword. The role of Irish in prestigious domains such as the legal system was not considered seriously, thus perpetuating the perceived uselessness of Irish as a modern vernacular language. This message was also transmitted strongly to the schoolchildren struggling to learn Irish: where could this virtually foreign language be used in the "real" world? In conjunction with the merely symbolic use of Irish at official level, Irish language education policy thus thwarted the potential of Irish as a vibrant vernacular language. In contemporary Ireland, the regurgitation of this flawed philosophy of language policy has left the Irish language "in danger of being respected to death".[2] This Chapter focuses on one aspect of language policy in the legal sphere which continues to be largely ignored, i.e. the evolution of Article 8 itself, the cornerstone on which all related policy measures rely for justification. The following discussion of two related issues illustrates the fatal lack of co-ordination that remains persistently evident in contemporary linguistic policy—the interpretation of Article 8 in the courts, and the use of the Irish language for official purposes.

INITIAL PRINCIPLES DEVELOPED FROM ARTICLE 8

The problems highlighted below in the context of judicial interpretation of Article 8 are a direct result of its vague yet potentially ambitious wording. What significance should be attached to the "national" language of a state? What exactly does its status as *first* official language mean? Indeed, how best can these terms be interpreted in light of the fact that they refer to a language not spoken fluently by a large majority of the Irish people?

In the absence of legislative clarification of these issues, the task of interpreting Article 8 landed squarely on the shoulders of the judiciary. The opportunities to do so have been infrequent and not well publicised. As a pre-

---

[2] J. A. Fishman, *Language and Ethnicity in Minority Sociolinguistic Perspective* (Clevedon, Multilingual Matters Ltd, 1989), at 221.

liminary observation then, it is useful to relate the incidence of these cases to the corresponding social and political climates. The first case relevant to Article 8 was not brought until 1963, almost thirty years after the enactment of the Constitution.[3] It has been suggested that the creation of an independent State may have *discouraged* an awareness of Irish language issues: it may have been seen as no longer necessary to promote the language as a banner of separate identity for the now self-governing Irish people.[4] The following decades remained curiously barren until a relative spate of litigation in the 1980s, spilling over into the early 1990s. This could be said to coincide with the corresponding increase in support for the Irish language among the middle and upper classes, most notably in urban areas. A parallel phenomenon was observed regarding the use of the Welsh language in the courts: this similarity is particularly evident when reference is made to the "protest cases", such as, for example, the deliberate failure to obtain a television licence.[5] Thus, when the seemingly random incidence of court proceedings is linked to the relevant social and political concerns of a given time, a more enlightening approach to understanding the otherwise haphazard occurrence of litigation in this area is revealed, rather than the making of a blanket assumption of popular disinterest in the Irish language.

Two distinct approaches can be discerned from judgments relating to the use of the Irish language for official purposes, such as in court proceedings. First, and particularly in earlier decisions, the courts referred to the principles of natural justice, i.e. that a citizen should be allowed to use the language that he speaks and understands in the courts, using suitable interpretation and translation services where necessary.[6] But from the very first judicial pronunciation on Article 8, the courts have assumed an implicit constitutional rights guarantee therein. In a case relating to the Free State Constitution, Kennedy CJ referred to Article 4 as conferring a "double right" on citizens in respect of official use of Irish:

> "It would seem to me to be a requisite of natural justice, particularly in a criminal trial, that a witness should be allowed to give evidence in the language which is his or her vernacular language. . . . The Irish language, however, is not merely the vernacular of most, if not all, of the witnesses in question in the present case, but it holds a special position by virtue of the Constitution of the Saorstát in which its status is recognised and established as the national language of the Saorstát, from

---

[3] *Attorney General* v. *Coyne and Wallace*, 101 ILTR 17 (1963). It should be noted that cases brought in respect of Art. 4 of the Free State Constitution were of considerable importance to the subsequent interpretation of Art. 8 and will be discussed where relevant.

[4] J. A. Andrews and L. G. Henshaw, *The Welsh Language in the Courts* (Cardiff, Cardiff University Press, 1984), ch. 10, at 87 ff.

[5] J. A. Andrews and L. G. Henshaw, "The Irish and Welsh Languages in the Courts: A Comparative Study" (1983) 18 *Ir. Jur.* 1–22.

[6] See *Attorney General* v. *Joyce and Walsh* [1929] IR 526; *The State (Buchan)* v. *Coyne*, 70 ILTR 185 (1936); *The State (Conneely)* v. *Governor of Limerick Prison* (*The Irish Independent*, 3 Feb. 1937).

which it follows that, whether it be the vernacular language of a citizen or not, if he is competent to use the Irish language, he is entitled to do so."[7]

The use of "rights" terminology is significant in itself since nothing in the wording of either Article refers to rights of any nature. Similarly, the introduction of the individual citizen's right to language choice was an extremely progressive innovation. This interpretation has been followed and developed in all subsequent cases, including those relating to Article 8 of the 1937 Constitution. Most notable in this context is the judgment of O'Hanlon J in *An Stát (Mac Fhearraigh)* v. *Mac Gamhna*,[8] in which the legal principles in respect of official use of the Irish language that had been enunciated to that date were summarised and confirmed. In particular, O'Hanlon J stressed that the issue of actual competence of the citizen in question to use the *English* language was not a matter into which the court could inquire. Furthermore, he concluded that any costs or delays that might result from the employment of interpretation facilities would have to be borne in order to comply with the Constitution.

In addition, Kennedy CJ had also attached legal significance to the term "national language" over and above any symbolic representations it might also have. He developed this concept in Ó *Foghludha* v. *McClean*:

> "The declaration by the Constitution that the national language of Saorstát Éireann is the Irish language does not mean that the Irish language is, or was at that historical moment, spoken by the people of the Saorstát, which would be untrue in fact, but it did mean that it is to rank as such in the nation and, by implication, that the State is bound to do everything within its sphere of action . . . to establish and maintain it in its status as the national language and to recognise it for all official purposes as the national language."[9]

Ironically, Kennedy CJ failed to identify an obvious discrimination against the status of Irish as national language in that case itself. Legislation demanding that an Irish language version of a summons must be accompanied by an English translation did not require a similar translation in respect of English language summonses, yet was considered to be acceptable. Thus, the conflict of principle with reality becomes clear. In theory, Article 8 introduces an implicit constitutional right to use the Irish language for official purposes without discrimination. Furthermore, the corollary duty of State responsibility in this context had been identified, in recognition of the fact that a citizen cannot exercise his/her right to use Irish for official purposes without the necessary procedural support on the part of State institutions. The plain words of Article 8 have the potential to justify an entirely bilingual administrative system in light of the specific prioritising of official languages in favour of the Irish language therein. And yet, the "first" official language is in fact a minor-

---

[7] *Attorney General* v. *Joyce and Walsh* [1929] IR 526 at 531.
[8] Unreported, High Court, 1 July 1983 (Judgment delivered in Irish).
[9] [1934] IR 469 at 486–7.

ity language. How then can these principles be reconciled by the judiciary in the absence of legislative guidelines?

Judicially developed principles based on language rights were applied without question in cases where, for example, a citizen was denied absolutely the right to use either Irish, or indeed English, in oral proceedings.[10] But it is easy to pronounce with authority where rights have been so blatantly infringed. At the periphery, there are questions that are not quite so straightforward in legal or indeed moral terms, such as those relating to the translation of official documents and the right to demand other official services in Irish. Here, the judiciary has fumbled and backtracked, stalling the exploration of the implications of Article 8, availing of escape hatches presented by the make-up of particular cases rather than tackling the issues directly. The contradictory patterns outlined below have thus tainted the jurisprudence initially developed in good faith and, more seriously, have compromised the rights of people who choose to use Irish for official purposes to an unacceptable, yet alarmingly accepted, extent.

SUBSEQUENT INTERPRETATION AND APPLICATION OF ARTICLE 8

The translation of official forms and documents has always been a contentious issue, necessarily requiring the judiciary to interpret the implications of Article 8 in the absence of operative legislation.[11] The issue first rose for consideration in *Ó Foghludha* v. *McClean*,[12] which addressed the translation of summonses. Despite the importance attached to the constitutional status of Irish by Kennedy CJ, in *Ó Foghludha*, it was not deemed necessary that a summons issued in the English language should be accompanied by an Irish translation, notwithstanding a similar provision in respect of Irish summonses, or the equal official status of both languages in Article 4 of the Free State Constitution. In *The State (Conneely)* v. *Governor of Limerick Prison*,[13] Gavan Duffy J held, *obiter*, that *native* Irish speakers were entitled to have all legal documents presented to them in that language. He did not, therefore, adopt the "linguistic choice" thesis developed by Kennedy CJ in *Ó Foghludha*.

---

[10] See *The State (Buchan)* v. *Coyne*, 70 ILTR 185 (1936); *R. (Ó Coileáin)* v. *Crotty*, 61 ILTR 81 (1927).

[11] S. 4 of the Irish Legal Terms Act 1945 provides that "[t]he Minister [for Justice] may, after consultation with the [Irish Legal Terms Advisory Committee], from time to time make such arrangements as he thinks proper for the preparation and publication of forms and precedents in the Irish language of legal instruments and documents". This provision, however, lies dormant to date. In particular, the *Fasach Report* (Fasach, *An Ghaeilge agus an Dlí: Tuarascáil* (Dublin, Fasach, 1986)) outlines the difficulties encountered by those seeking to obtain forms and documents in the Irish language: see ss. 3.1 and 3.2 of the *Report*. (Note: "Fasach" is an organisation established by Irish lawyers to examine the status and use of the Irish language in the legal system.)

[12] *Supra* n. 9.

[13] *Supra* n. 6.

It would thus seem that despite lyrical oration and the best of intentions, the courts were eager to restrict the ambitious doctrines that they themselves deduced, in light of the minority position of the Irish language. The fact that this was not done in an honest, open manner is regrettable. Introducing broad principles that could not be applied to the linguistic reality merely exhibits further the symbolic nature of the State's language policies, which cannot in turn address the very real concerns of Irish speaking citizens.

The contradiction between the positive legal interpretation of Article 8 and its uncertain application in the case law has been accentuated in light of the strengthened status of Irish as the "first" official language. *Attorney General v. Coyne and Wallace*[14] produces a rather peculiar result. First, the Supreme Court decided that a written notice in Irish, in respect of the Road Traffic Act 1933, did not need to be accompanied by an English translation since the recipient could have it translated if he did not understand Irish. This reasoning would appear to contradict that expressed in Ó *Foghludha*, but cannot be taken as an enhancement of the status of Irish, in light of the subsequent comments by Kingsmill Moore J on Article 8.3, with which Walsh J expressly agreed:

> "It was argued for the Attorney General that the true meaning of the Article was that either [Irish or English] might be used unless provision had been made by law that one language only was to be used for some one or more official purposes. On consideration, I consider this construction to be correct."[15]

Kingsmill Moore J failed to tackle the plain words of Article 8, that Irish was the *first* official language of the State, since it would then surely have been necessary to conclude that, in the absence of a legal provision to the contrary, Irish must be used for official purposes. Linguistic choice was thus taken from individual citizens and granted instead to those exercising official functions on behalf of the State.

This interpretation has never been challenged directly in the courts and remains authoritative in spite of its dubious accuracy. In *An Stát (Mac Fhearraigh)* v. *Mac Gamhna*,[16] O'Hanlon J sought to reduce the prohibitive effects of the Supreme Court decision when he confirmed that:

> "[u]ntil the Oireachtas uses the powers conferred on it by the provisions of the Constitution, it must always be accepted that it is a citizen's privilege to demand that it be used for official purposes throughout the State".

The operation of the doctrine of precedent would prevent a direct overrule by the High Court but, in fact, O'Hanlon J himself has since reverted to the position adopted by Kingsmill Moore J. This is especially evident in *An Stát (Mac Fhearraigh)* v. *Neilan*,[17] where he held that the applicant could not com-

---

[14] *Supra* n. 3.
[15] *Ibid.*
[16] *Supra* n. 8.
[17] Unreported, High Court, 1 June 1984.

pel the defendant to issue a summons in the first official language, even though the defendant in question was a Minister of Government. It is impossible to reconcile this decision with O'Hanlon J's reasoning in *Mac Gamhna*. More recently, the applicant in *Delap v. The Minister for Justice, Ireland and the Attorney General*[18] attempted to place on the defendants a general duty of translation in respect of the Rules of the Superior Courts. While he succeeded in obtaining a translation of the Rules he required specifically, O'Hanlon J refused to grant the more general order. He side-stepped the issue completely, basing his decision on the unenumerated constitutional right of access to the courts and not on Article 8 itself.

In two subsequent cases, *Ní Cheallaigh v. An t-Aire Chomhshaoil*[19] and *Mac Cárthaigh v. Éire, An t-Árd-Aighne agus Stiúrthóir na n-Ionchúiseamh Poiblí*,[20] the limitations of Kingsmill Moore J's precedent were further entrenched by the High Court. In the former case, O'Hanlon J confirmed once again that a Minister may use Irish or English as s/he wishes, irrespective of the specific choice of language made by an individual citizen. In *Mac Cárthaigh*, it was decided that an Irish-speaking defendant was not entitled to insist on the appointment of an Irish-speaking jury.[21] In dealing with the issue as one of procedure rather than language rights, O'Hanlon J referred to an earlier Supreme Court decision, *Ó Monacháin v. An Taoiseach*.[22] In that case, the applicant had sought to secure the appointment of an Irish speaking District Justice to a case in respect of alleged breaches of planning laws, in accordance with section 71 of the Courts of Justice Act,1924, which provided:

> "So far as may be practicable having regard to all the relevant circumstances, the Justice of the District Court assigned to a District which includes an area where the Irish language is in general use shall possess such a knowledge of the Irish language as would enable him to dispense with the assistance of an interpreter when evidence is given in that language."

The Supreme Court was of the opinion that the above section did not actually preclude the appointment of interpreters where necessary, and relied heavily on the opening phrase, "so far as may be practicable having regard to all the circumstances". The Court was thus spared from a potentially embarrassing scenario: declaring that the appointment of the District Justice in question was invalid, notwithstanding the fact that he had occupied the position for over twenty years at that date. In *Attorney General v. Joyce and Wallace*,[23] one the of official court stenographers, competent to report spoken Irish, had failed to record evidence given in the Irish language but had instead recorded

---

[18] Unreported, High Court, 13 July 1990.

[19] Unreported, High Court, 4 June 1992.

[20] Unreported, High Court, 14 Sept. 1994.

[21] In this context, the Welsh Language Board had recommended that the right to have trial proceedings conducted through the medium of the Welsh language implied the right to a Welsh-speaking jury. See *Recommendations for a New Welsh Language Act* (Cardiff, 1991), 22, para. 73.

[22] [1986] ILRM 660.

[23] *Supra* n. 7.

the interpreter's version in the English language. Despite his decision that all citizens had a constitutional right to use the Irish language in court proceedings, Kennedy CJ was of the opinion that since the accuracy of the interpreter's translations had not been called into question, the stenographer's omission was not fatal.[24]

It is somewhat frustrating, however, that the Court was not obliged to deal with the substantive issues raised in both Ó *Monacháin* and *Mac Cárthaigh*. In particular, the implicit rights supposedly conferred on the applicants by Article 8 were not given the degree of consideration they surely deserve. Evidence of such contradictory reasoning can also be found in respect of other policy areas concerning the use of the Irish language for official purposes. In Ó *Murchú* v. *Registrar of Companies and the Minister for Industry and Commerce*,[25] the applicant instituted High Court proceedings against the defendants on two occasions: first, in order to obtain Irish language versions of administrative forms and, secondly, to seek costs for the original proceedings. In awarding costs to the applicant, O'Hanlon J felt that it was "reasonable" for the defendant to initiate the proceedings, since any person who chooses to use the Irish language for official purposes "should not suffer any impediment or incur any liability or disability by reason of the language he uses". It is somewhat paradoxical that the initiation of High Court proceedings to ensure the provision of an Irish language document could be considered "reasonable". In *Delap*, the applicant sought to challenge this state of affairs when he argued for judicial declaration of a general translation duty yet his proposals were not seriously considered.

In *The Minister for Posts and Telegraphs* v. *Bean uí Chadhain*, the defendant had been prosecuted for failure to possess a television licence, stating in her defence that the Broadcasting Authority had failed in its statutory duty under section 13 of the Broadcasting Authority Act 1976, which provides that:

> "In performing its functions, the Authority shall in its programming—(a) be responsive to the interests and concerns of the whole community, . . . ensure that the programmes reflect the varied elements which make up the culture of the people of the whole island of Ireland and have special regard for the elements which distinguish that culture and in particular for the Irish language."

While dismissing the appeal on technical grounds, Henchy J, in the Supreme Court, did comment on broadcasting duties in general, expressing difficulty in seeing "how it could be said that there has been an infringement of those aims and duties if the only evidence in support of such a claim was that only a certain percentage of programmes was in the Irish language". Henchy J did not,

---

[24] This position contrasts with that adopted by the Canadian Supreme Court in *Andre Mercure* v. *Attorney General for Saskatchewan* [1988] SCR 234, where it was held at 237 that "when proceedings are required by law to be recorded, a person using one or other of the official languages has the right to have his remarks recorded in that language".

[25] High Court, unreported, 20 June 1988.

however, attempt to clarify the nature of the evidence that would be required were such a case to be initiated.

The courts do appear to have accepted the principle that Irish language requirements may be enforced as a precondition of employment or qualification. In *The State (Cussen)* v. *Brennan*, Henchy J, speaking for the majority in the Supreme Court, attributed this permissible differentiation to both the status of the Irish language as first official language in Article 8, and the power of the state, in Article 40.1, to recognise differences of capacity.[26] Judicial support for this principle stands in direct contrast, however, to the implementation of the Legal Practitioners Act 1929, which requires that all legal practitioners should be competent to carry out their professional duties through the medium of the Irish language if necessary. Both branches of the legal profession have introduced examinations in the Irish language as part of the qualification procedure, yet the extremely basic standard and resulting lack of relevance to actual legal practice have been sharply criticised by Fasach.[27] While recognising that the strict implementation of the statutory requirement would be impractical, Fasach recommend that an optional but specialised and extensive legal Irish course be introduced instead of the present mandatory but meaningless regime, thus ensuring that an appropriate number of legal practitioners would be competent to deal with Irish-speaking clients where necessary.

At present, then, an Irish citizen who exercises his constitutional right to use the national and first official language in the courts may encounter the following difficulties: he may have some trouble finding a legal professional competent to deal with proceedings through the medium of the Irish language; he may not be able to obtain the requisite forms and documents in Irish, irrespective of whether his case involves another private citizen or the State itself, but should he be required to initiate court proceedings to this end, it is highly likely that he will succeed and be rewarded costs; if his case does involve the State, he may claim that it is his privilege to use the first official language, and he will be free to exercise that right in respect of his side of the case but the State may choose to proceed with its side of the case in the English language; his evidence may not be recorded in the Irish language as spoken, which places an additional burden on his counsel to ensure that the interpreter is translating the evidence correctly, since the judge, and jury where appropriate, will probably not be able to understand the Irish testimony. It is hardly surprising to realise then that citizens who do choose to use Irish for official purposes have been relegated to a position of considerable disadvantage, in comparison to English speaking citizens, a situation that persists in blatant contradiction

---

[26] [1981] IR 181, at 194. This aspect of state language policy has also been upheld by the European Court of Justice, in Case 379/87 *Groener* v. *Minister for Education and the Dublin Vocational Education Committee* [1989] ECR 3967. See O'Leary, "The Reciprocal Relationship Between Irish Constitutional Law and the Law of the European Communities" in this volume.

[27] *Fasach Report, supra* n. 11, ss. 10.2–10.4.

to their constitutional rights and to the corollary State duty to protect and enforce those rights.

CONCLUSION

The Irish language is the vernacular language of a numerical minority in contemporary Ireland, as it was when both Article 4 of the 1922 Constitution and Article 8 of the present Constitution were adopted. This is a fact that does not seem to have inspired serious consideration by the policy-makers when it was decided that the Irish language should be the first official language of this State, as well as its national language. It was surely expected that independent Ireland would soon become Irish-speaking, assisted in no small way by the language revival policies engineered by the governments of both the Free State and the Republic. It has been shown, however, that the broad, yet vague, formulation of Article 8 has been stringently limited by judicial interpretation, to the extent that speakers of the Irish language often cannot enjoy the implicit constitutional rights that they have been deemed to possess. Both the substantive text and interpretation of Article 8 are entirely unsuitable to ensure the legal protection necessarily required in a minority language situation. Opponents of the "minority" terminology might do well to consider more carefully the failure of the present constitutional status of the Irish language upon which they depend. According status to the abstract concept of language alone cannot protect adequately the rights of the speakers of that language. Focusing on implicit rights has not secured the equality and dignity deserved by Irish speakers since the implicit limitations on these rights have suppressed any original commitment to this end.

Demotion of the present constitutional status of the Irish language is not, however, an acceptable alternative solution, as was proposed by the Constitution Review Group in 1996.[28] The Report recommended that the first and second sections of Article 8 be replaced by provisions similar to the following:

> "1. The Irish language and the English language are the two official languages.
>
> 2. Because the Irish language is a unique expression of Irish tradition and culture, the State shall take special care to nurture the language and to increase its use."[29]

The Report did not examine the present text (or interpretation) of Article 8.3. The provision outlined above would accord equal status to two very unequal concepts, which would certainly perpetuate the inequality even further. The concept of a "national language" has been dismissed, without consideration of either the symbolic or legal consequences of that phrase developed by the courts. While acknowledging and approving of the implicit rights of Irish

---

[28] *Report of the Constitution Review Group* (Dublin, Stationery Office, 1996).
[29] *Ibid.*, at 15.

speakers in light of Article 8, the Report stresses in another context that the very nature of implicit rights creates problems in respect of judicial discretion and should thus be avoided.[30] A weak attempt to introduce constitutionally a degree of State duty has once again been developed in terms of the language rather than its speakers. Overall, the Group failed to give serious consideration to an area of constitutional law long neglected. While recognising that Article 8 as it is presently constructed does not reflect Ireland's linguistic reality, it did not appreciate the complexities of linguistic policy or its effects on the speakers of the language(s) in question.

The relationship between the Irish language and the Irish people is indeed a complex one. Its factual minority position seems to contradict the intensity of the majority's respect for and appreciation of its unique reflection of Irishness. Its constitutional status has evolved in a manner that has reduced the potential of Article 8 to facilitate the use of Irish for official purposes. Several aspects of this evolution are constitutionally suspect, yet have not been addressed by the judiciary, who have increasingly been able to deal with relevant cases without examining the labyrinth of jurisprudence on Article 8 itself. It may be acceptable to dismiss the efforts of the Free State Government in this context, or to write off an over-ambitious linguistic experiment to the patriotic zeal still operative in the formulation of the 1937 Constitution. But it is not acceptable that, sixty years later, a blatant and persisting violation of the constitutional rights of Irish speakers engenders concern typically on the part of those speakers alone.

---

[30] *Ibid.*, in the Group's consideration of Art. 40.3.1.

20

This Side of Paradise—The Constitution and the Irish Language

MICHAEL CRONIN

INTRODUCTION

In the summer of 1948 Chiang Yee climbed the innumerable steps to the top of the Nelson Pillar. At the top he looked out over Dublin Bay and the Wicklow Mountains but not being able to identify much more of the surrounding landscape, he began to listen in to other people's conversations:

"I had not realised that Dublin was so very cosmopolitan. Several foreign languages were being spoken, but there were a great many more Irish people than tourists. I can distinguish fairly accurately the main languages of the world, though that does not mean that I can speak them: but here were two gentlemen whose language I had never heard before. I suppose they must have come from some small East European country. Somebody pushed me from behind and I was obliged to lean against one of the strangers. He turned his head without saying anything and I apologised hastily. Then I suddenly decided to play one of the tricks employed by London children. I asked him: 'Can you tell me the time, Sir?' He smiled, but still said nothing. I made sure that he and his companion had just arrived in Dublin and knew no English. But when in the evening I told my host of the incident he asked if I had noticed a badge on their coats. I was able to tell him that each of them had a small metal ring in their buttonhole. 'Then they were members,' replied my host, 'of the Irish Language Association. They speak only the ancient Irish language, and refuse even to answer a question in any other language.'"[1]

Chiang Yee's surprise is surprising. Nobody had informed this experienced traveller that Ireland was a bilingual country with two official languages, Irish and English. Yet, at another level, Yee's linguistic bewilderment is perfectly understandable, the presence of Irish seeming exotic and "foreign" in the overwhelmingly English-speaking capital of an officially bilingual State. This essay will focus on the question of language in the Irish Constitution of 1937, a Constitution that gives pre-eminent place to the Irish language, and consider

---

[1] C. Yee, *The Silent Traveller in Dublin* (London, Methuen, 1953), 23–4.

the distance that exists between rhetoric and reality, a distance that gave rise to the perplexity of a Chinese tourist on the top of a Dublin monument.

THE CONSTITUTION AND CULTURAL NATIONALISM

Article 4 of the Constitution of the Irish Free State (1922) provided:

> "The National Language of the Irish Free State (Saorstát Éireann) is the Irish language, but the English language shall be equally recognised as an official language. Nothing in this Article shall prevent special provisions being made by the Parliament of the Irish Free State (otherwise called and herein generally referred to as the "Oireachtas") for districts or areas in which only one language is in general use."

The position of Irish was further strengthened in the 1937 Constitution in Article 8:

> "1. The Irish language as the national language is the first official language.
> 2. The English language is recognised as a second official language."

Article 25.4.6 of the same Constitution provides "[i]n case of conflict between the texts of a law enrolled under this section in both the official languages, the text in the national language shall prevail".

This in effect means that the translation of a text has superior status over the original as bills in the *Oireachtas* are always drafted initially in English and only later are the bills when they become law translated into Irish. In the debate on the Constitution, a Fine Gael Senator, Frank Mac Dermot, sought an amendment to Article 8 that would read that "[t]he Irish and English languages are recognised equally as national and official languages." He claimed:

> "I am moving my amendment because to call the Irish language the sole national language is to fly in the face of facts. . . . There is at least as much of Irish culture, history and tradition embodied in the English language as there is in the Irish language. A far larger number of inhabitants of Éire or Ireland are able to speak in the English language than in the Irish language, and this artificial and mischievous Gaelicisation does not do a single thing to advance the prestige or culture of our country but serves as an extra and unnecessary barrier between ourselves and the Northern Unionists."[2]

De Valera's reply to Mac Dermot was a succinct statement of the ideological justification for Article 8 as it appeared in the Constitution:

> "I do not know that I need speak about the question of what is intended by the 'national language.' It is the language that is most associated with this nation; the language that is in accordance with the traditions of our people. We are a separate people, and our language was spoken until little over 100 years ago generally by our people. The English language was the language of those who came as invaders."[3]

[2] Cited in S. Ó Riain, *Pleanáil Teanga in Éirinn 1919–1985* (Dublin, Carbad, 1994), 25–6.
[3] *Ibid.*, at 26.

Cultural nationalism had been the crucible for the movement for Irish independence. The Gaelic League had a profound influence on the thinking of the majority of the signatories to the 1916 Proclamation and on those who were later to become active in the War of Independence. The origins of cultural nationalism are various but a crucial, formative text was Fichte's *Addresses to the German Nation*, where nationality is predicated on language:

"we give the name of people to men whose organs of speech are influenced by the same external conditions, who live together, and who develop their language in continuous communication with each other".[4]

For revolutionary Irish nationalists, political independence without cultural independence was worthless, form with no content. The only conceivable legitimacy for Irish claims to independence was cultural and culture was primarily a matter of language. Indeed, the complete absence of the Irish language from Neil Jordan's film *Michael Collins* obscured this fundamental tenet of the thinking of Collins and his fellow nationalists. Collins himself argued in *The Path to Freedom* that the "biggest task will be the restoration of the language. How can we express our most subtle thoughts and finest feelings in a foreign tongue?"[5] The official status given to the Irish language in the 1922 and 1937 Constitutions was then very much in keeping with the linguistic relativism that was rooted in the German romantic origins of European and Irish cultural nationalism.

IRISH, LAW AND THE INDIVIDUAL

The pre-eminent position given to Irish as the first official language in the 1937 Constitution would appear to satisfy the wishes of the most ardent language revivalist. It can be argued, however, that the current constitutional position of Irish does nothing but breed cynicism in Irish language activists and hostility in their opponents.

Article 8.1–2 is expressed as a declaration, not as a right. Tomás Ó'Máille has demonstrated that it has been the understanding of the courts—as evidenced by the remarks of Kennedy CJ in the case of O Foghludha v. McClean[6] and those of Justice O'Hanlon in Ó Murchú v. *Registrar of Companies and the Minister for Industry and Commerce*[7]—that the constitutional position of Irish places substantial obligations on the state.[8] In other words, the constitutional declaration entails individual rights. In order to have these rights defended, however, Irish speakers have to have constant recourse to the

---

[4] J. G. Fichte, *Addresses to the German Nation* [1808] (New York, Harper, 1968), 49.
[5] M. Collins, *The Path to Freedom* (Dublin, Talbot Press, 1922), 17.
[6] [1934] IR 469.
[7] Unreported, High Court, 20 June 1988.
[8] Tomás Ó Máille, *The Status of the Irish Language: A Legal Perspective* (Dublin, Bord na Gaeilge, 1990), 1–19.

courts, as each time they must be redefined in different contexts given the generality of the constitutional declaration. In the case cited above, Helen Ó Murchú had to go all the way to the High Court to seek an order of mandamus compelling the Registrar of Companies to provide the Irish version of forms necessary for the incorporation and registration of an association, *Comhar na Múinteoirí Gaeilge*. She obtained the order but then had to institute legal proceedings to recover the costs of the case which the State refused to pay, claiming that it was not under an obligation to provide this documentation in Irish. Thus, in order to obtain a simple set of forms in Irish, Helen Ó Murchú had go through the long, complex and financially perilous procedure of going to the courts, not once but twice. It is little wonder, then, that many Irish speakers find the constitutional provision more symbolic than real. It is far easier to assent to the English-speaking *status quo* than to begin the long journey through the legal system to have any—even the most minor—rights vindicated. In addition, although Ó Máille asserts that Article 8 places substantial obligations on the State, he enters the important caveat that this may apply only to the legal area and not in "social, economic and cultural contexts".[9] The onus, then, is on the individual to establish the protection of his/her language rights, but it is precisely the "individualisation" of these rights that has stifled rather than enabled linguistic diversity in Ireland.

De Valera, speaking to Seanad Éireann on 7 February 1939, claimed that the restoration of Irish was not merely a matter for government but for the individual:

"Each individual must understand that they have a particular duty with respect to the Irish language because in the final analysis the language cause depends on the spirit and zeal of the individual" (author's translation).[10]

At the first meeting of the *Coimisiún um Athbheochan na Gaeilge* in July 1958, de Valera reiterated his belief in the primacy of the individual in language policy, "it is the people who ultimately will save Irish and each one of us, personally, has our own share of responsibility towards the language".[11] Individuals are not monads and language is first and foremost an act of communication in a social context so that external forces rather than internal desires dictate language choice. As Seán Ó Riain argues:

"It is not true that an individual speaks whatever language he wants. He accepts the existing decision made by society—the norms of usage."[12]

[9] Tomás Ó Máille, *The Status of the Irish Language: A Legal Perspective*, (Dublin, Bord na Gaeilge, 1990), at 18.
[10] "Ní mór gach duine ar leith á thuiscint go bhfuil dualgas le comhlíonadh aige féin i dtaobh na Gaeilge, mar is ar spiorad agus ar dhúthracht an duine ar leith atá cúis na teanga ag brath sa deireadh thiar thall": *Official Report of Parliamentary Debates: Seanad Éireann* (Dublin, Oifig an tSoláthair, 1940), XXII, 989.
[11] "Ach is é an pobal sa deireadh a shlánóidh an Ghaeilge agus . . . titeann a chion féin den dualgas i leith na teanga ar gach aon duine againn . . . go pearsanta": *An Coimisiún um Athbheochan na Gaeilge: An Tuarascáil Dheiridh* (Dublin, Oifig an tSoláthair, 1974), xii.
[12] "Ní fíor go labhraíonn an duine aonair pé teanga is mian leis. Glacann sé le cinneadh réamhdhéanta na sochaí—na noirm úsáide." Ó Riain *supra* n. 2, at 92.

Individuals are powerfully conditioned by their immediate social circumstances, and unless animated by unusual zeal they tend to accept consensual norms. In strongly Anglophone environments, it is easier, less conflictual and less time-consuming simply to accept the dominant language. Indeed, to do otherwise is to be taxed as a zealot, a dreaded *Gaeilgeoir*, disrupting the lives of decent people with unreasonable demands and dangerous fanaticism.[13] In many situations, therefore, the notion of Language Freedom or Freedom of Choice is a fiction for Irish speakers in modern Ireland.

THE MYTH OF INSIGNIFICANCE

The fallacy of individual choice in turn sustains the myth of insignificance. Kevin Myers articulated this myth most clearly in a broadside against Irish where he claimed, "[t]he Irish language is the source of the greatest State-driven hypocrisy in political life in this country. Virtually nobody speaks the language, nobody does business in it."[14] Irish speakers, in other words, are a tiny, insignificant section of the population who never use the language anyway. The studied vagueness of "virtually nobody" empties the assertion of any concrete meaning, and it is possible to counter the claim with statistics showing that many Irish people do in fact speak the language.[15] However, rather than playing a numbers game, it is more useful to examine the assertion that "nobody does business" in Irish as this brings us to the origins of the myth. In a report prepared for *Bord na Gaeilge* and *Udarás na Gaeltachta* by the Social Sciences Research Centre, University College Galway, the authors found that:

> "Like other communities in other fields the Gaeltacht community and the Irish speaking public do not make use of a poor or mediocre service to the same extent as an excellent service. It would appear from the report that as far as the availability of services through Irish is concerned they make good use of a satisfactory service, a limited use of a mediocre service and they seldom bother to complain of lack of service or poor quality service from a great number and variety of organisations. This contradicts the claims of those organisations who equate no complaints about poor service with customer satisfaction and accordingly deduce that there is no demand for better services through Irish. It is clear that the great majority in the Gaeltacht and Irish-speaking communities use high quality services through Irish when they are available to them without question."[16]

[13] See M. Cronin, "The Imaginary Gaeilgeoir", 6 *Graph* 16–18.
[14] K Myers, *Irish Times*, 17 Jan. 1997.
[15] For detailed figures of the numbers of Irish speakers in Ireland, see *The Irish Language in a Changing Society* (Dublin, Bord na Gaeilge, 1986). The report estimates that the proportion of the population who use Irish intensively at some stage in their lives is around 15%.
[16] *Provision of Services through Irish by the Public Service in the Galway Area* (1996), 9. This is a bilingual summary of the main conclusions of M. Ó Cinnéide and S. Ní Chonghaile, *An Ghaeilge san Earnáil Phoiblí i gCeantar na Gaillimhe* (Galway, Coláiste na hOllscoile Gaillimh, 1996).

In their detailed study of the provision of services through Irish by public bodies in the Galway area, O Cinnéide and Ní Chonghaile showed that in the vast majority of cases where an individual started a conversation in Irish, the representatives of many public sector agencies simply carried on the conversation in English, ignoring the wishes of the Irish speaker. These agencies included bodies that have a very direct impact on the lives of people living and working in the Connemara Gaeltacht: the Department of Agriculture, Food and Forestry, Teagasc, Galway County Council, Galway Corporation, the Western Health Board, the Department of Social Welfare, Telecom Éireann, the Office of Public Works, the Revenue Commissioners, Bus Éireann, Iarnród Éireann and the tourism agency, Fáilte an Iarthair.[17] In a 1995 survey of bilingualism in the state sector, Bord na Gaeilge found that only 17 per cent of public sector organisations displayed notices at point of contact with the public welcoming the use of Irish while just under a quarter (23 per cent) issued this invitation on headed notepaper.[18] Out of the twenty-five public agencies studied in the Ó Cinnéide and Ní Chonghaile report only four made available to their officials copies of the "Expanding Bilingualism in Irish Society: Guidelines for Action in the State Sector". In only nine agencies out of twenty-five did those responsible for management and personnel have copies of the guidelines.[19] The guidelines taken from the *Programme for Partnership Government 1993–1997* contain a list of specific steps to be taken by public agencies so as to respect the rights of Irish speakers in relation to services to the public, staffing and administrative practices and the visibility of Irish. Irish speakers find themselves, therefore, part of a vicious circle of non-representation. Faced with a majority of public agencies that are at best indifferent and at worst hostile, they opt for the monolingual solution and use English. This in turn leads to the justification for the provision of even fewer services in Irish on the basis that there is no demand. Anglophone intolerance is rewarded and Irish speakers' tolerance of English leads to further marginalisation and cultural and political disenfranchisement.

The term "business" in Myers' claim is significant. If nobody does business in Irish (an untrue claim as is shown by the record of Údarás na Gaeltachta) it does not occur to him that it might be because nobody *can* do business in Irish. The provision of services in Irish by the private sector in Ireland is pitifully inadequate and is wholly dependent on the goodwill of individual companies. Here the weakness of the present constitutional provision for Irish becomes obvious as Article 8, in the absence of a proper Language Act governing all areas of social life, has been narrowly defined to relate to dealings with the State. In addition, as we have seen previously, few individuals are prepared to undertake costly litigation that is unpredictable as to its income

[17] M. Ó Cinnéide and S. Ní Chonghaile, *An Ghaeilge san Earnáil Phoiblí i gCeantar na Gaillimhe*, (Galway, Coláiste na hOllscoile Gaillimh, 1996), ibid.
[18] *Bilingualism in the State Sector* (Dublin, Bord na Gaeilge, 1996), 63.
[19] Cinnéide and Ní Chonghaile, *supra* n. 16, at 148–9.

for the sake of having a cheque card or an insurance certificate available to them in Irish. The tendency of Irish-language activists to focus on the responsibilities of the State, partly because of the constitutional position of Irish, has had the unfortunate effect of obscuring the equally important questions of the language rights of Irish speakers in their dealings with the private sector. The narrow focus on interaction with the state is reflected in the *Report of the Constitution Review Group*[20] where they recommend that Articles 8.1, 8.2 and 8.3[21] be amended to read:

> "1. The Irish language and the English language are the two official languages.
>
> 2. Because the Irish language is a unique expression of Irish tradition and culture, the State shall take special care to nurture the language and increase its use."

In their commentary on these suggested changes the authors of the report state, "The Review Group considers that there is an implicit right to conduct official business in either official language and that the implementation of this right is a matter for legislation and/or administrative measures rather than constitutional provision."[22] Legislation for the conduct of official business through Irish is of limited value in a society where citizens as consumers have extensive dealings with the private sector and where indeed the public sector is declining due to the advent of deregulated markets and privatisation. In addition, the restriction of the use of Irish to the official domain further strengthens the stereotypical identification of Irish with State intervention in formal schooling. Thus, the Constitution Review Group unwittingly perpetuate residual clichés about Irish even if their call for legislation is timely.

ECONOMIC EVOLUTION AND DEMOCRATIC WILL

In asymmetrical bilingual situations where one language is dominant and is supported in this by powerful economic and cultural influences from elsewhere, doing nothing is doing something. That is to say, passivity is a form of activism, providing a linguistic safe house for a monoglot, Anglophone Ireland. Policy makers are, however, placed in an invidious position. For a language that finds itself in a minority position, it must be protected and promoted through proactive measures if it is to continue to exist. Ó Máille, in fact, argues that:

> "The mere granting of formal equality to any group (minority or otherwise) can be of little use unless accompanied by more constructive measures to ensure both the continued existence and natural development of the group in question."[23]

[20] (Dublin, Stationery Office, 1996).
[21] Art. 8.3 provides: "Provision may, however, be made by law for the exclusive use of either of the said languages for any one or more official purposes, either throughout the State or in any part thereof". See discussion *infra*.
[22] *Supra* n. 20, at 15.
[23] Ó Máille, *supra* n. 8, at 23.

The position of the dominant language and its expansion will appear *natural* while the intervention of the State to protect a weaker language will appear *unnatural*. The efforts of States actively to promote languages in a minority position is equally derided by the Left (the unacceptable face of ethnic nationalism) and the Right (Kevin Myers' complaint about "thousands of millions of pounds . . . confiscated from the taxpayers of Ireland"). Underlying both positions is a deeply conservative commitment to the rightness of pragmatic materialism. In this vision of things, material circumstances are immutable, the Irish changed language for material reasons, "there is no doubt English was . . . the language of survival and social advancement"[24] and any attempt to counter the implacable logic of this materialist monoglossia is seen as either another example of the interventionist monstrosity of central government (Right) or a further example of suspect bourgeois idealism (Left). The fact that the majority of Irish people have consistently supported the Government's commitment to the promotion of the Irish language which involves allocation of resources, and have since independence voted for political parties committed to the restoration of Irish, and later bilingualism, is blithely ignored in this particular version of linguistic Darwinism.[25] The strong language will become stronger and any attempts to check this process constitute unnatural interference with the process of economic evolution.

The question of democratic will needs to be taken seriously, not only by opponents of Irish but also by its supporters. In this respect, a lesson has been learnt in that policies that are formulated around the notion of rights have much greater democratic appeal than policies centred on obligations (such as the language bar that used to exist for State examinations and civil service appointments). This is not say that rights do not carry obligations. If someone wishes to exercise the right to use Irish, someone else has a duty to respond. However, the daily experience of Irish speakers who are continually coerced into speaking English should remind them that coercion is damaging and alienating. There is another level at which the expression of a democratic will is important, and this relates to the nature of political activism and language policy in the Irish experience. The two most significant areas of change for the Irish language over the past two decades have been the media and education. *Raidió na Gaeltachta, Teilifís na Gaeilge* and the *Gaelscoileanna* do not exist, however, because of Government initiative. Rather, they exist because of Government response to popular initiative. In all three cases, it was years of campaigning by activists that forced a

[24] T. Crowley, *Language in History*, (London, Routledge, 1996), 110.

[25] There have been consistently high levels of popular support over recent decades for the maintenance and promotion of the Irish language. The two most comprehensive surveys of popular attitudes to Irish are: Committee on Irish Language Attitudes Research, *Report* (Dublin, Stationery Office, 1975); P. Ó Riagáin and M. Ó Gliasáin, *The Irish Language in the Republic of Ireland, 1983: Preliminary Report of a National Survey* (Dublin, Institiúid Teangeolaíochta Éireann, 1984).

Government response.[26] An insidious effect of Article 8 is the assumption that it is the State which has sole responsibility for the promotion of Irish, that bilingualism is an "official" task of government. The dramatic decline in the membership of *Conradh na Gaeilge* after independence was prompted by similar thinking. Now that Irish was enshrined in a constitutional provision and the restoration of Irish was official government policy, no more needed to be done. The placards were put away, the bicycles locked up and former *Conradh* members waited for the parousia of language. The movement died away and what replaced it was the chaotic chorus of individual complaint berating the State for failing to live up to its constitutional aspirations. Whereas it is true that the only effective instrument people have for the implementation of language policy in a democratic society is government, government will only respond in relation to the rights of a minority when these are actively pursued by a *movement*. Movement here refers to a group or groups that are base-driven, often focused on specific aims. With respect to both media and education, if Irish-language activists had not begun to take their own initiatives by setting up pirate stations and opening schools without official sanction, they would still be condemned to the prayer-wheel of denunciation.

In a sense, Article 8 provides status without substance. It provides a symbolic support that is the natural enemy of realism. To this extent, the Article has been disabling in that it appears to give Irish speakers a standing they do not in fact enjoy. Though it is difficult to quantify, there is no doubt but that Irish speakers themselves have found themselves paralysed by the double bind of constitutional rhetoric (you are free to speak the nation's first, official language) and linguistic reality (you are able only in the most restricted circumstances to speak the nation's first, official language). Movement is a way out of this double bind that combines a necessary pragmatism with a justifiable idealism. No Irish government will introduce an Irish Language Act unless it has to, no matter what the Constitution says. It will only do so in response to a strong, articulate movement for such a measure that draws on the concrete, daily experiences of Irish speakers rather than self-righteous reference to the founding principles of the State.

THE BIASES OF BILINGUALISM

In Appendix A to *Expanding Bilingualism in Irish Society: Guidelines for Action Programmes in the State Sector* there is the following declaration, "The national aim with respect to Irish is that the majority of our people would be truly bilingual" (author's translation).[27] The statement is in line with the

---

[26] For details of some of the campaigns, see R. Ó Glaisne, *Raidió na Gaeltachta* (Cló Chois Fharraige, Indreabhán, 1982) and D. Ó hÉallaithe, "Craoladh Bradach", *Foinse*, 26–27 Oct. 1996.

[27] "Is é an spriocaidhm náisiúnta i leith na Gaeilge ná go mbeadh formhór ár muintire fíor-dhátheangach": *Bilingualism in the State Sector*, *supra* n. 18, at 176.

post-1945 shift in government policy from restoration to bilingualism. Bilingualism appears decent, generous, open-minded and tolerant, while the restoration emphasis on monolingualism appears impractical, intolerant and illusory. The revivalist commitment to monoglossia is seen as the mirror-image of the imperial defence of one language, one empire.[28] Examples are given of the many societies where the population is bilingual or indeed multilingual.[29] The credo of bilingualism may be seen by policy-makers and language activists as a liberal sweetener, but does it make any sense? Can there be bilingualism without monoglossia? The examples that are given of bi- and multilingual groups are always examples of bi- and multilingualism occurring in the contact zone between monoglot groups. You speak the language of the other only because you have no other option. The choice is to learn the other's language or some international, vehicular language. The figure of bilingualism is inconceivable then without the ground of monoglossia. This is why all Irish speakers have become bilinguals—they have to communicate with their monolingual compatriots. However, the reverse process is unlikely to take place unless there is a similar need on the part of Anglophones to communicate with Irish speakers in monoglossic situations. Paradoxically, intolerance breeds tolerance. It is only by insisting on the right to monoglossia for Irish speakers that genuine two-way bilingualism can emerge in Irish society. The true Anglophone bilingual needs the Irish monoglot. In this respect, Article 8.3, which we have not examined and which is ignored in the Report of the Constitution Review Group, may turn out to be the most radical in its implications.

Based on a similar provision in the 1922 Constitution, Article 8.3 has been interpreted as facilitating an eventual reunification of Ireland by allowing the Government to waive its official language policy in Northern Ireland.[30] However, it can be interpreted as providing a basis for a monoglossia that is essential if polyglossia is to exist. The obvious site for this monoglossia is the Gaeltacht, but this at present covers less than 2 per cent of the national territory. There must be sites elsewhere, particularly in large cities, where monolingual Irish communities can sustain themselves. Otherwise, the national aim of a people that are truly bilingual is a fiction. The architects of Article 8.3, perhaps unwittingly, realised this when they allowed for selective monoglossia in the constitutional provision. The establishment of such communities will differ from the Israeli experience, in that Hebrew was a necessary vehicular language for settlers coming from many different language backgrounds. In Ireland, English can always fulfil that function, so that the motivation must initially lie elsewhere. The greatest challenge for intellectuals sympathetic to

[28] See Crowley, *supra* n. 24, at 131–46 for the most comprehensive development of this particular argument.

[29] Many examples of bi- and multilingual societies are given in John Edwards, *Multilingualism* (Harmondsworth, Penguin, 1995).

[30] Ò Máille, *supra* n. 8, at 3.

the Irish language is to provide a contemporary rationale—social, cultural and economic—for these communities potentially envisioned by Article 8.3.

CULTURE AND HERITAGE

The Irish language is almost invariably associated with culture and heritage in official pronouncements. The Constitution Review Group was no different in its express desire to have language and culture linked in a new constitutional provision, "[b]ecause the Irish language is a unique expression of Irish language and culture, the State shall take special care to nurture the language and increase its use." The danger, once again, is of reality falling out with aspiration. In 1995, three-quarters of printed/typed material in the culture and heritage area was in English only. Only half of the organisations concerned with cultural matters considered competence in Irish as a factor in recruitment.[31] Culture and heritage are increasingly linked to cultural tourism yet the Office of Public Works, a body entrusted with the protection and promotion of the material heritage of Irish culture had not one employee in the Galway area who could work competently through Irish. This was similarly the case with CERT, the tourism training authority, which works through the medium of English only and refuses to use Irish in its dealings with the public.[32] CERT's dogged monolingualism is not without its ironies. The same organisation has for a number of years now embarked on an ambitious programme of foreign language training for employees in the tourism sector, out of deference to the linguistic and cultural sensibilities of European visitors to Ireland.[33] This deference does not extend to the Irish-speaking natives who are expected presumably to put up (with English) or shut up.

An important function of language is, of course, to act as a form of collective memory, keeping alive traditions and networks of influence and allusion that constitute the specificity of a people's experience of a particular place. However, totemic status for Irish as the sign of Culture and Tradition is worthless if the language is not included in both its form and substance in cultural and heritage policy. Formal inclusion means providing Irish speakers with the same range of documentation and services that are available to users of other languages. Otherwise, cultural institutions by default champion hegemony over diversity, a poor basis for any cultural reinvigoration of Irish society. Substantial inclusion means the informed incorporation of Irish-language history and experience into the presentation of Irish heritage and culture. It is

---

[31] *Bilingualism in the State Sector, supra* n. 18, at 65–6.

[32] Cinnéide and Ní Chonghaile, *supra* n. 16, at 151 and 162.

[33] For details of this programme and the accompanying rationale, see J. Péchenart and A Tangy, "Gifts of Tongues: Foreign Languages and Tourism Policy in Ireland" in B. O'Connor and M. Cronin (eds.), *Tourism in Ireland: A Critical Analysis* (Cork, Cork University Press, 1993), 162–80.

astonishing, for example, that one of the most vibrant periods of Irish culture, the Irish-language renaissance of the late Middle Ages, is almost wholly ignored in our media, museums and heritage centres. Unless there is informed inclusiveness we risk offering both ourselves and others a truncated misrepresentation of our past and present that is an eternal hostage to monolingual, Anglophone perspectives.

A contributor to *The Nation* newspaper in 1842 noted the following with respect to Irish:

> "Its importance need not be questioned, even if we begin with the Garden of Eden— and in doing so I do not for a moment think we assume too high a position. We find the meaning of the first word that had necessarily been spoken by the Creator to his creature pure Irish—Adam, that is *Ead, am—As yet fresh*, which was very appropriately addressed by the object he had just created in his own likeness, and hence was our first father called Adam."[34]

Eden was not eternal and banishment followed on bliss. The site for one of the wilder fantasies of folk linguistics in the 1840s was tragically ambiguous, as Irish speakers saw not paradise but the inferno in the form of famine and exile in the years that followed the Edenic comparison. Irish does not thrive in utopias, constitutional or otherwise. A fall from being the first official language would lead not to the death of hope but to the birth of ambition. An ambition that would be finally grounded in the defence of real rights rather than empty symbols.

---

[34] Cited in Crowley, *supra* n. 24, at 108–9.

21

National Sovereignty in the European Union

ANTHONY WHELAN*

INTRODUCTION

The term "sovereignty" is used in at least two ways, both in the Constitution and more generally. There is the sovereignty of the State and that of the people. In constitutional terms, State sovereignty derives from that of the people and permits the State to act for the people in external relations on a footing of equality with other States. The sovereignty of the people may be understood as their constituent authority regarding all aspects of governance, both domestic and external. Because membership of the European Communities and Union is undertaken by means of international instruments, but those instruments are the basis of constitutional claims which affect profoundly and directly the domestic legal order of Member States, this essay is chiefly concerned with the effects of membership on sovereignty in the second, more extended sense of the sovereignty or constituent authority of the people.

The Constitution, as adopted in 1937, conceives of Ireland as a sovereign State. This sovereignty, deriving from the authority of the nation and the people, can be contrasted with the ambiguous status and source of authority of the Irish Free State. State sovereignty was restricted by accession to the European Communities, and by the later ratification of the Single European Act (SEA) and the Treaty on European Union (TEU). This restriction of State sovereignty was authorised through specific amendments to Article 29.4 of the Constitution which were approved by the people by referendum. However, in European Community law, the ratification by the Member States of the founding Treaties is deemed to establish the constitutional authority of the resulting Communities and their law, which is not dependent on further domestic constitutional authorisation. There has been extensive debate over the degree to which the claims of European Community law have been accommodated in Irish law by Article 29.4.3–5 of the Constitution.

* I am grateful to my colleagues Kieran Bradley, Steven Cras, Georges Dellis, Leo Flynn, Diarmuid Rossa Phelan and Noel Travers for their criticisms and suggestions. All responsibility remains my own. All views expressed are personal, and in no way represent the position of the Court of Justice or of any member thereof.

In this essay, I will examine the question whether the limitation of State sovereignty in international law by accession to the Community and Union Treaties also entails the limitation of popular sovereignty or constituent authority and, in particular, the hypothetical problems regarding the location of constituent authority which would arise if the people were to repeal Article 29.4.3–5 and the State were to attempt to leave the Union unilaterally. I venture one possible response, which is speculative and perhaps provocative in character, but which would also resolve the more real problem of interpretation of Article 29.4.3–5 in a case of profound conflict between Community law and important substantive principles of Irish constitutional law. It would involve acceptance, in Irish constitutional law that, by authorising ratification of the Treaties, the people have consented to a partial but permanent transfer of their sovereignty. I do not make any case in favour this approach, other than to suggest that it is logically tenable and that it would provide an unambiguous solution to the current, somewhat schizophrenic, approaches to the place of Community law in Irish law. I do not argue that it is the most likely, or, in Irish constitutional terms, the most convincing response by the Irish Courts to a future dispute.

SOVEREIGNTY OF THE NATION AND THE PEOPLE

The Preamble to the Constitution states, in relevant part, that "[w]e, the people of Éire . . . [d]o hereby adopt, enact, and give to ourselves this Constitution." Article 1 of the Constitution states: "The Irish nation hereby affirms its inalienable, indefeasible and sovereign right to choose its own form of Government, to determine its relations with other nations, and to develop its life, political, economic and cultural, in accordance with its own genius and traditions." Article 5 of the Constitution states: "Ireland is a sovereign, independent, democratic state."

Article 6 of the Constitution states:

"1. All powers of government, legislative, executive and judicial, derive, under God, from the people, whose right it is to designate the rulers of the State and, in final appeal, to decide all questions of national policy, according to the requirements of the common good.

2. These powers of government are exercisable only by or on the authority of the organs of State established by this Constitution."

The Irish courts have relied upon the Preamble and on Articles 1, 5 and 6 of the Constitution as establishing that sovereignty is vested in the people, who act through the State.[1] Budd J observed in *Byrne* v. *Ireland*[2] that the nation could only be understood as the people, and that Articles 1 and 6 of the Constitution "indicate that it is recognised in the Constitution itself that

---

[1] *Per* Walsh J in *Webb* v. *Ireland* [1988] IR 353.
[2] [1972] IR 241.

there is a higher authority than the State. . . . It is the people who are paramount and not the State." Walsh J added that:

> "Our constitutional history, and in particular the events leading up to the enactment of the Constitution, indicate beyond doubt, to my mind, that the declaration as to sovereignty in Article 5 means that the State is not subject to any power of government save those designated by the people in the Constitution itself, and that the State is not amenable to any external authority for its conduct."

In *Re Article 26 and the Regulation of Information (Services outside the State for Termination of Pregnancies) Bill 1995*[3] (hereinafter the *Information Bill* case), the Supreme Court rejected the argument that the people were bound by natural law when amending the Constitution. Hamilton CJ cited Articles 5 and 6 of the Constitution, reviewed the case law on natural law and personal rights and stated that the courts "at no stage recognised the provisions of the natural law as superior to the Constitution". He continued: "The People were entitled to amend the Constitution in accordance with the provisions of Article 46 of the Constitution and the Constitution as so amended . . . is the fundamental and supreme law of the State representing as it does the will of the People."

Hamilton J (then President of the High Court) also observed in *Attorney General, ex rel. Society for the Protection of Unborn Children (Ireland) Ltd* v. *Open Door Counselling Ltd*[4] that the decisions of the people in final appeal, referred to in Article 6 of the Constitution, include their decisions on constitutional amendments.

EXTERNAL SOVEREIGNTY OF THE STATE

Ireland's external relations are entrusted to the Government by Article 29.4.1 of the Constitution. The sovereignty of the State was characterised by the Supreme Court in *Crotty* v. *An Taoiseach*[5] as "the unfettered right to decide: to say yes or no". In that case, a majority of the Supreme Court judges decided that, in the absence of an enabling constitutional amendment, the State was not constitutionally entitled to ratify the SEA, insofar as its Title III established a form of foreign-policy cooperation among the Member States outside the scope of Community law. Walsh J, one of the judges of the majority, stated:

> "In enacting the Constitution the people conferred full freedom of action upon the Government to decide matters of foreign policy. . . . In my view, this freedom does not carry with it the power to abdicate that freedom or to enter into binding agreements with other States to exercise that power in a particular way or to refrain from exercising it save by particular procedures and so to bind the State in its freedom

[3] [1995] 1 IR 1.
[4] [1988] IR 593. The relator is referred to hereinafter as SPUC.
[5] [1987] IR 713.

of action in its foreign policy. The freedom to formulate foreign policy is just as much a mark of sovereignty as the freedom to form economic policy and the freedom to legislate. The latter two have now been curtailed by the consent of the people to the amendment of the Constitution which is contained in Article 29.4.[3–5]. If it is now desired to qualify, curtail or inhibit the existing sovereign power to formulate and pursue such foreign policies as from time to time to the Government may seem proper, it is not within the power of the Government itself to do so."[6]

A few further observations are necessary to the discussion below. Ireland is a dualist State: no international agreement shall be part of the law of the State save as may be determined by the Oireachtas.[7] Thus, international treaties must be specifically incorporated into Irish law if they are to be lawfully applied in such a manner as to affect legal rights, and to be enforced by the courts.[8] The obligations contained in the international convention then have the status in Irish law of the incorporating measure—a status inferior to the Constitution. It is therefore possible for the implementing measure to be challenged for unconstitutionality before the Irish courts, resulting in an inconsistency between the State's domestic and international obligations.[9]

The Irish courts will interpret domestic legislation, where possible, to conform with the State's international obligations.[10] It does not seem that they will expressly do so when construing the Constitution,[11] although there is evidence that they will have regard to international instruments and case law when applying concepts like public policy, which are of particular importance in the area of fundamental rights.[12]

THE "SOVEREIGNTY" OF THE EUROPEAN COMMUNITIES

The Court of Justice of the European Communities has long insisted that the treaties establishing those Communities are not to be treated simply as international agreements instituting an advanced form of co-operation between sovereign States. The Court stated in *Van Gend en Loos* v. *Nederlandse Administratie der Belastigen*:[13]

---

[6] [1987] IR 713, at 783.

[7] Art. 29.6 of the Constitution.

[8] *In Re Ó Laighléis* [1960] IR 93.

[9] *The State (Gilliland)* v. *Governor of Mountjoy Prison* [1987] IR 401. The courts also appear to be willing to review the constitutionality of the State's accession and adherence to international agreements even if they are not incorporated into Irish law, if they undermine the constitutional order: see *McGimpsey* v. *Ireland* [1990] 1 IR 110; see comments about the necessity of review before ratification in *Crotty* v. *An Taoiseach* [1987] IR 713, discussed further below; see generally J. Casey, "*Crotty* v. *An Taoiseach*: A Comparative Perspective" in J. O'Reilly (ed.), *Human Rights and Constitutional Law—Essays in Honour of Brian Walsh* (Dublin, Round Hall Press, 1992), 189.

[10] *Ó Domhnaill* v. *Merrick* [1984] IR 151; *The State (Director of Public Prosecutions)* v. *Walsh* [1981] IR 412.

[11] *Norris* v. *Attorney General* [1984] IR 36.

[12] *Desmond* v. *Glackin (No. 1)* [1992] ILRM 490; see also the judgments of Denham and Keane JJ in *SPUC* v. *Grogan and others (No. 4)*, unreported, Supreme Court, 6 Mar. 1997.

[13] Case 26/62 [1963] ECR 1, at 12.

"[The EEC] Treaty is more than an agreement which merely creates mutual obligations between the contracting states. This view is confirmed by the preamble to the Treaty which refers not only to governments but to peoples.[14] It is also confirmed more specifically by the establishment of institutions endowed with sovereign rights, the exercise of which affects the Member States and also their citizens."

The Court concluded:

"[T]he Community constitutes a new legal order of international law for the benefit of which the states have limited their sovereign rights, albeit within limited fields, [15] and the subjects of which comprise not only Member States but also their nationals. Independently of the legislation of Member States, Community law therefore not only imposes obligations on individuals but is also intended to confer upon them rights which become part of their legal heritage."[16]

The Court of Justice also stated, in *Costa* v. *ENEL:*[17]

"By contrast with ordinary international treaties, the EEC Treaty has created its own legal system which, on the entry into force of the Treaty, became an integral part of the legal systems of the Member States and which their courts are bound to apply."

In that case, the Court based its analysis on the creation of a Community "of unlimited duration, having its own institutions, its own personality, its own legal capacity of representation on the international plane and, more particularly, real powers stemming from a limitation of sovereignty or a transfer of powers from the States to the Community". The Court of Justice concluded:[18]

"The integration into the laws of each Member State of provisions which derive from the Community, and more generally the terms and the spirit of the Treaty, make it impossible for the States, as a corollary, to accord precedence to a unilateral and subsequent measure over a legal system accepted by them on a basis of reciprocity . . . The transfer by the States from their domestic legal system to the Community legal system of the rights and obligations arising under the Treaty carries with it a permanent limitation of their sovereign rights, against which a subsequent unilateral act incompatible with the concept of the Community cannot prevail."

In *Les Verts* v. *Parliament,*[19] the Court of Justice referred to the EEC Treaty as "the basic constitutional charter" of the Community. This was repeated in

---

[14] The Preamble to the European Community (EC) Treaty, formerly the European Economic Community (EEC) Treaty, states that the contracting States are "[d]etermined to lay the foundations of an ever closer union among the peoples of Europe".

[15] The ECJ reiterated this formula in *Opinion 1/91 on the draft European Economic Area Agreement* [1991] ECR I–6079, para. 21, but referred to the Member States having limited their sovereign rights "in ever wider fields".

[16] *Supra* n. 13, at 12.

[17] Case 6/64 [1964] ECR 585, at 593.

[18] [1964] ECR 585, at 593–4.

[19] Case 249/83 [1986] ECR 1339, para. 23 of the judgment.

Opinion 1/91 on the draft European Economic Area Agreement.[20] In that case, the Court of Justice summed up:

"The essential characteristics of the Community legal order which has thus been established are in particular its primacy over the law of the Member States and the direct effect of a whole series of provisions which are applicable to their nationals and to the Member States themselves."

The root of title of the Communities' constitutional charter, the Treaties, is their ratification by all the Member States. In *San Michele* v. *High Authority*,[21] the Court of Justice rejected a claim that application of the European Coal and Steel Community Treaty should be suspended until the *Corte Costituzionale* (the Italian Constitutional Court) had assessed its constitutionality in Italian law. It stated that "the Court of Justice, as the institution entrusted with ensuring that in the interpretation and application of the Treaty the law is observed, can only take into consideration the instrument of ratification, which itself was deposited on behalf of Italy on 22 July 1952 and which, together with the other instruments of ratification, brought the Treaty into force". The Court continued:

"[I]t is clear from the instruments of ratification, whereby the Member States bound themselves in an identical manner, that all States have adhered to the Treaty on the same conditions, definitively and without any reservations other than those set out in the supplementary protocols, and that therefore any claim by a national of a Member State questioning such adherence would be contrary to the system of Community law."

The Court stated, in *Internationale Handelsgesellschaft*[22] that "the law stemming from the Treaty, an independent source of law, cannot because of its very nature be overridden by rules of national law, however framed". The fact that sovereignty has been transferred to the Communities only in certain fields is very important, and was confirmed by the insertion of Article 3b into the EC Treaty by the TEU.[23] Thus, Community law expressly recognises the continuing autonomous sovereignty of the Member States in non-Community matters, and the distinct character of their national legal orders. Temple Lang puts the Community-law position thus:

"States' powers are not derived from the Community constitution: the Treaty is the basis of the Community's constitutional law, but not that of the States' constitutions. There are [16] *grundnorms* in the Community. But in so far as Community rules now form part of the States' constitutional laws, the States can alter them only by amending the Treaty."[24]

---

[20] [1991] ECR I–6079, para. 21 of the Opinion.
[21] Joined Cases 9 and 58/65 [1967] ECR 1, at 28–9.
[22] Case 11/70 [1970] ECR 1125, para. 3 of the judgment.
[23] See also *Opinion 2/94 on the proposed accession to the European Convention on Human Rights* [1996] ECR I–1759, paras. 23–25, 30.
[24] "The Development of European Community Constitutional Law" (1991) 13 *DULJ* 36, at 47.

The EC Treaty and the TEU were concluded for an unlimited period.[25] They can be amended only by the unanimous agreement of the Member States.[26]

It is evident that the European Community doctrines of supremacy and direct effect derived from the constitutional Treaties are inconsistent with the retention of exclusive national legislative, executive and judicial power. Conflicts with other constitutional provisions, such as those regarding fundamental rights, cannot be excluded.[27] These problems were addressed in Ireland by the adoption of the Third Amendment to the Constitution, which was approved by the people in a referendum in 1972. This inserted in the Constitution a specific authorisation to join the Communities, and a specific provision on the supremacy of Community law and on the lawfulness of acts done pursuant to the obligations of membership. The relevant provisions of Article 29.4 of the Constitution, inserted by the Third Amendment of 1972, and later amended by the Tenth Amendment of 1987 and the Eleventh Amendment of 1992, are as follows:

"(3) The State may become a member of the European Coal and Steel Community . . . , the European Economic Community . . . , and the European Atomic Energy Community . . . The State may ratify the Single European Act. . . . [28]

(4) The State may ratify the Treaty on European Union signed at Maastricht on the 7th day of February, 1992, and may become a member of that Union.

(5) No provision of this Constitution invalidates laws enacted, acts done or measures adopted by the State which are necessitated by the obligations of membership of the European Union or of the Communities, or prevents laws enacted, acts done or measures adopted by the European Union or by the Communities or by institutions thereof, or by bodies competent under the Treaties establishing the Communities, from having the force of law in the State".

These constitutional provisions are phrased either in permissive terms (Article 29.4.3–4) or in negative terms (Article 29.4.5). Thus, while they might enable the State to apply Community law without constitutional obstacle, they would not, in the ordinary course, oblige it to do so. Within the dualist paradigm of the Constitution of Ireland, it was deemed necessary to adopt a further act of domestic incorporation of the Treaties which, once ratified, would activate, and also benefit from, the constitutional immunity contained in Article 29.4.5 of the Constitution. This was ensured by section 2(1) of the

---

[25] Article 240, EC Treaty; Article Q, TEU.

[26] Article N, TEU.

[27] For an analysis of such conflict in the Irish constitutional context, see S. O'Leary, "The Reciprocal Relationship Between Irish Constitutional Law and the Law of the European Communities" in this volume.

[28] The place and date of signature of the respective Treaties is omitted.

European Communities Act, 1972,[29] which states that "the treaties governing the European Communities and the existing and future acts adopted by the institutions of the Communities and by the bodies competent under the said treaties shall be binding on the State and shall be part of the domestic law thereof under the conditions laid down in those treaties".

These domestic legal provisions will ordinarily ensure that Community law is received and applied without obstacle in the Irish legal system. Costello J stated in *Pigs and Bacon Commission* v. *McCarron*[30] that the effect of these domestic provisions was that Community law "takes effect in the Irish legal system in the manner in which it itself provides". This is the purported effect of section 2(1) of the 1972 Act; however, the existence of such national acts of reception appears implicitly to belie Community law's claims to give rise to *autonomous* principles of supremacy and direct effect. These national measures are, in the words of Carroll J in *Tate* v. *Minister for Social Welfare*,[31] "the conduit pipe through which Community law became part of domestic law"—a device which would not be necessary if Community law were automatically recognised as operating "independently of the legislation of Member States".

However, because Community law recognises the distinct existence of national constitutional orders, it can, simultaneously, lay claim to its own autonomous force and apparently tolerate the operation of "the principle of the mirror image",[32] whereby nationally effective devices like incorporation and constitutional immunity are used to give practical domestic application to Community law, including its primacy and direct effect.[33]

This may not seem to be consistent with the statement by the Court of Justice in *Commission* v. *Italy*[34] that "the primacy and direct effect of the provisions of Community law do not release Member States from their obligation to remove from their domestic legal order any provisions incompatible with Community law, since the maintenance of such provisions gives rise to an ambiguous state of affairs in so far as it leaves persons concerned in a state of uncertainty as to the possibilities available to them of relying on Community law". This statement illustrates a difference in outlook, however. From the Community perspective, national measures granting the required effect to Community law may be necessary, given the existence of separate

---

[29] No. 27 of 1972. The Act has been much amended since Ireland's accession. A consolidated and annotated version can be found G. Hogan and A. Whelan, *Ireland and the European Union: Constitutional and Statutory Texts and Commentary* (London, Sweet and Maxwell, 1995), at 166–81.

[30] High Court, 30 June 1978 [1978] JISEL 77.

[31] [1995] 1 ILRM 507, at 521.

[32] P. Rawlings, "Legal Politics: The United Kingdom and Ratification of the Treaty on European Union" [1994] *Public Law* 254, at 258.

[33] See the discussion in G. Hogan and A. Whelan, *supra* n. 27, at 10–11, and in D. R. Phelan and A. Whelan, "National Constitutional Law and European Integration: Ireland" in M. Froment (ed.), *National Constitutional Law vis-à-vis European Integration* (Baden-Baden, Nomos Verlagsgesellschaft, 1996), 292, at 313.

[34] Case 104/86 [1988] ECR 1817, para. 12 of the judgment.

national constitutional systems, merely in order to safeguard the individual from legal uncertainty about rights granted independently and directly by Community law. For national law (and for dualist systems in particular), on the other hand, such national measures are traditionally regarded as necessary conditions for the applicability of Community law. Community law conceives of itself as having independent and supreme authority in its field of competence, while national competence is merely residual and is not opposable to Community law. From the perspective of most, if not all, Member State legal systems, Community law, however extensive its scope, is perceived to be exceptional, and to have been accommodated by special concessions within the national legal order. On this traditional view, the national legal order remains the overarching source of authority of both national law and, within that State's territory, of Community law, however deferential it may be *de facto* to Community law's "constitutional" requirements of supremacy and direct effect.

All may be well, so long as the national courts do not identify a flaw in the mirror which prevents, from the point of view of national law, the full application of Community law. Problems could arise under this regime if the Irish courts did not accept the interpretation of Community law by the Court of Justice in a particular case, or if it gave rise to such a profound conflict with fundamental principles of the national legal order that the Irish courts felt obliged to limit the apparently sweeping terms of Article 29.4.5 in the light of other provisions of the Constitution.[35] Problems would also arise if the competent national authorities were to revoke the measures by which Community law is received into the domestic legal order. This could occur in Ireland either by the repeal of section 2(1) of the European Communities Act 1972 or by the repeal of Article 29.4.3–5 of the Constitution. Such a step would shatter the mirror image of Community law received into Irish law.

I wish to outline one possible solution to such potential conflicts with Community law. This is full acceptance of the claims to authority of Community law, on its own terms, in Irish constitutional law, by virtue of the people's approval, in three referendums, of a progressive and permanent cession of sovereign constituent authority.

---

[35] See e.g. the remarks of Walsh J and, more ambiguously, of McCarthy J in *SPUC* v. *Grogan* [1989] IR 753, regarding the definition of services in Community law and the relationship of the Third and the Eighth Amendments of the Constitution. See the discussion in G. Hogan and A. Whelan, *supra* n. 27, Part I, in particular chaps. 1 and 8; D. R. Phelan, *Revolt or Revolution: The Constitutional Boundaries of the European Community* (Dublin, Roundhall Sweet and Maxwell, 1997); D. R. Phelan, "Two Hats, One Wig, No Halo" in B. Treacy and G. Whyte (eds.), *Religion, Morality and Public Policy* (Dublin, Dominican Publications, 1995), 130; D. R. Phelan and A. Whelan, *supra* n. 31. For a *communautaire* approach to the interpretation of Art. 29.4.3–5, see J. Temple Lang, "The Widening Scope of Constitutional Law" in D. Curtin and D. O'Keeffe (eds.), *Constitutional Adjudication in European Community and National Law* (Dublin, Butterworths, 1992), 229.

CONFLICT OF LEGAL ORDERS AND THE CITIZEN OF THE UNION

In the event of a repeal of Article 29.4.3–5 of the Constitution by an Amendment of the Constitution Act adopted pursuant to a referendum, and of a repeal of section 2(1) of the European Communities Act 1972, the resulting crisis would probably fall to be resolved by political means. However, I shall assume for the purposes of the present discussion that a diligent and litigious Union citizen will be able to bring a dispute which turns on the resulting legal conflict before the courts in advance of any general political compromise.

The directly effective Community-law rights of a Union citizen are not dependent on a national act of reception for either their direct effect or their primacy over contrary national law.[36] The national courts are under a direct Community-law duty to secure the enjoyment of those rights. Even if Ireland were unilaterally to denounce the Treaties—an unlawful act, in international law,[37] which, none the less, is within the capacity of sovereign States, subject to compensation—the Community-law position would probably remain formally unchanged, as the only authority which can alter the Treaties and the rights derived by individuals therefrom is the Member States acting by common accord to ratify Treaty amendments in accordance with their respective constitutional requirements.[38] This highlights how, from the point of view of Community law, the exclusive sovereignty and constituent authority of the Irish people has been permanently ceded, in fields governed by the Treaties, to another sovereign and constituent authority, the Member States acting in common.[39]

The position in Irish law after the enactment of a law repealing the incorporation of Community law into Irish law and of an amendment of the Constitution repealing Article 29.4.3–5 is rather less promising for the Union

---

[36] As regards rights which are not directly effective, she may be entitled to damages against the Member State in question if it fails to transpose them into national law: see Joined Cases C–6/90 and C–9/90 *Francovich and Bonifaci* v. *Italian Republic* [1991] ECR I–5357.

[37] See Articles 5, 54, 56 and 62 of the Vienna Convention of the Law of Treaties, 1969, 8 I.L.M. 679; N. Feinberg, "Unilateral withdrawal from an International Organization" (1963) 39 B.Y.I.L. 189; M. Akehurst, "Withdrawal from International Organizations" (1979) Current Legal Problems 143; J. Hill, "The European Economic Community: The Right of Member State Withdrawal" (1982) 12 Georgia J. I. Comp. L. 337; F. Harhoff. 'Greenland's Withdrawal from the European Communities (1983) 20 CML Rev. 13.

[38] Art. N of the TEU. Rights derived from secondary Community legislation are, similarly, open to alteration only by the appropriate legislative body, be it the Council, the Council and Parliament, or the Commission, subject to general principles of Community law regarding proportionality, protection of legitimate expectations, etc. It is open to debate whether the Member States' constituent authority extends to Treaty amendments which are in breach of these principles.

[39] The cession is permanent only on the part of the constituent authorities of the individual Member States. The constituent authority of the Communities/Union is free to restore or repatriate sovereignty to the Member States, in whole or in part, in accordance with the provisions of Art. N of the TEU. While the ECJ referred in *Van Gend en Loos*, *supra* n. 13, to the participation of the peoples of Europe in the political life of the Communities, they have no constituent authority distinct from that of their States.

citizen. A traditional interpretation of Article 29.6 of the Constitution would indicate that Community law was no longer part of the domestic law of the State. Thus, Irish courts would not be entitled to give it effect.[37] In that event, there would exist a direct conflict between the duties of the Irish courts under Community law and under national law, both of which would claim directly to bind those courts.[41]

However, the Union citizen could argue that, even as a matter of Irish constitutional law, the people, by authorising membership, partially ceded their sovereignty and original constituent authority to the Communities/Union. She could submit that, by expressly referring in Article 29.4.3–4 to the various Treaties, the people accepted the constitutional principles contained in those Treaties and already clearly identified by the Court of Justice: *inter alia*, supremacy, direct effect, and the ultimate interpretative authority of the Court of Justice. Having done so, the people, by the exercise of their own original sovereign authority, bound themselves to abide by the Treaties and to submit themselves, in fields governed by the Treaties, to the sovereign power of a new constituent authority, the Member States acting by common accord. They could not reappropriate the sovereign power so alienated save in accordance with the will of the new constituent authority.

Some remote support for this view can be found in the judgments of the Supreme Court majority in *Crotty v. An Taoiseach* in respect of ratification of Title III of the SEA. However, this is subject to the very important caveat that this aspect of the decision related to provisions of the SEA which were not part of Community law as such. The decision of the Supreme Court majority regarding Title III was founded upon the premise that ratification would restrict the Government's sovereign foreign-policy power, conferred by the people. Walsh J spoke of the curtailment or inhibition of sovereign power granted to the Government.[42] Henchy J stated that "each Member State will immediately cede a portion of its sovereignty and freedom of action in matters of foreign policy".[43] Ratification, in Hederman J's view, would "fetter powers bestowed unfettered by the Constitution".[44] The Government, as a creature of the Constitution, could not place itself in a position of being bound to act inconsistently with it, such as by committing itself to conduct its foreign policy otherwise than exclusively for the common good of the people.[45] Thus, a constitutional amendment would be necessary in order to permit ratification.

---

[40] Rights derived from directives which were transposed into Irish law by Acts of the *Oireachtas* would still be applicable, unless they were inconsistent with the Constitution. Directives implemented by ministerial regulation under s. 3 of the European Communities Act 1972 would presumably become ineffective: see *Meagher v. Attorney General* [1994] 1 IR 329.

[41] See further D. R. Phelan, "Two Hats, One Wig, No Halo", *supra* n. 33, at 130–1.

[42] *Supra* n. 5, at 783.

[43] *Ibid.*, at 786.

[44] *Ibid.*, at 794. Hederman J also concurred with the judgments of Walsh and Henchy JJ.

[45] *Ibid.*, at 777–8 (Walsh J) and 787 (Henchy J).

Two fundamental points emerge from the majority's analysis in *Crotty* v. *An Taoiseach*. First, the necessity for pre-emptive judicial review, before ratification, and the requirement of popular approval of ratification by constitutional amendment, were both based on the fact that the State would be bound by the resulting international commitments. Secondly, the people are free to permit the State so to bind itself. Walsh J stated that "[t]he foreign policy organ of the State cannot, within the terms of the Constitution, agree to impose upon itself, the State or the people the contemplated restrictions upon freedom of action. To acquire the power to do so would, in my opinion, require recourse to the people."[46] Walsh J also observed that the State would still be bound in international law by the treaty, even if it were found, after ratification, to be unconstitutional.[47] Henchy J stated that, under the SEA, Ireland "would be bound in international law to engage actively in a programme which would trench progressively on Ireland's independence and sovereignty". It would be "an imperative under international law".[48]

It may be possible to explain away these comments by reference to the traditional dichotomy between domestic and international law. Obligations under the latter need not be seen as operative in the constitutional order of a dualist State. However, the Supreme Court majority clearly saw such international obligations as being, in some sense, constitutionally relevant. If they were not, the Court could simply have declared that the Government would remain bound by its constitutional duty regarding foreign affairs, whether it ratified the SEA or not, just as an unconstitutional statute will be struck down by the courts to ensure that the organs of the State act constitutionally on the domestic front. The Supreme Court majority clearly saw a conflict between constitutional and international law as being more problematical, in domestic terms, in a case where basic sovereignty was perceived to have been partially ceded, than it normally is where acts of the State appear to be inconsistent with treaty obligations.[49]

It may be that the judges felt that they had greater freedom to ensure that the State's constitutional and international obligations did not conflict, without in any sense compromising the content of constitutional law, because the international obligation had not yet been undertaken. Such preventive reasoning may not operate in reverse, to permit the courts to restrain, or ignore, acts of the State or the people which purport to render constitutionally impossible the domestic observance of international obligations already undertaken.

It is important to note that the subject-matter of *Crotty* was at one remove from that of the present discussion: it related to obligations which the Government, a creature of the Constitution, proposed to undertake within the framework of the existing provisions of the Constitution, rather than to the

---

[46] *Crotty* v. *An Taoiseach* [1987] IR 713, at 783.
[47] *Ibid.*, at 780.
[48] *Ibid.*, at 788–9.
[49] See *Ó Laighléis* and *Norris, supra* nn. 8 and 11.

obligations which the people, the constituent authority, can undertake by changing the Constitution to accommodate them. It remains the case, however, that the Supreme Court's reasoning appears to apply to both stages of analysis. If the international obligations and cession of sovereignty entailed by ratification of the SEA by the State were such as to prevent the Government acting constitutionally, there is nothing in the Court's *dicta* to suggest that the constituent authority would not have been similarly disabled from exercising its normal powers. As a matter of international law, the people have no sovereign power greater than that of their State, and the Supreme Court took the view in *Crotty* that international obligations could inhibit, in some circumstances at least, the exercise of constitutional authority.

It is therefore worth posing a question of principle: can a sovereign people bind itself, and permanently alienate some or all of its sovereignty? The idea that the constituent authority can entrench constitutional provisions against its own amending power is not novel. In France, the constitutional provision providing for a republican form of government (Article 1) cannot be amended.[50] The same is true of the German constitutional provisions regarding the democratic and federal character of the State and the dignity of the individual (Articles 1, 20 and 79).[51] Entrenchments of specific features of the system of representative democracy can also be found in Article V of the US Constitution and in section 128 of the Constitution of Australia. The Indian Supreme Court has held that the constituent authority cannot alter the basic structure or framework of the Constitution.[52] Furthermore, it was deemed possible to entrench certain substantive matters in the Constitution of *Saorstát Éireann*. That constitution was adopted as a schedule to the Irish Free State (*Saorstát Éireann*) Constitution Act passed by *Dáil Éireann* "sitting as a constituent assembly" in 1922. This Act was "the one and all-sufficient root of title" of the Constitution,[53] but it limited the amending power of the *Oireachtas* to amendments which were "within the terms of the scheduled [1921 Anglo-Irish]

---

[50] The French *Conseil constitutionnel* (Constitutional Council) found that the TEU did not infringe Art. 1, although it did entail a reduction in national competence in respect of certain essential elements of State sovereignty, which necessitated a constitutional amendment to permit ratification: *Re Ratificationof the Treaty on European Union* [1993] 3 CMLR 345.

[51] The *Bundesverfassungsgericht* (German Constitutional Court) found that these principles would not be breached by ratification of the TEU. However, despite the supplementary democratic support provided to actions of the Communities by the representatives of the peoples of the Member States in the European Parliament, the basic democratic legitimation of the Communities was to be found in the national statute assenting to accession. As each of the peoples of the individual Member States was the starting point for State power relating to that people, this set certain limits to the extension of the Communities' functions and competences: *Re Brunner* [1994] 1 CMLR 57, paras. 37–40, 44. It added, at para. 55, that Germany, as a sovereign State, could ultimately revoke its adherence to the Union by a contrary act.

[52] *Kesavananda's Case* [1973] Supp. SCR 1, [1973] ASC 1461.

[53] Meredith J, *Cahill* v. *Attorney General* [1925] IR 70; see also Murnaghan J in *Fogarty* v. *O'Donoghue* [1926] IR 531, and Kennedy CJ and Fitzgibbon J in *State (Ryan)* v. *Lennon* [1935] IR 170. See the view of the UK courts that the Constitution derived validity from the Irish Free State Constitution Act, 1922, passed by the UK Parliament: see *Moore* v. *Attorney General* [1935] IR 472.

Treaty".[54] These are all examples of the constituent authority binding itself not to alter fundamental elements of the national constitutional order, but the constituent authority could equally commit itself irrevocably to a fundamental change in that order.

The possibility of the people binding themselves is not excluded by the decision in the *Information Bill* case. In that case, the Supreme Court indicated that the people possessed original constituent authority which, exercised in accordance with the procedures set out in Article 46 of the Constitution, could not be restrained by principles of natural law, whether identified in the constitutional text itself (the people's creation) or from an external, transcendent source (such as a theory of human worth or a system of morality). The Supreme Court did not address the question whether the people were free to bind themselves, either expressly or by implication, by the terms of their own Constitution or by committing themselves to a form of government inconsistent with the continued, unrestrained exercise of their own sovereignty. Indeed, by rejecting the possibility that natural law could trump the people's will, the Supreme Court may have shown that the people are not subject to any fundamental substantive principles which might restrain their alienation of their own sovereignty.[55] Thus, for example, the people may be free to exercise the right of the Irish nation to choose its own form of government, set out in Article 1 of the Constitution, by opting for union with another State. In the case of a total merger, the people would lose their distinct political and legal identity, and would therefore impede decisively any later effort to regain their sovereignty other than by the means provided for in the constitutional arrangements of the new entity, or by revolution. The choice of form of government, once made, would not be reversible by recourse to the sovereignty of the people. The same argument can be made about the partial merger of the people's sovereignty with that of other States in the Communities and, latterly, the Union, whose conception of their autonomous constituent authority and constitutional principles was well known.

Of course, it may be countered that, in the *Information Bill* case, the Supreme Court rejected only one form of transcendent values—natural individual rights—as a trump on the popular will, and that the transcendent rights of the nation as a whole preserve, even against their own actions, the sovereignty of the people. Article 1 of the Constitution describes the sovereign rights of the nation as being

---

[54] Art. 51 of the Constitution of Ireland provided for amendment of the Constitution by the *Oireachtas* for three years after the first President had come into office, but was itself unamendable by this procedure. However, it was thereby entrenched only against amendment by the temporary delegatee of constituent authority, the *Oireachtas*; the People itself remained free to extend or repeal Art. 51.

[55] For a discussion of substantive principles which would restrict the alienation of popular sovereignty, see A. Whelan, "Constitutional Amendments in Ireland: The Competing Claims of Democracy" in G. Quinn, A. Ingram and S. Livingstone (eds.), *Justice and Legal Theory in Ireland* (Dublin, Oak Tree Press, 1995), 45. On the possibility of natural law constraints on popular sovereignty, see D. R. Phelan, *Revolt or Revolution, supra* n. 33.

"inalienable" and "indefeasible", so that a fair case can be made that that provision is entrenched. In *Ryan* v. *Attorney General*,[56] Kenny J defined as inalienable "that which cannot be transferred or given away". In *Re Article 26 and the Criminal Law (Jurisdiction) Bill 1975*, the Supreme Court observed that one of the theories underlying Articles 1–3 of the Constitution "was that a nation, as distinct from a State, had rights; . . . that a nation has a right to unity of territory in some form . . . ; and that the Government of Ireland Act 1920, though legally binding, was a violation of that right to national unity which was superior to positive law."[57] A number of responses to this argument are possible. One could argue that the rights of the nation are only "relatively inalienable", as was said of certain family rights by Walsh J in *G* v. *An Bord Uchtála*.[58] Although it is by no means clear what Walsh J meant—relative to whom or what can rights be either alienated or inalienable?—his *dictum* clearly indicates that rights described as inalienable may not be so in all circumstances. Secondly, a provision which is not expressly stated to be entrenched (as was Article 46, against legislative amendment, for the first three years of the Constitution) is arguably subject to amendment in the ordinary course, including to implicit amendment. Article 29.4.3–5 of the Constitution could be taken to constitute just such an implicit (and irrevocable) amendment of Article 1.[59] Article 29.4.3–5 would then be concluded to be effectively entrenched, in that it envisages the transfer of a bundle of original sovereign rights to an external body, from which they cannot be reclaimed simply by further recourse to the mechanisms for constitutional amendment. (Of course, it can be countered that Article 46 of the Constitution provides an unrestricted procedure for constitutional amendment which permits the people to exercise undiluted sovereignty, even contrary to the terms of prior external commitments undertaken by the State with the authorization of the people.) Thirdly, even if Article 1 of the Constitution were deemed to have been entrenched, and if a permanent, partial alienation of popular constituent authority were deemed, none the less, to have taken place in 1973 or afterwards (in 1987 or 1992), it could also be contended that a constitutional revolution had already occurred, and that Article 1 had to that extent been supplanted by a new legal reality.[60] One can, however, dissent from this view on the basis of historical or

---

[56] [1965] IR 294.

[57] [1977] IR 129. The aspirational aspect of the Supreme Court's analysis was rejected by the Supreme Court in *McGimpsey* v. *Ireland*, in which the reintegration of the national territory was described as "a constitutional imperative".

[58] [1980] IR 32.

[59] On the possibility of implicit amendment of provisions of the Constitution, see the remarks of Walsh J on the relationship of Arts. 29.4.3 (now 5) and 40.3.3 of the Constitution in *SPUC* v. *Grogan, supra* n. 33.

[60] It may be instructive in this regard to examine the case law on the Articles of Union between England and Scotland of 1707: *MacCormick* v. *Lord Advocate*, 1953 SC 396; *Sillars* v. *Smith*, 1982 SLT 539. A "constitutional revolution" takes place when there is a break in legal continuity by departing from pre-existing rules regarding constitutional change, such as occurred when the 1937 Constitution was adopted in Ireland; see *J. M. Kelly, The Irish Constitution* (G. Hogan and G. Whyte (eds.), Dublin, Butterworths, 1994), at 1–3; A. Honoré, "Reflections on Revolutions" (1967) 2 *Ir. Jur.* 268. D. R. Phelan has suggested that such a revolution can also occur by judicial

originalist arguments about the supposed original intentions of the people when they voted for membership of the Communities in response to any suggestion of a permanent partial cession of sovereign power.

CONCLUSION

This is, of necessity, a very brief rehearsal of some of the arguments that could be deployed for acceptance in Irish constitutional law of the partial, autonomous sovereignty of the Community legal order. If the people were deemed to be bound by their acceptance of Community and Union membership on the terms set out by the Court of Justice, this would have important consequences not only for the improbable case of an attempted unilateral withdrawal opposed by the other Member States, but also for more foreseeable instances of conflict between national and Community law which are normally resolved by the Irish courts by recourse to Article 29.4.5 of the Constitution. That provision could then be seen, as it would be by Community law, merely as a device to clarify in domestic law the autonomous primacy of the Community-law rights and duties of the individual. The same could be said of section 2(1) of the European Communities Act 1972.

In the light of the *Information Bill* case, the most fundamental tenet of the Irish constitutional order appears to be the sovereignty of the popular will. If it were deemed to be the people's sovereign will to effect a binding transfer of a part of that sovereignty to the Communities/Union (including recognition of the Court of Justice as the authoritative interpreter of the conditions and extent of that transfer), this would compel the Irish courts, as a matter of Irish constitutional law, to support the primacy of Community law in any conflict, however profound, with other substantive principles of Irish constitutional law. Article 29.4.5 could then be read as the concrete expression in Irish constitutional law of that obligation.

This is not to say that Ireland would be trapped within the Union, any more than the State was unable to escape from the monarchical system imposed by the Anglo-Irish Treaty and the Constitution of the Irish Free State. Provided the State retains the political and other resources necessary to effect its withdrawal (including continued recognition as a sovereign State in international law), it can presumably do so, even over its partners' objections, just as the Irish Free State did under Mr de Valera. However, on the theory just outlined, such withdrawal would necessitate, as it did in 1937, a domestic constitutional revolution.[61]

means, through the application of a constitution in a way which is inconsistent with its foundational principles, *Revolt or Revolution, supra* n. 33.

[61] A very different argument has been made, on the basis that natural-law principles constitute the foundation of the Irish constitutional order, and that acceptance by the national courts that Community law could override natural constitutional rights would amount to a revolution: see D R Phelan, *Revolt or Revolution, supra* n. 33; G. Hogan and A. Whelan, *supra* n. 28, at 10, 141–2.

22

The Reciprocal Relationship Between Irish Constitutional Law and the Law of the European Communities

SÍOFRA O'LEARY*

INTRODUCTION

It should perhaps be recalled from the outset that as a consequence of the principle of supremacy, European Community (EC) law takes precedence over all national norms, even constitutional norms concerning the protection of fundamental rights.[1] This principle remains one of the fundamental pillars of the constitutional architecture of the European Communities. Indeed, the object of the Third Amendment to the Constitution, which added a new sub-section 3 to Article 29.4, and, subsequently, the insertion of sub-sections 4, 5 and 6, was variously to permit accession to the EC, to accommodate the principle of supremacy and to provide a means generally to receive European Community law into Irish law.[2] The warmth of the Irish reception of EC law is reflected in the following statement by one former member of the Supreme Court:

"It is as if the people of Ireland had adopted Community law as a second but transcendent Constitution, with the difference that Community law is not to be found in any single document—it is a living growing organism and the right to interpret

---

* All views expressed are personal and in no way represent the position of the Court of Justice or of any member thereof.

[1] See e.g. Case 11/70 *Internationale Handelsgesellschaft* [1970] ECR 1125.

[2] See also the European Communities Act 1972. The Tenth and Eleventh amendments of the Constitution in 1987 and 1992 were to enable the adoption of the Single European Act (SEA) and the Treaty on European Union (TEU). Note that Art. 29.4.5 of the Constitution provides as follows: "No provision of this Constitution invalidates laws enacted, acts done or measures adopted by the State which are necessitated by the obligations of membership of the European Union or of the Communities, or prevents laws enacted, acts done or measures adopted by the European Union or by the Communities or by the institutions thereof, or by bodies competent under the Treaties establishing the Communities, from having the force of law in the State."

it and give it conclusive judicial interpretation is reserved to the institutions of the Community and to its Courts."[3]

Nevertheless, in Ireland, as in other Member States, the principle of the supremacy of European Community law has not gone unchallenged and relations between national courts and the Court of Justice have not always run smoothly.[4] When granting the interlocutory injunction sought by the Society for the Protection of the Unborn Child (SPUC) in *SPUC* v. *Grogan*, for example, Walsh J emphasised that "any answer to the reference received from the European Court of Justice will have to be considered in the light of our own constitutional provisions" and Finlay CJ held further that:

> "if and when a decision of the European Court of Justice rules that some aspect of European Community law affects the activities of the defendants impugned in this case, the consequence of that decision for these constitutionally guaranteed rights and their protection by the [Irish] courts will fall to be considered by the [Irish] Courts".[5]

The litigation surrounding the interpretation of Article 40.3.3 of the Constitution[6] and, more particularly, the issue of the right to abortion information is perhaps the most celebrated example of conflict between the substantive guarantees afforded by the Irish Constitution and the EC Treaty. Nevertheless, other questions concerning sensitive national interests have also been referred to the Court of Justice pursuant to the Article 177 EC reference procedure which, if answered differently, might have provoked an equally hostile domestic reaction. Some commentators have stressed, shocked it seems by the prospect of a non-Irish court having something to say about Ireland's protection of fundamental rights, that there would be a constitutional revolution in Ireland if the primacy of Community law were to be accepted by the Irish courts in a situation of profound normative conflict with fundamental features of the Irish constitutional order which could be regarded as so fundamental as to be unamendable.[7]

---

[3] S. Henchy, "The Irish Constitution and the EEC" (1977) *DULJ* 20, at 21, 23.

[4] On tension between the protection of fundamental rights by national courts and the Court of Justice, see e.g. S. O'Leary, "Aspects of the Relationship Between Community Law and National Law" in N. Neuwahl and A. Rosas (eds.), *The European Union and Human Rights* (Dordrecht, Martinus Nijhoff, 1995), 23; and B. De Witte, "Community Law and National Constitutional Values" [1991] *Legal Issues of European Integration* 1, at 5–6 and 10 ff.

[5] [1989] IR 753, at 768 and 765, respectively. See also McCarthy J, "The sole authority for the construction of the Constitution lies in the Irish courts", at 770 and T. O'Higgins, "The Constitution and the Communities—Scope for Stress" in J. O'Reilly (ed.), *Human Rights and Constitutional Law—Essays in Honour of Brian Walsh*, (Dublin, Round Hall Press, 1992), 227, at 229, where he argues that whether or not a national legal measure is "necessitated" by EC membership falls to be determined by the High Court pursuant to Art. 34.3.2.

[6] Art. 40.3.3 provides that "The State acknowledges the right to life of the unborn and, with due regard to the equal right to life of the mother, guarantees in its laws to respect, and, as far as practicable, by its laws to defend and vindicate that right."

[7] See e.g. D. R. Phelan, *Revolt or Revolution: The Constitutional Boundaries of the European Community* (Dublin, Roundhall Sweet and Maxwell, 1997); and "Right to Life of the Unborn v. Promotion of Trade in Services: The European Court of Justice and the Normative Shaping of the European Union" (1992) 55 *MLR* 670.

The purpose of this Chapter is to reflect on the influence of EC law on the protection and development of individual rights guaranteed by the Irish Constitution. It is suggested that one of the inevitable consequences of increased European integration is that democratic, social and even moral standards may no longer be almost exclusively defined with reference to national criteria. Although this sort of incorporation of "supranational" standards has already provoked controversy, as the long and tortuous abortion/abortion information/right to travel saga illustrates,[8] and no doubt will do so again, integration and its effects should not be viewed in a purely negative light as fettering, if not undermining, the protection of fundamental national interests. Indeed, as one of the cornerstones of the EC judicial system—the Article 177 reference procedure—indicates, the relationship between the two legal orders is a reciprocal one,[9] something which the Court of Justice has anxiously and regularly reaffirmed throughout its jurisprudence. In addition, one commentator has suggested that the penumbra of unenumerated constitutional rights which "result from the Christian and democratic nature of the state"[10] be used as inspiration for the EU and for Member States such as the United Kingdom, which do not have a legislative or constitutional text of rights.[11] Extension of the Irish courts' jurisprudence on enumerated rights post-*Ryan* may, at first

---

[8] The litigation initiated by SPUC gave rise initially to numerous decisions of the High Court and Supreme Court: *Attorney General (SPUC)* v. *Open Door Counselling Limited and the Dublin Well-Woman Centre Limited* [1988] IR 593, [1988] IR 618; *SPUC* v. *Coogan and Others* [1989] IR 734; *SPUC* v. *Grogan and others, supra* n. 5; *SPUC* v. *Grogan and Others*, unreported, Supreme Court, 6 Mar. 1997; a reference to the Court of Justice: Case C–159/90 *SPUC* v. *Grogan and others* [1991] ECR I–4685; decisions of the European Commission and Court of Human Rights in *Open Door Counselling Ltd & Dublin Well Woman Centre Ltd* v. *Ireland*: Applications Nos 14234/88 and 14236/88, see the Report of the Commission of 7 Mar. 1991 and the decision of the Court, 1992, Series A, No. 246, 15 EHRR 244. Fears that EC law would spawn future conflicts on the issue of abortion led to a protocol being annexed to the TEU, further fears concerning the right to travel and the right to information then led to a subsequent interpretative Declaration on 1 May 1992. The High Court and Supreme Court have also handed down their decisions in *Grogan* following the Court of Justice's answer to the 1989 reference, *SPUC* v. *Grogan and others* [1992] IR 471 and the judgment of the Supreme Court of 6 Mar. 1997, which upheld the students' appeal on the ground that the law had changed since 1992 following the amendment of the Constitution by the Fourteenth amendment and the adoption of the Regulation of Information (Services Outside the State for Termination of Pregnancies) Act 1995. Also on the subject of abortion and the right to travel see the decisions of the High and Supreme Courts in *Attorney General* v. *X* [1992] ILRM 401 and 414, respectively. Following the Thirteenth and Fourteenth amendments to the Constitution, Art. 40.3.3 now also provides that it shall not limit freedom to travel between the State and another State, or the freedom to obtain and make available, in the State, subject to such conditions as may be laid down by law, information relating to services lawfully available in another State.

[9] See also P. Gallagher, "The Constitution and the Community" (1993) 1 *Irish J of Euro. L* 129, at 137: "the relationship between EEC law and Irish constitutional law is not entirely onesided in the sense of the former always influencing the latter. Irish constitutional law has had an influence, albeit very restricted, on the development of fundamental rights in EEC law. It is an influence which could be expanded because undoubtedly the constitutional principles developed by the Irish Courts have a relevance beyond Ireland."

[10] *Ryan* v. *Attorney General* [1965] IR 294.

[11] J. Temple Lang, "The Duties of National Courts under Community Constitutional Law" (1997) 22 *Euro. L Rev.* 3 at 11.

sight, appear attractive, but one should remember that the idea of a catalogue of rights based on the Christian nature of the State may be the mistaken path for a supranational, multicultural Community, on the verge of expansion eastwards, to follow.[12] The acknowledgement of several identifiable "Irish exceptions" in the jurisprudence of the Court, combined with a better understanding of the derogations permitted by the Treaty, as well as the Court of Justice's awareness of the delicate nature of its relationship with national courts which refer questions to it, may mean that the Irish courts,

> "which in general displayed a marked reluctance to entertain the European dimension to the [Grogan] dispute and an equal hostility to having the matter discussed by any European tribunal",[13]

will be more prepared in future to admit a supranational perspective in response to what may once have been purely Irish questions. A marked improvement in this respect is already discernible in the judgments of certain members of the Supreme Court in its 1997 decision in *SPUC* v. *Grogan*.[14] Citing the decision of the European Court of Human Rights in *Open Door Counselling*,[15] Keane J noted that that decision, albeit unbinding, was powerful support for the view that the comprehensive nature of the injunction against the students could not be reconciled with the right to communicate, and to receive, information relating to abortion in certain circumstances.[16]

MECHANISMS IN THE EC TREATY FOR THE PROTECTION OF NATIONAL INTERESTS

A number of provisions in the EC Treaty were specifically designed to permit Member States to derogate from the fundamental principles which it establishes, for example, in the area of free movement. Article 36 EC permits derogations justified on grounds of public morality, public policy or public security; the protection of the health and life of humans, animals or plants; the protection of national treasures possessing artistic, historic or archaeological value; or the protection of industrial and commercial property. Although these derogations are interpreted strictly by the Court of Justice, which ensures that the action taken by Member States thereunder does not

---

[12] For a re-evaluation of the *Ryan* case see G. Hogan, "Unenumerated Personal Rights: *Ryan's* Case Re-Evaluated" (1990–92) 25–27 *Ir. Jur.* 95.

[13] See F. Murphy, "Maastricht: Implementation in Ireland" (1994) 19 *Euro. L Rev.* 94, at 96. On this reluctance fully to embrace Community jurisprudence and doctrine see also D. Curtin, "Some Reflections on European Community Law in Ireland" (1989) 11 *DULJ* 207, at 216 ff. who cites not only the *Open Door* case, but also the High Court's decision in *McDermott and Cotter* v. *Minister for Social Welfare*, unreported, 10 June 1988 and *Browne* v. *An Bord Pléanala* [1989] ILRM 865.

[14] Unreported, Supreme Court, 6 Mar. 1997.

[15] *Supra* n. 8.

[16] See *supra* n. 8, where Denham J regarded the Strasbourg decision as a persuasive analysis and, in contrast to Walsh J in the *Grogan* decision prior to the Art. 177 EC reference, Hamilton CJ held that "[t]he ruling of the European Court of Justice is binding on the national court".

constitute a means of arbitrary discrimination or a disguised restriction on trade between Member States, the objective of Article 36 EC is to ensure that where vital national interests are at stake, Articles 30 to 34 EC shall not preclude prohibitions or restrictions on imports, exports or goods in transit. Similar provisions are found in Articles 48(3) and 56 EC as regards the free movement of persons and services. Derogations from these fundamental Treaty freedoms are permitted when justified on grounds of public policy, public health and public security. The Court of Justice has held, for example, that the public policy derogation in Article 48(3) EC is applicable to "genuine and sufficiently serious threat[s] to the requirements of public policy affecting one of the fundamental interests of society".[17] Articles 48(4) EC permits a further derogation in the context of certain types of employment in the public service which involve direct or indirect participation in the exercise of powers conferred by public law and duties designed to safeguard the general interests of the State or of other public authorities,[18] while, in the context of establishment and services, Article 55 EC permits a similar derogation as regards the exercise of activities which involve direct and specific participation in the exercise of official authority.[19]

Further exceptions to the prohibition on restrictions of free movement, whether it be with respect to goods, persons or services, have also been fashioned by the Court of Justice itself. Its case law now goes beyond the prohibition of directly or indirectly discriminatory national rules and prohibits, in addition, non-discriminatory national rules which are liable to impede or obstruct free movement.[20] These indistinctly applicable restrictions are only permissible if they can be justified with reference to imperative requirements of public interest. The public interests which the Court has recognised to date are meant to reflect the social, moral and cultural diversity which exists between the Member States. In the field of establishment and services, for example, Member States have been allowed to derogate from the Treaty provisions on free movement with respect to, amongst others, professional rules designed to protect the recipients of services,[21] the protection of intellectual property,[22] the protection of workers,[23] the protection of consumers,[24] or the conservation and protection of national artistic and historical heritage.[25]

---

[17] Case 30/77 *R.* v. *Bouchereau* [1977] ECR 1999, at para. 35.
[18] Case 149/79 *Commission* v. *Belgium* [1980] ECR 3881, at para. 10.
[19] Case 2/74 *Reyners* v. *Belgian State* [1974] ECR 631.
[20] See e.g. Case 120/78, *Rewe Zentrale AG* v. *Bundesmonopolverwaltung für Branntwein*, [1979] ECR 649 (goods); Case C–415/93, *Union royale belge des sociétés de football association ASBL* v. *Bosman* [1995] ECR I–4921 (workers); Case C–55/94, *Gebhard* v. *Consilio dell'Ordine degli Avvocati e Procuratori e Milano* [1995] ECR I–4165 (establishment); and Case C–76/90, *Sager* v. *Dennemeyer* [1991] ECR I–4221 (services).
[21] Joined Cases 110–111/78 *Ministère Public* v. *Van Wesemael* [1979] ECR 35.
[22] Case 62/79 *Coditel* [1980] ECR 881.
[23] Case 279/80 *Webb* [1981] ECR 3305.
[24] Case 205/84 *Commission* v. *Germany* [1986] ECR 3755.
[25] Case C–180/89 *Commission* v. *Italy* [1991] ECR I–709.

It could also be argued that the Court of Justice has been careful not to substitute a "European" standard in areas where no such standard could be said to exist. The question referred to in *The Netherlands* v. *Reed*[26] concerned the right of the unmarried companion of a British national working in the Netherlands to join her partner and to receive a residence permit for this purpose. Although secondary Community legislation provided for a right of residence and other socio-economic rights for the spouse and family members of a migrant worker, no such rights were explicitly provided for unmarried partners. When rejecting the argument that the notion of "spouse" in Regulation 1612/68[27] should be extended to unmarried partners the Court replied that such an extension would be unjustifiable, given the absence of consensus and the lack of a "general social development" amongst all Member States which would justify such a broad construction. Article 10 of the Regulation was held to refer to marital relationships only. Moreover, the Court held that:

> "any interpretation of a legal term on the basis of social developments must take into account the situation in the whole Community, not merely in one of the Member States"[28]

Similarly, when analysing whether the Treaty precluded the United Kingdom's legislation banning lotteries for reasons related to social policy and the prevention of fraud in *Customs and Excise* v. *Schindler*,[29] the Court recalled the moral, religious and cultural aspects of lotteries and other types of gaming in the Member States. Such considerations led Member States to limit and even prohibit lotteries and gaming to prevent the practice from becoming a source of personal enrichment. Furthermore, given the amount of money which they generate, lotteries involve high risks of crime and fraud and they invite people to spend, which has its own harmful social and individual consequences. These factors led the Court to hold that the national authorities of each Member State should enjoy a sufficiently wide margin of appreciation to determine how to protect lottery participants and, given the socio-cultural characteristics of each Member State, to determine how lotteries are operated, the size of the stakes and the allocation of profits. As long as the restrictions imposed by Member States were not discriminatory, it was up to them to decide whether it was necessary, not only to restrict lottery activities, but also to ban them.[30]

However, this deference to the standards adopted by different Member States is a double-edged sword, particularly when it comes to determining if

---

[26] Case 59/85 [1986] ECR 1283.

[27] 1968 JO L257/2.

[28] *Supra* n. 26, at para. 13. In the event, the Court held that the right of a worker to be accompanied by his or her unmarried partner constitutes a social advantage within the meaning of Art. 7(2) of the Regulation. To the extent that Dutch nationals enjoyed such an advantage, it had to be extended to workers from other Member States.

[29] Case C–275/92 [1994] ECR I–1039.

[30] *Ibid.*, at paras. 59–61.

the activity in question constitutes a service within the meaning of the Treaty in the first place. Thus, in *Grogan*, when defining abortion as a service and, in response to SPUC's arguments that a grossly immoral activity could not be considered as such, the Court stated that:

> "It is not for the Court to substitute its assessment for that of the legislature in those Member States where the activities in question are practised legally".[31]

Phelan and Whelan have suggested that the Court could, or indeed should, have considered Ireland's constitutional norms when defining abortion as a service, rather than deferring

> "to the more permissive rules adopted in other Member States pursuant to their assessment of this moral question, which permitted the commercial termination of pregnancy in a variety of circumstances".[32]

However, such an approach would fly in the face of the Court's broad approach to the definition of key Treaty terms such as goods, workers and services, which delimit its personal scope. Moreover, the argument that a "service" which is illegal in one Member State cannot be regarded as one "normally provided for remuneration" pursuant to Articles 59 ff. is a non-starter. The service in question in *Grogan* was provided in a Member State where, although subject to legislative restrictions and conditions, it was legal.[33]

In the same vein, the Court rejected the arguments submitted to it by a number of Member States in *Schindler* to the effect that lotteries could not constitute economic activities within the meaning of the Treaty provisions on services since they were subject in a number of Member States to strict control due to their harmful nature and were often limited to objectives of general interest such as public fund-raising. Pointing out that lotteries were in fact rather commonplace in the Community, the Court stated that even if the morality of such lotteries was at least questionable, it was not for the Court of Justice to substitute its assessment for that of the legislatures of the Member States where such activities are practised legally.[34]

---

[31] Case C–159/90, *supra* n. 28, at para. 20.

[32] See D. R. Phelan and A. Whelan, "National Constitutional Law and European Integration" (Berlin, Report for the XVII FIDE Conference, 1996), 292, at 315.

[33] See also Case 15/78 *Société Générale Alsacienne de Banques SA* v. *Koestler* [1978] ECR 1971 (stock-exchange transactions regarded as an illegal wagering contract in one Member State but not in another) and *Schindler* (lotteries), which suggest that provided a remunerated activity is lawful in one Member State it will constitute a service within the meaning of the Treaty. As regards the public or private nature of a service and the consequences for the criterion of remuneration, see S. O'Leary, *The Evolving Concept of Community Citizenship: From the Free Movement of Persons to Union Citizenship* (London, Kluwer, 1996) 65, at 75 ff.

[34] *Supra* n. 29, at para. 32. See further J. M. Fernández Martín and S. O'Leary, "Judicial Exceptions to the Free Provision of Services" (1995) 1 *Euro. LJ* 308, where the authors discuss whether the Court has been consistent when fashioning judicial exceptions to free movement.

AN OVERVIEW OF THE EUROPEAN COMMUNITY SOLUTIONS TO IRISH
PROBLEMS

Handoll has argued that Community law places a straitjacket on the assertion of national powers and interests which in some way affect the operation of the Community.[35] To illustrate this point he cites the Court of Justice's rulings in *Campus Oil* v. *Minister for Industry and Energy*,[36] *Groener* v. *Minister for Education and the City of Dublin Vocational Education College*[37] and *Grogan*.[38] In *Campus Oil* the Court is said to have insisted that an exception to the fundamental principle of free movement could be justified only if it was necessary to protect the interests which the Member State sought to secure and did not create obstacles to free movement which were disproportionate to those objectives. In *Groener* the Court is said to have placed conditions on the imposition of the linguistic requirement which it ultimately allowed to pass muster, and in *Grogan*, although the Court was able to avoid a head-on conflict between national constitutional law and European Community law on the free provision of services, Handoll points out that Advocate General van Gerven's Opinion stressed that the national rule, which he regarded as coming within the scope of Community law, must comply with the requirements of objective necessity and proportionality. The latter requirement, according to the Advocate General, would not be satisfied in the case of a ban on pregnant women going abroad, or their being subject to unsolicited examinations on their return.

A number of commentators have discussed the tensions which may result from a supranational entity such as the EU placing different values on rights or interests than those placed at national level.[39] As De Witte points out, although when it protects fundamental rights the Court of Justice seeks inspiration from the European Convention of Human Rights (ECHR) and the constitutional traditions common to the Member States:

> "[C]onstitutions are not mere copies of a universalist idea, they also reflect the idiosyncratic choices and preferences of the constituents and are the highest legal expression of the country's value system."[40]

Rules adopted in the course of implementing the Community's objectives may come into conflict with the values enshrined in national constitutions and the

---

[35] See J. Handoll, "The Protection of National Interests in the European Union" (1994) 2 *Irish J of Euro. L* 221, at 239.

[36] Case 72/83 [1984] ECR 2727.

[37] Case C–379/87 [1989] ECR 3967.

[38] Case 182/83 *Fearon* v. *Irish Land Commission* [1984] ECR 3677 is also discussed by J. Handoll, *supra* n. 35, at 240.

[39] See, *inter alia*, J. Handoll, *supra* n. 35; D. G. Metropoulos, "Human Rights, Incorporated: The European Community's New Line of Business" (1992) 29 *Stanford LJ* 131, 152; and B. De Witte, *supra* n. 4.

[40] B. De Witte, *supra* n. 4, at 8.

fact that common constitutional traditions do not always exist, suggests that such conflict is unavoidable. Realisation that membership of the EC prevents Member States from universally protecting their national interests may provoke shock and even anger at national level.[41] However, Handoll implies with respect to the aforementioned cases that the Court of Justice failed to display a suitable degree of discretion when faced with a conflict between national interests and Community policies.[42] This interpretation of the *Campus Oil*, *Groener* and *Grogan* cases is misleading, since these three cases are prime examples of the Court persevering to find a Community response to Article 177 references which would accommodate what were essentially national problems.

At issue in *Campus Oil* was an Irish legislative requirement that petrol importers purchase 35 per cent of their requirements from a state-owned oil refinery at prices fixed by the Irish government. This obligation was regarded by the Court of Justice as a measure equivalent to a quantitative restriction which fell within the scope of the prohibition in Article 30 EC. The Irish government argued that the importance of oil for the life of the country meant that Ireland must be able to maintain its own refining capacity and that the objective of the impugned legislation was simply to ensure that the products of the national refinery could be marketed. Despite the fact that Community legislation concerning the protection of oil supplies existed, albeit not comprehensive legislation, and despite the unmistakeably economic nature of the underlying issue—whether the national refinery should operate at a profit or loss—the Court held that:

> "in the light of the seriousness of the consequences that an interruption in supplies of petroleum products may have for a country's existence, the aim of ensuring a minimum supply of petroleum products at all times is to be regarded as transcending purely economic considerations and thus as capable of constituting an objective covered by the concept of public security".[43]

Although the Court added the usual rider regarding the proportionality of such derogations,[44] the obligation on importers to purchase over a third of their requirements at a fixed price from the national refinery survived.

The *Groener* case concerned the compatibility with Community law, and the principles of free movement and non-discrimination in particular, of the

---

[41] The Art. 177 EC reference concerning the compatibility of the state alcohol monopoly in Sweden with the Treaty provisions on the free movement of goods has provoked fierce controversy and debate at national level, with government ministers implying that a finding of incompatibility by the Court might not be followed. See the outcome of Case C–189/95 *Allmänna Åklagaren* v. *Harry Franzén* [1995] judgment of the Court of 23 Oct. 1997 (not yet reported). Sweden regards the State alcohol monopoly as an essential public health measure. In his Opinion of 4 Mar. 1997, Elmer AG interpreted Arts. 30 and 37 EC as precluding such a monopoly and held that, taken as a whole, such a scheme could not be justified with reference to the protection of human health in Art. 36 EC.

[42] *Supra* n. 35, at 239 and 245.

[43] *Supra* n. 36, at para. 35.

[44] *Ibid.*, at para. 37.

Irish legislative requirement that employees in the public sector be competent in the Irish language. After two years' employment on a part-time basis, Mrs Groener, a Dutch national, applied for a permanent post as an art teacher in a vocational college in Ireland. She was recommended for the post but was not appointed, having failed a special oral test in Irish. She alleged that the language criterion, which applied indistinctly to nationals and non-nationals, constituted indirect discrimination contrary to Article 3 of EC Regulation 1612/68 on the free movement of workers within the Community. An exception is provided by the latter provision with respect to "conditions relating to linguistic knowledge required by reason of the nature of the post to be filled". The Court of Justice found that the nature of the post sought by Mrs Groener—the teaching of art essentially or exclusively through English—was such that knowledge of Irish was not required for the performance of the duties which such teaching entails.[45] Nevertheless, it held that this finding was not sufficient in itself to enable the national court to determine whether the linguistic requirement was justified within the meaning of Article 3(1) of the Regulation. The Court conceded that in furtherance of the policy for the protection and promotion of a language which is, by virtue of the Constitution, both the national and the first official language of a Member State, teachers can be required to have some knowledge of that language. Thus, the permanent teaching post in the public sector to which Mrs Groener aspired was covered by the language exception in the Regulation. The Court did, as Handoll points out, insist that the language requirement be imposed as part of a policy promoting the national language and that it be applied in a non-discriminatory and proportionate way. However, the underlying rationale of the judgment was clearly to facilitate Ireland's cultural and constitutional commitment to the promotion of its ailing language. The importance of cultural diversity and identity and the protection of minority languages in the Community, especially in the context of a Member State with a historical and cultural background as particular as Ireland's, was not lost on the Court.

Finally, in *Grogan*, SPUC had sought an injunction in the High Court to prevent university students' associations from distributing abortion information and a declaration to the effect that their activities were contrary to Article 40.3.3 of the Constitution. Having distinguished the *Open Door* case, where the Supreme Court had refused to make a reference on the ground that Community law was not relevant, Carroll J held that an Article 177 reference was necessary, since the issue in *Grogan* was the right to impart and receive information in one Member State as a corollary to the lawful provision of a service in another. In the event, however, the Court of Justice held that although the provision of abortion constitutes a service within the meaning of the EC Treaty, the link between the students' associations and the abortion clinics operating in another Member State was too tenuous for the prohibi-

---

[45] *Supra* n. 37, at para. 15.

tion on the distribution of information to be regarded as a restriction within the meaning of Article 59 EC. The Court's approach in *Grogan*, in contrast to that of the Advocate General, has been characterised as follows:

"One is left with the suspicion that [its] approach in *Grogan* is a clever judicial strat- agem, enabling it, with a great sigh of relief, to avoid dipping as much as its little finger in the murky waters of morality or to engage in a balancing exercise as to the relative strength of competing (highly sensitive) fundamental rights".[46]

Quite apart from the approach of the Court of Justice in the *Grogan* case, the protocol subsequently annexed to the TEU "illustrates an unprecedented degree of deference on the part of the Community constituent power to a fun- damental constitutional commitment of a Member State".[47]

Rather than the free movement provisions of the Treaty strait-jacketing national interests, the latter were clearly given precedence in these cases, despite the discriminatory nature of the national legislation at issue or, at the very least, its capacity to distort or impede free movement.

THE NOTION OF A EUROPEAN DEMOCRATIC SOCIETY

One commentator has suggested that the resolution of the conflict in the X case between the constitutional ban on abortion and the fundamental free- doms guaranteed by EC law required that socio-political sacrifices and com- promises be made in order to achieve some form of economic unity.[48] Similarly, the Court of Justice was said in *Grogan* to have used the rhetoric of human rights to extend its jurisdiction into areas previously reserved to Member States' courts, thereby expanding the scope and impact of Community law.[49] Although one of the Community's fundamental economic freedoms was partially at issue in that case—the free provision of a service legally provided in the United Kingdom—the key issue related to the right to travel, a fundamental right which Member State nationals enjoy regardless of their involvement in any economic activity. A narrow reading of X (or at least the judgment of Costello J in the High Court) and *Grogan* which focuses on a possible limitation by virtue of EC law of the fundamental right to life of the unborn in favour of the free exercise of the Community's fundamental economic freedoms is misguided. As De Búrca points out, a number of fun- damental rights were competing in *Grogan* and if the Court of Justice had fol- lowed the Advocate General, any "justificatory test" would have constituted, not an attempt to promote trade at the expense of national interests, but

[46] See D. Curtin's annotation of Case C–159/90, (1992) 29 *CML Rev.* 585, at 596.
[47] See D. R. Phelan and A. Whelan, *supra* n. 32, at 319.
[48] See S. S. Stoffregen, "Abortion and the Freedom to Travel in the EEC: A Perspective on *Attorney General* v. *X*" (1993) 28 *New England L Rev.* 543, at 544.
[49] See J. Coppell and A. O'Neill, "The European Court of Justice: Taking Rights Seriously?" (1992) 29 *CML Rev.* 669, at 692.

rather an attempt to settle or reconcile two conflicting claims by accepting the compatibility of a national aim pursuing a genuine interest while ensuring that it did not unduly restrict other important human rights and freedoms.[50] In his judgment in the 1997 decision in *SPUC* v. *Grogan*,[51] Keane J was clearly willing to balance and reconcile different constitutional rights.

The existence of competing rights and freedoms was not lost on the European Court of Human Rights, which held in the *Open Door* case that the prohibition of non-directive counselling imparting information to pregnant women concerning abortion facilities outside Ireland was contrary to the freedom of expression enshrined in Article 10 of the European Convention on Human Rights (ECHR). The Court accepted that Article 40.3.3 of the Constitution is based on profound moral values concerning the nature of life. Furthermore:

> "it is not possible to find in the legislative and social orders of the Contracting States a uniform European conception of morals, and the State authorities are, in principle, in a better position that the international judge to give an Opinion on the exact content of the requirements of morals as well as on the "necessity" of a "restriction" or "penalty" intended to meet them. However, this power of appreciation is not unlimited".[52]

Given the absolute nature of the Supreme Court injunction, imposing a perpetual restraint on the provision of information, the fact that no link had been established between the provision of information and the destruction of unborn life, the fact that similar information was available elsewhere and that the injunction had been largely ineffective in preventing large numbers of Irish women from continuing to obtain abortions in Great Britain,[53] the Court of Human Rights held that the restriction was not proportionate to the legitimate aim pursued by the constitutional guarantee of the right to life.

While he concurred with the Opinion of the European Commission of Human Rights in the *Open Door* case, Schermers had based his decision on the fact that the prohibition of non-directive counselling by welfare clinics in Ireland constituted interference with the clinics' freedom of expression contrary to Article 10 ECHR. In particular, he considered that such a restriction was not necessary in a democratic society:

> "The Convention is a European convention. Therefore the European democratic society must be the model. Traditionally, European society is a society of nation States. Each European State has its own cultural and moral values which may not be identical to the values of the other European States . . . it is therefore justified to look first at the meaning of necessity for the State concerned. . . . But what is necessary for the State concerned cannot be decisive. The Convention requires that

---

[50] G. De Búrca, "Fundamental Human Rights and the Reach of European Community Law" (1993) 13 *OJLS* 283, at 299.

[51] *Supra* n. 14.

[52] *Supra* n. 8, at para. 68.

[53] *Supra* n. 8, at paras. 73–76.

restrictions on freedom of expression must be necessary in a democratic society in general. Account must therefore be taken of other democratic societies as well."[54]

A similar notion of common European standards also flows from the Opinion of Advocate General Jacobs in *Christos Konstantinidis*.[55] That case involved a Greek national, resident and working in Germany in a self-employed capacity who argued that the incorrect transcription of his name in latin characters in the civil register hampered his free movement, since it could cause confusion amongst his clients. Advocate General Jacobs argued that:

"a Community national who goes to another Member State as a worker or self-employed person under Articles 48, 52 or 59 of the Treaty is entitled not just to pursue his trade or profession and to enjoy the same living and working conditions as nationals of the host State; he is in addition entitled to assume that, wherever he goes to earn his living in the European Community, he will be treated in accordance with a common code of fundamental values, in particular those laid down in the European Convention on Human Rights. In other words, he is entitled to say 'civis europeus sum' and to invoke that status in order to oppose any violation of his fundamental rights."[56]

The evolving nature of the rights guaranteed by the Irish Constitution has been accepted by the Irish Courts. Walsh J emphasised in *McGee v. Attorney General*,[57] for example, that:

"It is but natural that from time to time the prevailing ideas of these virtues [prudence, justice and charity] may be conditioned by the passage of time; no interpretation of the Constitution is intended to be final for all time. It is given in the light of prevailing ideas and concepts".

In contrast, the Supreme Court's decision in *Norris* seemed to be premised on the idea that a sacred trust was placed by the Constitution on the Irish State to uphold the morality and "Christian beliefs" of Irish society.[58] Walsh's vision of an evolving Constitution is to be preferred, but it is suggested that the passage of time is no longer the only factor which will breathe life into and condition the values and interests guaranteed by the Constitution. "International" judges, as the European Court of Human Rights emphasised in *Open Door*, must remain sensitive to the margin of appreciation enjoyed by national authorities when sensitive national interests are at stake.

---

[54] *Ibid.*

[55] Case C–168/91 [1993] ECR I–1191.

[56] *Ibid.*, at para. 46. Note that the Court of Justice decided the issue on narrower grounds. See, however, Case C–334/94 *Commission v. France* [1996] ECR I–1307, where, in a case concerning the registration of vessels not used in the exercise of an economic activity, Fennelly AG, at 1328, held that the bounds of rights enjoyed as corollaries to free movement must be defined by reference to the essential human as well as economic needs of those who avail of the primary Treaty right. The Court, at para. 21, also regarded access to leisure activities as a corollary to the freedom of movement guaranteed by the treaty.

[57] [1974] IR 284, at 319.

[58] *Norris v. Attorney General* [1984] IR 36, at 64.

Nevertheless, membership of the EU and accession to human rights conventions such as the ECHR mean that, on the one hand, the Irish courts are no longer the sole judicial bodies to which recourse may be had when individual (fundamental) rights are infringed and, on the other, the values and interests to which Irish society adheres may no longer be restricted to those prevalent when the Constitution was adopted in 1937.[59]

The European Court of Human Rights and the European Court of Justice will no doubt become embroiled again in problems relating to the protection of national interests, the answers to which would once have been sought and found within the confines of the State. It is not one of the objectives of the EC that a Member State should be obliged to set at nought the constitutional guarantees for the protection within the State of fundamental human rights guaranteed in the Constitution.[60] Indeed, Article F.1 of the TEU expressly provides that the Union shall "respect the national identities of its Member States, whose systems of government are founded on the principles of democracy" and Article F.2 repeats the principle oft-cited in the jurisprudence of the Court, that the European Union shall respect fundamental rights, as guaranteed by the ECHR and as they result from the constitutional traditions common to the Member States. When the Member States' constitutional traditions are not shared, problems will emerge regarding the correct balance to be achieved between diverse and even competing national interests and the interests of the Community. However, twenty years after accession to the then EEC, is it surprising that restrictions of the right to information or the right to travel to another Member State to avail of a service practised legally there provoked dismay, criticism and even judicial censure at European level?

---

[59] See *supra* n. 14, where Denham J spoke in the 1997 Supreme Court decision in *Grogan* of constitutional rights and duties in an "ongoing situation".

[60] See Walsh J, *supra* n. 5, at 769.

23

Politics Beyond Parties and the Irish Constitution

STEPHEN LIVINGSTONE

INTRODUCTION

It is a paradox of the late twentieth century that, just as free elections and representative democracy are becoming an international norm,[1] political representatives in advanced democracies have rarely been less popular. Membership of political parties is generally in decline, and recent studies of political engagement indicate that many people, notably young people, display little interest in joining or becoming involved in the work of political parties. Revelations of financial scandals involving politicians, notably the beef scandal in Ireland,[2] have served to increase cynicism over the extent to which politicians act in the public interest. However, these same studies do not indicate widespread political apathy or a retreat into consumerism but rather a growing interest in the work of non-governmental groups, such as Amnesty International or Greenpeace, which seek to campaign on specific issues such as human rights or the environment without seeking electoral office. Politics, it seems, is still a matter of public interest, but it is taking on new forms and new questions.

That politics should be carried on beyond political parties is not, of course, an entirely new phenomenon. Since the birth of parliamentary democracies and, perhaps even more significantly, the administrative state, pressure groups have formed on issues which government had responsibility for but which did not always seem to find an adequate hearing in the political process. Prison administration and the welfare of children are two obvious examples. In addition governments and political parties have often thought it wise to interact with associations representing significant social or economic interests, such as employers, trade unions, churches or the professions. As we shall see in more

---

[1] See e.g. J. Crawford, "Democracy and International Law" (1993) *British YB of Int. Law* 113, and "Democratization and International Law: Building Institutions of Civil Society" (1994) 88 *Proceedings of the American Society of International Law* 197.

[2] See F. O'Toole, *Meanwhile Back at the Ranch: The Politics of Irish Beef* (London, Vintage, 1995).

detail later, the Irish State has a particularly significant history of engagement with the idea that sectoral or vocational interests should play a role in formation and execution of State policy. While traditional pressure groups and sectoral interests remain important, there are a number of features of these new forms of politics beyond political parties which suggest this phenomenon poses new challenges for political decision-making and the organisation of the State.

First, such groups tend to be self-defining in character, as opposed to being the representatives of particular interests, and to have organised around personal or cultural issues which have not previously featured highly on politicians' agendas. Moreover the issues on which such groups have organised, such as the environment, gender or sexuality, are not necessarily the preserve of one government department alone or even exclusively of the State. Environmental groups, for example, have targeted multinational corporations just as much as State agencies and have sought to influence both. Secondly, such groups now operate in a variety of fora, rather than simply seeking to lobby national politicians and the national media. Some, like Amnesty or Greenpeace, are large international organisations themselves which are used to operating in a variety of national settings as well as in international fora such as the United Nations or European Union. Even groups whose focus is on issues in one particular State have sought to utilise international organisations to put pressure on their own State to act or bypass them to obtain resources to carry out a project themselves.[3] Many an advocacy group has found that thinking locally but acting globally is just as important as doing the opposite. Thirdly, many of these groups are much better organised than their predecessors. Again this is especially true for the larger, international, organisations many of whose tasks are now carried out by a professional staff of career activists. However a whole industry has also arisen in most advanced democracies to provide training and support for even local women's groups or community organisations. As a result they are likely to be much more adept at obtaining media coverage (which itself has expanded with the growth of media outlets) and dealing with State agencies than was true of some of the pressure groups of the past.

Why this growth of interest and involvement in non-governmental groups has come about is a matter of conjecture. Anthony Giddens' recent account of the political challenges facing the modern world[4] provides one provocative suggestion. Giddens argues that we live in a world characterised by increasing *social reflexivity*, where an increasingly well-educated and well-informed populus has become less willing to accept the views of tradition or authority

---

[3] For examples from Northern Ireland of this phenomenon, see J. Morison and S. Livingstone, *Reshaping Public Power: Northern Ireland and the British Constitutional Crisis* (London, Sweet and Maxwell 1995), ch. 6.

[4] A. Giddens, *Beyond Left and Right: The Future of Radical Politics* (Cambridge, Polity Press, 1994).

with regard to its conduct. As he observes, "[i]n a world of clever people, however, most people most of the time know most of what the government knows".[5] One consequence of this development of social reflexivity is that people become less willing to trust the State to solve their problems or even look to it at all, thus fuelling calls for the "downsizing" of government and the transfer of its functions to the private sector or voluntary organisations. Another is that people become more prepared to redefine the political agenda to deal with what they see as their particular needs, and more confident in acting on this agenda rather than deferring to the expertise of the State. If this analysis is correct then it would suggest that the recent development of extra-parliamentary activity in advanced democracies and the way in which this has redefined the issues for public concern are unlikely to be a temporary phenomenon. Existing governments and political parties need to find ways of interacting with this new sector and its concerns (without seeking to absorb or colonise them) if political decision making is not to be drained of popular commitment and eventually of popular legitimacy.

POLITICS BEYOND POLITICAL PARTIES AND THE IRISH CONSTITUTION

The 1937 Constitution clearly makes party politicians the central political actors in the State. By requiring that the *Taoiseach* and all but two members of the Government must be members of *Dáil Eireann*,[6] by requiring the *Taoiseach* to resign if he does not continue to enjoy the support of *Dáil Eireann*,[7] and by vesting all executive power in the Government[8] and all legislative power in the *Oireachtas*,[9] the Constitution ensures that the direction of the State is a matter for the leaders of political parties.

However things could have been otherwise. In the 1930s arguments for the development of the State in a corporatist or vocationalist direction gained significant levels of support among Irish intellectuals.[10] Drawing inspiration from Pius XI's encyclical *Quadragesimo Anno* (issued in 1931), the vocationalists sought to present their version of corporatism as a "middle way" between communism and fascism. Their primary objective was the creation of a Vocational Council composed of representatives of occupational groupings. By establishing what they claimed would be a disinterested body acting in the public good the vocationalists argued citizens would be protected against either capitalist exploitation or bureaucratic oppression. The most extensive

---

[5] *Ibid.*, at 94.
[6] See Articles 28.7.1 and 28.7.2 of the Constitution
[7] Art. 28.10.
[8] Art. 28.2.
[9] Art. 15.2.1.
[10] For a discussion of the vocationalist movement see T. Brown, *Ireland: A Social and Cultural History* (London, Fontana, 1985), 161–5, and J. J. Lee, *Ireland 1912–1985: Politics and Society* (Cambridge, Cambridge University Press, 1989), 271–7.

statement of the vocationalist position came in the report of the Commission on Vocational Organisation, published in 1944. As Lee observes, this report was incisively critical of the performance of the Irish Civil Service and contained much thought-provoking material.[11] However, its long and prolix character of 300,000 words, failure to cost proposals or explain how the proposed Vocational Council would relate to the *Oireachtas* made its acceptance unlikely by politicians or civil servants; especially by a *Fianna Fáil* government which had just won a handsome majority in the 1944 election and saw little reason to share power with another organisation. Lee observes that the vocationalist arguments were not so much confronted as squashed.[12]

Moreover the date of the report, seven years after the new Constitution was established, showed that the vocationalists had already lost the main argument. The Commission was very much a consolation prize. Nevertheless the 1937 Constitution did show some traces of contemporary vocationalist thinking in the "special position" for the Catholic Church,[13] the power for the *Oireachtas* to "provide for the establishment or recognition of functional or vocational councils representing branches of the social and economic life of the people",[14] and the composition of the *Seanad*. The third of these is the most obvious bow in the corporatist direction with Article 18.7.1 providing that forty-three of the sixty members of the upper house should be elected from five panels representing aspects of national life. As Brown observes, however, the fact that vocationalist ideas were given recognition only in the largely powerless *Seanad* shows how muted their reception was.[15] Moreover, the electors for the panel system are composed of *Dáil* Deputies, outgoing Senators and members of country councils and country boroughs. As a result party politics has reasserted itself and the composition of the *Seanad* proves not to be significantly different from that of the *Dáil*. When this is added to the fact that the designation of aspects of national life has remained unaltered since 1937 and does not include groups, such as women or travellers, who might be thought appropriate for representation now, it is not surprising that the Constitutional Review Group came to the conclusion that "[t]he current system of *Seanad* representation is in theory vocational but, as we have argued, in practice is not".[16]

Nor have the other vocational elements of the Constitution proved a great success. The special position of the Catholic Church proved increasingly controversial within the Republic and a significant impediment to better relations with the Protestant population of Northern Ireland. It was eventually repealed

---

[11] J. J. Lee, "Aspects of Corporatist Thought in Ireland: The Commission on Vocational Organisations 1939–43" in A. Cosgrove and D. McCartney (eds.), *Studies in Irish History Presented to R. Dudley Edwards* (Dublin, 1979), at 324.

[12] See Lee, *supra* n. 10, at 277.

[13] Art. 44.1.2, subsequently repealed by the Fifth Amendment to the Constitution Act 1972.

[14] Art. 15.3.1.

[15] See T. Brown, *supra* n. 10, at 165.

[16] *Report of the Constitution Review Group* (Dublin, Stationery Office, 1996), 69.

by the Fifth Amendment of the Constitution Act in 1972. The Article 15.3.1 provision on the establishment or recognition of "functional or vocational councils" has never been used, and Casey, writing in 1987, took the view that it "is now probably redundant".[17]

However the vocational influences are not the limit of the Irish Constitution's extension of political power beyond political parties. Two other devices, those of referendums to amend the constitution and judicial review, stand out as more successful examples of the way in which the Irish constitution has moved beyond the exclusive focus on political parties characteristic of the Westminster system. Although under the 1937 Constitution a referendum to amend the constitution may be initiated only by *Dáil Eireann*,[18] unlike its Free State predecessor which permitted initiation on the basis of a petition of 75,000 voters, governments have increasingly resorted to referendums to deal with some of the most contentious political issues of the day. These include divorce, abortion and membership of the European Union. While political parties have often campaigned vigorously on one side or other of a proposal for constitutional amendment, referendums have also offered the opportunity for non-party organisations to become more significantly involved in the resolution of important questions of State policy. Judicial review has functioned as a vehicle for non-governmental groups to influence political decision-making since the Supreme Court began the development of the fundamental rights provisions in *Ryan v. Attorney General*.[19] Where such groups can identify a fundamental right which legislation or government action infringes they can utilise the courts to challenge such action. In recent years the use of the courts in this way, notably by pro-life and pro-choice groups in relation to abortion information, has forced political parties to deal more seriously with issues they might prefer to ignore and engage with viewpoints they might otherwise avoid.

NEO-CORPORATISM AND CONSTITUTIONAL CHOICES

While the vocational elements of the Constitution may currently be in decline the 1990s have witnessed a significant flourishing of corporatist institutions and practices in Irish political life. Examples include the Council on the Status of Women and the National Youth Council of Ireland. Both of these organisations facilitate the filtering to government of the views of a large number of groups representing interests which have traditionally found themselves marginalised or indeed excluded from the concerns of traditional political parties. Most significantly there has been the evolution of the idea of "social partnership" in the area of economic and social policy. Via the institution of the

---

[17] J. Casey, *Constitutional Law in Ireland* (London, Sweet and Maxwell, 1987), 90.
[18] Art. 46.2.
[19] [1965] IR 294.

National Economic and Social Forum the experiment in social partnership has brought together senior civil servants with the representatives of trade unions, employers and farmers to agree on wide-ranging social policies including wage restraint, health spending, taxation and welfare reform. In addition to establishing the initial programme the social partnership experiment has provided for ongoing review and dialogue between all the social partners. The initial *Programme for National Recovery* (1987–90), followed by the subsequent *Programme for Economic and Social Progress* (1990–3) and *Programme for Competitiveness and Work* (1993–6) are credited with making a significant contribution to reversing the indebtedness of the Irish economy and providing the basis for economic growth. Moreover, far from inhibiting effective decision-making, a regular criticism of the consultation requirements implicit in corporatist arrangements, social partnership appears to have improved it. As O'Donnell and O'Reardon observe:

"following a decade of political drift, the ability of government to take strategic, non pragmatic decisions, seems to have increased considerably under the new regime of social partnership"[20]

In common with many other advanced democracies Ireland has also witnessed an expansion of involvement in non-governmental organisations concerned with social and political issues, such as the environment, human rights or the position of travellers. It may also be argued that the advent of near permanent coalition government itself indicates a trend towards a more pluralist style of politics. Whereas in the past political parties may have seen their best electoral strategy as lying in assembling a package of policies designed to prove more convincing to a majority of voters than the package offered by rival parties, now it may be more advantageous to focus on issues particularly dear to the hearts of one section of the public even if this alienates others. Where government has engaged with groups other than political parties in recent times it has largely been on a voluntary basis. Organisations such as the Council on the Status of Women or the National Economic and Social Forum do not have any statutory basis, nor is the government's relationship to the participant groups legally defined. For observers of the Constitution the issue is whether they should be, and indeed whether the Constitution itself should give recognition to such developments. When the Constitution Review Group came to examine such issues it did recognise that developments had taken place and expressed the view that:

"the fact that so many new participatory structures have been established is itself an indication of the weakness of the existing systems of representation and the lack of flexibility within them to allow for change".[21]

---

[20] R. O'Donnell and C. O'Reardon, *Ireland's Experiment in Social Partnership 1987–96* (Dublin, National Economic and Social Council, 1996), 6.
[21] See *Report of the Constitution Review Group, supra* n. 16, at 42.

However its recommendations went no further than a proposed amendment to Article 15.3.1 to substitute "advisory or consultative bodies representing branches of the social, community, voluntary and economic life of the people, with a view to improving participation in and the efficiency of, the democratic process" for the now outdated "functional or vocational councils". Commentators have observed that this essentially reflects a concern with tidying up the constitution and does not fully explore the implications of such new forms of political organisation.[22] The Report also recommended further consideration of the membership of the *Seanad* in the light of criticisms of its representative character. Some members would be prepared to go further in updating the vocational groups from which it draws its membership to include groups such as the National Women's Council of Ireland or travellers' groups.[23] However, while its powers remain limited and it has to deal with a wide range of issues, it is unlikely that a reconstituted *Seanad* will satisfy the needs of many non-governmental organisations. Indeed, if this were all that was on offer they may well see it as a step backwards, swapping the direct access to ministers and civil servants that many such groups have now for a more distant influence on legislation in a body where they would be heavily outnumbered by the representatives of established political parties.

In terms of a way forward three options suggest themselves. One would be to build on the recommendations of the Constitution Review Group, limited though they are. This would involve giving formal recognition to civil society groups through advisory or consultative councils. One could create such a council to correspond to each government department. The consultation process might then operate much as the present social partnership arrangements through the National Economic and Social Forum do, whereby government and the council members might agree a programme of action which would be made public and subject to regular review within the council framework. Strengthening the Article 15.3.1 requirement from one where the *Oireachtas* may create such arrangements to one where it is required to do so would ensure that such non-governmental organisations have a guaranteed place in government decision-making. Ultimate executive power and responsibility would remain with elected politicians, but a constitutional obligation to provide for consultation would require those politicians to consider ideas and arguments beyond those developed within their own parties. The formal character of such arrangements would also ensure that the extent to which civil society groups were consulted did not depend on the vagaries of media fashion or ministerial idiosyncrasy.

However, obvious problems exist with such an approach. One is that such consultation requirements paralyse decision-making and prevent governments responding sufficiently quickly to the rapid pace of events. However, as

---

[22] See e.g. J. Morison, "'A Disposition to Preserve and an Ability to Improve': The Report of the Constitution Review Group in the Republic of Ireland" [1997] *Public Law* 55.

[23] See Appendix 7 to the Report by Kathleen Lynch.

earlier discussion of the Economic and Social Forum experience demonstrates, this may not be such a problem as expected, even in an area (such as financial decision-making) where a premium is often placed on the need to respond rapidly to events. More serious may be difficulties over deciding who is sufficiently representative to be appointed to such consultative bodies. One of the consequences of the growth of civil society organisations is the fragmentation of a particular sphere within it and a greater degree of uncertainty as to who can claim to be representative. Should the State consult with a national organisation claiming to represent women or a local women's group in the area affected by a particular decision? Does this require the State to engage itself in establishing a set of criteria by which a group is regarded as representative? Moreover the extent to which a particular group is representative may change over time. Observers of German and Swedish corporatism have observed that the partnership between government, employers' federations and unions may become less able to deliver stable economic policies as either the employers' federations become less representative due to an influx of foreign capital or the unions due to the displacement of the manufacturing sector by the rise of the service sector.[24] No doubt many in the Ireland of 1937 felt that the Catholic Church could represent their interests, especially on social and moral questions, but this is clearly no longer the case.[25] These problems are not insurmountable. Many within the civil society sector are well aware of the problem of representativeness and are capable of taking steps to resolve it, for example by national organisations seeking themselves to consult with local groups, but this issue does need to be carefully examined in any more formal arrangement lest what might be an exciting form of partnership becomes an ossified ritual.

A second way forward might be to leave the constitutional relationship between the State and civil society groups where it is, one of informal arrangements at best, but take steps to empower such groups to make better use of these arrangements. Such an approach leaves the issue of who influences the vagaries of prevailing political dynamics but avoids the need for the State to specify any formal criteria of representation. Public sector reforms such as a Freedom of Information Act, 1997, which might enable civil society groups to obtain better information on the workings of government, or a stronger role for parliamentary committees, which in turn will need information from civil society groups to play this role, might go some way to achieving this.[26] Beyond these, government might assist the empowerment of such groups by providing funding for training of activists or guarantees of media access, perhaps through a public-access television channel. The courts can assist this

---

[24] Indeed some critics suggest that Ireland's partnership experiment may be vulnerable to similar pressures if the dependency on inward investment is not reduced: see R. O'Donnell and C. O'Reardon *supra* n. 20, at 6.

[25] See B. Girvin, "Church, State and the Irish Constitution: The Secularisation of Irish Politics?", 49 *Parliamentary Affairs* (1996) 599.

[26] For a discussion of such potential reforms, see T. Bourke, "Irish Public Sector Reform: A Review of Current Developments", 49 *Parliamentary Affairs* (1996) 485.

process by ensuring that *locus standi* rules are given a wide interpretation when civil society groups wish to subject government decisions to constitutional review.[27] One area of constitutional change which might be considered to assist this approach (although rejected by the Constitutional Review Group) is the provision that referendums may be initiated only by a resolution of *Dáil Eireann* rather than by a petition of citizens. However most of the government decisions which civil society groups seek to influence are unlikely to reach the level of constitutional amendment.

The two approaches discussed above retain the traditional model of civil society groups seeking to influence decisions taken by organs of the State. Both the executive and legislative power remains with the State and the issue is the extent to which groups other than politicians and political parties can influence or review such decisions. A third approach would be to devolve aspects of certain areas of government decision-making to such civil society groups themselves. Recent public sector reforms in the United Kingdom have come close to achieving this where, for example, the State contracts out care of the elderly to charities or the provision of public sector housing to housing associations.[28] Political theorists, such as Paul Hirst,[29] argue that while the impetus for such arrangements in the United Kingdom may have come simply from a desire to reduce public expenditure and weaken local government the model can be developed in a progressive direction to form the basis of a new partnership between the State and civil society. Drawing on ideas similar to those of Giddens, Hirst observes that the large bureaucratic welfare state may be less flexible and less accountable to the diverse needs of a plural citizenry than a variety of civil society groups. He suggests that the State may seek to devolve aspects of its social and economic functions to associations which may be able to perform these functions in a more imaginative and efficient way. Nevertheless Hirst acknowledges that such a strategy carries the risks of uneven levels of service provision throughout a State (one of the reasons why such functions were made the preserve of national welfare state provision in the first place) and of mistreatment of citizens by the association to which the function is devolved, for example by practising discrimination. Therefore the State should retain the role of setting minimum standards of service provision and guiding public standards, such as prohibitions against discrimination. One of the key features of Hirst's "associative democracy" is thus that it "bridges and transforms the division between state and civil society, 'pluralizing' the former and 'publicizing' the latter".[30]

---

[27] J. Casey, *supra* n. 17, at 279–82 observes that the Supreme Court took a somewhat restrictive view of standing in *Cahill* v. *Sutton* [1980] IR 269, but has not subsequently invoked it to deny *bona fide* applicants a hearing.

[28] For a summary of such developments, see C. Foster and F. Plowden, *The State Under Stress* (Buckingham, Open University Press, 1996), chs. 6 and 7.

[29] P. Hirst, *Associative Democracy: New Forms of Economic and Social Governance* (Cambridge, Polity Press, 1994).

[30] *Ibid.*, at 74.

Ireland has already had experience of a pluralist welfare state. In areas such as the provision of health or education, the State never assumed exclusive responsibility for the provision of public services, leaving the Church especially substantial involvement. However the State has not always ensured that the values by which the conduct of entirely public services are regulated have extended to other institutions providing services out of public money. As, in common with many other advanced democracies, Ireland struggles with how to reconstitute its welfare state in the twenty-first century, some elements of its experience may nevertheless be drawn upon to create a new partnership between the State and elements of civil society.

Moving political decision-making beyond the sphere of political parties may thus take a variety of forms. It may be indeed that different forms are appropriate for different types of decision; a consultative council for foreign policy, the contracting out of child protection to a variety of voluntary organisations etc. Irish constitutional history shows a recognition that a healthy democratic polity requires more than periodic public selection of political party representatives. The way in which this insight is developed may well determine the extent to which the exercise of State power continues to enjoy popular legitimacy.

24

Evaluating Constitutions—The Irish Constitution and the Limits of Constitutionalism

ADRIAN HUNT*

INTRODUCTION

F. F. Ridley has pointed out that "[h]aving a constitution seems to be a matter of self-respect: no state is properly dressed without [one]".[1] When considered at this level of abstraction on the sixtieth anniversary of Bunreacht na hÉireann we may all rightly celebrate the fact that we are at least dressed in some constitutional garb. However, whether or not we are properly or appropriately dressed is another matter, and this is one of the key questions which this volume seeks to address. How, one might well ask, is one supposed to do that? How can one measure appropriateness? As no doubt this collection of essays illustrates, people will differ about the degree of utility of our present constitutional arrangements. There is, however, inherent in the process of examining any set of constitutional arrangements, an assumption that in terms of function, constitutions are not merely abstract assertions embodying or symbolising some notion of statehood and independence. Rather it is assumed that constitutions "do things". Thus Brian Walsh wrote that the Irish Constitution:

> "is not simply a composition of exhortations or aspirations which it is hoped will be followed. It is the basic law which *distributes* powers and *imposes* obligations and *guarantees* rights . . . "[2]

This indicates that there is inherent in the process of constitution building, and the process of examining any set of constitutional arrangements, an implicit belief or trust in the functional, instrumental nature of constitutions.

It is this that I take as my starting-point in examining the appropriateness

* The author would like to thank Professor David Feldman for reading and discussing an earlier draft of this essay.

[1] F. F. Ridley, "There is no British Constitution: A Dangerous Case of the Emperor's New Clothes" (1988) 41 *Parliamentary Affairs* 340.

[2] J. Casey, *Constitutional Law in Ireland* (2nd edn., London, Sweet & Maxwell, 1992), p. vii (author's italics).

of the Irish constitutional arrangements as we enter the next millennium. That is to say that I shall examine the Irish Constitution in a functional or instrumental sense.[3] This requires first an examination of the formal constitutional scheme with a view to assessing whether or not the Irish Constitution actually delivers the type and form of government which, on the face of it, it purports to deliver. Secondly, it involves asking the question whether the Constitution addresses the types of matters which it ought to address. In short, does it purport to deliver what it is sensible, practical or reasonable to expect a constitution to deliver? In examining the Constitution in this way my objective is not so much to make specific prescriptions for the future. My concern is more with matters of nature, form and method, rather than substance. What follows, therefore, is more of a reflection on the role and functions of constitutions in a modern context than it is a definitive survey of the substantive constitutional provisions in a detailed sense. The essay adopts a twofold division as the basis for discussion of the issues mentioned above, which is largely dictated by the logic of the general constitutional scheme set out in the Constitution. First, the institutional dimension will be addressed. This involves examining the extent to which the Constitution actually delivers the type and form of government which the Constitution purports to establish. Secondly, the "rights" dimension will be addressed. This involves a consideration of the utility of "rights" as a distinct *legal* form of protection attaching to individuals within the Irish constitutional context.

THE INSTITUTIONAL FRAMEWORK

The most striking feature of the arrangements for government set out in the Constitution is the obvious disjuncture between the constitutional scheme at the institutional level on the one hand, and political reality on the other. The Constitution vests ultimate sovereignty in the people[4] and it establishes the *Oireachtas* as the dominant body for the making of ordinary law[5] and the Government as the body which exercises the "executive" power of the State.[6] In this way *Bunreacht na hÉireann* institutionalises:

> "the traditional liberal model with its notion of a representative assembly reflecting the will of the people in legislation and policy declarations that are put into effect by 'the executive' and the public service".[7]

---

[3] The term "functional" here is not used in the sense of being the antithesis to "normative"; see M. Loughlin, *Public Law and Political Theory* (Oxford, Clarendon Press, 1992), especially 59–62. Rather it is used in the sense that, from first principles at least, one is entitled to expect that a constitution has some kind of impact in controlling and exercising public power. Thus the term functional is being used here in the sense of being the opposite to "symbolic" or "irrelevant".

[4] See Arts. 6 and 47.

[5] See especially Art. 15.2.1°.

[6] See especially Art. 28.2.

[7] B. Chubb, *The Government and Politics of Ireland* (3rd edn., London, Longman, 1992), 153.

However, as Chubb also notes:

> "the *Oireachtas* as an institution is not an important, positive contributor to policy. This is due to the domination that the government has over it, a domination that is both accepted by almost all those involved and made the more effective by the habit of party loyalty and strict adherence to the party line in the voting lobbies."[8]

Now, perhaps this is by far the most pragmatic and sensible set of arrangements. However, even if one accepts this from a prescriptive standpoint, it raises the question of what function the formal constitutional provisions serve? Why do we maintain the legal fictions established by Articles 12 to 37, when the political reality is very much different? If we accept that:

> "[c]onstitutionalism is the political doctrine that claims that political authority should be bound by institutions that restrict the exercise of power [and that] . . . [s]uch institutions offer rules that bind both the persons in authority as well as the organs or bodies that exercise political power",[9]

then what version of constitutionalism do we possess in Ireland, where it is generally accepted that despite the formal scheme set out in the constitutional document, it is the Government, or political factions within Government, rather than the *Oireachtas*, which wields lawmaking power? Of course these developments might well be explained by saying that we should "not confine our use of the word constitution to an identifiable document".[10] This document will at best only define the general pattern of political and legal organisation and relationships, whereas

> "[t]he day-to-day operations of government will make necessary both the creation of a body of law dealing with matters too detailed to include in the constitution and the development of an ever-growing collection of laws and other legal instruments, court rulings, and statements of practice or norms that are not formal rules at all."[11]

Whilst this is true, it does not absolve those who claim to know about these things, such as lawyers and political scientists, from exploring the significance of the differences between the formal constitutional provisions and those other aspects of our constitutional *arrangements* which are not found in the formal document. Moreover, might one not also say that if our Constitution is very much broader than the formal constitutional arrangements indicate, then why should our judges not be entitled when adjudicating on matters which bear upon the institutional side of our constitution, to consider not only the scheme set out in the constitutional document itself, but also those broader concepts, rules and practices which make up the totality of our constitutional arrangements? Despite the activist role which the judiciary have

---

[8] *Ibid.*, at 192.

[9] J. Lane, *Constitutions and Political Theory* (Manchester, Manchester University Press, 1996), 19.

[10] B. Chubb, *The Politics of the Irish Constitution* (Dublin, Institute of Public Administration, 1991), 1.

[11] B. Chubb, *supra* n. 7, at 37.

adopted with respect to "rights", which is discussed below, when it comes to constitutional adjudication as regards the institutional dimension, there is a noticeable tendency to stick to the strict letter of the formal constitutional document. One of the best examples of this is to be found in the decision of the majority of the Supreme Court in *Attorney General* v. *Hamilton*.[12] Here, when addressing the question whether the Constitution requires an absolute rule of confidentiality as regards discussions at Cabinet meetings, Finlay CJ argued that since the Beef Tribunal[13] was:

"essentially, an exercise of the legislative power originated by the Executive as members of the legislature and implemented, and put into effect, by an order of the Executive pursuant to the resolution of both Houses of Parliament,"[14]

it followed that the principles which were relevant to deciding whether or not to compel disclosure were those which arose as a consequence of the constitutional arrangements for the relationship between the legislature and the executive.[15] Proceeding from this point the Chief Justice declared:

" . . . the question must . . . be raised as to whether under any circumstance both Houses of the *Oireachtas* could by resolution appoint some outside agent, and it need not necessarily be a member of the judiciary, to inquire into matters, and clothe him or her with much greater power, and a fundamentally different power, than they have themselves, in the procedure of the *Dáil*. Having regard to the provisions of Article 28, s. 10 of the Constitution, the members of the *Dáil* have the ultimate sanction and control, if they cease to support the decisions and policies of any government, to cause its dissolution or, in the alternative, to cause the declaration of a general election, permitting the People, if they see fit, to elect a different government. Bearing in mind that power, so fundamental to the democratic process, there would appear to be nothing inconsistent with the democratic constitution in permitting a government, whilst it retains the support of the *Dáil* and remains in office, the confidentiality with regard to its discussions, which is claimed in this case."[16]

Of course what this analysis ignores entirely is that the Tribunal had to be established precisely because the ordinary *Dáil* procedure of itself, when combined with government domination of the *Dáil*, was unlikely to be adequate

---

[12] [1993] 2 IR 250.

[13] The Beef Tribunal was established to inquire into allegations of illegal activities, fraud or malpractice in connection with the beef industry. Part of the inquiry concerned what transpired at a Cabinet meeting on 8 June 1988. At the Tribunal, a question was put to a witness who had been a government minister concerning the deliberations at that meeting. Objection to the question was taken by counsel for the Attorney General. He argued that Art. 28.4 of the Constitution, which provides that the Government shall meet and act as a collective authority and shall be collectively responsible for the Departments of State administered by the members of the Government, rendered discussions between members of the Government meeting together for the purpose of making decisions absolutely confidential, and as a consequence the content of such discussions could not be inquired into by the Tribunal.

[14] [1993] 2 IR 250, 270–1.

[15] *Ibid.*, 271.

[16] *Ibid.*, at 271–2.

to uncover the information which the *Dáil* needed in order properly to decide whether to exercise "its ultimate sanction and control". Indeed, as the sole member of the Tribunal, Hamilton J, ruefully noted:

" . . . if the questions that were asked in the Dáil were answered in the way they were answered here, there would be no necessity for this inquiry and an awful lot of money and time would have been saved."[17]

However, the majority of the Supreme Court seemed not to be interested in this type of analysis. They took the formal constitutional scheme as their touchstone and, as a consequence, they proceeded on a basis which, though arguably consistent with that scheme, failed entirely to take into account the reality of the balance of power as between the *Oireachtas* and the Government.

The discussion above brings us back, then, to the fundamental question about what the formal constitutional scheme is for. Within the Irish context, one might surmise upon reading *Bunreacht na hÉireann* that, at the institutional level, the Constitution seeks to deliver a version of democratic constitutionalism founded upon the notion that parliamentary democracy provides a basis for democratic popular input and control of the Executive. In fact, though the Constitution has failed to deliver this, as the Beef Tribunal Case indicates, it provides, in formal terms, a facade which serves both to mask, yet at the same time legitimise, power relationships which proceed on an entirely different basis. If it is accepted that this is the case, we must ask ourselves whether, at the institutional level, constitutions provide at best a limiting framework which operates only *in extremis*, and at worst a framework which legitimises and hides real power relationships. In both of these situations we need to acknowledge the difference between the idea of having a constitution on the one hand, and the "functional" or "instrumental" potential of constitutions on the other. At the institutional level at least, it is arguable that it is the fact of having a constitution, rather than having a constitution which actually delivers a particular type of representative government, which has been significant in Ireland. This is not necessarily to say that the Irish system is undemocratic as such. Rather, it indicates that whatever form or type of democracy we may have, it is not the sort set out in the Constitution.

The problem of the disjuncture between the *formal* Constitution and the *real* Constitution exists at least at two other levels in the institutional context. First, in line with "orthodox constitutionalism" the world over, the formal institutional provisions of the Irish Constitution are concerned "almost exclusively with the institutions of big government".[18] Whilst Ireland is probably

---

[17] Quoted in F. O'Toole, *Meanwhile Back at the Ranch: The Politics of Irish Beef* (London, Vintage, 1995), 241.

[18] For critiques of this approach generally, see G. Poggi, *The State: Its Nature Development and Prospects* (Cambridge, Polity Press, 1990); N. Chomsky, *World Order, Old and New* (London, Pluto Press, 1994); C. Offe, "Contradictions of the Welfare State" in J. Keane (ed.), *Contradictions of the Welfare State* (London, Hutchinson, 1984); J. March and J. Olsen,

the most centralised of States within the European Union, nevertheless a whole plethora of different institutions and organisations undertake public functions and exercise public power.[19] There is no evidence that this is a trend which is likely to disappear. Indeed the prospect of privatisation of certain public sector industries may well lead to an even greater proliferation of such bodies.[20] The exercise of public power through these organisations receives no explicit recognition in the formal institutional provisions of the Constitution. In their report, the Constitutional Review Group concluded that constitutional recognition "should be sparingly accorded on the basis that the Constitution should concern itself predominantly with the strategic elements in the organisation of the State".[21] Though the group did make recommendations regarding local government[22] and the Ombudsman,[23] the general thrust of the approach above indicates that they had a conception of "strategic elements in the organisation of the State" which corresponds with the artificial abstract conceptions of state favoured by eighteenth and nineteenth century political theorists. It certainly was not based upon a realistic examination of power relationships and networks in a "Post-Parliamentary democracy" of the late twentieth century.[24] Of course it ought to be pointed out that decision-making by "second-tier" bodies is subject to control by the application of administrative law principles. Leaving aside the problems which privatisation might present in this respect,[25] this is true. However, this makes it all the more pertinent to consider what the Constitution is for. As just noted, a host of other writers have traced the transformation of the "State" in the twentieth century. If the institutional aspects of constitutional schemes are to carry out the role which is traditionally ascribed to them, then surely the reality of power and decision-making processes must properly be recognised in

Democratic Governance (New York, The Free Press, 1995); and J. Morrison and S. Livingstone, *Reshaping Public Power: Northern Ireland and the British Constitutional Crisis* (London, Sweet & Maxwell, 1995).

[19] See B. Chubb, *supra* n. 7, chaps. 12–15; J. F. Zimmerman, "Irish State Sponsored Bodies: The Factionalization of Authority and Responsibility" (1986) 7 *Seirbhis Phoibli* 2; R. Keane, *The Law of Local Government in the Republic of Ireland* (Dublin, Incorporated Law Society of Ireland, 1982); J. F. Zimmmerman, "The Office of Ombudsman in Ireland" (1989) 27 *Administration* 258 and ch. 6 in D. Morgan and G. Hogan, *Administrative Law in Ireland* (2nd edn., London, Sweet & Maxwell, 1991).

[20] See F. Covery and M. McDowell (eds.), *Privatisation: Issues of Principle and Implementation in Ireland* (Dublin, Gill and Macmillan, 1990); C. Graham and T. Prosser, *Privatizing Public Enterprises: Constitutions, the State and Regulation in Comparative Perspective* (Oxford, Clarendon Press, 1991); and N. Lewis, "Regulating Non-Government Bodies: Privatisation, Accountability and the Public Private Divide" in J. Jowell and D. Oliver (eds.), *The Changing Constitution* (2nd edn., Oxford, Clarendon Press, 1989).

[21] *Report of the Constitution Review Group* (Dublin, Stationery Office, 1996), para. 12 p. xi.

[22] *Ibid.,* at 428–31.

[23] *Ibid.,* at 425–7.

[24] See C. Ham and M. Hill, *The Policy Process in the Modern Capitalist State* (London, Wheatsheaf, 1993).

[25] See G. Borrie, "The Regulation of Public and Private Power" [1989] *Public Law* 553; M. Freedland "Government by Contract and Private Law" [1994] *Public Law* 86.

the basic law of the constitutional document itself. It might be commented that such a change would inhibit the administrative process and reduce the opportunities for flexibility and adaptability as regards institutional design, and that this in turn would not be in the public interest.[26] I have some sympathy with this analysis. However, if it is to be accepted, it calls into question the whole justification for constitutions in the first place and serves once again to underscore the point made above that despite the "collective magic" and venerable status which surrounds the constitution itself, it is largely irrelevant as a mechanism for structuring and controlling the processes by which means we are governed.

The other level at which the institutional arrangements in the Irish Constitution are out of step with the real constitution relates to Europe. As Chubb has noted, with accession to the European Community:

> "A new dimension was added to the framework of limited government, for Ireland, it was said 'has two constitutions now'—namely *Bunreacht na hÉireann*, the domestic constitution; and the Community Treaties and other primary legislation, the 'offshore' constitution."[27]

As regards the "off-shore" constitution, we need but note that from the perspective of orthodox liberal constitutionalism, there is room for significant dissatisfaction regarding the democratic deficit at the Community level. If, as seems likely, the role of the Community continues to grow and develop, it will prove impossible, given the present decision-making arrangements, to square the lack of democratic input and control at Community level with traditional notions of constitutionalism upon which our formal constitutional arrangements (and indeed those of all other Member States) are grounded. This observation ought not to be interpreted as being "anti-Europe"; rather it is simply an observation that the Community's political system, being "a curious mixture of intergovernmental and supranational characteristics",[28] cannot be accommodated or explained within the conceptual framework which underpins notions of constitutionalism within a nation state. Nevertheless, it does serve once again to call into question our present understanding of the role and functions of constitutions such as *Bunreacht na hÉireann* in this new age. We will have to wait and see how this develops.[29] On the domestic front, of course, the incorporation of Community law within our own hierarchy of constitutional laws serves only to add further weight to the point made above,

---

[26] See J. M. Landis, *The Administrative Process* (New Haven, Conn., Yale University Press, 1938).

[27] B. Chubb, *supra* n. 7, at 305.

[28] B. Laffan, "An Overview of the Community's Institutional System" in P. Keatinge (ed.), *Studies in European Union, No 1, Political Union* (Dublin, Institute of European Affairs, 1991), 241.

[29] See, for instance, J. Temple Lang, "European Community Constitutional Law: The Division of Powers between the Community and Member States" (1988) 39 *NILQ* 209 and J. Schwarze, "Towards a Common European Public Law" (1995) 1 *Eur. Pub. Law* 227.

that the *Oireachtas* is largely irrelevant in the process of making policy and laws. It is true that the *Crotty* case[30] firmly establishes that where changes made are fundamental in the sense of being "history-making decisions [which] alter the Union's legislative procedures, rebalance the relative powers of EU institutions, or change the EU's remit",[31] then democratic approval by way of referendum is required. However, as regards any other species of Community lawmaking, or indeed the process of negotiation of policy undertaken at Council level, then the *Oireachtas* and even political parties "are conspicuous by their absence"[32] After considering the implications of the decision of the Supreme Court in *Meagher* v. *Minister for Agriculture*,[33] where the general practice of giving legal effect to EC directives by means of statutory instruments amending earlier primary legislation was upheld, the Constitution Review Group noted that

> "The extensive use of statutory instruments to implement directives has meant that hundreds of statutory provisions . . . have been expressly or impliedly repealed by statutory instruments often with a minimum of publicity. The use of statutory instruments ensures speedy and effective implementation of EC law but often at the expense of the publicity and debate which attends the processing of legislation through the *Oireachtas*."[34]

The implication here is that our law is capable of being changed, and is being changed, without any real substantive, albeit minimalistic, input from the supreme *legislative* body as established in the formal constitutional document.

None of the above should be taken to mean that this writer is opposed to membership of the European Union. Moreover, I acknowledge that the vast majority of the Irish population is extremely well disposed to membership and the perceived benefits which it has brought. My task here is to consider the role of our Constitution and its relevance to modern day Ireland. Taking the above analysis as a whole, it seems clear that in fact we practise a form of constitutional pragmatism which renders the formal constitutional scheme almost irrelevant. Our commitment to the form of constitutionalism established by our Constitution is patently superficial. To my mind this is a serious constitutional problem. This is not a constitutional problem in the sense that, say, the resignation of Cearbhall O'Dalaigh presented constitutional difficulties.[35] Individual difficulties such as that at least have the advantage of rendering the constitutional problem public and explicit. However, the disjuncture between the formal constitutional provisions and the real

---

[30] *Crotty* v. *An Taoiseach* [1987] IR 713.

[31] See J. Peterson, "Decision-making in the European Union: Towards a Framework for Analysis" [1995] *J of Eur. Pub. Policy* 69.

[32] See B. Chubb, *supra* n. 7, at ch. 17.

[33] [1994] 1 IR 329.

[34] *Report of the Constitution Review Group*, *supra* n. 21, at 115.

[35] See M. Gallagher, "The Presidency of Ireland: Implications of the 'Donegan Affair'" (1977) 30 *Parl. Affairs* 380.

Constitution at the institutional level is a serious problem precisely because we do not notice it. It is an insidious, incremental process, which calls into question the efficacy of liberal democratic constitutions such as ours to deliver what they might be expected to deliver. It is a result of the complacency which our form of constitution produces. As Loewenstein has noted:

> "The well-balanced constitution, with its liberty-guaranteeing checks and balances, was intended to establish, by functionally separated powers, the ideal equilibrium of social forces . . . the constitution was primarily a moral necessity and a functional achievement only subsidiarily. . . . In their naïve optimism the politicians and the political theorists themselves believed that all that was needed for a well-ordered society was a well-ordered constitution."[36]

With this in mind we might all have mixed emotions when reading Fintan O'Toole's analysis of the events which gave rise to the Beef Tribunal. He concluded that:

> "Over a period of five years, certain fundamentals of democratic government—accountability to parliament, the assumption that governments obey the law, the conduct of independent foreign policy, the rights of citizens to consent to the actions of their government—had been set aside."[37]

We might share his anger, but we should not be surprised.

THE RIGHTS FRAMEWORK

If the formal institutional elements of the Constitution seem to have failed to guarantee the type and form of democratic government which one might originally expect, it might still be argued, one can at least confidentally point to the fundamental rights provisions, and their application and development by the High Court and Supreme Court, as the "Jewel in the Crown" of constitutionalism Irish-style. A number of significant points might be made in support of this contention. First, these provisions have delivered significant protections to the ordinary citizen against the might of State power.[38] Secondly, it is arguable that a crucial aspect of these protections is that they operate to protect individuals regardless of the reality of the power relationships described above. Hence they serve to satisfy the Madisonian requirement that the Rule of Law necessitates mechanisms to minimise the impact of "factions" on the one hand, and the "tyranny of the majority" on the other.[39]

---

[36] K. Loewenstein, "Reflections on the Value of Constitutions in Our Revolutionary Age" in A. J. Zurcher (ed.), *Constitutions and Constitutional Trends Since World War II* (New York, New York University Press, 1951), 195.

[37] F. O'Toole, *supra* n. 17, at 275.

[38] See, for instance, *Ryan v. Attorney General* [1965] IR 294; *McGee v. Attorney General* [1974] IR 284 and *The State (C) v. Frawley* [1976] IR 365. For a more complete list of relevant case law, see *Report of the Constitution Review Group, supra* n. 21, at 246.

[39] See A. Hamilton, J. Madison and J .Jay, *The Federalist Papers* (New York, Mentor, 1961), 41–2.

Therefore, even if the Constitution has failed to deliver in institutional terms as regards the form of democratic representative government, nevertheless the fundamental rights of individuals cannot be affected by whatever power relationships exist at the level of making and executing ordinary law. Thirdly, in ontological terms,[40] the application of these provisions indicates that constitutions can have explicit instrumental or functional utility. Put simply, the fundamental rights part of the Constitution has delivered what, on the face of it, one might have expected it to deliver.

However, in considering the role and limits of constitutions, and evaluating the Irish Constitution in this respect, one must express doubts about the rights provisions in the Constitution from two perspectives. The first set of limitations flows from a consideration of the context in which these rights become significant. The second relates to the character of the rights themselves. As regards context, it has to be recognised that, despite the obvious prominence which the rights provisions of the Constitution have come to assume since the 1960s, these provisions become relevant only at the very end of the policy/law making process. In most cases this will be at the suit of an individual citizen.[41] Despite the use of such terms as "constitutional imperative" by the Irish courts on occasion,[42] the rights provisions do not proactively direct the lawmaking process. They operate generally not as a sword, but rather as a shield, which can be used only in certain limited legally recognised circumstances. There must be the constitutional equivalent of *lis inter parties*[43] and the form and culture surrounding the resolution of these matters is the narrow, legal context. The matter is handed over to the "professionals" (i.e. lawyers and judges) where the individual whose right or rights are being asserted is a spectator who generally has little or no control over, nor is he/she likely always to understand, the terms in which their rights are being asserted. Thus the rights provisions of the Constitution effect a "judicialisation" of political power which, though capable of delivering protection to individuals in particular circumstances, is nevertheless significantly divorced from the experience of ordinary citizens whose interests they champion. In this sense constitutional rights and their relationship/relevance to individual citizens stand in the same position as the theocratic, Christian, explanations of power and the state, which they might be thought to have supplanted. Just as

> "medieval christianity, though pervasive, was a *mediated* religion—the interpretation of its scriptures and the making of its doctrine a jealously guarded prerogative of the Church",[44]

---

[40] See generally K. Loewenstein, *supra* n. 36, at 191–224.

[41] Though see Art. 26 whereby the President may refer a Bill to the Supreme Court for a decision on whether the Bill, or provisions of it, are unconstitutional.

[42] See *McGimpsey v. Ireland* [1990] IR 110.

[43] See, for instance, *Cahill v. Sutton* [1980] IR 269; *Norris v. Attorney General* [1984] IR 36; and *Madigan v. Attorney General* [1986] ILRM 136.

[44] S. Trussler, "Introduction" in *Everyman* (London, Nick Hern Books, 1996), pp. xvii–xviii.

so, too, the extent and scope of constitutional rights within our type of constitution are mediated for us by the courts.

One of the most frequently mentioned difficulties which emerges from this is that it presents real problems regarding the proper constitutional role of the judiciary. This arises simply because in their role as constitutional adjudicators judges are arguably being "drawn into making . . . overtly political and highly contentious value choices".[45] Chubb argues that:

"It is the democratically elected representatives of the people who should be making public policy. . . . It is they who should be the architects of significant constitutional development . . . ".[46]

However, the fact that judges are called upon to perform such a role is not so disturbing as is sometimes asserted. The notion that judges ought not to be making decisions of this sort is based upon a peculiarly formalist view of what "law" is. It is arguable that curial adjudication is always "political" in one way or another, and this is perhaps inevitably so where the matter at issue falls within the "constitutional" category. As William Rehnquist, Chief Justice of the United States noted, " . . . a court operating under a written constitution and exercising the power of judicial review is sooner or later bound to be caught up in the political turmoil of the times".[47] What is worrying, however, is whether the substantive political or value choice being made is openly acknowledged as such. One of the problems which is attendant to the judicialisation of "rights adjudication" is that judges, in an attempt to maintain the façade of some form of peculiar legal objectivity as a way of maintaining the distinction between law and politics, express their decisions, and the reasons for their decisions, by reference to artificial legal constructions, without acknowledging the value basis for their reasoning. This not only has the consequence often of hiding the real basis for the decision. It also renders the rights aspects of the Constitution entirely inaccessible to the citizens for whose benefit it is said they were created. After all, they have not been "initiated" into the mystique and complexity of "the Law".

One of the finest examples illustrating the kind of difficulty mentioned above is the *Norris* case.[48] Here the plaintiff challenged the constitutionality of various sections of two nineteenth century statutes which were, of course,

---

[45] J. A. Smillie, "'Fundamental' Rights, Parliamentary Supremacy and the New Zealand Court of Appeal" (1995) 111 *LQR* 209 at 217. However, see A. Hunt, "Fundamental Rights and the New Zealand Bill of Rights Act" (1995) 111 *LQR* 565, especially 567–8.

[46] B Chubb, *supra* n. 10, at 77. It might be commented that this is actually a misrepresentation of the Irish constitutional scheme. It is the people, through the mechanism of constitutional referenda, rather than the politicians, who must/ought explicitly approve of "significant constitutional" change. However, the process of bringing such questions to the people (see Art. 46) lends a degree of weight to Chubb's analysis. See generally, *Report of the Constitution Review Group*, *supra* n. 21, at 397–405, 639–48.

[47] W. H. Rehnquist, "The American Constitutional Experience" (1989) 24 *Ir. Jur.* 87 at 98.

[48] *Norris* v. *Attorney General* [1984] IR 36; see also L. Flynn, "To Be an Irish Man: Constructions of Masculinity within the Constitution" in this volume.

passed prior to the establishment of the Irish state, and which had the effect
of criminalising various homosexual acts.[49] Reflecting on the decision, in
which he delivered judgment for the majority rejecting the plaintiff's claim,
the former Chief Justice commented extra-judicially that

> "The issue before the court was whether such provisions had been carried over into
> the law of the state. If these provisions were found to be in conflict with the
> Constitution, then they were not carried over and were not part of the law enforce-
> able in the state. Otherwise they were—and that in fact was the decision of the court
> arrived at by a majority. This case has often been referred to as one in which
> the Supreme Court condemned homosexuality. This is not so, because that issue
> simply did not arise."[50]

Now this is all quite correct from a formalist legal perspective. However,
considering whether the prohibition upon certain acts was repugnant to the
Constitution involved a consideration, from each individual judge's own
moral perspective, of whether these acts were or were not sufficiently "beyond
the pale" to be worthy of condemnation. As both the majority and minority
judgments indicate, one could devise numerous "legal" arguments, each of
which would be equally valid as a basis for supporting one conclusion or
another. This is generally the case when courts come to adjudicate upon these
type of "rights" issues, and if lawyers are honest they will admit as much. It
never ceases to amaze me how, when some or other constitutional issue comes
before the courts, serried ranks of distinguished legal experts rush into television and radio studios to proclaim what the constitutional answer will be. In
reality, all those legal experts can do is identify the possible lines of constitutional argument which might be used to steer the court to one conclusion or
another. Whilst undoubtedly this is a state of affairs which leads to uncertainty, and I accept that it creates difficulty for the *Oireachtas*[51] and the legal
profession,[52] it is not my point here that something should be done about it,
or indeed that it is really possible to do anything about it. Rather my point is
that this is a characteristic feature of constitutional adjudication of this type.
Consequently we need to be careful, and distinctly circumspect about our
assessment of the efficacy and utility of the rights provisions as part of our
overall constitutional scheme. The only honest assessment in this context,
which I offer in the knowledge that it is likely to confirm the worst suspicions
of the populace at large about lawyers, as well as being distinctly unwelcome
by our friends in the media, is that "it depends".

Quite apart from the difficulties which flow from the form and nature of
constitutional "rights" adjudication, a second matter which needs to be con-

---

[49] The provisions in question were ss. 61 and 62 of the Offences Against the Person Act 1861
and s. 11 of the Criminal Law Act 1885.

[50] T. F. O'Higgins, *A Double Life* (Dublin, Town House, 1996), 282.

[51] See J. M. Kelly, *Fundamental Rights in the Irish Law and Constitution* (2nd edn., Dublin,
Jurist Publishing, 1984), p. xxix.

[52] See D. Gwynn Morgan, *Irish Times*, 2 Feb. 1980.

sidered when assessing the rights provisions of the Irish Constitution against views about the function and utility of our Constitution arises when one considers the general character of the rights themselves. Two points are relevant here. First, in so far as *Bunreacht na hÉireann* has for most of its life contained provisions which promote a set of "Catholic ideological and social values",[53] the Constitution has actually institutionalised the "tyranny of the majority" in respect of certain key aspects of personal/private morality. Though it is true that the last three decades have seen the gradual acceptance of more secularist and pluralist attitudes in Irish society, our Constitution has acted as a formal institutional impediment to recognition of these developments in ordinary law. In this way the rights provisions of the Constitution have become an authoritative statement of an established conservative *status quo*, which, as the various divorce referenda indicate, are incredibly difficult to change. This is not meant to be an attack on such provisions in substantive terms. Rather, it is a recognition of the fact that one problem with written, entrenched constitutions is that one has to start somewhere. However, where and *when* one starts is vitally important. As Chubb notes:

> "The procedures followed by de Valera in drafting the Constitution, which involved consultation with clerics and the Vatican on matters which concerned the Church, were thoroughly in keeping with the cultural climate of the twenty-six counties at the time."[54]

I have no doubt that if we were starting the process today we would adopt a different approach. Thus the Constitutional Review Group concluded that

> "While the common good and morality should be in harmony, the Review Group considered it preferable that the Constitution should avoid moral prescriptions not generally acceptable to the citizens of the State."[55]

This secularist/pluralist approach was reflected in their consideration of Article 41 and the education and religion provisions of Articles 42 and 44 in so far as they affect the family. The group noted that Articles 41 and 42 were heavily influenced by papal encyclicals and that they were clearly drafted with one type of family in mind, namely the family based upon marriage. However they were also aware that

> "The mores of Irish Society have changed significantly over the past six decades. The traditional Roman Catholic ethos has been weakened by various influences including secularisation, urbanisation, changing attitudes to sexual behaviour, the use of contraceptives, social acceptance of premarital relations, cohabitation and single parenthood, a lower norm for family size, increased readiness to accept separation and divorce, and greater economic independence of women".[56]

---

[53] B. Chubb, *supra* n. 7, at 16, see also the essays by N. Browne, G. Whyte and D. M. Clarke in this volume.
[54] B. Chubb, *supra* n. 10, at 33.
[55] *Report of the Constitution Review Group, supra* n. 21, at para. 8, p. xi.
[56] *Ibid.*, at 319.

Hence they recommended that in recognising and protecting the role of the family, the Constitution ought not to define "family" by reference to families based upon marriage alone.[57] In a similar vein, the identification of unenumerated personal rights by reference to "the Christian . . . nature of the State" was thought to be unsatisfactory[58] and there also was some support for the removal of religious references from the Constitution as a whole.[59]

It is my contention, then, that if we were starting out writing our Constitution now, the type of approach recommended by the Constitutional Review Group would be the one adopted. Moreover, it is probably the case that there would be considerable, though perhaps not "majority", support for such an approach. However, we are not starting out from scratch and, despite the changing mores in Irish society, any attempt to change the *status quo*, by means of formally "secularising" the Constitution, is likely to be extremely contentious and perhaps politically impossible. In this way the character of certain "rights" provisions present us with a real problem, when we consider the role of our Constitution as we enter the next millennium. A significant minority reject the values which these provisions propound, but (and here I am merely surmising) a majority might not support the type of changes suggested by the Constitutional Review Group.[60] The issue of course is whether a suggestion that the underlying ethos of a constitution should be changed stands in the same position as a suggestion for changing a particular provision. To some degree this represents the difference in conceptual terms between merely *amending* the Constitution, and *reconstitution* itself. This difference was hinted at by the Constitutional Review Committee where it commented that its "commission was to *review* the Constitution, not to rewrite it or replace it."[61] This difficulty is perhaps inherent in the type of constitution which we possess. There are limitations on the extent to which the Constitution, and the values it espouses, can evolve incrementally into something entirely different through the normal processes of constitutional amendment. The prospect here then is the continuing disjuncture between the values

---

[57] *Report of the Constitution Review Group, supra* n. 21, at 336–7.

[58] *Ibid.,* at 251–2. Whilst one is inclined to suspect that this was based upon their acceptance that the rights which Art. 40.3 requires the State to defend and vindicate "are supposed to be common to all citizens regardless of belief", their argument for a changed approach was specifically linked to their argument that there was an illogicality in the constitutional scheme as it presently exists, because though the Preamble seems to suggest or imply that the State is a Christian State, other Arts. (i.e. 6 and 44) do not indicate that the State is to be regarded as an exclusively Christian State for the purposes of identifying personal rights. It might be commented that rather than openly admitting their preference on the basis of modern secularist values, here the Constitution Review Group took refuge in the kind of formalist constitutional analysis which I have associated with judges above.

[59] *Ibid.,* 3–6 (on the Preamble) and 13 (on Art. 6).

[60] This analysis is supported by the research in M. Fogarty, L. Ryan and J. Lee, *Irish Values and Attitudes: The Irish Report of the European Value Systems Study* (Dublin, Dominican Publications, 1984), though this study may be considered somewhat out-of-date now.

[61] *Report of the Constitution Review Group, supra* n. 21, at para. 8, p. x (emphasis in original).

and beliefs of a significant proportion of the population and the formal Constitution.

The second concern arising out of a consideration of the character of the rights provisions of the Constitution is that those which do not necessarily reflect a distinctly Roman Catholic view of world, such as those contained in Article 40, reflect a limited, narrow, conception of rights which are "fundamental" and those which are not. Thus, for instance, Article 40 declares the rights to equality and personal liberty and due process. These are the types of provisions which reflect the concerns of nineteenth century constitutionalists about the dangers of arbitrary state power. These are still important, however what is missing are provisions which reflect the concerns of ordinary citizens about the responsibilities of the State today. That is to say that if we are entitled to expect that constitutions are:

> " 'living' in the sense that they are essential to the life not of the professionals manipulating them but of the common people . . . [and that they are] instrumental for the pursuit of happiness of the people",[62]

then the rights provisions of the Irish Constitution fail to guarantee a whole plethora of social and political rights, which people today consider central to "happiness". The type of "rights" to which I am alluding is well illustrated in Franklin Delano Roosevelt's reflections on constitutional developments in the United States. In 1944 he explained:

> "This Republic had its beginning, and grew to its present strength, under the protection of certain inalienable, political rights—among them the right to free speech, free press, free worship, trial by jury, freedom from unreasonable searches and seizures. They were our rights to life and liberty . . . [but] these political rights proved inadequate to assure us equality in the pursuit of happiness. . . . We have accepted, so to speak, a second Bill of Rights under which a new basis of security and prosperity can be established for all . . . the right to a useful and renumerative job in the industries or shops or farms or mines of the nation; the right to earn enough to provide adequate food and clothing and recreation; the right of every farmer to raise and sell his products at a return which will give him and his family a decent living; the right of every businessman, large and small, to trade in an atmosphere of freedom from unfair competition and domination by monopolies at home and abroad; the right of every family to a decent home; the right to adequate medical care and the opportunity to achieve and enjoy good health; the right to adequate protection from the economic fears of old age, sickness, accident, and unemployment. . . . "[63]

Roosevelt was referring to the values inherent in the "New Deal", which never did achieve the status of "constitutional rights" in the traditional sense. Moreover, many of the ideas found here are reflected in the Directive

---

[62] K. Loewenstein, *supra* n. 36, at 222.

[63] Quoted in C. R. Sunstein, *After the Rights Revolution: Reconceiving the Regulatory State* (Cambridge and London, Harvard University Press, 1990).

Principles of Social Policy contained in Article 45 of *Bunreacht na hÉireann*, which are specifically designated as being non-justiciable.[64] Although the Irish courts have considered these provisions in certain cases,[65] they do not share the same status as enumerated or unenumerated rights.[66] The question, of course, is whether they ought to. Now this is a vexed issue, and I shall not address it in detail. My point is comparative, and methodological. In comparative terms the types of rights to which I am referring are just as important, if not generally more important for most people, than the justiciable rights which are found in the Constitution. The inclusion of certain types of rights and the exclusion of others requires that we reflect both on what we consider to be "fundamental" in substantive terms, as well as addressing what should be the role of the State and, by implication, the role of constitutions. Of course in methodological terms the key question is how these matters should be addressed. In its consideration of Article 45, the Constitutional Review Group concluded that the principle that Article 45 should not be cognizable by any court should remain.[67] The reason for this may well be indicated in the following:

> "Public advice to the Review Group ranged from 'if it ain't broken, don't fix it' to 'ensure its responsiveness to the ethos of 21st century Ireland' . . . . The Review Group holds the view that the Constitution, as a fundamental legal framework establishing powers, rights and responsibilities, should be as simple and clear as possible, leaving the treatment of particular or changing circumstances to be dealt with by the more flexible democratic process of legislation."[68]

Hence it seems that the view was that the social principles referred to in Article 45 reflect issues which should be dealt with by the more flexible process of legislation. Two points of general importance follow from this and upon these I will conclude this discussion. First, our Constitution in the traditional liberal democratic mode contains only some "rights" which might in a modern context be considered to be "fundamental". Secondly, here our consideration of rights joins up with our consideration of the institutional dimension. There is little merit in the suggestion that these matters can effectively be dealt with through the democratic legislative process, when we know that that process does not actually function in accordance with the values or principles implicit in the formal constitutional scheme.

---

[64] Art. 45 provides that the principles contained therein are "for the general guidance of the Oireachtas. The application of those principles in the making of laws shall be the care of the Oireachtas exclusively, and shall not be cognisable by any Court under the provisions of this Constitution."

[65] See *Murtagh Properties Ltd* v. *Cleary* [1972] IR 330; *Landers* v. *Attorney General* (1975) 109 ILTR 1; *Attorney General and the Minister for Posts and Telegraphs* v. *Paperlink Ltd* [1984] ILRM 373 and *Kerry Co-Operative Creameries Ltd* v. *An Bórd Bainne* [1991] ILRM 851.

[66] See especially the *Paperlink* case, *supra* n. 65.

[67] *Report of the Constitution Review Group*, *supra* n. 21, at 393.

[68] *Ibid.*, para. 8, pp. x–xi.

CONCLUSION

The reader may well wonder where the above analysis takes us. My view is that it indicates where constitutional scholarship, debate and inquiry should head in the future. As a starting point, we must eschew the approach which involves revering our Constitution in an abstract sense, and begin to examine the disjuncture between reality and idealised notions as to constitutional role and function. As part of such a project, lawyers in particular need to reassess orthodox Irish Constitutional Legal Method, which is typically characterised by an obsession with the minutiae of constitutional provisions and decisions of the courts about individual constitutional provisions. One of the disadvantages of having a detailed written constitution such as ours is that constitutional debate, and constitutional inquiry, tends routinely to concentrate upon individual matters of constitutional detail, rather than addressing questions such as: what objectives or functions the Constitution purports to address; whether these objectives or functions are appropriate in a modern context; whether our Constitution can be said to have succeeded in delivering upon such objectives; in what way is the Constitution failing to deliver; and why is this so? Though not all public lawyers will agree, it is my view that addressing such questions is central to public law scholarship, and should not be dismissed as being more appropriate for students of political science rather than law. Studying constitutional law involves an attempt to understand the nature and limitations of constitutional law as a *species of law*, as much as it involves trying to understand what the law is (if that can ever really be determined objectively anyway).[69]

Any such inquiry will ultimately present us with difficult substantive questions. These include whether the formal Constitutional provisions ought to be changed to reflect reality or whether the Constitution should be changed in some way to ensure that reality reflects the values inherent in the Constitution. It will also involve engaging in a debate about which matters should be decided, guaranteed or protected by means of the "highly structured legal process of party-controlled proof and argument"[70] which characterises adjudication on fundamental *constitutional* rights, and which matters should be consigned to the "largely unstructured process of pulling and hauling by

---

[69] The formalist approach to public law scholarship is not unique to Ireland. See, for instance, P. McAuslan, "Administrative Law and Administrative Theory: The Dismal Performance of Administrative Lawyers" (1978) 9 *Cambrian L Rev.* 40; T. Prosser, "Towards a Critical Public Law" (1982) 9 *J of Law and Society* 1; and R. de Friend, "Constitutional Law", 114–19 in I. Grigg-Spall and P. Ireland (eds.), *The Critical Lawyers' Handbook* (London, Pluto Press, 1992). Moreover, there is some indication that political scientists may not welcome such an intrusion by lawyers into what they consider to be their territory. See B. O'Leary, "What Should Public Lawyers Do?" (1992) 12 *OJLS* 404 and P. Craig, "What Should Public Lawyers Do? A Reply" (1992) 12 *OJLS* 564.

[70] C. S. Diver, "Policymaking Paradigms in Administrative Law" (1981–82) 95 *Harv. L Rev.* 393.

individuals directly accountable to the citizenry"[71] which characterises "politics" in the ordinary sense.

The need to engage in such a process of self-examination is perhaps more pressing now than ever. At the time of writing the *Oireachtas* has just established another Tribunal, this time to inquire into alleged payments by a major retail group to TDs, their relatives, political parties and other public officials.[72] It is remarkable that these matters arise only six months after the Constitutional Review Group declared that "the Constitution has, indeed, stood the test of time quite well".[73] One wonders exactly what criteria they employed to arrive at this self-satisfied conclusion. It seems to me that recent events not only make a mockery of this analysis, but also serve to underscore the responsibility of public lawyers, political scientists and others continually to explore, articulate and deconstruct the "dissonance between theory and practice" in constitutionalism Irish-style.[74]

[71] C. S. Diver, "Policymaking Paradigms in Administrative Law" (1981–82) 95 *Harv. L Rev.* 393.

[72] The resolution establishing the Tribunal was passed on 6 Feb. 1997. For the Tribunal's terms of reference see *Irish Times*, 7 Feb. 1997.

[73] *Report of the Constitutional Review Group*, *supra* n. 21, para 8, p. x.

[74] See P. McAuslan and J. F. McEldowney, "Legitimacy and the Constitution: The Dissonance between Theory and Practice" in McAuslan and McEldowney (eds.), *Law, Legitimacy and the Constitution* (London, Sweet & Maxwell, 1985).

Contributors' Profiles

Garrett Barden is Associate Professor of Philosophy at the National University of Ireland, Cork. His works include *Towards Self-Meaning* (Dublin, Gill and MacMillan, 1969) (co-authored with P. J. McShane) and *After Principles* (Notre Dame, Ind., University of Notre Dame Press, 1990), as well as several articles on the theory of knowledge and the epistemology of law.

Dr Noel Browne (1915–1997) was a founder member of *Clann na Poblachta* and TD for almost twenty years between 1948 and 1982. He was Minister for Health between 1948 and 1951 during which time a successful campaign to eliminate tuberculosis, a disease that claimed the lives of his parents and two siblings, was launched and the first national blood transfusion service established. Catholic Church opposition to his Mother and Child welfare scheme prompted his resignation from the cabinet in 1951 and the collapse of the Government. After his retirement from active politics in 1982 he continued to offer trenchant views on the failure of the Irish State to tackle emigration and poverty, publishing his autobiography in 1986, *Against The Tide* (Dublin, Gill and Macmillan, 1986).

Bozena Cierlik is a member of the Human Factors Resource Group at the Department of Applied Psychology, National University of Ireland, Cork, where she has also tutored in the Department of History. She was recently awarded a Ph.D by the National University of Ireland for a comparative study of aspects of political life in Poland and Ireland between 1918 and 1939. Previously she worked in the National Archive in Krakow, Poland, after studying history and archive studies at the Catholic University of Lublin.

Desmond M. Clarke is Associate Professor of Philosophy and Head of the Philosophy Department at the National University of Ireland at Cork. Currently General Co-editor of *Cambridge Texts in the History of Philosophy*, he has written extensively on issues about morality, law and the Irish Constitution including (as editor), *Morality and the Law* (Cork, Mercier Press, 1982) and *Church & State* (Cork, Cork University Press, 1984).

Michael Cronin is Director of the Centre for Translation Studies, Dublin City University. He is a founding member and former Chairperson of the Irish Translators' Association and is currently co-editor of the Irish cultural studies journal *Graph*. He is author of *Translating Ireland: Translation, Languages, Cultures* (Cork, Cork University Press, 1996) and is co-editor (with B. O'Connor) of *Tourism in Ireland: A Critical Analysis* (Cork, Cork University Press, 1993).

Dolores Dooley is a Senior Lecturer in Philosophy at the National University of Ireland, Cork. Her works include *Equality in Community* (Cork, Cork University Press, 1996) and *William Thompson's Appeal to One Half of the Human Race (1825)* (annotated student edition) (Cork, Cork University Press, 1997). She was one of the launch editors of the *Irish Journal of Feminist Studies*.

Garret Fitzgerald, former Leader of the *Fine Gael* Party and *Taoiseach* of Ireland, was called to the Irish Bar in 1947 and has been a lecturer, journalist and consultant. Among his works are *Planning in Ireland* (Dublin, Institute of Public Administration, 1968), *Towards a New Ireland* ((London, Knight, 1972) and an autobiography, *All in a Life* (Dublin, Gill and Macmillan, 1991).

Leo Flynn is a *référendaire* at the Court of Justice of the European Communities. He was previously a Lecturer in Law at King's College London, and remains a member of its Centre for European Law, and also at the University of Leeds where he taught European Community law and jurisprudence. His publications include contributions to journals and books on European law, law and gender and corporate law and *Law and Senses: Sensational Jurisprudence* (London, Pluto Press, 1996), co-edited with L. Bently.

Adrian Hunt is a Lecturer in Law at the University of Birmingham. He has researched and written on various aspects of public law and has a particular interest in administrative law and comparative constitutional form and method. He is currently engaged in research on the regulation of privatised industries.

Stephen Livingstone is Reader in Law and Co-Director of the Human Rights Law Centre at the University of Nottingham. He has previously taught at Queen's University Belfast and the University of Detroit. Among his publications is *Reshaping Public Power: Northern Ireland and the British Constitutional Crisis* (London, Sweet & Maxwell, 1995). He is currently working on a book on UK constitutional law with John Morison and Karen Morrow.

Irene Lynch is a Solicitor and Senior Lecturer in Law at the National University of Ireland, Cork, where she teaches company law and labour law. Her published works include *Labour Law in Ireland* (Dublin, Gill and Macmillan, 1993), which was co-authored, and *Corporate Insolvency and Rescue* (Dublin, Butterworths, 1996), written in consultation with two leading practitioners in the area.

Frank Martin is a Lecturer in family law and contract law at the National University of Ireland, Cork. He has published on a range of legal issues in several legal journals including The *Irish Law Times* and The *Irish Criminal Law Journal*. He holds postgraduate degrees in both Irish political history and law.

David Gwynn Morgan is Professor of Law and Head of the Law Department at the National University of Ireland, Cork. He has lectured on, and written about, public law in a number of common law jurisdictions and is a regular contributor on constitutional issues in the *Irish Times*. He is the author of *Constitutional Law in Ireland* (2nd edn., Dublin, Roundhall Press, 1990), *Administrative Law in Ireland* (with G. W. Hogan) (3rd edn., London, Sweet and Maxwell, 1998) and *The Separation of Powers in the Irish Constitution* (Dublin, Round Hall Sweet and Maxwell, 1997).

Siobhán Mullally is a Lecturer in human rights and public international law at the National University of Ireland, Cork. She is currently undertaking research for a Ph.D at the EUI, Florence, on "Gender and Multiculturalism". She has previously taught at the University of Hull, and has contributed to books and journals in the areas of gender, discrimination and the law.

Tim Murphy is a Lecturer in jurisprudence and constitutional law at the National University of Ireland, Cork. He has previously taught law in the United Kingdom, France and India. He is the author of *Rethinking the War on Drugs in Ireland* (Cork, Cork University Press, 1996).

John A. Murphy is Emeritus Professor of Irish History, National University of Ireland, Cork. His works include *Ireland in the Twentieth Century* (2nd edn., Dublin, Gill and Macmillan, 1989), *De Valera and his Times* (co-edited with J. O. O'Carroll) Cork, Cork University Press, 1983, and *The College: A History of Queen's/University College Cork, 1845–1995* (Cork, Cork University Press, 1995). He is a former Independent Member of *Seanad Eireann*.

Síofra O'Leary is a *référendaire* at the Court of Justice of the European Communities. Her works include *The Evolving Concept of Community Citizenship: From the Free Movement of Persons to Union Citizenship* (London, Kluwer, 1996), and (co-edited with A. Dashwood), *The Principle of Equal Treatment in EC Law* (London, Sweet and Maxwell, 1997), as well as a number of articles on the free movement provisions of the EC Treaty and on the protection of fundamental rights in the European Union.

Paul O'Mahony is a researcher and writer on Irish criminal justice. He was formerly a Lecturer in Psychology and Research Methods at Trinity College, Dublin and, for ten years, was Research Psychologist with the Irish Department of Justice. He is author of *Crime and Punishment in Ireland* (Dublin, Round Hall, Sweet and Maxwell, 1993), *Criminal Chaos: Seven Crises in Irish Criminal Justice* (Dublin, Round Hall, Sweet and Maxwell, 1996) and *Mountjoy Prisoners: A Sociological and Criminological Profile* (Dublin, The Stationery Office, 1997) and numerous articles on criminological and psychological topics. He is a founding member of the Irish Penal Reform Trust.

Brendan Ryan is a Lecturer in Chemical Engineering at Cork Regional Technical College. He was an Independant Member of *Seanad Eireann* from 1981 to 1992 and was re-elected to that position in 1997. He is the author of *Keeping Us in the Dark—Censorship and Freedom of Information in Ireland* (Dublin, Gill and MacMillan, 1995).

Niamh Nic Shuibhne teaches constitutional law at University College, Galway, where she completed an LL.M degree on the legal status of the Irish language. She is currently undertaking a Ph.D on legal aspects of minority language issues in the context of European unity at the Europa Institute, Faculty of Law, University of Edinburgh. She has published a range of articles on the Irish language, and other minority languages.

Patrick Twomey is a Lecturer in Law at the University of Nottingham and member of the Human Rights Law Centre. He has previously taught at the Universities of Durham and Liverpool. He is co-editor of (with D. O'Keeffe) *Legal Issues of the Maastricht Treaty*, (London, Chancery, 1994), (with G. Korella), *Towards a European Immigration Policy* (Brussels, European Interuniversity Press, 1993), and (with F. Nicholson) *Current Issues of UK Asylum Law and Policy* (London, Ashgate, forthcoming) and *Refugee Rights and Realities: Evolving International Concepts and Regimes* (Cambridge, Cambridge University Press, forthcoming).

Anthony Whelan is a *référendaire* at the Court of Justice of the European Communities and a Lecturer in Law at Trinity College, Dublin. He has edited *Law and Liberty in Ireland* (Dublin, Oak Tree Press, 1993) and co-authored *Ireland and the European Union: Constitutional and Statutory Texts and Commentary* (London, Sweet and Maxwell, 1995) (co-authored with G. Hogan), and (with J. Kingston) *Abortion and the Law* (Dublin, Roundhall Sweet and Maxwell, 1997) (co-authored with James Kingston, and Ivana Bacik).

Gerry Whyte is a Senior Lecturer at the Law School, Trinity College Dublin. His publications include (with G. Hogan) J. M. Kelly, *the Irish Constitution* (3rd edn., Dublin, Butterworths, 1994) and (co-authored with T. Kerr) *Irish Trade Union Law* (Abingdon, Professional Books, 1985). He also co-edited (with B. Treacy) *Religion, Morality and Public Policy* (Dublin, Dominican Publications, 1995).

Index

Index compiled by Stephanie J Dagg